The Myth of Judicial Independence

The Myth of Judicial Independence

Criminal Justice and the Separation of Powers

MIKE MCCONVILLE

Honorary Professor, University of Nottingham
Emeritus Professor and Honorary Fellow,
The Chinese University of Hong Kong

LUKE MARSH

Associate Professor, The Chinese University of Hong Kong
Door Tenant, 25 Bedford Row, London

OXFORD
UNIVERSITY PRESS

OXFORD
UNIVERSITY PRESS

Great Clarendon Street, Oxford, OX2 6DP,
United Kingdom

Oxford University Press is a department of the University of Oxford.
It furthers the University's objective of excellence in research, scholarship,
and education by publishing worldwide. Oxford is a registered trade mark of
Oxford University Press in the UK and in certain other countries

First Edition published in 2020

Impression: 1

Published in the United States of America by Oxford University Press
198 Madison Avenue, New York, NY 10016, United States of America

British Library Cataloguing in Publication Data
Data available

Library of Congress Control Number: 2020931643

ISBN 978–0–19–882210–3

Printed and bound by
CPI Group (UK) Ltd, Croydon, CR0 4YY

Acknowledgements

While researching and writing this book we have accumulated many debts to colleagues, friends, family, and institutions. We wish to pay thanks to our colleagues at the Faculty of Law, The Chinese University of Hong Kong, including its Dean, Lutz-Christian Wolff. The University Law Librarian, John Bahrij and his assistants Lily Ko and Agnes Cheung supported us by chasing down references from around the world. We similarly had support throughout from colleagues at the University of Nottingham and the University of Lancaster who encouraged the project from its inception.

We are indebted to all those who offered support and insight as we undertook our global search including: Professor Ian Dobinson; Professor Mark Finnane; Professor Gilbert Kodilinye; Professor Constantine Theophilopoulos; Professors Kris Gledhill, Ian Bryan, Sanoj Rajan, and the late Professor Geoffrey Wilson.

Professors David Ormerod and Jonathan Rogers kindly assisted by finding space for one of the authors at University College London's Centre for Criminal Law (despite the ongoing refurbishments to Bentham House). Professor Ingrid Eagly was equally generous with her time in overseeing the provision of research facilities at the School of Law, University of California, Los Angeles. Our thanks must also go to Professor Spyros Maniatis, Keith Ruddock, and Clare Priestly at the British Institute of International and Comparative Law for opening their doors towards the final stages of this book.

Jeremy Dein QC was a source of unsparing encouragement, helped clarify thoughts and came armed with the excellent clerking team at 25 Bedford Row, London, who in turn always made facilities available when required.

We owe a further great debt to Jamie Berezin, Commissioning Editor, Academic Law at OUP for having faith in the project when it was at an early stage of development, the anonymous reviewers who gave useful and positive advice, and to Catherine Rogers and Imogen Hill at OUP for their expert guidance, and to Arokia Anthuvan Rani and the Newgen team at Chennai for invaluable assistance during the publication process.

We had the constant assistance of staff at the National Archives and understanding and help from the Head of the Images Library, Hugh Alexander. We thank the National Archives for permission to use the Illustrations in this book and are most grateful to everyone at Middle Temple library and the British library.

Sonia McConville hunted down family and educational backgrounds of key figures in the research through massive archival endeavours and proof read the entire manuscript. Caspar McConville worked magic on archival material by reconfiguring fragile documents into readable form. Enormous gratitude is also owed for the support and encouragement of Mukesh, Bhauna, Madhuri, Neekita, and Sachin Joshi. Also, we thank Tania and Mike Gilpin and Gloria Mirsky for their constant inspiration and support. Margaret McGee, Mike Marsh, and Man Wai Chan require mention for their enduring support and Fiona and Richard Morgan for their timely visit to Hong Kong which boosted spirits enormously.

As will be clear from the book, we owe a huge debt to all the scholars who have come before us and who have not only laid the foundations for our own efforts but have been an inspiration. Any contribution that we make to the existing literature results in no small measure from those who have preceded us.

Finally, we thank all our other friends and family for their encouragement and forbearance throughout.

Mike McConville
Cambridge
Mikemcconville63@gmail.com

Luke Marsh
Hong Kong
Luke.marsh@cuhk.edu.hk

Contents

Table of Cases

Note on tables: *For the benefit of digital users, table entries that span two pages (e.g., 52–53) may, on occasion, appear on only one of those pages.*

UNITED KINGDOM

PRIVY COUNCIL CASES AND FOREIGN CASES

List of Illustrations

1
Introduction and Overview

> It has always been one of the pillars of freedom ... that the judges are no respecters of persons and stand between the subject and any attempted encroachments on his liberty by the executive, alert to see that any coercive action is justified in law.
>
> *Liversidge v Anderson* [1942] AC 206, 244, *per* Lord Atkin.

Events surrounding the Brexit case,[1] during the course of which the judges were publicly attacked and described in the press as the 'Enemies of the People',[2] have raised questions as to the politics of the judiciary, the relationship between the making of laws and their interpretation and, in that context, the role of the judiciary in being able to withstand external pressure when reaching a determination. This book directly addresses the major themes to which these debates have given rise: the politics of the judiciary, judicial independence, the rule of law, the role of the executive, and the separation of powers within the context of a democratic polity underpinned by the common law.

The Traditional View

In traditional understandings, under the so-called 'Westminster Model', the three branches of the British state have broadly separate functions: the power to *make and develop* the law lies with Parliament; the power to *interpret* the law and to decide what the law is rests with the judiciary; and *implementation* of the law is a matter for the executive. Under this constitutional arrangement, the rule of law requires that the three branches should, in general, be independent of each other; their functions should be distinct.[3] Those responsible for developing

[1] 'Brexit' symbolizes departure of the United Kingdom from the European Union. See *Miller & Anor, R (on the application of) v Secretary of State for Exiting the European Union* (Rev 3) [2017] UKSC 5 (24 January 2017). The proceedings which excited caustic press comment related to the earlier High Court ruling in *Miller & Anor, R (on the application of) v The Secretary of State for Exiting the European Union* (Rev 1) [2016] EWHC 2768 (Admin) (3 November 2016) (hereafter *Miller* [2016]).

[2] James Slack, *Daily Mail* (4 November 2015).

[3] The Judicial Executive Board has provided guidance to assist individual judges and the judiciary as an institution when considering whether, and how, to engage with the executive, particularly in relation to matters of policy and legislation. See Judicial Executive Board, *Guidance to the Judiciary on*

The Myth of Judicial Independence. Mike McConville and Luke Marsh, Oxford University Press (2020). © Mike McConville and Luke Marsh. DOI: 10.1093/oso/9780198822103.001.0001

and making the law should not be involved with interpreting or implementing it; those whose function is to interpret the law should neither make it nor put it into effect; and those who carry the law out should not make it or interpret it.

The constitutional arrangement set out is the result of a political process stretching over many centuries, as outlined by Lord Templeman:[4]

> Parliament makes the law, the executive carry the law into effect and the judiciary enforce the law. The expression 'the Crown' has two meanings: namely the Monarch and the executive. In the 17th century Parliament established its supremacy over the Crown as Monarch, over the executive and over the judiciary. Parliamentary supremacy over the Crown as Monarch stems from the fact that the Monarch must accept the advice of a Prime Minister who is supported by a majority of Parliament. Parliamentary supremacy over the Crown as executive stems from the fact that Parliament maintains in office the Prime Minister who appoints the ministers in charge of the executive. Parliamentary supremacy over the judiciary is only exercisable by statute. The judiciary enforce the law against individuals, against institutions and against the executive.

A recent restatement of this understanding was put forward by Lord Reed:[5]

> At the heart of the concept of the rule of law is the idea that society is governed by law. Parliament exists primarily in order to make laws for society in this country.
>
> Democratic procedures exist primarily in order to ensure that the Parliament which makes those laws includes Members of Parliament who are chosen by the people of this country and are accountable to them. Courts exist in order to ensure that the laws made by Parliament, and the common law created by the courts themselves, are applied and enforced. That role includes ensuring that the executive branch of government carries out its functions in accordance with the law.

Engagement with the Executive (July 2016) <https://www.judiciary.uk/publications/guidance-to-the-judiciary-on-engagement-with-the-executive/> accessed 1 January 2020. See also Cabinet Office, *The Cabinet Manual* (October 2011) <www.cabinetoffice.gov.uk> accessed 1 January 2020.

[4] *M v Home Office* [1994] 1 AC 377. *Miller* [2016] (n 1) provides a recent and authoritative exposition of the constitutional principle of parliamentary sovereignty, see paras 3, 40–46, 277–78 <https://www.supremecourt.uk/cases/docs/uksc-2016-0196-judgment.pdf>.

[5] *R (Unison) v Lord Chancellor* [2017] UKSC 51, 68. For comment on this decision, see Mark Elliott, 'The Rule of Law and Access to Justice: Some Home Truths' (case comment) (2018) 77(1) Cambridge Law Journal 5.

Within this constitutional model, the judiciary has to be, and be seen to be, independent of the other arms of the state. It is said to achieve this by acting under the rule of law. Lord Neuberger put the central argument this way:[6]

> Independence for the judiciary does not mean ignoring the legislature or the executive; it does not even mean having no discussions with the legislature or the executive. It means that the legislature and the executive should not be able to exert improper influence over the judges. It means in particular that neither the legislature nor the executive should be able (i) to interfere with, or influence, judicial decision-making (other than by advancing normal legal argument in cases) or (ii) to remove judges from office (save in those almost vanishingly rare cases where a judge has acted improperly and refuses to go).

In a similar vein, LCJ Thomas set out the view, widely shared by judges in other jurisdictions as well, that the judiciary is an essential part of the democratic settlement in England and Wales:[7]

> Why is the justice system therefore a pillar of democracy? There are a number of reasons . . . : first, the safeguarding of the rule of law, second, maintaining the certainty of the law while allowing for its development, third, providing public access to the law, fourth, providing openness and accountability and fifth, making decisions independently of interests.

In this account, not only is there an independent judiciary operating within the constitutional framework but the judiciary itself, as well as citizens more generally, are enjoined to ensure that that independence is not in any way compromised. As Lord Judge put it:[8]

> . . . [We] must remain vigilant against the slightest encroachment on judicial independence, not because judicial independence represents some traditional flummery, some bauble, some meaningless superficiality, but because without an independent judiciary the rule of law would collapse.

[6] Lord Neuberger, 'Judges, Access to Justice, the Rule of Law and the Court of Final Appeal under "One Country Two Systems"' (Lecture delivered at the University of Hong Kong, 13 September 2017). Neuberger described the *Daily Mail* headline (above n 2) as 'shameful' and added: 'A few politicians, who should have known better, joined in the attack, and many more senior politicians including the then-Lord Chancellor failed in their duty to stand up for the judges.'

[7] Lord Thomas, 'The Centrality of Justice: Its Contribution to Society, and its Delivery' (The Lord Williams of Mostyn Memorial Lecture, 10 November 2015) <www.judiciary.uk/wp-content/uploads/2015/11/lord-williams-of-mostyn-lecture-nov-2015.pdf> accessed 1 January 2020.

[8] Lord Chief Justice Judge, Speech at Lord Mayor's Banquet, 3 July 2013, 2 <www.judiciary.uk/wp-content/uploads/2015/11/lord-williams-of-mostyn-lecture-nov-2015.pdf> accessed 1 January 2020.

Such is the perceived threat that the vigilance required even extends towards members of its own ranks:[9]

> When carrying out their judicial function they must be free of any improper influence. Such influence could come from any number of sources. It could arise from improper pressure by ... other judges, in particular *more senior judges*.

However, defence of the formal constitutional arrangements and, in particular, the independence of the judiciary is especially important, it is said, because of the inherent threat to independence posed by the executive.[10] As Lord Phillips put it:[11]

> Because it is the executive that exercises the power of the State and because it is the executive, in one form or another, that is the most frequent litigator in the courts, it is from executive pressure or influence that judges require particularly to be protected.

Under this model, not only must the judiciary be protected from an overmighty executive but also there must be assurance under the rule of law that the imposition of the coercive powers of the state is the responsibility of the judiciary not that of the executive, as Lady Hale stated:[12]

> The rule of law means that everyone is expected to obey the law and to meet their legal obligations and should face punishment or enforcement if they do not. But the rule of law also means that these coercive powers of the state should not be arbitrarily meted out by unaccountable state officials. They should be imposed by an independent judiciary sworn, as I have sworn, 'to do right to all

[9] Judiciary of England and Wales, 'The Judiciary, the Government and the Constitution' <www.judiciary.uk/about-the-judiciary/the-judiciary-the-government-and-the-constitution/jud-acc-ind/independence/> accessed 1 January 2020 (emphasis supplied).

[10] In this context, accountability of the executive to Parliament does not alter the role of the courts. In *R v Inland Revenue Comrs, Ex p National Federation of Self-Employed and Small Businesses Ltd* [1982] AC 617, 644 Lord Diplock said: 'It is not, in my view, a sufficient answer to say that judicial review of the actions of officers or departments of central government is unnecessary because they are accountable to Parliament for the way in which they carry out their functions. They are accountable to Parliament for what they do so far as regards efficiency and policy, and of that Parliament is the only judge; they are responsible to a court of justice for the lawfulness of what they do, and of that the court is the only judge.' Cited with approval in *R (on the Application of Miller) (Appellant) v The Prime Minister (Respondent)* [2019] UKSC 41, para 33.

[11] Lord Phillips, 'Judicial Independence' (Lecture given at Constitution Unit, UCL, 8 February 2011) <https://www.supremecourt.uk/docs/speech_110208.pdf>.

[12] Lady Hale, 'Georgetown Commencement Speech' (23 May 2010) 4–5 <https://www.supremecourt.uk/docs/speech_100523.pdf>accessed 1 January 2020.

manner of people, after the laws and usages of this realm, without fear or favour, affection or ill-will.'

The background is accordingly constituted by a set of claims which underpin the idea of constitutionalism within the democratic polity. The judges are variously said to be apolitical, impartial, acting as a restraint on an oppressive government,[13] interpreting the law but not making it, and abstaining from policy-making. Central to all this is the democratic polity, supported by an administration that is both competent and uncorrupt, operating under the rule of law by which the judges are able to enforce recognized human rights and hold government accountable to the law.

The constitutional arrangements that are celebrated in this way are not only formalistic: they are said to rest upon and to have produced a judicial body that is unsurpassed in terms of quality[14] accounting for its emulation in other parts of the world:

> The judiciary of England and Wales has earned a well-deserved reputation for being the best in the world ... because it is impartial, independent and incorruptible (Sir Ian Burnett, Lord Chief Justice of England and Wales).[15]
>
> It is British justice rather than English or Scots law that has been the gift of British lawyers to the world. You cannot visit the countries of the Commonwealth without realizing that ... (Lord Devlin).[16]
>
> We are fortunate in England and Wales that the world, again and again, chooses our courts to resolve its disputes. We are fortunate that the reputation of our independent judiciary, the quality of our barristers and solicitors, the centuries-old respect for due process that characterizes our legal system and the total absence of corruption in our courts and tribunals, have all made England and Wales the best place in the world when it comes to resolving matters by law (Former Lord Chancellor).[17]

[13] Even today, some eminent individuals, by conflating government and legislature, have suggested that both ought to be immunized from judicial oversight by restrictions on judicial review. This has been convincingly demolished by Sir Stephen Sedley, 'Judicial Politics' *London Review of Books* (23 February 2012).

[14] Laudatory attitudes towards the judiciary have even manifested through those tasked with pioneering (still) leading forums for objective and critical engagement within the discipline of law. Sir Maurice Amos, founding member of the *Modern Law Review*, put it this way: 'English criminal justice is sustained and pervaded by the profound confidence of all classes of the population in the integrity of the English judges, and their complete inaccessibility to official pressure or other corrupt influences' in "Conclusion' of *British Criminal Justice* (Longmans, revised edition 1962).

[15] Transcript of speech made on 2 October 2017 <https://www.judiciary.uk/announcements/sir-ian-burnett-became-the-lord-chief-justice-of-england-and-wales-today/> accessed 1 January 2020.

[16] 'Judges and Lawmakers' (1976) 39 MLR 1, 8.

[17] The Rt Hon Michael Gove, MP, 'What does a one nation justice policy look like?' (Speech given at the Legatum Institute, 23 June 2015) <www.gov.uk/government/speeches/what-does-a-one-nation-justice-policy-look-like> accessed 1 January 2020.

> The British judiciary, the United Kingdom judiciary, is one of the great glories of our constitution—they are independent … Believe me, around the world people look at our judges with awe and admiration (The Prime Minister of the United Kingdom, 2019).[18]

Of course, central to all these claims is the implicit understanding that the independence of the judiciary is indivisible within the legal system. It cannot be qualified or segmentized into different branches of the law, rather independence is said to be universalistic in character.

Our Research

The principal lens through which we examine these notions is the way in which police powers of detention and interrogation came to be regulated principally through the Judges' Rules. These Rules, which until 1985 governed such things as police cautioning, detention, interrogation, and access to a lawyer, have a continuing influence on the structure of police–citizen relationships not only in England and Wales but in many other jurisdictions. At the same time we address two other fundamentally connected issues: first, so-called 'plea bargaining' (or what we term 'state-induced guilty pleas') under which suspects and defendants are pressed into making confessions and/or pleading guilty; and second, the role and impact of the Criminal Procedure Rules (CrimPR), under which trial judges are re-cast as case managers with defendants and their lawyers bound into a co-operative relationship with the prosecution. As will become clear, the fine drafting details of these measures are subordinate to how they fit into the rule of law and the adversary system, their origin, structure, integrity, and legality.

The Data: Sources and Limitations

The principal sources of data are derived from internal Home Office files,[19] decided cases, biographical material, and information secured through Freedom of Information requests. The internal files, some released publicly long in advance of their 'sealed' date, trace the way in which Home Office officials were assigned significant responsibility for regulating police–citizen interactions in relation to the investigation of crime and, in the process, with the assistance of government

[18] 'Kwasi Kwarteng Criticised for "biased judges" Comment' (*BBC News Online*, 12 September 2019) <https://www.bbc.com/news/uk-politics-49670901>.

[19] Located at the National Archives in Kew, London. The National Archives is a non-ministerial government department.

ministers acting outside the parliamentary framework, assumed an extraordinary measure of influence and control over the senior judiciary.

As with all 'information' of an official character, the disclosed files have to be read with care, cross-checked, and supplemented wherever possible by external material. We simply draw the reader's attention to this as others have discussed in detail the ethical and political dimensions associated with such official practices.[20]

Access to the files is, accordingly, not an unproblematic golden harvest for a number of reasons. Files have to be read guardedly. The Home Office, like other government departments, has a developed art in writing 'Minutes' which are plausible but imperfect records of events; records of correspondence are sometimes incomplete, the thread often broken at what appears to be critical moments; and many meetings of some historical significance are simply mentioned without a record or can only be deduced as having taken place, not having been noted at all.

Another limitation derives from the fact that, in the early period up to 1930, a number of internal files are marked as having been 'destroyed' by the Home Office itself while others are missing and it is unclear whether these have also been destroyed or are still retained by the Home Office.[21] On top of this, there is an official policy under which sensitive official documents, in addition to those formally classified as containing 'state secrets', are withheld from public view by being 'sealed' for long time periods (fifty or seventy-five years). We indicate in the text where documents are withheld and where we believe that they have been destroyed, thus escaping the risk of disclosure.[22]

Although from time to time we discuss decided court cases, in general we are not concerned with analysing individual case determinations. As we will explain, we do not seek to tease out the 'political' views of individual judges from legal

[20] See eg: Christopher Moran, *Classified: Secrecy and the State in Modern Britain* (CUP 2013); David Vincent, *The Culture of Secrecy: Britain 1832–1998* (OUP 1997); Peter Hennessey, *Whitehall* (Secker & Warburg 1989); Peter Kellner and Lord Crowther-Hunt, *The Civil Servants: An Inquiry into Britain's Ruling Class* (Macdonald 1980); David Leigh, *The Frontiers of Secrecy* (Junction Books 1980); Gavin Drewry and Tony Butcher, *The Civil Service Today* (Wiley-Blackwell 1988); John Arundel Barnes, *Who Should Know What? Social Science, Privacy and Ethics* (CUP 1979). The problem of secrecy extends also to local government. See eg: 'Secret State' *The Times*, Leading Article, (6 October 2018). And the colonial regime is now notorious for its destruction of records relating to such matters as massacres, torture, and other violations of human rights. See Ian Cobain, Owen Bowcott, and Richard Norton-Taylor, 'Britain Destroyed Records of Colonial Regimes' *The Guardian* (18 April 2012); Shohei Sato, '"Operation Legacy": Britain's Destruction and Concealment of Colonial Records Worldwide' (2017) 45(4) The Journal of Imperial and Commonwealth History 697.

[21] The unaccountable disappearance of archival material relating to controversial periods of history by civil servants is known elsewhere: 'Government Papers Missing from the National Archives' *The Times* (27 December 2017).

[22] In the more modern era, government departments are supposed to be regulated in relation to the preservation of records. For a full statement, see National Archives, *Records Management Retention Scheduling* (2012) <www.nationalarchives.gov.uk/documents/information-management/sched_info_management.pdf> accessed 1 January 2020. cf Phil Miller and Oliver Wright, 'Whitehall Addiction to Secrecy Getting Worse, Warns Watchdog' *The Times* (3 August 2017). It should be noted in this context that s 3(4) Public Records Act 1958 allows Whitehall departments to withhold records from the National Archives indefinitely for 'administrative reasons' or 'for any other special reason'.

judgments or from their extra-curial writings. The aspect of the book dealing with the 'politics' of the judiciary focuses instead on the development of 'policy' by senior judges and the process by which this reaches maturity. We are not concerned with the motivations of individual judges but instead upon their role in policy-making and the consequent effect upon the system. For this purpose, the internal confidential departmental files of the Home Office[23] have provided a rich source.

Research Focus

In this book we challenge the core constitutional notions set out above and, in particular, the idea that the judiciary, as an institution, is independent of the other arms of the state. We demonstrate, among other things, that in matters directly bearing upon the liberty of the individual, specifically the rights and freedoms enjoyed when confronted with police power, that the executive has interfered with the judicial role and has done so in secret while concurrently deceiving Parliament; the judiciary, for its part, being forced by executive intimidation to jettison common law principles it historically celebrated.

We will argue that some senior judges who have taken a significant role in shaping the structure of the criminal justice system have acted 'politically' and thereby compromised the independence proclaimed under the rule of law and transgressed core precepts of the common law. Much of the story speaks of clandestine links with the executive represented here by government ministers and Home Office civil servants.

Our concern with the senior judiciary is at an *institutional* level and with the concept of an independent judiciary. The actions of individual judges who attract media attention for breaking the law or engaging in other unacceptable conduct are *not* part of our account.[24] We focus exclusively upon the role of the *senior judiciary* in the formation of *policies* which have re-engineered the adversary system away from its foundational principles. In this, we demonstrate that the question to what extent does an unelected judiciary control the executive, framed usually as a government or press complaint, should rather be to what extent are the judges controlled by the executive.

As part of this account, we challenge commonly held notions regarding the quality and competence of the Civil Service which has now played a vital role in

[23] The files of the Lord Chancellor's Department have been scoured by others although they do not appear to have thrown light on the areas of our interest. See Robert Stevens, *The Independence of the Judiciary* (OUP 1993).

[24] See the insightful account of Stephen Sedley, *Lions Under the Throne: Essays on the History of English Public Law* (CUP 2015): 'Impartiality is a state of mind—in the vocabulary of the judicial oath, the absence of affection or ill-will. Independence is a state of being—freedom from what the judicial oath calls fear of favour' 279.

shaping the criminal justice system for over a century. In conventional accounts, in the latter part of the nineteenth century, Gladstonian reforms transformed an amateur service based on patronage into one founded in intellectual excellence, in which civil servants displayed core values still celebrated today and expressed in these terms:[25]

- 'integrity' is putting the obligations of public service above your own personal interests
- 'honesty' is being truthful and open
- 'objectivity' is basing your advice and decisions on rigorous analysis of the evidence
- 'impartiality' is acting solely according to the merits of the case and serving equally well governments of different political persuasions

We show, to the contrary, that civil servants often lacked the necessary intellectual powers to deal with matters under their responsibility, were far from truthful and honest in handling policy issues, did not base advice on a rigorous analysis of the evidence, and failed to demonstrate impartiality in assessing evidence and advising ministers.

A necessary implication of our account is to challenge the underpinnings of the 'Westminster Model' of governance under which the three arms of the state are independent and independent of each other. We show how it has been possible for Parliament to be removed from the democratic equation by disinformation and deception leaving policy to be forged by the relevant government department, acting at the behest of an unseen (but subsequently vocal) police lobby, persuading the judges to abandon their own principles and ultimately forcing the senior judiciary to accept its diktats under political threat.

The book is not about the performance of the police, their compliance with Codes of Practice, or more pointedly departures from the law and corruption within the police, although that necessarily has a prominent place in our account. Rather, the state of policing itself at all points in the history that concerns us is an essential backcloth to understanding the actions of the Civil Service and the judges in determining the boundary between the citizen and the state and between formal and less than formal styles of regulation.

While our research has a principal focus on England and Wales, it has major implications for countries (and other former colonial territories) around the world which have, through the reach of the Empire or through emulation of an admired system of governance, incorporated the system of regulating policing and restructuring adversary justice into their own jurisdictions.

[25] UK Government, *The Civil Service Code* (London 2015) <www.gov.uk/government/publications/civil-service-code/the-civil-service-code> accessed 1 January 2020.

The Structure of the Book

Given the responsibility of the Home Office since 1782 for the administration of criminal justice through its function of ensuring the 'maintenance of the Queen's Peace', it is essential that the role of its civil servants who participate in managing the system on a day-to-day basis is understood. This involves both reviewing the technical capacity of these officials, the extent of their involvement in policy, and their overall integrity. We begin that examination by looking at the operational structure and work practices of Home Office personnel around the time the Judges' Rules were first being considered through its ancillary responsibility for dealing with Petitions (against conviction or sentence) in Chapter 2. Many of the key figures involved in responding to Petitions became central to the Home Office responsibility for dealing with policing and the need in the early years of the twentieth century to rationalize its regulation. This led ultimately to the development of the Judges' Rules in 1912 and their subsequent augmentation in 1918. The process by which the Rules took the form they did is described in Chapter 3. Thereafter, Chapter 4 deals with the aftermath of the 1918 Rules which continued in existence until 1964. As drafting deficiencies and enhanced concerns over police detention and interrogation practices came to the surface, a process of revision was inaugurated, the first phase of which is analysed in Chapter 5. Chapter 6 tells the story of how the revised Rules came into existence in 1964. Chapter 7 records the aftermath of the 1964 revision, which not only saw considerable interpretive discretion vested in the judges but also, against a background of police corruption scandals, a volte-face in the disposition of judges towards the rights of individuals with new policies applied in the form of inducements to plead guilty and to forego trial.

In Chapter 8 we consider how the forms of judicial policy-making described in Chapter 7 fit in with the rule of law and other foundational precepts of the common law, the bedrock of judicial claims regarding the role of judges in the law-making process. In Chapter 9 we address the issue of judges and constitutionalism within the Westminster Model, the tripartite arrangement for the separation of powers between Parliament, the executive, and the judiciary. Chapter 10 directly engages with the ongoing debates as to whether the judiciary can be said to be political or whether, as claimed, it is above politics and neutral. In so doing, we examine the methodologies that might be applied to answer that question in the context of existing theoretical approaches. In Chapter 11 we show how the actions of senior judges in England and Wales are not jurisdictionally specific but instead have had, and still have today, enormous repercussions for other territories, especially those that are part of the colonial heritage. Chapter 12 underlines why, as a matter of historical record, the senior judiciary as an institution cannot be said to be independent in criminal justice matters, pulls together the threads of the book's argument concerning the rule of law and the common law, and raises questions about the moral compass of the Civil Service, the judiciary, and the executive that, at identifiable historical moments, combined to create major policy initiatives out of parliamentary and public view.

Endnote

Overall, and with a focus on criminal justice, our book is intended not simply as a critique of fairy tales[26] concerning the independence of the judiciary, its fidelity to the rule of law and the Westminster Model with its so-styled three 'independent' arms of the state; instead, we draw attention to the need for a democratic and more transparent polity which is truly committed to fairness and integrity in the protection of its subjects rather than one shrouded in secrecy and sheltered behind facile and repetitive rhetoric which serves only to hide a disturbing reality.

[26] Lord Reid once observed 'We do not believe in fairy tales any more, so we must accept the fact that for better or for worse judges do make law' (1972) The Journal of Public Teachers of Law 22.

2

The Management of Criminal Justice

An Early Challenge

Introduction

The arcane court system originating from the Middle Ages extraordinarily lasted until reforms instituted by the Judicature Acts (1873–75). While these replaced the old courts with a Supreme Court of Judicature consisting of a High Court of Justice and a Court of Appeal in civil cases, it was not until 1907 that there was a right of appeal against criminal convictions with the creation of the Court of Criminal Appeal.[1] Until then, decisions in criminal cases, in respect of both convictions and sentences, could be reversed only through the intercession of the Home Secretary. The role of the Home Office, which had general responsibility for the administration of criminal justice through its function as 'maintenance of the King's Peace',[2] was accordingly of crucial significance in determining whether there had been a wrongful conviction.

Home Office Officials

Until the mid-nineteenth century, all government departments relied heavily upon patronage for their staffing requirements. A key figure at the Home Office was the permanent Under-Secretary, an administrative adviser to the Home Secretary, a non-political appointee who remained in office with the passing of government. The permanent Under-Secretary was supported by junior and more established clerks. New clerks were nominated by the Home Secretary either through office or family connections[3] tying them to the culture and traditions of the department.

This conservative and self-reproducing system was supposed to change following the Civil Service Commission in 1855 established in response to a series

[1] The Court for Crown Cases Reserved could rule on a point of law on reference by the trial judge.
[2] See Sir Edward Troup, *The Home Office* (Putnam 1925) (hereafter Troup, *Home Office*).
[3] Jill Pellew, *The Home Office 1848–1914* (Heinemann Educational Books 1982) 10 (hereafter Pellew, *Home Office*).

The Myth of Judicial Independence. Mike McConville and Luke Marsh, Oxford University Press (2020). © Mike McConville and Luke Marsh. DOI: 10.1093/oso/9780198822103.001.0001

of investigations[4] culminating in the Northcote-Trevelyan reforms[5] which established the principle that recruitment should be through open competitive examination with promotion based on merit. The reform was opposed by the Home Office on the ground that its work particularly required a level of trustworthiness that could be secured only through a personal appointments process as set out in the Home Secretary's response to the Treasury's invitation to begin implementation of open competition:[6]

> The personal knowledge possessed by the Secretary of State of young men appointed by him to clerkships affords a guarantee for their character and honour which has hitherto proved sufficient, and which could not be supplied by unrestricted competition and mere testimonials as to character ...

However, with the arrival of Robert Lowe (later Viscount Sherbrooke) as Home Secretary in 1873, the Home Office resistance to open competition ended.

The new system initially did little to alter the background of new entrants but the reforms began to take effect after 1880[7] with the appointment of Edward Troup[8] as the first open competition recruit to a junior clerkship. Thereafter, entry became dominated by university graduates although these, in turn, were almost exclusively drawn from Oxford and Cambridge[9] coming from a social background not dissimilar from their predecessors. It was into this slowly evolving structure that the case of Adolf Beck fell in 1896.[10]

[4] See, John Greenaway, 'Celebrating Northcote/Trevelyan: Dispelling the Myths' (2004) 19(1) Public Policy and Administration 1. Greenaway emphasizes that the Northcote-Trevelyan Report came 'at the end of a long-drawn out series of investigations over the previous five years into the organisation of various departments to ensure both efficiencies and economies', 2.

[5] The reforms proposed in 1854 are reproduced in the Fulton Report, *The Civil Service, Report of the Committee* (1968).

[6] Response of Home Secretary Henry Bruce cited by Pellew, *Home Office* (n 3) 20–21.

[7] ibid 22.

[8] We will refer to him as Edward Troup although in the literature he is variously referred to as 'Charles'. On entering the Home Office, Troup was said to have 'represented the new generation, not limited to one social class or one profession'. As permanent Under-Secretary of State, Troup was described as 'perhaps over-cautious and *no believer in bringing the expert into policy discussions*': Lord Allen of Abbeydale, 'State Service: Reflections of a Bureaucrat' in *The Home Office: Perspectives on Policy and Administration—Bicentenary Lectures* (1982) 26 emphasis supplied.

[9] Pellew reports that nine of the twelve graduates who entered the Home Office between 1880 and 1896 had degrees from Oxford and every first division graduate entrant between 1896 and 1914 came from Oxbridge, *Home Office* (n 3) 33–34. The position today has hardly improved. A 2016 study on the socio-economic backgrounds of those accessing the Civil Service 'Fast Stream' revealed its intake was 'less diverse than the student population at the University of Oxford', see Executive Summary <https://www.gov.uk/government/publications/socio-economic-diversity-in-the-fast-stream-the-bridge-report>.

[10] See generally, Eric Watson (ed), *Trial of Adolf Beck* (William Hodge 1924) (hereafter Watson, *Beck*); Tim Coates (ed), *The Strange Story of Adolf Beck* (TSO 1904); National Archives, Crim 8/17; George Sims, *The Martyrdom of Adolf Beck* (serialized in *Daily Mail* 1904).

The Beck Saga: An Overview

Beck was wrongly convicted in 1896 for crimes perpetrated by another person (William Wyatt) calling himself 'John Smith',[11] who had been convicted of identical crimes in 1877. During Beck's time in prison the frauds stopped. After his release in 1901, the frauds started again and Beck was again wrongfully convicted in 1904. These had again been carried out by Smith. Beck was saved only when Smith was arrested and his true identity established. An Inquiry concluded in 1904 that there was 'no shadow of foundation for any of the charges made against Mr Beck or any reason for supposing that he had any connection whatever with them'.

The case of 'John Smith'

The background to Beck's case was the conviction of 'John Smith' in 1877 for frauds on twenty different women. Smith represented himself as 'Lord Willoughby' with a substantial residence in St John's Wood. The women would be offered a position as mistress of his house and given a cheque to purchase better quality clothes. By various pretexts they would be relieved of their rings, other jewellery, and cash. The cheques were worthless. Smith disappeared until seen again by one of the victims who caused his arrest. 'John Smith' was defended by Montague Williams, prosecuted by Forrest Fulton, and following conviction sentenced to five years' penal servitude. He never disputed his conviction but filed a petition to the Home Office complaining of the severity of his sentence. It was after almost identical crimes started up again in 1894 that Adolf Beck[12] came into the picture.

The Crimes of 1894–95

In November 1895 Ottalie Meissonier, a German music teacher, met a man purporting to be a rich aristocrat who by various false pretences reminiscent of the earlier frauds, including giving her a worthless cheque to buy clothes, took from her a ring, watch, and other items. She reported the losses to the police and described the fraudster. A month later, Ottalie saw Adolf Beck, a Norwegian seaman, and confronted him as the man who had defrauded her. Beck, believing her to be a prostitute, walked away but Ottalie followed until she saw Constable Frederick Edwards. Once Ottalie said that she would charge him and Beck said that he was willing to go to the police station, Edwards took both to the police station at Rochester Row.

[11] Wyatt, a German national, had other aliases including 'Thomas'.
[12] Beck's forename was reported variously as Adolf, Aldof, and Aldophus.

After their arrival, the police brought in Daisy Grant who had made a complaint in July 1895 that she had been defrauded by a person calling himself 'Lord Wilton'. An identification parade was held at which both Daisy and Ottalie picked out Beck as the fraudster. Following the charge and committal proceedings, newspaper reports brought forth another eighteen complainants. A second parade was then held at which a range of complainants picked out Beck, although four or five did not.

The police proceeded to deal with Beck as 'John Smith', the identity of the two being 'confirmed' by PC Spurrell and another officer who had arrested Smith fifteen years earlier. A handwriting expert, Thomas Gurrin, stated that the handwriting in the cheques was identical to the exhibits taken from Smith's case. Applications by Beck's solicitor to have access to and examine Smith's record were turned down.

At Beck's Old Bailey trial, the prosecution was undertaken by one of the Treasury Counsel, Horace Avory.[13] Avory had been called to the Bar in 1875 and was a lawyer of vast experience having appeared in over 800 cases.[14] He was an austere, tight-lipped barrister who adopted a quasi-judicial, dispassionate style of advocacy.[15] Avory's biographer concluded that the Beck case is particularly noteworthy for the fact that 'Avory's scrupulous sense of fairness contributed so largely to the tragic miscarriage of justice'.[16]

The prosecution could have proceeded by way of a *misdemeanour* indictment involving ten counts to reflect the ten complainants or by *indictment* for felony and larceny in which the previous conviction (as 'Smith') was charged. The logical approach was to proceed by indictment since the instructions to Avory assumed that the identity of Beck as Smith was indisputable. Nonetheless, Avory proceeded only on the misdemeanour indictment and PC Spurrell who had arrested Smith was accordingly not called to give evidence for the prosecution. Later, Avory sought to justify his decision on two grounds of fairness: (i) that many of the individual offences amounted in his view only to misdemeanours; and (ii) that in a trial upon one indictment for a felony, it might be difficult for the defendant to establish a defence either by alibi or otherwise whereas it would be easier to prove alibi at ten different dates.[17] Even if this explanation is accepted, this points up a tragic error because Avory could have charged the previous conviction in the misdemeanour indictment under the Prevention of Crimes Act.[18]

[13] The prosecution papers were prepared by a clerk who was neither a solicitor nor barrister.

[14] *The Proceedings of the Old Bailey: London's Central Criminal Court 1674–1913* <www.oldbaileyonline.org/forms/formMain.jsp> accessed 1 January 2020.

[15] Stanley Jackson, *Mr. Justice Avory* (Victor Gollancz Ltd 1935). His loyal clerk described him as a 'detached, stand-offish man ... [who] had no small talk and little interest in events which did not find their ultimate expression in briefs', F W Ashley, *My Sixty Years in the Law* (The Bodley Head 1936) (hereafter Ashley, *Sixty Years*) 57.

[16] Stanley Jackson, ibid 55.

[17] This justification does not bear analysis. Ordinarily, it would have been difficult, if not impossible, to provide alibis (unless provably absent abroad) because the allegations covered an uncertain period of between eighteen months to two years, upon unspecified days and at uncertain times.

[18] 34 & 35 Vict C 112 sec 8. This undermines the wafer-thin defence of Avory put forward by his clerk F W Ashley who attended the trial and ventured that 'the martyrdom of an innocent man was brought

Charles Gill, defending Beck, began cross-examining Gurrin as to the handwriting in Smith's case in order to get Gurrin to confirm that the documents in each case were written by the same person,[19] in which event Beck had a defence, supported by impeccable witnesses, namely, that he had been in South America in 1877 and over the period when the earlier crimes were committed.[20] However, Avory objected because 'that was a collateral issue, and should not be inquired into until after the Jury had returned their verdict, lest it should afterwards be said that the prisoner had been improperly convicted'. This was another serious error on the part of Avory for at least two reasons, as Watson points out.[21] First, who was in a position to complain that the line of defence chosen had led to an improper conviction? Obviously, it would not be the defence. Secondly, if, as Avory conceded, the identity of Beck with Smith could properly be inquired into *after* verdict, on what basis could the defence be stopped from going into it *before* verdict?

The Common Serjeant (trial judge), who was, extraordinarily, Sir Forrest Fulton, the very person who had prosecuted Smith in 1877,[22] ruled that the question whether Beck was the man convicted in 1877 was not admissible on the ground that it related to another and distinct issue, and one calculated to mislead the jury. This was another serious error: the prohibition debarring the prosecution from referring to a previous conviction did not debar the defendant from introducing it, if it was in any way material to his defence. In this case, the evidence regarding the previous conviction was directly relevant to Beck's defence because it was the first step in a chain of reasoning leading to the conclusion that Beck was not the man: 'Two crimes were committed by one and the same person. Beck could not have committed the first. Therefore, he did not commit the second.'

As a result of Fulton's ruling, that part of the evidence of Gurrin—that the exhibits of 1896 and those of 1877 were unquestionably in the same handwriting—never appeared in evidence and the core of Beck's defence was brushed aside. With an adverse summing up, the jury returned a verdict of guilty in a few minutes. Beck was sentenced to seven years' penal servitude and removed to Portland Prison. In prison, Beck was treated as if he were Smith and given the number 'DW 523' which indicated a previous conviction. Given that the judge had refused to certify a point of law, the matter could not go before the Court for Crown Cases Reserved and Beck's fate would be dependent upon any Petition that he might file.

about by several chapters of accidents, and the *only explanation* one can proffer or hazard is that by a malign conspiracy of Fate Beck was *predestined* to undeserved mental and physical suffering': *Sixty Years* (n 15) 142 (emphasis added).

[19] The prosecution briefs stated that the 1877 exhibits had been examined by Gurrin and that 'as is obviously the fact . . . they are in the same handwriting as the documents in the present case . . .'.

[20] Actually, Beck left England in 1868 and did not return until 1885 and, consistent with his alibi, he does not appear in the Census of 1871 or that of 1881.

[21] Watson, *Beck* (n 10).

[22] Given this, Fulton should have recused himself and, arguably, even been a witness for Beck.

Beck's Petitions

Almost immediately after Beck's incarceration, his solicitor, Mr Duerdin Dutton, filed a Petition on his behalf. The Home Office had a settled practice in dealing with criminal Petitions set out in a Memorandum given to the Committee of Inquiry ('Beck Inquiry') in 1904 by Sir Kenelm Digby, permanent Under-Secretary from 1895 to 1903. Essentially, faced with four thousand Petitions each year (relating principally to sentence but also some to verdict), the Home Office would not, save in very exceptional cases, go behind the opinion of the judge even where 'a doubt is still entertained'.

This guarded approach is evident in the statistics offered by Digby. Altogether, free pardons on the ground that the prisoner's innocence had been established totalled five by 1904 while over the same period some ninety cases of sentence had been remitted because of a doubt arising over the propriety of the conviction. Beck's Petition, accordingly, faced an uphill struggle.

Mr Dutton's Petition set out the defects which led to Beck's conviction. Dutton pointed out that the offences committed in 1877 and in Beck's case were identical in character; the documents in each case were 'undoubtedly in the same handwriting … in the same way and so much alike that they might be photographs of each other'; the fraudulent documents in each case had been mostly written on Bill of Exchange Forms; the evidence of Mr Gurrin was that the documents 'were undoubtedly written by the same person'; the man who committed the offences in 1877 committed the offences alleged against Beck in 1894 and 1895; the prosecution had before the magistrate at committal a retired police officer to prove that Beck was the same man who had been convicted in the name of John Smith at the Old Bailey in May 1877 for a series of similar offences; Beck could establish by reputable witnesses[23] that he was in South America between 1873 and 1884 'which embraces the whole period during which John Smith was engaged in committing the offences of which he was convicted and the time he was in Prison in England'; the prosecution 'could have included in the Indictment [against Beck] the previous conviction but this was not done;' and the entry of a *nolle prosequi* on the other felony charges had denied Beck the means of proving that the prosecution identification witnesses were mistaken.

In response, the first Home Office Minute (dated 1 June 1896) was dismissive, describing the Petition as an attempt to get the Secretary of State to 'overrule the decision of the Court on a point of law and then to go on to declare that the verdict is wrong.' The Minute continued in dispositive tones:

> He was identified with one John Smith who was convicted of similar offences in 1877, and this former conviction was charged in the indictments.

[23] Mr Dutton set out the identity and standing of the alibi witnesses stating that 'there can be no doubt as to the correctness of the evidence of all these gentlemen … '.

> The argument of the petition is that the handwriting of the swindler in this case is the same as that of John Smith, and all the details of the frauds are precisely similar. Therefore, all the present set of frauds were committed by John Smith. But the prisoner cannot be John Smith, because he was in Peru from 1873 to 1884, while Smith was convicted in 1877. Therefore the prisoner is innocent. Prisoner's counsel tried to raise the question of the prisoner's identity with Smith in the course of his trial on the specific charges of fraud, but the Common Serjeant ruled that it was irrelevant ..., and even if the prisoner is not Smith the evidence of his guilt is overwhelming. He was identified by ten women whom he had defrauded quite positively. There was also the evidence of Mr. Gurrin as to the handwriting on the forged cheques and its identity with the prisoner's writing.

The judgment of the Beck Inquiry on this Minute was scathing, stating that it was not:

> such a minute as a trained lawyer, who had read and understood the petition and realised the full effect of the learned judge's ruling in excluding all the evidence in favour of the prisoner, could possibly have written for the guidance of his superior. It suggests no inkling on the part of the writer of any miscarriage. It assumes as concluded beyond discussion the ruling itself which is the real ground of appeal, and assumes as conclusive evidence which was only conclusive because all evidence to the contrary was excluded by the ruling impugned.

Although the Beck Inquiry's stinging public rebuke was in generalized terms there was an equally significant point of concern: the Minute had been written by a junior clerk (initialled: AJE) and overseen by another (initialled: HBS) who had ten years' service in the criminal department.

The author of the Minute was, in fact, Arthur John Eagleston, the son of an ironmonger, educated at Oxford High School and Oxford University where he took a First in Classics. Eagleston, with fewer than two years' experience within the Home Office and without legal training, had been entrusted with drafting the first response to Beck's Petition. How could such a task be delegated to a novice without a legal background? The concern is hardly reduced by the fact that the Minute had been approved by a junior clerk, Harry Butler Simpson (HBS), also an Oxford graduate with a First in Classics but who had been called to the Bar. Despite the fact that he had never practised and a paper qualification as a barrister was at the time undemanding,[24] it is remarkable that Simpson was regarded within the Home Office as an expert in criminal law.[25]

[24] See Viscount Simon, *Retrospect: The Memoirs of The Rt. Hon. Viscount Simon* (Hutchinson 1952) 45 where he discloses that Leo Amery passed the whole Bar examinations on three weeks' reading.

[25] Sir Harold Scott, *Your Obedient Servant* (Andre Deutsch 1959) 61.

The practice of the Home Office in respect of Petitions (and, indeed, other items of work) was to delegate such tasks to those lowest in the hierarchy. Junior clerks were given initial responsibilities on the basis that, as Harold Scott, a junior clerk from 1911, stated:[26] 'we were not expected or allowed to exercise any initiative or responsibility. It was our job to look for precedents, and to draft letters for the approval of our seniors ... Tradition and precedent were ... powerful factors in our lives.' The devolvement of initial responsibility to Arthur Eagleston was, accordingly, usual practice and, for his part, Eagleston would have received no formal training for this work.[27]

While the Beck Inquiry's criticism may have been plausible in respect of the first Minute, the same accusation could hardly be levelled against the next. The author of that Minute was Charles Stewart Murdoch, who, although not qualified as a lawyer, had progressed from junior clerk in 1856 to become assistant Under-Secretary in 1896 thereby having some thirty years' experience in the criminal branch.[28] The Minute (dated 16 June 1896) read as follows:

> Mr. Gill [counsel for Beck] tried very hard to raise the point now put forward in the memorial, that the writing of the cheques was the writing of the man convicted in 1877, and, if he had succeeded, he had witnesses to prove that Beck could not be the man, as he was out of the country. Mr. Avory objected and the Common Serjeant supported him. It was a clever ruse, for how could his witnesses' evidence have been disproved. It would have been very difficult indeed, I should think ... The Common Serjeant, in passing sentence ... said 'the jury had convicted the prisoner on what he himself considered overwhelming evidence found not in one direction, but in every direction, of a most base and wicked crime, one which was entirely heartless.'

The Beck Inquiry's response was withering. It was not such as a trained lawyer could have written. It suggested that the alibi defence was a 'ruse' because it would have been difficult for the Crown to answer it. Yet the defence was not open to the usual objection, namely that the defendant could have been at that other place but on another day because the presence of Beck in Peru on any single day in the whole period embracing Smith's frauds and his imprisonment would have sufficed to prove his plea.

The Beck Inquiry itself, however, overlooked one important feature of this Minute. While it might have been correct to remark that such a Minute would not have been written by a trained lawyer, Murdoch's note had in fact been approved

26 ibid.

27 Even by 1911, as Scott observes, no formal training was offered to junior clerks: individuals were 'expected "to pick it up as you go along"' ibid 29.

28 Murdoch had been appointed under the old patronage system, his father being Chairman of the Colonial Land and Emigration Commission.

by Sir Kenelm Digby, the permanent Under-Secretary who was a barrister and sometime County Court judge.[29] The lack of engagement with Beck's Petition,[30] therefore, went to the top of the Home Office.

After further efforts failed, Beck's luck appeared to have changed. In 1898, Beck's solicitor learned that John Smith had been circumcised and, since Beck was a Christian, the issue of identity could be easily resolved. He communicated this to the Home Office when requesting an interview on 17 May 1898. Charles Murdoch, although appearing to have his mind already closed to the significance of such an outcome ('this does not prove that Beck was not guilty of the many offences of the same kind of which he was convicted'), asked the Prison Department on 23 May 1898 for a statement of the marks of the two men in detail. The next day, the Prison Department furnished a report entitled '**Distinctive Marks of:**' which catalogued differences, as between Smith and Beck, as seen in **Illustration 2.1.**[31]

The Prison Report was dispositive: Beck and Smith *were* different people. When the papers were reviewed by Simpson, he continued the official scepticism. Simpson conceded that while the circumcision evidence must be taken as conclusive against Beck being Smith 'on the other hand' there was both:

> ... personal similarity which led to Beck's identification and similarity in their handwriting—though there are obvious differences such as might be expected after 20 years ... The fact that the similarity of handwriting was urged by the defence at Beck's trial suggests that he knew more than he admits about Smith.

Simpson concluded with the observation that 'Beck's undoubted frauds were very extensive and of a singularly mean & bad kind—7 years is not an exceptionally severe sentence considering all things.'

However, because Beck was not circumcised and discrepancies in other details were apparent,[32] Murdoch belatedly wrote a Minute on 27 June, agreed to by Kenelm Digby, in the following terms:

> ... Though the present conviction is not affected by the representations made by Mr. Dutton, I think the papers should go to the Common Serjeant for his opinion & observations.

[29] Digby, a graduate of Oxford, had been called to the Bar in 1865, had written a text on real property, and had acted as a County Court judge in Derbyshire. He was brought in to the Home Office in 1896.

[30] Bernard O'Donnell reported that 'once in prison, [Beck] bombarded the Home Office with sixteen petitions', *The Trials of Mr. Justice Avory* (Rich & Cowan 1935) 52.

[31] It is not apparent how the (red) 'X' marks were entered on the document.

[32] The Home Office should have taken account of the important difference in eye colour and scars.

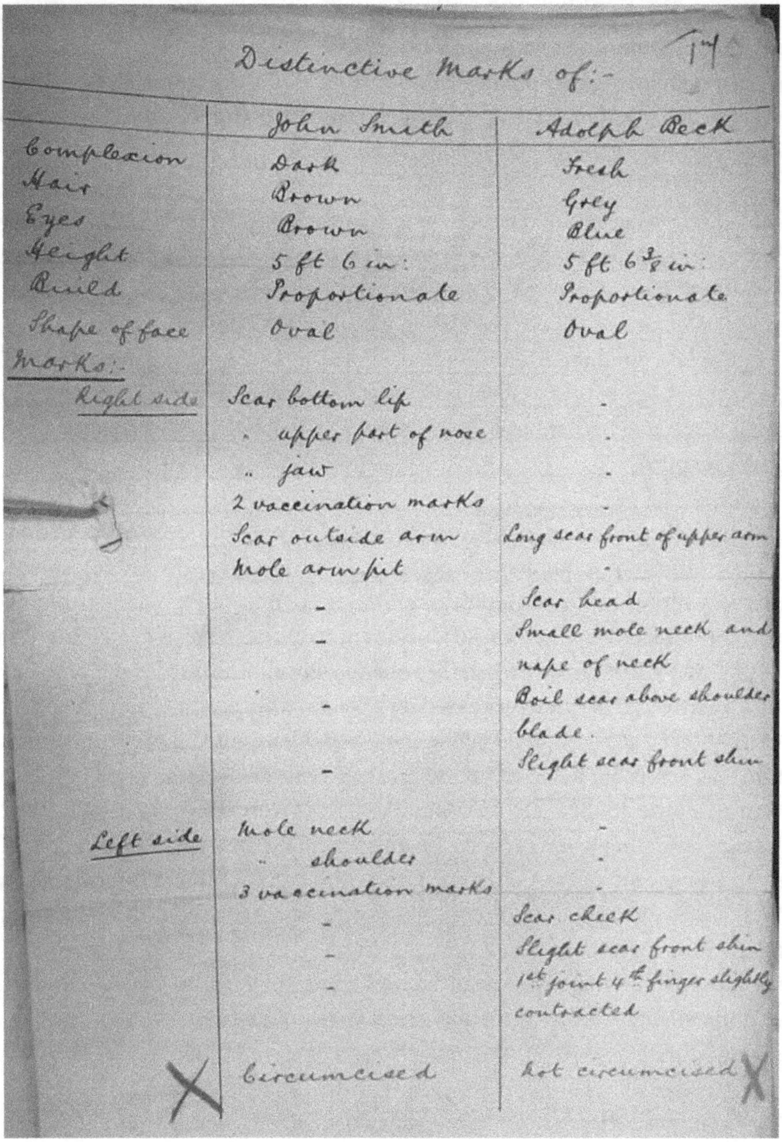
Distinctive marks of:-

	John Smith	Adolph Beck
Complexion	Dark	Fresh
Hair	Brown	Grey
Eyes	Brown	Blue
Height	5 ft 6 in:	5 ft 6 3/8 in:
Build	Proportionate	Proportionate
Shape of face	Oval	Oval
Marks:-		
Right side	Scar bottom lip	-
	" upper part of nose	-
	" jaw	-
	2 vaccination marks	-
	Scar outside arm	Long scar front of upper arm
	Mole arm pit	-
	-	Scar head
	-	Small mole neck and nape of neck
	-	Boil scar above shoulder blade.
	-	Slight scar front shin
Left side	Mole neck	-
	" shoulder	-
	3 vaccination marks	-
	-	Scar cheek
	-	Slight scar front shin
	-	1st joint 4th finger slightly contracted
	Circumcised	Not circumcised

Illustration 2.1 Prison Comparison of Description of Smith and Beck (May 1898)

The Common Serjeant, Sir Forrest Fulton, was accordingly written to on 8 July 1898. Fulton stated that the evidence of identity was 'most overwhelming', that Beck had had the benefit of being defended by Charles Gill who, despite being a 'most skilful cross-examiner' had been unable to shake any of the witnesses, and he regarded the evidence of alibi with 'great suspicion, particularly having regard to the source from which it comes'.[33] Fulton's opinion was, however, clearly influenced by the Home Office communication.

The accompanying document from the Home Office detailing the 'Distinctive Marks' did not indicate that it emanated from the prison authorities.[34] Fulton's letter in response contained the following statement:

> I did not investigate the question as to whether he was John Smith, although I have very little doubt that he and Beck were one and the same person. *I do not understand if the paper sent to me purporting to be a record of the marks of the person of Smith and Beck respectively is official or not.* I observe that Mr. Dutton in one of his communications says he is informed that Smith was a Jew and was circumcised. It is of course obvious that if at the time of his conviction Smith was circumcised, and Beck is not so, they cannot be one and the same person . . . (emphasis supplied)

This important section of Fulton's letter should have led to immediate action by the Home Office for a number of compelling reasons. First, the judge's statement 'I have very little doubt that [Smith] and Beck were one and the same person' was clearly contradicted by the official document in possession of the Home Office regarding the 'Distinctive Marks'. This in and of itself informed the Home Office that Fulton's overall opinion was based on a *factual* misunderstanding. Second, the letter went on to accept that this view could not be sustained if Mr Dutton's information was correct: it asserted on the one hand that Fulton remained of the view ('I *have* very little doubt . . . ')[35] that Smith and Beck were one and the same person, and on the other that it was obvious that this would not be so if Smith were circumcised and Beck not. Since the Home Office knew that Dutton's information was correct, it was incumbent on them to inform the judge without delay of the true position. They did nothing.

The letter from Fulton was dealt with by Simpson who, we have seen, was almost unpersuadable as to a possible miscarriage of justice. Simpson drafted the following Minute:

> The Common Serjeant has not the slightest doubt that Beck is the man who robbed (sic) the women in 1895: whether he is also the man who was convicted of

[33] This is nonsense and should have been seen as such by the Home Office officials. The 1877 crime was committed by Smith and, indeed, in his Petition to the Home Office he admitted guilt. Given this, there was no question of Beck being the wrongdoer in 1877 and his geographical location was irrelevant.

[34] The Home Office stamp on the document merely signified that the Home Office had copied it.

[35] In its efforts to help the judge, the Beck Inquiry was later to suggest that, because his letter had been dictated to his clerk, the clerk had misunderstood the judge saying: 'I *had* very little doubt . . . ' Fulton confirmed that this was plausible adding: 'It is impossible if I had known that the examination [of Beck's marks] had been made that I could have said that I thought he was the same man.'

a similar offence in 1877 is open to doubt, but this is really immaterial as Beck is being punished only for the offence proved in 1896 [Nil to Petition][36] but let convict be given a fresh prison number so that his identity with D 523 [Smith] should not be affirmed.

As the Beck Inquiry found, this Minute (initialled by both Charles Murdoch and Kenelm Digby) 'discloses a want of appreciation of the facts and the legal aspect of the case'. On the substance, it was clear that once the separate identities of Smith and Beck had been confirmed, instead of alibi (which was not before the jury) the first step in Beck's defence was made good. The other step (which was set out in his first Petition) was that whoever committed the first crime (ie, now clearly Smith) committed the crimes in 1894–95 where the same story, the same cheques, the same handwriting, and the same signature were repeated. Although the documents in the Smith case were held at the Old Bailey rather than at the Home Office, it would, as the Inquiry stated, have been easy to compare them so that: 'Had these documents been examined the inference must have been irresistible that all were the work of the same man, and have forced the conclusion that relief could not be withheld.'

But nothing of the kind was done. No one sought to inform the Common Serjeant that the documentation regarding the distinctive marks *was* an official document. Furthermore, no one told the police or Public Prosecutor that Smith had been circumcised until July 1904 when Smith was arrested for new frauds. And further still, this was not simply the failing of a junior clerk: the deficiency went all the way in the chain of subordination up to the permanent Under-Secretary. After this, further protests from Beck were brushed aside,[37] he was given a new prison number (W 78) and served his sentence before being released on licence in 1901.

Following Beck's release, the frauds started up again and he was re-arrested and appeared at the Marylebone police court in London on 15 April 1904 charged with stealing a ring, a gold watch, and a sovereign from Pauline Scott, a domestic servant. The circumstances of the fraud were similar to the earlier frauds with the fraudster representing himself as 'Lord somebody', offering a cheque for £120 in her favour to buy dresses, jewellery, shoes etc and taking the items on various pretexts. The publicity surrounding Beck's arrest brought forward further complainants. So, on 30 April 1904, Adolf Beck appeared again at police court charged with defrauding Rose Reece, Caroline Singer, and Grace Campbell and on 12 May 1904 he was charged with defrauding Lily King. Beck was committed

36 'Nil' was how the Home Office recorded a failed Petition.

37 Thus, in response to a letter from Beck, a Home Office Minute (12 October 1898) simply records that he 'again pleads innocence' and that he 'naturally makes the most of the alteration of the [prison] number'.

for trial on 19 May 1904 and tried before Grantham J at the Central Criminal Court on 27 June 1904.

These events were widely reported in the press. Indeed, the basic storyline, 'The Servant and the "Lord": Credulous Girl's Adventure', set out in the *Nottingham Evening Post* on the 16 April 1904, the day following Beck's initial court appearance, excited interest in England and elsewhere[38] as indicative banner headlines below illustrate:

- '"Peer's" Fascinations: Said To Have Borrowed Rings And Money From Women' (*Daily Mail*, 2 May 1904)[39]
- 'London Police Courts: West-End Adventurer' (*Daily Telegraph*, 2 May 1904)
- 'He Said He Was A Lord. Two Servant Girls Duped. Strange Adventures in London Streets' (*Evening Telegraph, Dundee* 3 May 1904)
- '"Peer's" Lady Friends. Women As Dupes Of An Affable Stranger' (*Evening Telegraph* (Dundee), 14 May 1904)
- 'Victimising Girls' (*Daily Mail*, 20 May 1904)
- 'Easily Duped Girls. Tempted by a "Cellar Full Of Wine And An Orchard"' (*Evening Telegraph*, 21 May 1904)
- 'Singular Charge of Fraud. "Peer" And His Cheques' (*Cheltenham Chronicle*, 21 May 1904)

The story gripped the whole country.

Inexplicably, in spite of the nationwide ferment amid extensive press publicity,[40] the Home Office made no attempt to alert the authorities that there might be some dreadful mistake.

In evidence to the subsequent Inquiry, Edward Troup[41] stated incredulously that the Home Office knew nothing of Beck's second arrest until *after* his trial and conviction. If this is correct, the Home Office was grossly negligent in discharging its responsibility for a case where the original conviction had been throughout contested, closely monitored by its officials at all levels, and very much in the public domain. However, it beggars belief that no one in the Home Office was seized of a case which was now a *cause célèbre*. It is more likely that the Home Office was fully apprised of the situation (how, indeed, could it be otherwise) and, through moral cowardice, decided not to act at all or, almost inconceivably, decided to wait for Beck's conviction to vindicate its earlier handling of his Petition.

[38] See eg, 'The Great Judicial Scandal' *Evening Post* (New Zealand 14 October 1904).

[39] This story and its headline were repeated in the Derby *Daily Telegraph* (2 May 1904).

[40] In addition, an amateur criminologist, George Sims, lobbied strenuously on Beck's behalf in a series of articles which appeared in the *Daily Mail* and the *Referee* with other accounts in the *Daily Telegraph* and *Truth*.

[41] It seems that, as the department's high-flier, Troup was chosen to present the Home Office case.

As the Beck Inquiry was later to observe 'an innocent man was convicted through the ignorance of the police and the Public Prosecutor of a material fact which was in the possession of the prison authorities and the Home Office'. By good fortune, Grantham J postponed sentence because of concerns he had about the case. In the interim, William Wyatt alias 'Thomas', alias 'Smith', was then arrested on similar charges based upon acts committed while Beck was in custody.[42] He was then identified as 'Smith', alias 'Lord Wilton' thereby leading to Beck's release.[43]

Allocating Responsibility

Against a background of press agitation,[44] the Beck Inquiry had the unenviable task of sorting out who was responsible for this calamity.

The Inquiry confronted the process that led to the exclusion of alibi evidence at Beck's first trial, although it abjured from anything approximating a cross-examination of the relevant parties.[45] As a result of Avory's objection and the ruling of Fulton, Beck was convicted on evidence from which, as the Inquiry concluded, 'everything that told, or might be thought to tell, in his favour was excluded. His case was never tried.' The Inquiry concluded that Fulton's ruling could not be supported on the principle that evidence adduced by a prisoner relevant to his defence cannot be excluded although it be relevant to a collateral issue which is not under trial.[46]

Fulton, it will be recalled, had acted as prosecutor against Smith in 1877, which should have raised difficult questions about his role as trial judge in the Beck case. Fulton sought to justify himself by telling the Inquiry that he 'had not the faintest recollection either of the [Smith] case or the man' and that he expected that he 'only held the brief ... for a friend' having 'very little business at the Old Bailey at that time'. This would have been open to the objection that a rare case would have

[42] After his release on licence in 1881, it seems that 'Smith' did not engage in frauds for many years.

[43] The real fraudster was sentenced to five years' in prison.

[44] There is a general account in Watson, *Beck* (n 10) 31–33.

[45] As Watson remarked, the Beck Inquiry 'were almost morbidly anxious that no aspersion should be suffered to rest on any member of the legal profession' (ibid 45). This judgment is fully justified in the light of the remarks by the Chairman when introducing Fulton: '[I]t would be nothing less than a public scandal if any question in the nature of cross-examination were addressed to a judge who, for public reasons, has thought it fitting on a public occasion to state such facts as he thinks material that have come before him in his judicial capacity on the trial. Therefore, in this inquiry no questions will be addressed to Sir Forrest Fulton upon his statement, except as may occur to us as necessary to enable us to understand fully that which he desires to say.'

[46] Subsequently, the judgment on Fulton's ruling was much more severe. Thus, the Lord Chancellor, speaking of the Beck case on the Second Reading on the Criminal Appeals Bill said: 'There was an undoubted misdirection in that case; evidence was refused admission which was palpably proper evidence to have been allowed. The Judge was confident that he was right, although he was transparently wrong; he refused to grant a case; and no remedy against his refusal was possible.' HL Deb 27 March 1906 vol 154 cols 994–95.

been more memorable but the records show that Fulton was no stranger to the Old Bailey at the time. Indeed, prior to the Smith case, he had appeared as both prosecutor (eg, *Charles Carter* February 1877; *William Stunt and George Cole* March 1877; *George Godfrey Harman* September 1876) and as defence counsel (eg, *Silas Barlow* November 1876; *Rachel Roland* December 1876; *Charles Gower and Charles Malles* December 1876).

The Inquiry found no fault in the prosecution conduct of the trial. In view of the case he held, Avory was not in error in taking the objection in the first place and the justification he offered for proceeding on the misdemeanour indictment had no possible effect in narrowing the area of Beck's defence.[47] In this respect the Inquiry withheld criticism of Avory's justification for shutting out the 1877 case—that it was to prevent the jury being prejudiced against Beck by knowledge of the conviction in that case—when it is clear that its introduction was a matter for the defence. The Inquiry dealt with it in breathtakingly dismissive terms:

> Mr. Avory, as counsel for the Crown, in view of the case which he held, was perfectly justified in taking the objection, as well as in every step he took in the conduct of the prosecution. He has given his reasons in evidence, and it would be quite superfluous to refer to them here.

In the result, after looking cursorily into the actions of the defence solicitor and the prison authorities, the Inquiry reserved its main criticism for the Home Office officials.

It was left to Edward Troup, then assistant Under-Secretary and with no connection with the case before 1904, to recite the sorry tale of Home Office involvement. This evidence consisted in reading out the various Petitions, describing the Distinctive Marks, reciting the flawed internal minute of Charles Murdoch in May 1898 in which the lack of identity was said not to prove that Beck was innocent of the later offences, and the sending of the papers to Forrest Fulton. Extraordinarily, Troup asserted that the Home Office knew nothing of Beck's second arrest (despite its wide and sensational coverage in the press)[48] until after his conviction adding that the Home Office now regarded Beck's innocence as established beyond doubt. The next, and key,[49] Home Office witness was Sir Kenelm Digby.

What Digby had to say amounted to a general defence of Home Office inertia in respect of the handling of Petitions which was deference to the opinion of the trial judge, *any* trial judge at whatever level. The Inquiry, accepting the need for the two

[47] Here the Inquiry simply reflected the legal position that the evidence Beck wished to bring out ought not to have been excluded whatever the form of the indictment.

[48] Prior to Grantham J sentencing Beck, which was adjourned following the second trial, Avory's clerk explained that the Beck case was 'the burning topic of the day', Ashley, *My Sixty Years* (n 15) 147.

[49] Charles Murdoch also appeared as a witness but his involvement was clearly established by the Minute he had written in May 1898 and his lack of action thereafter.

jurisdictions to be kept apart, considered that even on the facts stated in the first Petition, the Home Office might have realized that there had been 'a miscarriage so grave as to call for interference had they deemed themselves bound to look at the case with a fresh eye'. Referring to Digby the Inquiry pointedly observed:

> That accomplished lawyer who then held the post of permanent Under-Secretary[50] could not have failed to realise the extent of the miscarriage had he felt himself at liberty to canvass the role of the judge.

The Inquiry was most concerned with the way in which the Home Office dealt with the case in 1898 after obtaining from the prison authorities the distinctive marks of Smith and Beck. The Home Office were faulted for failing to explain to the Common Serjeant with sufficient clarity that the information regarding the distinctive marks was derived from official sources; and also for failing to ascertain 'the indisputable fact that the incriminating documents of 1896 were in the same handwriting as those of 1877'. The failure led to two consequences, said the Inquiry: 'it led to Mr. Beck's continued detention in prison; it indirectly led to his re-arrest and conviction in 1904'.

The Immediate Lessons

Despite the failings of the Petition system revealed by the Beck case, the Home Office opposed the establishment of a Court of Criminal Appeal.[51] Before the Inquiry, Digby refused to concede a direct right of appeal but, extraordinarily, only one by leave of the Home Office. Deference appears to have operated in both directions, the Inquiry (headed by the Master of the Rolls, Henn Collins) not recommending the establishment of a Court of Criminal Appeal.

The Longer Term

The actions of its subordinate staff and the evidence of its top officials are indicative of an ineffective department yet to come to terms with its responsibilities. Deference to judges left it blind to clear failings in criminal justice.[52] The system

[50] Digby had ceased to act in this capacity in 1903.

[51] Troup (in *Home Office* (n 2)) glosses over this when he says that the establishment of the Court of Criminal Appeal 'had for many years been advocated by legal reformers and by more than one Home Secretary' referring to a Bill prepared by Sir William Harcourt towards the end of his term of office as Home Secretary (1880–85).

[52] The problematic corollary of such deference is further underscored by Alan Dershowitz, who remarks that the Beck case 'goes to show that when a judge believes that a defendant did it (in this case because he erroneously believed he had done it before) he or she will become blind, deaf and oblivious

of Petitions, on which the fate of wrongly convicted prisoners largely rested, was assigned to those lowest in the hierarchy of experience. Slavishly following precedents and fearful of departing from departmental practice, clerks responded to claims of prisoners with a mixture of deflection, defensiveness, and lassitude. Their responses were then passed up the chain of command to the next individual in seniority who would initial the Minute, agree it, or add his own Minute or annotation and so on up the ladder. The evidence shows, however, that, like those at the foot of the ladder, their superiors lacked independence of mind, did nothing to inculcate good practice in junior clerks, if they knew what that might be, and exhibited an absence of intellectual engagement with any of the serious issues raised.

There is no doubt that deference to the opinion of judges could not explain the series of blunders which characterized the handling of Beck's petitions. Apart from the failure to act on the first Petition, no effort was made to compare the handwriting of the documents in Beck's case with those in Smith's case; no effort was made to obtain the Distinctive Marks document until prompted by Beck's solicitor; once the separate identities of Beck and Smith were established, these were not communicated to the Common Serjeant in a clear manner; no effort was made to clarify the status of the Distinctive Marks document after Fulton had written to say that he was unsure in this regard; no one in the Home Office then or thereafter informed the Public Prosecutor or the police that official documentation proved that Beck was not Smith; despite a frenzy of publicity, no one in the Home Office responded in 1904 to requests for help from Beck on his re-arrest; and no one in the Home Office on the occasion of Beck's second arrest sought to inform the Public Prosecutor of the lack of identity between Beck and Smith. These were failings of the highest order with the fault lines running throughout the chain of command. This left the important question: what would the Home Office learn from this fiasco?

The Home Office Response

It is clear from internal Home Office documents that its staff found difficulty in accepting responsibility for the Beck fiasco. Thus, following Beck's release from prison on 18 July 1904, a Memorandum and accompanying Minute written by Troup on 9 August 1904 sought to elevate the importance of the role of the Home Office: 'It was *in consequence of the inquiries made by the Home Office in 1898* that the fact came to light that John Smith was circumcised' (original emphasis); and continuing to assert that, despite the fact that it was then known that Beck was not Smith, 'the evidence against him was still so "overwhelming" that no interference

to exculpatory evidence no matter how persuasive', 'Introduction' in Eric Watson, *The Trial of Adolf Beck* (Gryphon Editions 2014 (Special Edition, Notable Trials Library)).

was possible'. This highly selective reading of the facts suggested defensiveness approaching denial.

The key formal Home Office response[53] came in the report to the Cabinet by the Home Secretary, Aretas Akers-Douglas, in 1904 following the exoneration of Beck and the grant of a free pardon.[54] This Report utterly failed to engage with the Inquiry's wholesale critique and posted worrying signs for the future intelligent involvement of the Home Office in criminal justice matters.[55]

The Report first sought to put the focus at the bottom of the hierarchy:

> They [the Beck Inquiry] pass a somewhat severe criticism on the *subordinate members* of the Home Office for failing to see that the evidence which the Judge excluded ought to have been considered; and for failing to see the full bearing on the case of the fact, discovered by the Home Office in 1898, that Smith was circumcised and Beck therefore could not be Smith; and they suggest that *if the subordinate officers of the Home Office had been trained lawyers this mistake could not have been made* (emphasis supplied).

Even allowing for the measured language of the Inquiry, this summary amounts to a misrepresentation of its findings which in terms indicted those at the apex of the hierarchy, the assistant Under-Secretary (Murdoch) and the permanent Under-Secretary (Digby).

The first step in deflecting criticism was quickly followed by the next:

> I cannot but think that the [Beck Inquiry] have—unintentionally and in good faith—done something less than justice to my Department, and that in their (very proper) desire to shield the Judge they have cast an undue proportion of blame on the Home Office. This appears to me to be indicated at the outset of their Report, where they say that Judges, however able and experienced, are fallible but imply that it is not permissible for the reviewing authority to be so too.

This led to the extraordinary proposition that the Home Secretary could not think that 'a lack of legal training was the cause of the error in the Department, when a Judge of exceptionally great criminal experience made on the same information exactly the same mistake' and that the error, therefore lay in 'deferring too readily' to what was plainly the opinion of the judge, namely, that no further inquiry was

[53] National Archives, CAB 37/73.

[54] Suffering from pleurisy and bronchitis, Beck died in Middlesex Hospital in 1909.

[55] Top Home Office officials continued their attempts to exonerate the Department from blame. See eg, Troup: 'In that case the Home Office, relying on Beck's identification by no less than ten independent witnesses as well as by the evidence of the first expert in handwriting, failed, as the court had failed, to follow up a clue which would have established Beck's innocence, and he underwent seven years penal servitude for a crime of which he was innocent. Whether a Court of Criminal Appeal would have done better may be doubted' Troup, *Home Office* (n 2) 59–60.

necessary. Such an opinion would nearly always be decisive and it would be 'absurd for [Home Office staff] to attempt to re-try on paper cases already heard in open Court before a jury; and any effort on their part to do so would necessarily be received with disfavour by the Judges'.

It hardly needs saying that this was not the issue at all: the issue was whether the opinion of the Common Serjeant was based on a full understanding of the papers submitted to him by Home Office staff, the answer to which lay self-evidently in the terms of the opinion itself. If the report of Aretas Akers-Douglas set out to bury the past it also sought to leave the future of the Home Office in its own hands.

The Home Secretary began by conceding that he was prepared to strengthen the criminal branch on the basis that it was 'over-worked'. It did not follow, however, that this should consist, as the Beck Inquiry suggested, with the addition of 'trained lawyers' since:

> The mistake, if any, made by the Home Office in 1898 was one of fact, not of law, and the Department does not deal with criminal Petitions on any legal or technical grounds, but on principles of common sense.

As can be seen, under the pretext of setting out the boundaries of Home Office responsibilities in regard to petitions, the defence of the Department now moved to contesting whether it was guilty of any shortcomings at all!

This led the Home Secretary into a line of argument that spoke eloquently of its core weaknesses:

> To add to the Home Office staff lawyers of recognised ability and position at high salaries, with the idea of independently revising judicial errors, would bring the Department at once into conflict with the judicial Bench and indeed with the Constitution of the country; while if I should attempt to place lawyers in the now existing subordinate posts, I fear that the barristers, who would be attracted by the salaries paid to junior clerks, would be men of less general ability than the latter, and would not be likely to possess legal knowledge or training of any value.

In this way, the Home Secretary, whilst conceding that the conditions of service in the junior posts would not attract lawyers of ability, sought to assert that the existing junior staff were people of greater 'general ability' than any such barrister despite the obvious fact that they had (in combination with more senior staff) failed in matters of fact and law and had been subject to severe criticism by the Beck Inquiry.

The line of defence set up by the Home Secretary was assiduously pursued by the Prime Minister in the House of Commons:[56]

[56] 4 Hansard 143 690 ff (21 March 1905).

> In his opinion, and he could not state it too clearly, it was not the duty of the Home Office to deal with the state of the law. Mistakes in law were properly dealt with by a judicial tribunal; and the Home Office was bound to take the law as laid down at a trial by a Judge of the Superior Court, or of Assize or Central Criminal Court, upon the interpretation of a statute or the admissibility of evidence...
>
> The original mistake was one of law,[57] and in that he did not think the Home Office was to blame. Where he thought it was to blame was when it was discovered, as it was, after the unfortunate man had been two years in prison by evidence beyond all cavil, that his supposed identity with Smith, a person convicted of a similar offence, was disproved. When the identity of the two men was disproved by the new evidence the Home Office did right in forwarding that new evidence to the learned Judge who tried the case; and, seeing that the actual documents were forwarded, how the Judge could have treated it as other than official evidence, when if he had read it he would have seen that it was the official document[58] of the prison authorities showing that one man was circumcised and the other was not, remained an unexplained mystery. Where the Home Office went wrong was when they acquiesced in the opinion of the learned Judge that, whether or not the two men were the same, the stream of other evidence was sufficient to convict. When the Home Office discovered that Smith and Beck were not the same person they should have pursued the investigation further. Here they committed an error of judgment.

The government did indicate that it would seek to strengthen the department as a consequence of this case. As the Prime Minister put it:

> ... there should be a strengthening of the Criminal Department of the Home Office by an infusion of gentlemen with practical experience of the administration of the law. He dissented altogether from the censure which had been applied to the clerks at the Home Office who prepared the minutes. The high qualifications of first-class clerks in the Civil Service were universally recognised, and anybody with experience at the Home Office must acknowledge with gratitude the efficient service the clerks of that Department rendered. But the burden cast upon them should not be too heavy. They should be adequate in numbers.

The outcome was an addition of one junior clerk and a legally qualified assistant Under-Secretary (Ernley Blackwell)[59] to reinforce the criminal department. This was far from the root and branch review that the Home Office appeared to require.

[57] The Home Secretary, as noted above, asserted that the mistake was one of fact!

[58] To the contrary, the document as submitted to the judge bore no indications whatever that it was an official prison document or, indeed, an official document of any kind.

[59] For details regarding Ernley Blackwell and his involvement in Home Office responsibilities, see ch 3.

Conclusion

It is tempting to see the Home Secretary's report to Cabinet and the Prime Minister's statement as both a natural defence of the Department and an object lesson in the art of dis-information. However viewed, the real questions went unanswered. These included: whether Home Office deference to the judiciary extended beyond respect for considered and reported legal opinions in decided cases; whether staff who had been criticized by the Inquiry would be given further training and, if so, what form it might take; whether staff who had been criticized by the Inquiry would be given additional, and, if any, which, criminal justice responsibilities following the effective end of the Petition system with the establishment of the Court of Criminal Appeal; whether those at the top of the chain of command would have a greater supervisory role in the oversight of junior staff; and whether staff, at all levels, would display greater wisdom, discernment, and judgment in the discharge of their responsibilities. These very questions immediately came up for consideration over the issue of another Home Office responsibility: the police questioning of suspects in the course of criminal investigations, to which we now turn.

3

The Origin of the Judges' Rules

Introduction

The responsibility for handling policing issues necessarily involved both the Home Office, which was charged with maintaining the King's Peace, and the judges who regulated the admission of evidence at trial. While these functions were distinct, they came together as the investigative role of the police expanded in advance of formal legal regulation. At the same time, differential policies as between police forces and conflicting decisions of lower courts called for a more coordinated response. In the absence of parliamentary intervention, the locus of this response came in the creation of the so-called Judges' Rules in 1912, extended in number from four to nine in 1918.

In this chapter, we examine how and why the Judges' Rules were created. Our account primarily draws upon material in the National Archives.[1] We preface our discussion with a short introduction to policing over this period[2] as a backcloth to more detailed analysis of the regulatory framework.

General Policing Issue

The official (and sympathetic) historian of the Metropolitan Police (Met), David Ascoli, described the police in 1900 as 'a kind of urban peasantry, largely illiterate, grossly underpaid ... '[3] This assessment was broadly in line with that of

[1] See generally National Archives: HO 144/10066 which contains papers for the period 1899–1929 regarding the history and procedure adopted in cautioning and interrogating offenders. We have retained references to individual files. Of the sixty-five relevant Home Office files for this period the following have been marked as 'destroyed': A 52392/1; A 52392/2; A 52392/3; A 52392/7; A 52392/8; A 52392/13; A 52392/14; A 52392/16; A 52392/18; A 52392/20; A 52392/24; A 52392/25; A 52392/26; A 52392/27; A 52392/28; A 52392/59. Eighteen other files could not be located in the bundles and are probably destroyed.

[2] See generally, Thomas Alan Critchley, *A History of Police in England and Wales* (2nd edn, Patterson Smith 1972) (hereafter Critchley, *History of Police*); Clive Emsley, *The Great British Bobby: A History ofBritish Policing from the 18th Century to the Present* (Quercus 2010) (hereafter Emsley, *British Bobby*); Clive Emsley, *The English Police: A Political and Social History* (2nd edn, Longman 1996) (hereafter Emsley, *English Police*).

[3] David Ascoli, *The Queen's Peace* (Hamish Hamilton 1979) 179 (hereafter Ascoli, *Queen's Peace*). See also James Morton, *Bent Coppers: A Survey of Police Corruption* (Warner Books 1993) (hereafter Morton, *Police Corruption*); Emsley, *British Bobby* (n 2); Emsley, *English Police* (n 2); Critchley, *History of Police* (n 2); Douglas Browne, *The Rise of Scotland Yard: A History of the Metropolitan Police* (George G. Harrap & Co Ltd 1956) (hereafter Browne, *Scotland Yard*); Robert Reiner, *The Politics of the Police*

The Myth of Judicial Independence. Mike McConville and Luke Marsh, Oxford University Press (2020). © Mike McConville and Luke Marsh. DOI: 10.1093/oso/9780198822103.001.0001

Tom Critchley, a former Home Office civil servant, who described the life of a policeman as involving 'almost unremitting hard work performed under conditions of severe discipline, in exchange for a weekly wage that left him, particularly the married man with a family, near the breadline'.[4] The police were paid no more than a labourer's wage and, as Ascoli notes, inflation during the First World War created increasing hardship and 'in many cases destitution'.[5] In such circumstances, it was inevitable that some would be tempted into various forms of graft[6] and others might disrespect rules and regulations in more enterprising ways.[7] Despite some advances in criminal science,[8] police training was minimal,[9] comprising little more than drilling exercises, and did not begin to be meaningfully confronted until after the reports of the Desborough Committee appointed in 1919 following police strikes in Birmingham, Liverpool, and London.[10] The Police Act 1919 gave effect to the key recommendations of Desborough introducing standard terms and conditions for all police forces in England and Wales.[11]

Policing at the start of the twentieth century was far removed from policing of today in terms of its structure, organization, and management. Following the establishment of the Met in 1829, the County and Borough Police Act 1856 made it compulsory for a police force to be established in any county which had not previously formed a constabulary. Policing authority was diffuse, the Royal Commission into Police Powers and Procedures (RCPPP) (1929) reporting, for example, that there were 180 different police forces spread across the country.[12] Whereas the Commissioner of the Met was directly responsible to the Home Secretary, the provincial police were agents of local government with Chief Constables in the boroughs responsible to Watch Committees and those in the counties, after 1889,

(3rd edn, OUP 1985); William Melville Lee, *A History of the Police in England* (Methuen 1901); Mike Brogden, *The Police: Autonomy and Consent* (Academic Press 1982).

4 Critchley, *History of Police* (n 2) 150.

5 Ascoli, *Queen's Peace* (n 3) 196.

6 According to Critchley many officers and their families were, by 1918, undernourished and 'the temptations held out by bribes of food and money must at times have been irresistible' *History of Police* (n 2) 184.

7 Browne (*Scotland Yard* (n 3)), eg, notes the conviction of a constable for perjury and two others for drunk and disorderly behaviour in 1908. Police Constable Rolls, acquitted of planting an offensive weapon on a sleeping cabinet-maker, was subsequently convicted and sentenced to five years' penal servitude; and Police Constable Ashford was convicted of assault: see Morton, *Police Corruption* (n 3) 58ff.

8 At the start of the century, a Criminal Record Office was established and fingerprinting introduced.

9 Edward Henry initiated a small training school for detectives in 1902 but the first Police Training School was not established until 1907 at Peel House in Westminster.

10 In response to poor conditions, a Police and Prison Union was formed illegally in 1913 and attracted members nationally despite the threats of instant dismissal.

11 The Act also barred the police from belonging to a trade union outlawing the existing National Union of Police and Prison Officers, established the Police Federation as the representative body for all police officers up to the rank of Chief Inspector, and the Home Secretary was given power to regulate police pay and conditions of service.

12 *Report of the Royal Commission on Police Powers and Procedure* (HMSO 1929) (hereafter RCPPP, *Report* (1929)) 99 para 261.

responsible to county police authorities.[13] Apart from Home Office authority over the Met, however, the creation of Inspectors of Constabulary by the County and Borough Police Act imported a degree of central influence[14] since government grants could be made for police forces deemed to be 'efficient'.[15]

Against this background, the Home Office was not only responsible for the Met but also for mediating between the problems presented by the divergence between, on the one hand, each force with its distinctive Instruction Book and, on the other, the generalized demands of the common law. It is in this setting that the origins of the Judges' Rules are to be found.

Cautioning and Questioning Suspected Persons

When investigating alleged crimes at the end of the nineteenth century,[16] the guidance offered to police officers by the law was at best unhelpful. The core problem is probably traceable to the unclear implications of the common law principle, *nemo tenetur prodere seipsum*—no one shall be compelled to betray or incriminate himself.[17] With the rejection of torture by the common law courts[18] came the principle that in order for statements of prisoners to be admissible at trial they had to be 'voluntary' and with that came the question whether voluntariness had to be secured by a caution[19] and whether questioning by a person in authority compromised the free will that the common law came to insist upon. These general principles gave rise to four major issues: whether a suspect should be cautioned; whether an arrested person should be cautioned; in either event, the form of any caution; and whether it was permissible to question persons arrested for crime.

The answers given by the courts were unclear[20] with ensuing divergence in approach as between police forces and the need for Home Office advice. In the

[13] The committees were established by the Local Government Act 1888.

[14] The Inspectors, though reporting their plans to the Home Office, established a degree of independence by dealing directly with local Chief Constables, watch committees, and other representatives of local government.

[15] The influence of the Home Office increased after 1874 when the Treasury grant available was enlarged from one-quarter to one-half of overall costs.

[16] For accounts of earlier periods, see James Fitzjames Stephen, *A History of the Criminal Law of England*, vol i (1883); John Henry Wigmore, *Evidence in Trials at Common Law* (1904, revised by Chadbourn 1970); Sir John Fox, *The History of Contempt of Court* (Clarendon Press 1927); Peter Mirfield, *Confessions* (Sweet & Maxwell 1985); John Langbein, 'The Criminal Trial Before Lawyers' (1978) 45 University of Chicago Law Review 263; Ian Bryan, *Interrogation and Confession* (Dartmouth 1997); John Langbein, *The Origins of Adversary Criminal Trial* (OUP 2003).

[17] *R v FitzPatrick* (1631) 3 St Tr 420 *per* Chief Justice Hyde.

[18] Torture had been used on charges of treason before the King's Council and was notoriously a feature of the Court of Star Chamber. See generally, Glanville Williams, *The Proof of Guilt* (Stevens & Sons 1963).

[19] An early reference to a form of caution occurs in *R v Broderick* (1730) Sess Pap V 12.

[20] The case law presented difficult interpretive problems. See Salim Ali Farrar, 'The Role of the Accused in English and Islamic Criminal Justice' (PhD thesis, University of Warwick 1999) <www.go.warwick.ac.uk/wrap/36414> accessed 1 January 2020.

aftermath of the Beck Inquiry the criminal department of the Home Office was little changed but reinforced with the addition of a junior clerk and, in 1906, the appointment of Ernley Blackwell as assistant Under-Secretary to take some of the workload off Edward Troup. Blackwell was Scottish but offered additional legal expertise having been called to the English Bar in 1892.[21]

Throughout this period, much of the burden of initial review still fell on the shoulders of Simpson who had been heavily criticized by the Beck Inquiry.[22] According to a colleague, Harold Scott, who entered the criminal department in 1911, the feeling that he had been made a scapegoat had 'tended over the years to sour [Simpson] and to accentuate his eccentricities'.[23] As a result, Scott stated, 'it was difficult to work with him, for he was quite capable in his capriciousness of deciding a matter in contrary sense on successive days'.[24] Nevertheless, Simpson became the key figure in addressing core policing problems.

A major source of confusion lay in apparently contradictory statements by Lord Denman CJ. In answer to an inquiry from the Royal Commission on Criminal Law and Procedure in 1843 he stated that:

> The rule laid down, as, I believe, by all the judges, is that the arresting officer shall apprise his prisoner of the cause of his arrest, and leave him free to speak or keep silence. But this rule has been misunderstood by officers, who fancy themselves bound to stop the prisoner's mouth by a caution against criminating himself, or by the use of language which leads to the invention of falsehoods and the suppression of truth.

However, advice in Denman's Introduction to *Vincent's Police Code* first published in 1882 appeared to state the opposite:

> [O]n arresting a man the constable ought simply to read his warrant or tell the accused the nature of the charge upon which he is arrested, leaving it to the person so arrested to say anything or nothing as he pleases. For a constable to press any accused person to say anything with reference to the crime of which he is accused is very wrong ... There is, however, no objection to a constable listening to any mere voluntary statement which a prisoner desires to make and repeating such statement in evidence ... Perhaps the best maxim for a constable to bear in mind with respect to an accused person is: 'Keep your eyes and ears open and your mouth shut.'

21 Sir Ernley Blackwell spent his career in Whitehall retiring in 1933.
22 In the early years, Simpson still had assistance from Arthur Eagleston.
23 Sir Harold Scott, *Your Obedient Servant* (Andre Deutsch 1959) 61.
24 ibid.

In the light of this latter statement and in line with general concerns about the alleged unfairness of Continental (particularly French) procedures, it was said to have become widespread practice for constables to caution arrested persons[25] although some forces deemed a caution unnecessary. Thus, a Cornish Police Regulation of 1882 which stipulated, on the apparent authority of Lord Denman, that constables were not to caution prisoners,[26] attracted criticism from Grantham J. The Home Secretary's formal reassurance to the House of Commons, based on a Minute drafted by Simpson[27] that this was an isolated case, proved short-lived, a sharp exchange between a judge and chief of police occurring within a short time.

The row was sparked by an Order issued in 1899 by the Chief Constable of Hampshire, Major Warde, to the effect that prisoners were not to be cautioned.[28] Warde instructed his officers that this was to be rigidly adhered to and that, 'an instance having recently occurred of a Constable cautioning a prisoner in custody, it is notified for general information that no excuse will be accepted in future for any similar disregard of instructions'.[29] In the course of a case heard at Quarter Sessions held at Bournemouth, the Recorder, Robert Kinglake, criticized this Order as 'thoroughly inimical and ... very irregular ... and illegal'. In drawing the attention of the Home Secretary to this, the Recorder said that:

> ... it has constantly been laid down that when a Constable is merely making enquiries he need not caution, but he must not cross-examine a person when he intends to apprehend. When taking a person into custody or is charging him he ought to caution him.

The public rebuke caused great offence to Warde as it could not, in his view, 'fail to have a tendency subversive of discipline' in the ranks of his force.[30]

This exchange pointed up an area of law that was not in fact settled.[31] As Troup set out in a Minute in May 1903, while judicial opinion had been unanimous in

[25] The judges in various cases said that a caution should be administered: *R v Kerr* (1837) 8 C & P 176 where Park J said: 'I should not myself ... put a question to a prisoner without cautioning her' 451.

[26] See *The Times* (3 February 1899) reporting on the case of William Collins.

[27] The case gave rise to a question in Parliament when the Secretary of State stated, in line with Simpson's note, that: 'I understand that the statement in question is to be omitted from the regulations for the Cornish police. I am not aware that a similar statement is to be found in the regulations of any other police force, and I have therefore at present no reason to think that a general circular is called for': HC Deb 20 February 1899, vol 66, col 1429.

[28] The relevant Order read: 'A Constable is not to try to *draw a statement from a prisoner; but he should not caution a prisoner not to make a statement, nor should he stop a prisoner if he is about to speak*; it is a breach of duty in an Officer to put questions to prisoners *in his custody*, and learned judges have, in many cases, reprobated such conduct ... ' (original emphasis).

[29] General Order 34/98, Hants Constabulary.

[30] Letter to Troup (25 May 1903).

[31] See, eg, Pollock CB that a prisoner 'should be cautioned not to criminate himself' in *R v Baldry* (1852) 2 De C C 430. Some other cases, by contrast, stated that the constable should listen to anything the prisoner had to say but that it was no part of his duty to caution him: *R v Howell*, Lincoln Assizes, 1864.

condemning the examination of prisoners in custody by constables, there was by no means similar unanimity in holding that a prisoner who voluntarily wishes to make a statement must be cautioned. Nevertheless, Troup acted as a conciliator, and advised that the Home Secretary would suggest to Warde the desirability of revising his Orders at an early opportunity pointing out that 'so long as most of the judges will not admit statements made by [prisoners] who have not previously been cautioned, it is not advisable to issue orders which may lead to the exclusion of valuable evidence'. Extracts from the Metropolitan Police General Orders S xvii (1903)[32] were included for reference:

> 231. Whenever a Prisoner is brought to a Station on a charge of felony, the Officer on duty is not to suffer any statement in the nature of a confession to be extracted from the person charged, either by the Police or by any other person. The accused should be warned that anything he says may be used in evidence against him.

Additionally, Rule 364 made clear that while any promise or inducement was 'likely to render' any statement involuntary, a statement made without such promise etc was 'admissible as evidence against him'. None of this or informal contacts with police forces resolved the embedded contradictions and they soon resurfaced.

In May 1904, the Chief Constable of Denbighshire, Major Leadbetter, wrote to the Home Office asking for a legal opinion on the following question:

> Is it the duty of a Policeman on apprehending a prisoner to immediately caution him and thus close his mouth and stop him from giving what may be very important evidence and which probably after the excitement of arrest had passed off he would not give, by telling him that it will be given in evidence against him at trial.

He said that he was aware that 'various Chiefs of Police' had given different instructions on this and that judges had also differed on this question but that, while he had always given an order not to caution, on a recent visit the Government Inspector 'seemed to disagree with my Order on the subject'.[33] He said that he had had a conversation with the permanent Under-Secretary, Sir Kenelm Digby, about a year earlier and was told that this was receiving attention by the Home Office but that he had heard nothing since. This inquiry excited consideration given to some more formal general intervention.

[32] The Orders and Regulations were voluminous and difficult for anyone to comprehend. See, eg, the *Royal Commission Upon the Duties of the Metropolitan Police*, 1 (1908) 35.

[33] He attached various press cuttings of remarks by judges to illustrate the confusion.

Simpson drafted a Minute (13 May 1904) which posed the question:

> Would it not be possible to get the L.C.J.'s assent to a letter in more general terms wh. Could be sent to the police whenever they inquire on this subject? Statements by a prisn on arrest may be most valuable as evidence, but as a general rule a prisn is not likely to make any statement of value for this purpose if he has been formally cautioned first...

He pointed out that doubts had been expressed as to admissibility unless a caution was administered and that if this was a view generally held by judges, it would clearly be right for a constable to always caution adding:

> ... but the H. O. has no sufficient evidence as to this; and if at present the prevailing view is that 'uncautioned statements' are admissible, a caution would only tend to defeat the ends of justice and help criminals to escape conviction. If there is a general agreement among H. M. judges on the subject—as to wh. We know nothing, most of the dicta having been given by late judges whose dicta do not bind the present Bench—the police would be greatly helped by knowing it.

Troup annotated Simpson's Minute the next day: 'If the matter is to be submitted to the L. C. J. we ought first to have a complete & reasoned statement of the whole subject.' The reply to Major Leadbetter (draft 12 May 1904) stated that while judicial opinion has not been unanimous, an order *never* to caution may lead to the exclusion of valuable evidence and this consideration 'will apply especially when the cases are to be tried before a Judge who is known to object to evidence of such statements being given . . . '.[34]

Despite judicial statements that it was the duty of a constable not to caution a prisoner in custody,[35] some courts thought that questions could be asked following a caution and it gradually became police practice to put at least some questions to prisoners following arrest and detention.[36]

The 1912 Rules

The introduction of the Judges' Rules proper began with a false start. The General Post Office (GPO) in London, which had been involved in a number

[34] The Secretary of State also pointed out that it was the experience of the Metropolitan Police that 'in certain classes of cases particularly cases where the accused is a foreigner or infanticide cases where young women are charged it is very necessary that a caution should be given' (Draft letter for approval, 12 May 1904).

[35] For example, in *R v Reason* (1872) 12 Cox 228.

[36] *R v Best* (1909) 1 KB 692.

of prosecutions, contacted the Home Office after learning from a report in *The Times*[37] that the Lord Chief Justice (LCJ), Lord Alverstone had said:

> ... [W]e have noticed lately that there is a disposition on the part of the police to question a prisoner unduly. Now it must be understood that, although it is quite right to ask questions to a man before he is charged, or at times after he is charged, neither before nor after ought questions to be put in the nature of cross-examination ... The Judges had to consider this matter (i. e. the questioning of suspected persons) formally some two or three years ago, and they issued a circular, which was circulated among the authorities ...

No such Circular existed. However, Lord Alverstone was under the impression that in October 1906 the judges had considered this matter writing to Troup: 'I wrote a letter on behalf of the Judges to the Chief Constable of Birmingham but I cannot find out whether any circular was issued from the Home Office.' Troup replied that he had *not* written to the Home Office on this question and that the Home Office had never issued any such general circular adding: 'I think such a circular would be very useful, and if you will communicate the opinion of the Judges to the Home Secretary I am sure he will be glad to make it known to the Police.' Lord Alverstone responded positively: 'If the Home Secretary desires it I will prepare a circular respecting interviews by the police of persons charged ... Perhaps you will let me know if it is really desired.'[38]

The correspondence with the Chief Constable of Birmingham, Charles Rafter, had it been unearthed then,[39] would not have resolved matters. After referring to differences of view that had emerged in London, Rafter pointed out that 'even in Birmingham the Stipendiary and the Magistrates Clerk hold different opinions on the subject, and that during one Circuit two Police Officers were censured by different Judges at Warwick and at Birmingham—one for having cautioned the prisoner and the other for having omitted to do so.'[40] The correspondence with

[37] *The Times* Report, 20 June 1912, concerned the case of *William Charles Croker* for wilful murder. One of the Grand Jurors in the case as well as the Clerk to the Hertfordshire Court of Quarter Sessions also requested copies of the Circular. The GPO was concerned that the remarks attributed to Lord Alverstone appeared more restrictive of the questioning of suspected persons than the decision of the Court of Criminal Appeal in the Post Office case of *R v Booth and Jones* (1910) 5 Cr App R 179. The remarks of Lord Alverstone are also reported in 'Questioning or Cross-examination of Persons under Arrest by the Police—Important Warning by the Lord Chief Justice' The Justice of the Peace LXXVI 340 (29 June 1912).

[38] A Minute by Ernley Blackwell notes that the Chief Constable of Birmingham was unable to find the LCJ's letter of 1906 adding: 'It would be useful to have the views of the Judges though I doubt if they would be unanimous.'

[39] It was later found following a request from the RCPPP (1929).

[40] Rafter had been recruited from the Royal Ulster Constabulary where police officers were under instructions to caution prisoners on arrest in indictable cases.

Lord Alverstone being inconclusive, Rafter did not issue any new instructions in Birmingham.[41]

The initial iteration of the Judges' Rules was issued by Lord Alverstone in 1912 following, it was said,[42] a meeting of the judges of the King's Bench. The four Rules were as follows:

> (1) When a police officer is endeavouring to discover the author of a crime, there is no objection to his putting questions in respect thereof to any person or persons, whether suspected or not, from whom he thinks that useful information may be obtained;
> (2) Whenever a police officer has made up his mind to charge a person with a crime, he should first caution such person before asking any questions, or any further questions, as the case may be.
> (3) Persons in custody should not be questioned without the usual caution being first administered.
> (4) If the prisoner wishes to volunteer any statement the usual caution should be administered.
>
> It is desirable that the last two words of the usual caution should be omitted, and that the caution should end with the words 'be given in evidence.'

The Rules got off to a bad start. The Home Office was at fault in failing to accompany the Rules with a Circular. The Rules (described in internal Home Office documents as 'somewhat ambiguous'[43]), although noted in a few publications,[44] were not known to some forces until later[45] and did not feature in decided cases for some years.[46] Indeed, Lord Sumner's authoritative summary of the common law position

[41] The Birmingham Instruction Book forbade constables from questioning prisoners following arrest.

[42] In his autobiographical reflections, Lord Alverstone makes no mention of the Judges' Rules: see Viscount Alverstone, *Recollections of Bar and Bench* (Edward Arnold 1914).

[43] See a file note by Harry Butler Simpson, Assistant Secretary (A 52392/17).

[44] Thus, the *Police Chronicle* noted that the Standing Joint Committee of the Herts County Council had submitted a copy of the Rules for the information of Justices of the County: Letter from Major Law, Chief Constable of Birmingham (24 February 1913). The four Rules first appeared in the second edition of Archbold (1918) (this volume was dedicated to Darling J). Archbold states only that they are 'from an authoritative source' (p18) (original text located at UCLA Law Library, California).

[45] Thus, in February 1913 (the Rules having been issued in November 1912), Major Law, the Chief Constable of Birmingham, having noticed that a Memorandum from the judges had been submitted to the Standing Joint Committee of Hertfordshire, requested the Chief Constable of Hertfordshire to give him 'some particulars of these' as it related to a matter on which he had had correspondence with the LCJ 'when no definite decision was arrived at on the subject' (A 52392/56). In thanking the Chief Constable of Hertfordshire, Major Law said that, now that he had the Memorandum, 'the matter to my mind remains as it was before' adding, 'Also I do not think para 3 [of the Rules] is sufficiently clear.'

[46] *Ibrahim v R* [1914] AC 599 (hereafter *Ibrahim*). The revelation of the Rules came about in *R v Voisin* [1918] 1 KB 531 (hereafter *Voisin*) as a footnote. None of the distinguished counsel involved—including (for the Crown) Richard Muir (one of the greatest lawyers of his day) and Percival Clarke (Junior Treasury Counsel); and L Morgan May for Voisin—made reference to the Rules, nor did the trial judge (Darling J).

in respect of police questioning issued two years later[47] makes no reference to the Rules which made their more public entrance only as a footnote in a case in 1918.[48]

If there was confusion as to status, there was equal uncertainty as to their interpretation and meaning. Against a background of divergent judicial views[49] and constabulary practice, the Judges' Rules added to the confusion because of their atypical and chaotic history. Thus, whereas the letter from the Chief Constable of Birmingham in 1906 to the LCJ sought guidance on the *cautioning* of prisoners on their arrest, Lord Alverstone replied as though the issue had been about the *questioning* of prisoners.[50] The release of the Rules in 1912 did not feature in decided cases for some years. Their interpretation was far from clear. Whether, for example,[51] persons in custody could be questioned at all or only to clear some ambiguity led to divergent interpretations within the police and by judges.[52] On one interpretation, the Rules seemed to offer greater latitude than existing police practice, as Ernley Blackwell noted in comparing the General Orders ('G. O.') of the Metropolitan Police: 'The G.O. says it is as a rule improper to question such a person except (1) as to identity & (2) to obtain explanation which may avoid necessity of arrest. The Judges on the other hand seem to say "Question as much as you like but caution first".'

The 1912 Rules and Procedure

The decision to promulgate the first set of Judges' Rules was in breach of established and available procedure. The issues regarding whether and when the police should caution a citizen should have been ventilated in the Court of Criminal Appeal.[53] This much was acknowledged in 1914 in internal Home Office records drafted by Simpson[54] and Blackwell, then assistant

[47] *Ibrahim* (n 46).
[48] *Voisin* (n 46).
[49] While some judges insisted on a caution, others thought that no caution should be administered.
[50] In the letter of 26 October 1906, Lord Alverstone said that 'whenever a constable determines to make a charge against a man he should caution him before taking any statement from him. Whether there is any necessity for a caution before a formal charge is preferred must depend upon the particular circumstances of the case; no definite rule can be laid down.' A further attempt at clarification brought the issue no nearer to resolution with Lord Alverstone stating that he considered that 'in some circumstances persons who are charged ought to be cautioned and I do not think that a hard and fast rule can be laid down in such a matter.'
[51] Although the Rules appeared to permit questioning after a caution, Sankey J stated in *R v Crowe and Myerscough* (1917) JP 288, *The Times* (27 June 1917), that '... if a police constable has determined to arrest a person, or a person is in fact in custody, then he should ask no questions which will in any way tend to prove the guilt of the person in custody from his own mouth.'
[52] On 18 June 1915, eg, Low J at the Essex Assizes, before stopping the case, criticized a police officer for asking questions of a man in custody saying that he 'had no right to do so' adding: 'Where a person is in custody and asks to be allowed to make a voluntary statement, all that the Police Officer ought to do is to take down that statement. He has no business to ask him questions or cross-examine him about it. It materially destroys the whole value of the statement.' (A 53292/17).
[53] The Court, established by the Criminal Appeal Act, 1907, began sitting in May 1908.
[54] Simpson noted that as an earlier letter (in 1912) intimated the Secretary of State's intention 'to communicate to the Police the judges' views on the question a circular to Police seems necessary—but

Under-Secretary of State, when consideration was being given to reformulating the Rules, Blackwell's Minute, also agreed by Troup ('C.E.T'), stating that: 'I think this might stand over for the present. If the Judges want to lay down Rules on the subject they have opportunities of doing so in the Crt. C. A.' as seen in **Illustration 3.1**.

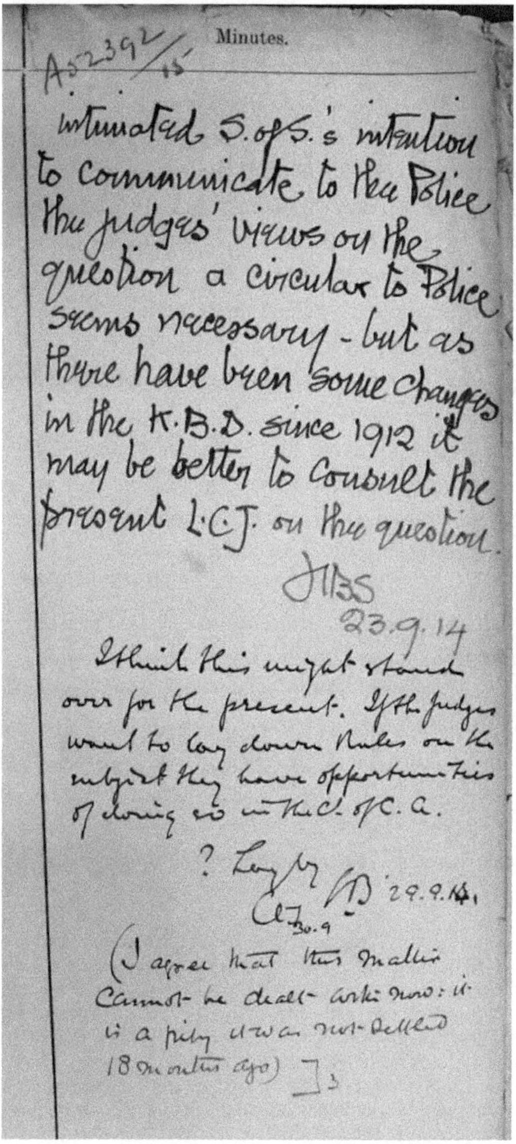
A52392/15

Minutes.

intimated S. of S.'s intention to communicate to the Police the judges' views on the question a circular to Police seems necessary - but as there have been some changes in the K.B.D. since 1912 it may be better to consult the present L.C.J. on the question.

JHBS
23.9.14

I think this might stand over for the present. If the Judges want to lay down Rules on the subject they have opportunities of doing so in the Ct. of C. A.

29.9.14.

CET
30.9

(I agree that this matter cannot be dealt with now: it is a pity it was not settled 18 months ago)

Illustration 3.1 Home Office Minute Regarding Venue for Reviewing Judges' Rules (September 1914) (National Archives)

This was not, however, a merely procedural error. Had the matter gone before the Court of Criminal Appeal there would have been an opportunity to subject earlier decisions to proper forensic examination by experienced counsel with close consideration given to drafting any rules or guidelines. Whatever their actual provenance and whether the Home Office was involved,[55] the 1912 Rules could not be said to have been carefully drafted.

Further Concerns Regarding the Rules

While the Home Office recognized shortcomings in some of the Rules,[56] they appeared to be embarrassed by the form of the Rules as a whole. An indication of this was revealed when a Parliamentary Question in 1915[57] asked what were the regulations in the Met with respect to the taking down of statements by persons in custody and with respect to the questioning of such persons or of persons suspected of offences? The obvious answer—reference to the Judges' Rules of 1912—was not one the Home Office was prepared to advise the Minister.

Simpson began the process of addressing the Question by noting that the Metropolitan Police Instructions 'are lengthy & do not altogether accord with the somewhat ambiguous memo on the subject settled by the judges of the K. B. D. in 1912. To give them in full might lead to unprofitable controversy.' Accordingly, the Minister's answer, drafted by Simpson, was restricted to a general precis of the General Orders of the Met:[58]

> The Metropolitan Police are instructed not to question persons who are in custody or are about to be taken into custody. Exceptions to this rule may have to be made for the purpose of identifying the person named in a warrant of arrest. When a person is merely under suspicion questions may be put to him if the answers to them may remove the suspicion or obviate the necessity of an arrest, but as there have been some changes in the K. B. D. since 1912 it may be better to consult the present L. C. J. on the question.'

[55] We note that the Home Office has destroyed (without explanation) at least five internal files immediately preceding or co-terminus with Lord Alverstone's announcement of the Rules.

[56] Thus, Sir Ernley Blackwell annotated a copy of the Rules amending 'the usual caution' in Rule 3 to read 'a caution' and marking Rule 4 ('If a prisoner wishes . . . ') with a side note: 'I think this must mean "If the [prisoner] states that he wishes etc." Otherwise how is the Officer to know that [prisoner] wishes etc? I do not think that it means that a voluntary statement blurted out by a [prisoner] is inadmissible in [evidence] because no caution has been administered' (original emphasis). However, Blackwell then referred to a ruling by Horridge J excluding such a statement by a prisoner on that ground.

[57] Question by Mr King, *Daily Debates* (17 June 1915).

[58] Simpson drew attention to a decision of Low J reported in the *Police Review* (18 June 1915) disapproving of questioning suspects in custody.

> police officers are instructed to use the utmost discretion in doing this, and not to ask questions of a suspected person the answers to which may have an incriminatory character, without first cautioning him. Voluntary statements made by persons in custody are reduced to writing and preserved.

The Home Office was forced into further action following the decision in *Voisin*[59] in February 1918 in which Lawrence J said that there had been 'so much doubt among the police' in 1912 that the judges, at the request of the Home Secretary, had drawn up four Rules, the contents of which he set out in his judgment. Reports of this case prompted inquiries directed to the Home Office from the Chief Constable of Bath[60] and others for copies of the 1912 Rules causing the Home Office to give thought to the structure and drafting of the Rules themselves.

The process of revision of the Rules was effectively launched by a Minute from Simpson in the same correspondence. After dealing with the inquiries arising from *Voisin*, Simpson added the following note dated 26 June 1918:

> It would seem desirable that a H. O. circular shld now be issued—but it wld be well to add to the Judges' memo. & certain additions which experience since 1912 has shown to be desirable to allow (i) statements made before there has been an opportunity of 'administering the usual caution'... and of questions put for the purpose merely of removing ambiguity in a voluntary statement ... The Judges of today should be consulted as to the actual terms of the circular ...

Simpson stated that an extended circular would prove useful to the police:

> ... instead of a number of dicta relating to cases of very diverse character & of different degrees of authority. A newspaper report of Darling J's judgment[61] is scarcely sufficient to serve the purpose.

In agreeing to Simpson's suggestion, the assistant Under-Secretary, Ernley Blackwell, added: '? Draft circular for submission to the Judges.' This short observation by Blackwell,[62] agreed to by Edward Troup,[63] set in train the process of revising the 1912 Rules.

[59] There was an additional approving reference to *Voisin* (n 46) by Darling J in *R v Cook* [1919] 1 KB 531 (hereafter *Cook*).

[60] The Chief Constable asked for a dozen copies of the Rules stating that: 'As I have not received the circular I would feel obliged if I can have a dozen copies of this statement as it is very essential that police should comply as far as possible with the wishes of the Judges of the High Court.' The Home Office short response was to simply say that 'no such circular ... has been issued from this office'.

[61] *Cook* (n 59).

[62] 26 June 1918.

[63] 27 June 1918.

The Process of Revision of the Rules

Almost immediately, Simpson had a draft prepared and his proposals were approved by Sir Ernley Blackwell. Simpson's draft left Rule 1 and Rule 2 intact. His draft would have modified Rule 3 ('Persons in custody should not be questioned without the usual caution being first administered') only by substituting 'a caution' for 'the usual caution'. This was a serious error because the questioning of persons in custody was a highly contentious issue.

Simpson also proposed addressing two issues that had arisen:

(i) the question of the admissibility of statements made before there was an opportunity of administering a caution; and
(ii) whether questions could be put directed merely to remove ambiguities in a purely voluntary statement as opposed to questions going to its material parts or in the nature of cross-examination.

For this purpose, Simpson suggested amending Rule 4 and adding two further Rules. The precise arrangement of Simpson's draft [Draft A] need not be gone into here because Troup intervened[64] and decided that they ought not to alter the four rules which the judges laid down in 1912. He added that Simpson's points could be put into the form of additions[65] which, if approved, would be sent in reply 'to questions which are frequently asked by the judicial authorities of the Colonies' as shown in **Illustration 3.2.**

This Minute was initialled by the Secretary of State (Sir George Cave) on 9 July 1918 who then wrote to Darling J[66] on 17 July 1918.

In essence, Troup adopted the proposals made by Simpson with minor changes so that the amendments would read:

(5) The caution to be administered to a prisoner, when he is charged, should therefore be in the following words: 'Do you wish to say anything in answer to the charge? You are not obliged to say anything unless you wish to do so, but whatever you say will be taken down in writing and may be given in evidence.'

A similar form of words should be employed before asking the prisoner questions or before he makes a voluntary statement. Care should be taken to avoid any suggestion that his answers can only be used in evidence against him, as this may prevent an innocent person making a statement which might assist to clear him of the charge.

[64] 6 July 1918.
[65] Set out in his 'Draft B'.
[66] Darling, rather than the LCJ, Lord Reading (Rufus Isaacs), liaised with the Home Office.

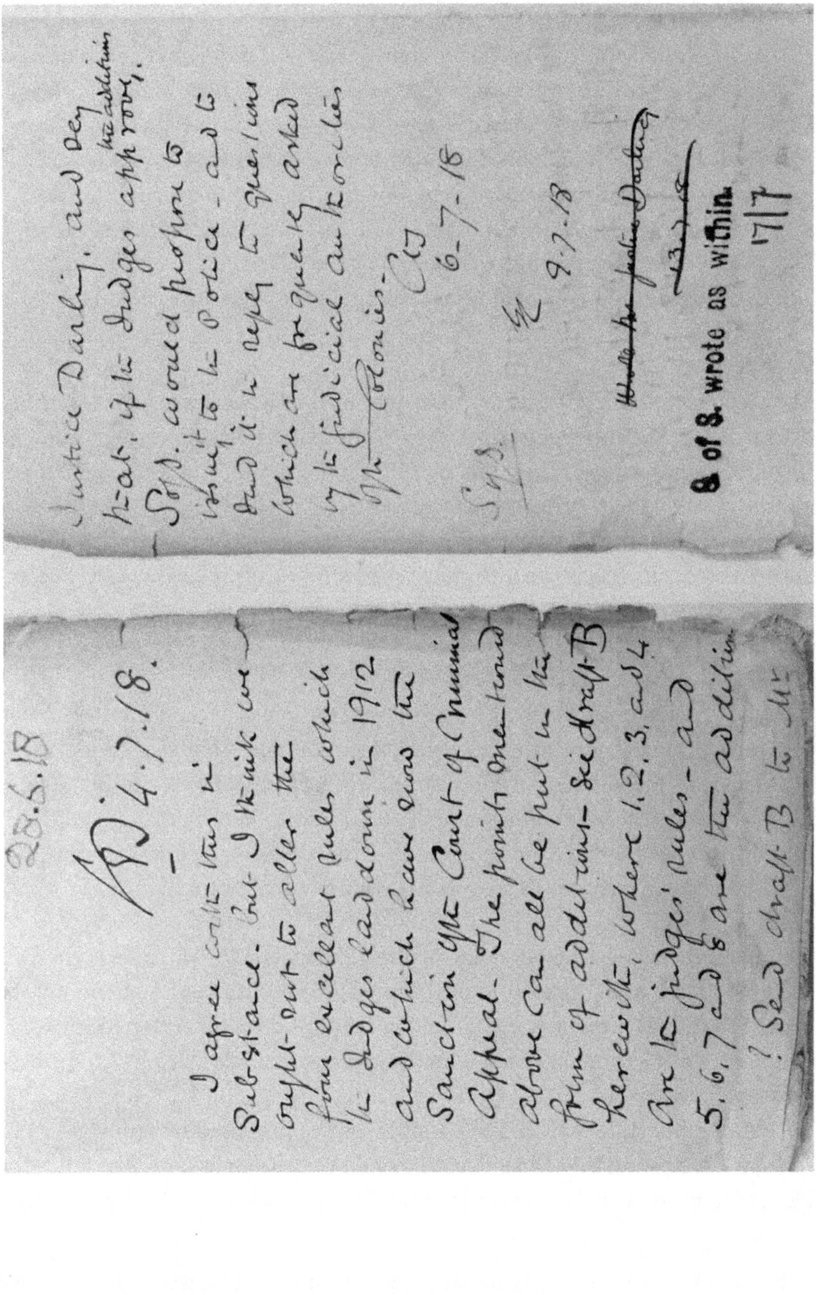

28.6.18

4.7.18.

I agree with this in substance. But I think we ought not to alter the form [of the] excellent rules which the Judges laid down in 1912 and which have now the sanction of the Court of Criminal Appeal. The points mentioned above can all be put in the form of additions – see Draft B herewith, where 1, 2, 3, and 4 are the Judges' rules – and 5, 6, 7 and 8 are the additions.

? Send draft B to Mr Justice Darling, and say that, if the Judges approve the addition, S of S. would propose to issue it to the Police – and to send it in reply to questions which are frequently asked by the judicial authorities in the Colonies.

CJ 6.7.18

9.7.18

~~Write to Justice Darling~~

13.7.18

S of S. wrote as within. 17/7

Illustration 3.2 Minute of Edward Troup on Draft Judges' Rules (June 1918) (National Archives)

(6) A statement made by a prisoner before there is time to caution him is not rendered inadmissible in evidence merely by reason of no caution having been given, but in such a case he should be cautioned as soon as possible.
(7) A prisoner making a voluntary statement must not be cross-examined, and no questions should be put to him about it except for the purposes of removing ambiguity in what he has actually said. For instance, if he has mentioned an hour without saying whether it was morning or evening, or has given a day of the week and a day of the month which do not agree, or has not made it clear to what individual or what place he intended to refer in some part of his statement, he may be questioned sufficiently to clear up the point.
(8) Any statement made in accordance with the above rules should, wherever possible, be taken down in writing and signed by the person making it after it has been read to him and he has been invited to make any corrections he may wish.

In the absence of the LCJ,[67] this draft was sent by the Home Secretary to Darling J on 17 July 1918. Darling replied on 22 July 1918 advising that copies had been sent to 'the K.B. Judges who will meet on July 29th to consider the matter & I will let you know the result of their deliberations'.

In large measure, the suggested amendments were approved by the judges. A substantive change was the introduction of a new Rule, which was to become Rule 8, the draft rule 8 of Troup becoming Rule 9. The new Rule 8 was intended to cover the case of multiple suspects:

(8) When two or more persons are charged with the same offence and statements are taken separately from the persons charged, the police should not read these statements to the other persons charged, but each of such persons should be furnished by the police with a copy of such statements and nothing should be said or done by the police to invite a reply. If the person charged desires to make a statement in reply, the usual caution should be administered.

Other relatively minor changes made by the judges were: (i) 'when he is charged' in Rule 5 to read 'when he is formally charged'; (ii) in Rule 5, the deletion of the sentence: 'A similar form of words should be employed before asking the prisoner questions or before he makes a voluntary statement'; and (iii) in Rule 7, 'purposes' changed to 'purpose'.

In addition, the judges altered the draft Preamble proposed by Troup as can be seen from **Illustration 3.3**. The judges amended the introduction—'The following rules which have been *laid down* by His Majesty's Judges of the King's Bench

[67] The Earl of Reading was serving as Ambassador to the United States of America, a position he held until 1919.

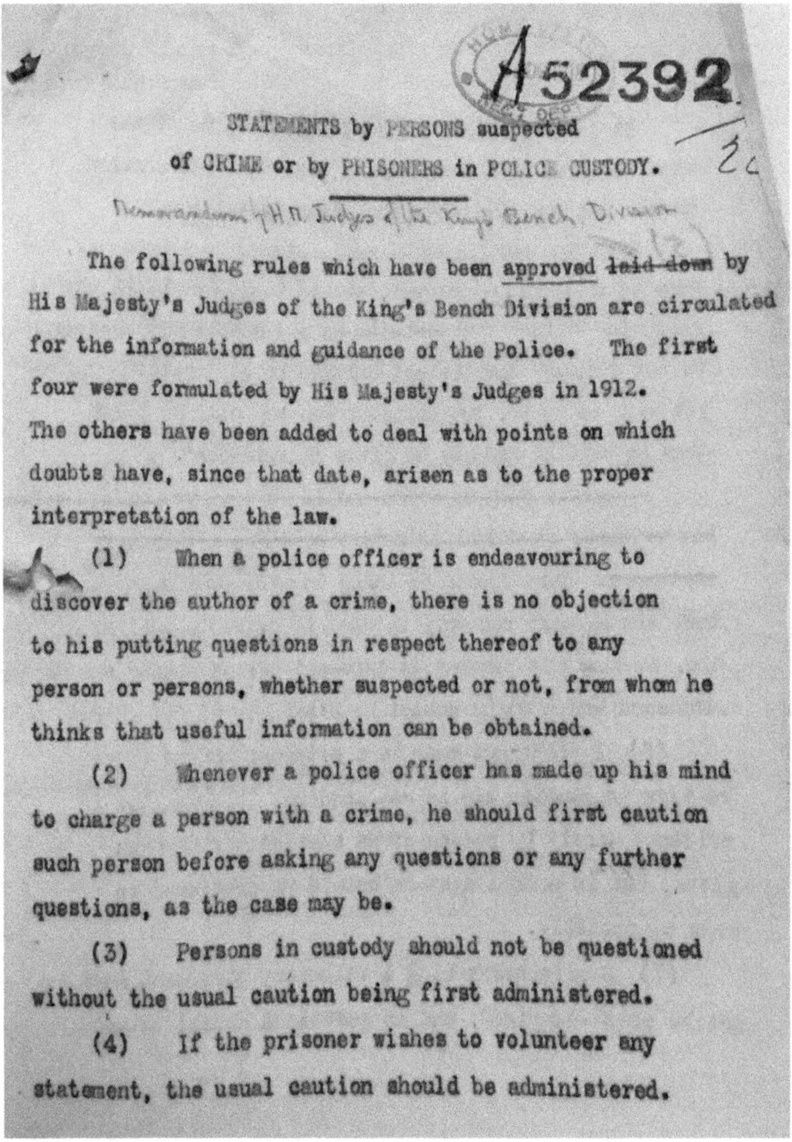

A52392

STATEMENTS by PERSONS suspected of CRIME or by PRISONERS in POLICE CUSTODY.

Memorandum of H.M. Judges of the King's Bench Division

The following rules which have been approved ~~laid down~~ by His Majesty's Judges of the King's Bench Division are circulated for the information and guidance of the Police. The first four were formulated by His Majesty's Judges in 1912. The others have been added to deal with points on which doubts have, since that date, arisen as to the proper interpretation of the law.

(1) When a police officer is endeavouring to discover the author of a crime, there is no objection to his putting questions in respect thereof to any person or persons, whether suspected or not, from whom he thinks that useful information can be obtained.

(2) Whenever a police officer has made up his mind to charge a person with a crime, he should first caution such person before asking any questions or any further questions, as the case may be.

(3) Persons in custody should not be questioned without the usual caution being first administered.

(4) If the prisoner wishes to volunteer any statement, the usual caution should be administered.

Illustration 3.3 Memorandum on Statements of Detained Persons Amended by the Judges (August 1918) (National Archives)

Division … ' (emphasis supplied)—so that it instead read: 'The following rules which have been *approved* by His Majesty's Judges of the King's Bench Division … ' (emphasis supplied).

Given that the Home Office had in essence drafted the new Rules, it was improper for Troup to suggest that the Rules had been *laid down* by the judges.

Though the judges recognized this, the formulation they adopted continued to convey the impression that the judges had actually written the Rules (their name alone—'*Judges' Rules*'—suggesting as much), which is what gave them gravitas and authority,[68] and commentators thereafter all assumed authorship in the judges.[69]

The Success of the Redrafted Rules

The atypical process adopted in drafting the Rules in 1912 resulted in both a failure to properly disseminate the Rules and continued uncertainty as to the procedures the police should follow in questioning citizens. Attempts to clarify the resulting confusion by the addition of five new Rules in 1918 proved unsuccessful.[70] An internal Home Office Note in 1929 accurately summed up the position: 'The Rules ... have given rise to questions from the outset. Their peculiar form is due to the peculiar manner in which they grew up.' In the same vein, Lord Devlin, reviewing the Rules in 1960, by which time further 'clarifications' had been found necessary, concluded:[71] 'As they have been put together in this piecemeal way, the whole does not constitute a well-drafted document; and they are in fact lengthy and repetitive.' The problems, however, were much deeper than infelicitous drafting.

Although the Rules were devised to provide guidance to police officers, they contained no statement on the key issue of admissibility, the only reference to evidence

[68] As RCPPP, *Report* (n 12) confirmed: 'Rules approved by Your Majesty's Judges, and issued by the Home Office, are *naturally regarded as constituting a most authoritative document* and we can understand the reluctance of a Chief Officer to add glosses or interpretations of his own to a Memorandum emanating from *such high quarters*' 72, para 186, emphasis supplied.

[69] See, eg, Thomas Eric St Johnston, 'Judges' Rules and Police Interrogation in England Today' (1966) 57(1) Journal of Criminal Law and Criminology 85 stating that requests were made by Chief Constables for clarification regarding the caution: 'Following this, many similar requests were made until 1912 when the Judges formulated the first four Judges' Rules. In 1918 they prepared another five rules and in 1930, issued a statement clearing points of ambiguity in the nine rules they had made.' Darling was no stranger to disguising written work under false names. Outside the law, Darling had a journalistic bent and was known for the way he habitually 'cloaked the authorship of his writings' (Derek Walker-Smith, *The Life of Lord Darling* (Cassell and Company 1938) 64). Whilst Darling was said to have 'considerable literary power' this was off-set by him having given 'no sign of legal eminence' according to *The Times* (26 October, 1897) which went as far to comment: 'To speak of him as an eminent lawyer, or even a distinguished advocate would be absurd. If he is raised to the Bench, it will be on political grounds' (quoted by Walker-Smith, ibid 92). The article made little difference and two days later, Darling's appointment was announced, swiftly followed thereafter by further public condemnation. *The Daily Chronicle*, eg, took a fierce line: 'Mr Darling has only two conceivable qualifications for a judgeship—that he is an extreme partisan of the Government now in office, and that his seat is supposed to be safe. He is clever with a certain shallow cleverness. On any subject to which he has publicly addressed himself, he has shown himself incapable of a broad judicial view. He has no serious knowledge of the Law, and has never handled any important practice at the Bar, The whole transaction is grossly scandalous' (quoted by Walker-Smith, ibid 93–94).

[70] This was noted in the Police Order issued by Major Law, the Chief Constable of Birmingham, after the Judges' Rules were issued in 1918 in which he said: 'the memorandum is not yet quite clear in regard to one or two points. If any further information is received with regard to it, it will immediately be published in Police Orders.' (A 52392/56)

[71] Patrick Devlin, *The Criminal Prosecution in England* (OUP 1960) 33.

is in Rule 6 where the reference is incidental to the purpose and direction of the Rule. This in and of itself created doubts among police as to the necessity of compliance with the relevant provisions. Worse still, any officer who sought to follow the Rules would have found them contradictory thereby leading to differences of practice as between police force areas and, indeed, within individual forces.

The prime example of internal contradiction, and, as we shall see, one that was to have long-term consequences for policing, was located in the conflict between Rule 3 and Rule 7.

> Rule 3: Persons in custody should not be questioned without the usual caution being first administered.
>
> Rule 7: A prisoner making a voluntary statement must not be cross-examined, and no questions should be put to him about it except for the purposes of removing ambiguity in what he has actually said …

On one view, once a prisoner was cautioned, Rule 3 would appear to have permitted questioning without restriction contrary to earlier judicial rulings and on its face inconsistent with Rule 7. Although it might be possible to reconcile these Rules through strained interpretation,[72] some police forces saw themselves free to question prisoners whereas others did not.

Beyond this basic contradiction in the Rules lay other problems. These included: whether there was significance in the use in Rule 3 of the phrase 'persons in custody' which occurred nowhere else in the Rules, the word 'prisoner' being used in the four following Rules;[73] whether the reference to 'the usual caution' in Rules 3 and 4 meant the same as reference to 'caution' in Rule 6 and, more significantly, the text of the caution in Rule 5;[74] and whether a constable was permitted, by reason of Rule 7, to cross-examine or otherwise question a person on any reply made following a caution under Rules 2 or 3.

What is evident is that the blame for drafting problems cannot be laid at the door of lowly officials. The Home Office learned little from the Beck Inquiry beyond a small reinforcement to the staff dealing with criminal justice matters, the principal

[72] Thus, some have argued that Rule 3 might apply only to occasions on which the police wished to question a prisoner, whereas Rule 7 to occasions on which a prisoner wishes to make a voluntary statement. Another attempt at reconciliation would confine Rule 3 to cases on which the prisoner is questioned about some charge other than that with which he is charged and on which he is held in custody (this interpretation is not supported by *R v Booker* [1924] 18 Crim App Rep 47 which indicates that a person in police custody on another charge comes under both Rule 1 and 3).

[73] This is not a matter of mere semantics but raises the technical issue of the moment at which a person becomes a prisoner and additionally whether a person detained by the police is necessarily a 'person in custody'.

[74] Interpretation is not straightforward for a number of reasons. First, there was reference to 'the usual caution' in the 1912 Rules prior to the coming into existence of the text in Rule 5. Second, the form of the 'usual caution' in Rule 5 presupposes a formal charge and, accordingly, appears inapplicable to Rules 2, 3, and 4.

work still devolved on those low in the hierarchy. If there was additional internal 'training' it was nowhere evident in the efforts of officials to iron out contradictions in the Rules in the redrafting process. Despite the addition of the barrister Ernley Blackwell, the moving force in dealing with police forces and the rules relating to questioning citizens remained Harry Simpson. After dealing with Petitions in a far from professional manner, Simpson was permitted to stray into the area of legal drafting without displaying a gift for this challenging task. Even though he had been the receptacle of concerns from the police, his suggestions for adding to the 1912 Rules displayed a failure to understand their basic shortcomings. Simpson was far from the only one at fault. There was no rigorous oversight of Simpson's work either by Blackwell or by Troup, the permanent Under-Secretary. More extraordinary, Troup, without having the benefit of legal practice,[75] felt himself qualified to pronounce the existing 1912 Rules fit for purpose when they clearly were not and then to propose additional Rules which, so far from clarifying existing problems, magnified them further.

Conclusion

The organization of criminal justice, its management, personnel, and judicial oversight was such as to require wholesale and transparent review. Statutory intervention of a comprehensive kind would have been preferable rather than the piecemeal, murky, and irregular intervention that the Judges' Rules represented. Even if the judges deemed the issue of police questioning to be within their purview given their responsibility for the admissibility of evidence, the process of determining what rules would be appropriate should have been subject to consideration in the Court of Criminal Appeal where the matter could have been fully aired and tested through the normal forensic process.

So far as the police were concerned, the localization of policing inevitably led to disparities in the Instruction Books and General Orders that each force produced. In principle, local police rules could not be sustained where they conflicted with judicial rulings, but this apparent truism was for many years falsified by the fact that judges differed in what should be done and none of the rulings were authoritative. In this setting, the Home Office quite properly acted as an advisory body to individual police forces or as mediator where judicial criticism had been directed at a police force.

Once Home Office officials took upon themselves the role of drafting procedural rules, however, serious questions are raised. It might be defended, on one view, on the basis that any suggestions would be advisory and based upon observing the

[75] Troup had been called to the Bar in 1888 but this required little except passing an undemanding examination.

effects on police forces of divergent judicial rulings; and their proposals were no more than proposals, always open to acceptance, modification, or rejection by the judges. Even if that view is accepted, however, a more fundamental question arises because the judges would be predisposed to accept Home Office proposals, as they did in large measure, assuming that its officials were both knowledgeable and competent and that the additional Rules advanced would resolve the ambiguities and uncertainties that had caused difficulties for individual police forces and embarrassing discordance as between judges. It is to that question that we now turn.

4

The Aftermath

1918–60

Introduction

The way in which the Judges' Rules came into existence was likely to cause problems in regard to interpretation and implementation if only because they had been authored by different hands (some without legal training), at different times, and with different objectives. But, as a subterranean Home Office policy began to crystallize and as the judiciary more overtly entered the policy arena, technical considerations became subordinate as the Rules came to have an even greater impact on police culture and practices and, in consequence, the experiences of citizens who fell into the category of 'suspects'. It is to these issues that we turn in this chapter.

Technical Disarray over the Rules

The Home Office was fully aware that the Rules were poorly drafted. When the Royal Commission into Police Powers and Procedures (RCPPP) (1929) was looking into police questioning, a Home Office Memorandum[1] was frank in this regard. While no point of substance arose on the first four Rules, the Memo stated that the 1918 additions 'introduced, by way of Rule 7 as finally redrafted in the Home Office, elements of very grave doubt which time and discussion have gradually brought fully to light'.

The author drew attention to the following: did the limitations in Rule 7 apply to the questioning of the persons referred to in Rule 2; and did they apply to the questioning of the persons referred to in Rule 3? If in either case they did not apply (ie, if questions need not be confined to removing ambiguity), what limitations *did* apply? The Memo added that Mr Dixon[2] and Mr Houston shared these views and that the Home Office legal advisers had drafted a Memorandum outlining the difficulties.

[1] Memorandum (27 October 1928) prepared by Arthur Locke (joined in 1890 and became Junior Clerk in 1911).

[2] Arthur Dixon, later Sir Arthur Dixon, was joint head of the Police Division of the Home Office who became assistant Under-Secretary of State.

The Myth of Judicial Independence. Mike McConville and Luke Marsh, Oxford University Press (2020). © Mike McConville and Luke Marsh. DOI: 10.1093/oso/9780198822103.001.0001

The Legal Memorandum in question had been prepared by L S Brass[3] and O F Dowson[4] the more important points of which are:

> Rule 3 applies, it is submitted, to all persons in police custody for whatever cause.[5] There is no real contrast between this Rule and Rule 2, which are complementary. The caution to be administered under both rules should be the usual caution
>
> A real doubt arises regarding the position of 'persons detained by the Police.' On the whole, it appears that such persons were probably not contemplated by the framers of the rules, since Rules 1, 2 and 3 seem to relate to the stages of a normal criminal investigation in chronological sequence. If, however, it is considered that the rules do provide for such persons, it is submitted that Rule 3 is the rule that is applicable since such persons are in custody ...[6]
>
> Rule 7 applies expressly to prisoners (i.e. persons coming within Rule 3). It is submitted that in practice it should be regarded as applicable to a person making a voluntary statement after caution whom the officer has made up his mind to charge (i.e. Rule 2) ...
>
> 'Voluntary statement' must include a statement volunteered spontaneously and a statement voluntarily made in reply to a general invitation.
>
> A real doubt, however, arises as to whether this rule should be applied also to a reply to a question asked after caution as laid down in Rule 3. In other words, is a constable permitted to cross-examine a person in custody on particular replies to such question? The answer appears to be that he should not do so. A similar point arises as to replies to questions after caution under Rule 2.
>
> A real doubt also arises as to whether the prohibition in this rule applies only to questions in the nature of cross-examination, i.e. questions put to test the accuracy of something said in the statement.[7] It is submitted that the prohibition is so limited and the words 'about it' are to be so construed. It is clear that the mere making of a voluntary statement cannot have the effect of altogether precluding a constable from thereafter asking questions as authorized in Rule 3. If the submission is wrong, the proper course must be for the constable to ask his question after the voluntary statement is concluded and so obtain a supplementary statement ... (original emphases)

[3] Brass was then legal adviser.

[4] Dowson was then assistant legal adviser.

[5] The side note states: 'The judgment of the Ct. of C. A. in Booker's Case 18 CAR 47 indicates that a person in police custody on another charge comes under both Rules 1 & 3'. The reference is *Booker*.

[6] The side note states: 'Voisin's case removes this doubt. It seems clear that such persons are to be regarded as persons in custody.'

[7] The side note states: '[cf. Grove J in R v Adams Staffs Assizes Feb. 1926. News report].'

The correctness of these observations is supported by a Memorandum sent to Hewart LCJ by Lord Lee, Chairman of the RCPPP in March 1929 in which 'some of the difficulties' over interpretation of the Rules were set out.

Lord Lee prefaced the central points by indicating that the evidence submitted to the Commission had made clear that:

> there are marked divergencies (sic) of opinion amongst Police authorities as to the meaning of the Rules, and that these divergencies (sic) are reflected in variations of practice, not only throughout the country but in some cases within the same Force.

Lord Lee indicated the areas of difficulty along similar lines to those set out by the Home Office legal advisers, drawing particular attention to the clash between Rule 3 and Rule 7. After setting out no fewer than four different interpretations advanced to reconcile these Rules, Lord Lee said that:

> Owing, doubtless to these difficulties of interpretation, some [Police] Forces base their practice on the passage in Lord Brampton's Address, 'Neither Judge, magistrate, nor juryman can interrogate an accused person, … much less then ought a constable to do so' and ignore the permission to question a person in custody, after caution, which appears to be inferred from Rule (3)

In evidence to the RCPPP, while the great majority of police forces reported that they followed the advice of Lord Brampton, others admitted of no questioning of prisoners on any matter connected with a criminal offence; yet others limited the application of the principle to the charge for which the suspect was in custody while approving of questioning prisoners regarding any other offence; and a few claimed, by virtue of Rule 7, a right to question prisoners on the charge for which they were in custody, although even these said that it should be done very sparingly.[8] These disparities, concluded the RCPPP, had 'become a real stumbling-block to many responsible police officers'.

The RCPPP, concerned about the disadvantageous position of persons in custody, recommended:

> We recommend a rigid instruction to the police that no questioning of a person in custody about any crime or offence with which he is or may be charged should be permitted. This does not exclude questions to resolve elementary and obvious ambiguities in a voluntary statement …

[8] *Report of the Royal Commission on Police Powers and Procedure* (HMSO 1929) 99 (hereafter RCPPP, *Report* (1929)) para 162.

This was set aside by a Home Office Circular (1930)[9] which purported to provide definitive guidance on the status of Rule 3 by declaring, in the words of Leonard Hoffmann (later Lord Hoffmann), 'implausibly but authoritatively',[10] this to mean that persons in custody should not be questioned *at all*.

The source of this Circular arose out of correspondence between the LCJ and the RCPPP. Having failed to arrange a meeting with the judges, the RCPPP received a 'copy of the memorandum by Mr Justice Avory, countersigned by the Lord Chief Justice, and dated the 18th March, 1929'.[11] This short Memorandum became the basis of the Home Office Circular and the claims in it that 'His Majesty's Judges have advised … '

There was a certain irony in the involvement of Avory. Horace Avory had, it will be recalled, made disastrous legal mistakes in the Beck prosecution before gaining a reputation as a hard-working junior.[12] Avory belatedly took silk in 1901 but was not elevated to the Bench until the age of fifty-nine in 1910. There he acquired a reputation for harshness because of the large number of death sentences he passed. This, combined with his aloof, impassive, and emotionless presence[13] led to the widely applied sobriquet, 'The Hanging Judge' or, even more grimly, 'Acid Drop'. Had the true origins of the Memorandum and Circular been known, the now seventy-seven-year-old Avory would have been subjected to fierce criticism despite the fact that he was said to have been fair, if stern,[14] and the failings here went to the substance and procedure rather than the man.

The Avory/Hewart Memorandum presented the rules regarding police–citizen encounters as unproblematic when both knew of the historical problems that this area had presented. Thus, in *R v Gardner and Hancox*, Avory J delivering the judgment of the Court of Criminal Appeal said:[15]

> That statement, made by Hancox, was obtained in pursuance of a practice which [Crown Counsel] tells us prevails among the police; it is a practice, after men have been separately charged, of charging them together with the same offence with which they have already been separately charged, and reading over to them

[9] Circular 536053/23 issued on 24 June 1930.

[10] Leonard Hoffmann, 'The Judges' Rules' (1964) 23 The Lawyer 25 (hereafter Hoffmann, 'Judges's Rules').

[11] Letter to A L Dixon, Home Office from E E Bridges, Secretary to the RCPPP (5 April 1929).

[12] He is described at that stage of his career as 'the embodiment and *beau-ideal* of a Senior Treasury Counsel': Stanley Jackson, *Mr. Justice Avory* (Victor Gollancz Ltd 1935) (hereafter Jackson, *Avory*) 92.

[13] His biographer described Avory as having a 'white and shrunken face, rigid bones and trimmed smile': ibid 16. A crime reporter who attended Avory's big trials, described him thus: 'Emotionless—austere almost—he holds the scales of justice in skinny, attenuated hands' Bernard O'Donnell, The Trials of Mr. Justice Avory (Rich & Cowan 1935), 'Preface'.

[14] See, eg, the summation by a 'well-known silk' in Archibald Edgar Bowker, *A Lifetime with the Law* (W. H. Allen 1961) 76–77: 'If I were sent to trial and was innocent, I would rather be tried by Avory than by any other Judge; but if I were guilty and came before Avory, I should know that I must expect the worst.'

[15] (1916) 11 Cr App R 265 269.

> statements made by the others behind their backs. That is a practice which must certainly be condemned. It is a form of cross-examination after arrest, and the police have been told over and over again from the bench that they have no right to cross-examine a prisoner after he has been arrested and charged. *The difficulty is that, notwithstanding that the practice is to be condemned, there are decisions that when the practice is followed, and the advice given to the police disregarded, if the prisoner answers the statement, and makes anything in the nature of a confession, or says anything material, his statement cannot be excluded in evidence ... Some day the authorities may have to be reconsidered*, but the Court is not prepared to say that the statements made by Hancox were not admissible in evidence, while repeating that *if the practice is followed for the purpose of obtaining confessions or admissions it is reprehensible and ought to be discontinued* (emphasis supplied).

The Avory/Hewart Memorandum asserted as fact that Rule 3 was never intended to encourage or authorize the questioning or cross-examination of a person in custody *after he had been cautioned on the subject of the crime for which he was in custody* but did not explain the obvious contradiction with the actual terms of Rule 3, viz, persons in custody should not be questioned *without the usual caution being first administered* (emphasis supplied). This had particular significance because earlier condemnations were not conditioned upon the administration of a caution but upon the practice of police subjecting prisoners to questioning, as stated by the Court of Criminal Appeal (in which Avory J was one of the appellate judges) in *R v Grayson*:[16]

> This sort of proceeding—it was in fact an informal preliminary trial in private by the police—is not fair to prisoners and, as this Court has already observed, is not in accordance with principles of English justice.

Although the wording of Rule 3 appeared to sanction post-caution questioning, the Home Office accompanied the Circular with a note to Chief Officers seeking to reinforce the message conveyed in the Avory/Hewart Memorandum:

> A rigid instruction should be issued to the Police that no questioning of a prisoner, or a 'person in custody', about any crime or offence with which he is, or may be, charged, should be permitted. This does not exclude questions to remove elementary and obvious ambiguities in voluntary statements, under No. (7) of the Judges' Rules, but this prohibition should cover all persons who, although not in custody, have been charged and are out on bail while awaiting trial.

[16] (1922) 16 Cr App R 7. To the same effect: *R v Taylor* (1924) 17 Cr App R 109, where Avory J (sitting with Hewart LCJ and Sankey J) in the course of argument stated: 'This Court has laid it down as a rule that the police must not examine accused persons after they are in custody' 110.

The impact of this instruction was, however, unlikely to be effective since Rule 3 remained in place and since the courts had previously stated that statements made by persons in custody in answer to police questioning were admissible subject to the discretion of the court.[17]

A second concern related to the significance of the term 'persons in custody' in Rule 3 in contrast to 'prisoner' in the four following Rules which raised the question when a person becomes a prisoner. The answer of Avory/Hewart was unconvincing: the terms were synonymous and, extraordinarily, a person detained for enquiries who is allowed to go after the enquiries have been made 'cannot be regarded as in custody'. Of course a person who is *released* cannot be said to be in custody but the person is released *from custody*. Yet, by this sleight of hand, detention for questioning was authorized.

A third area of concern related to the form of the caution where the person has not been formally charged. The Avory/Hewart Memorandum avoided the difficulty by stating that 'before the formal charge is made the usual caution is or should be . . .' when the question related to situations in which there had been *no formal charge*.

If Avory's opinion is extraordinary, that of Hewart LCJ is astonishing. Not only had Hewart participated in cases where the interpretation of the Rules was frequently at issue, Lord Lee had indicated to him, in terms, the widespread problems that the RCPPP had uncovered. Yet Hewart handed over this keg of dynamite to a judge who was out of touch and whose outlandish opinion he endorsed without comment.

Police Practice prior to 1930

The unsatisfactory character of the Avory/Hewart Memorandum had another side: it flew in the face of practice in some police forces as known to the Home Office itself. There is clear evidence that both the judges and the Home Office were aware that the temptation to question prisoners, with or without legal authority, was, at least occasionally, too great to resist. As early as 1912,[18] Lord Alverstone said to the Grand Jury that:

> We have noticed lately in the Court of Criminal Appeal . . . that there is a disposition on the part of the police to question a prisoner unduly.

The Home Office also recognized that the interpretation by some judges of Rule 3 opened the door to police interrogation subject only to a caution being administered.[19] Although judges discouraged the questioning of arrested persons,

[17] *Ibrahim v R* [1914] AC 599; *R v Winkel* (1912) 76 JP 191; *R v Matthews* (1919) 14 Cr App R. 23; *R v Turner* (1926) 19 Cr App R 171.

[18] *R v George Day* (*The Times* 20 June 1912). The point had not been lost to the Home Office, a Memorandum of Locke in 1928 specifically referring to it: A/52392/54.

[19] Minute of Sir Ernley Blackwell: A52392/15.

the Home Office was made aware in 1924 by the distinguished HM Inspector of Constabulary, Sir Leonard Dunning[20] that some police were interpreting the Rules as a licence to question persons before and after arrest and whilst in police custody as shown in his Memorandum reproduced in **Illustration 4.1**.

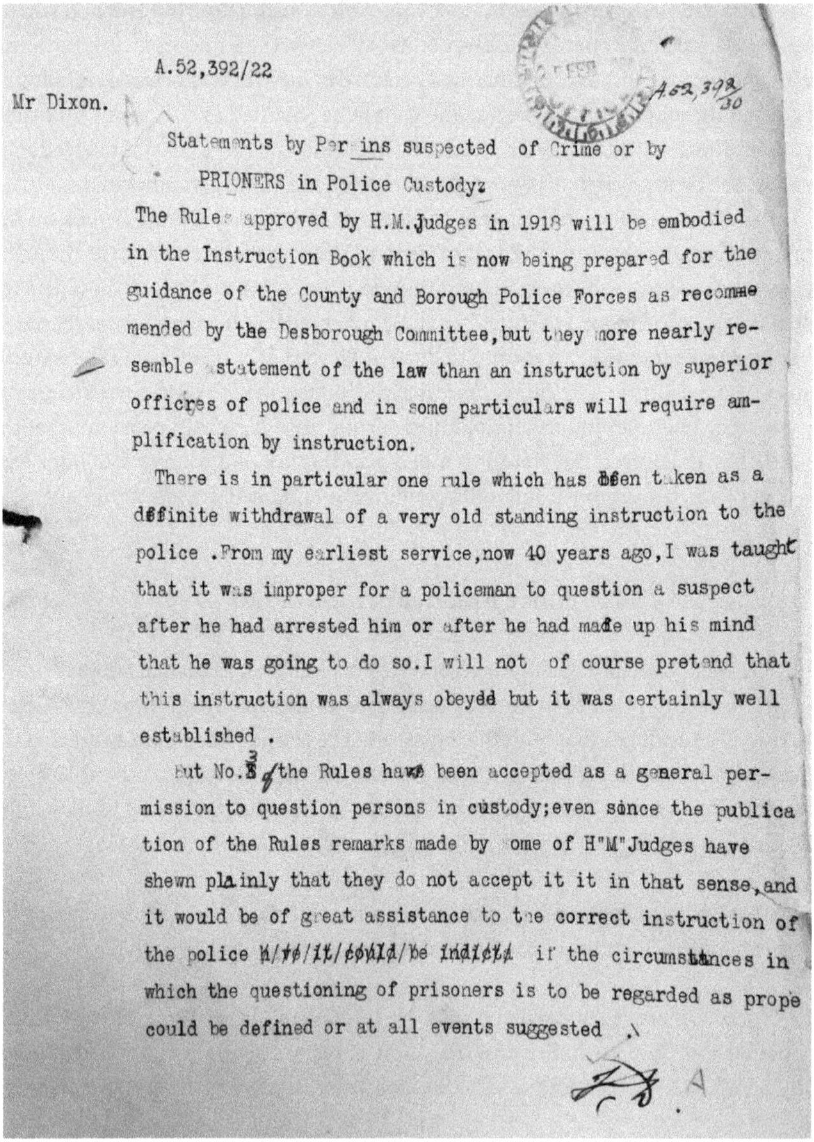

A.52,392/22

A.52,392/30

Mr Dixon.

Statements by Per ins suspected of Crime or by

PRIONERS in Police Custody.

The Rules approved by H.M.Judges in 1918 will be embodied in the Instruction Book which is now being prepared for the guidance of the County and Borough Police Forces as recommended by the Desborough Committee, but they more nearly resemble statement of the law than an instruction by superior officers of police and in some particulars will require amplification by instruction.

There is in particular one rule which has been taken as a definite withdrawal of a very old standing instruction to the police. From my earliest service, now 40 years ago, I was taught that it was improper for a policeman to question a suspect after he had arrested him or after he had made up his mind that he was going to do so. I will not of course pretend that this instruction was always obeyed but it was certainly well established.

But No.3 of the Rules have been accepted as a general permission to question persons in custody; even since the publication of the Rules remarks made by some of H"M"Judges have shewn plainly that they do not accept it in that sense, and it would be of great assistance to the correct instruction of the police ~~it could be indicated~~ if the circumstances in which the questioning of prisoners is to be regarded as proper could be defined or at all events suggested.

Illustration 4.1 Memorandum of Sir Leonard Dunning Regarding Police Questioning (February 1924) (National Archives)

[20] Formerly Head Constable of the Liverpool City Police.

Dunning's concern was with the contradiction of the Denman injunction to officers ('keep your mouth shut') by Rule 3 (seemingly authorizing questioning after a caution) and the practice of officers[21] accepting Rule 3 '*as a general permission to question persons in custody*'. While Dunning's knowledge was based on first-hand experience, the Home Office was dependent upon communications from Chief Constables who were unlikely to say that constables were regularly disregarding the Rules. Indeed, in response to Dunning's Report, Simpson's internal note stated that the Home Office had not heard of any practice of constables attempting to cross-examine prisoners.[22]

In the light of this, the adoption in the Home Office Circular of Avory/Hewart's dogmatic pronouncement is unlikely to reflect Home Office naivety as to constabulary practice.[23] Rather than simply being disingenuous, it seems that, guided by the permanent Under-Secretary, Sir John Anderson,[24] the Home Office decided that latitude should be accorded to the police in questioning suspects. Since the judges were not prepared to alter or amend the Rules, the Home Office did so by default.

Police Practice after the Home Office Circular

Whether the police would question those taken into their custody during an investigation into possible crime depended on: (i) police culture and practice; (ii) the ambiguous terms of the Judges' Rules; and (iii) the attitude of the judges towards police departures from the Rules. Given that police practice was less influenced by tenderness towards suspects, the tendency was to seek an explanation from those they regarded as probably criminals. The Home Office clerk Simpson drafted a Minute in 1915[25] in which he discussed police General Orders ('G.O.') and police compliance with them in these terms:

> PCs are much more likely to be guided in practice by custom & what they have been told than by the terms of the G.O.

The standing of the Rules as 'administrative directions' for the guidance of police officers rather than rules of law combined with their ambiguous nature also gave

[21] A52392/30.

[22] A52392/30 (5 March 1924). Internal annotations by Simpson's superiors show little appetite for change: 'These Rules were settled by the Judges after much discussion and consideration. I see no need to alter them. They are explicit enough. A prisoner must always be cautioned and he can hold his tongue if he likes—and very often does.'

[23] cf Hoffmann, 'Judges's Rules' (n 10).

[24] Sir John Anderson assumed office in 1922.

[25] A52392/17 (19 July 1915).

the police some basis for more extended questioning than a rigid interpretation might suggest.

In addition, over time there was a perceptible change in the attitude of judges towards police practices and the 'rights' of suspects. In the early years of the twentieth century and soon after the 1930 Circular, judges showed a distaste for police 'cross-examination' of suspects which they saw as a matter for court.[26] This attitude appears to have continued up to the Second World War with, for example, the House of Lords insisting that a police officer arresting an individual must give that person the true reason for the arrest.[27] However, in the ensuing years, judges came to stress that the Rules were merely administrative directions[28] and actions of the police which formerly attracted judicial disapproval came to be disregarded[29] or condoned.

The Home Office Circular of 1930 had set out what was expected at interrogations as follows:

> In carrying out their duties in connection with the questioning of suspects and others [police officers] must, above all things, be scrupulously fair to those whom they are questioning, and in giving evidence as to the circumstances in which any statement was made or taken down in writing, they must be absolutely frank in describing to the Court exactly what occurred . . .

However, to avoid difficult cross-examination in court, police officers developed the practice of backing each other up with identical evidence while telling the court that the evidence of each was entirely independent and tendered without prior collaboration. Such perjury was, in an *obiter dictum*, condoned by the judges in *Bass*:[30]

> This court has observed that police officers nearly always deny that they have collaborated in the making of notes, and we cannot help wondering why they are the only class of society who do not collaborate in such a matter. It seems to us that nothing could be more natural or proper when two persons have been present at an interview with a third person than that they should afterwards make sure that they have a correct version of what was said. Collaboration would appear to be a better explanation of almost identical notes than the possession of a superhuman memory.

[26] This was also the view taken by the RCPPP, *Report* (1929) (n 8).

[27] *Christie v Leachinsky* [1947] AC 573.

[28] See, eg, *R v Wattam* (1952) 36 Cr App R72.

[29] See, eg, *R v J E Smith* (1961) 46 Cr App R 51. See, Gerald Abrahams, *Police Questioning and the Judges' Rules* (Oyez Publications 1964) 26 ff.

[30] *R v Bass* (1953) 1 Q B 680 *per* Byrne J 686.

Taking stock in 1961, Glanville Williams said that the former interpretation of the Rules:[31]

> ... may now be said to be a dead letter. Notwithstanding the [Home Office Circular of 1930], the police still interrogate persons in custody, and the judges admit the resulting confessions in evidence.

He concluded that police questioning in some forces continued without check; that 'the judges have given up enforcing their own rules'; and that 'English Judges maintain in theory an idealist rule, while conniving at police practices which set it at defiance.'

As the Home Office stood by, the judges were inaugurating changes that were to have profound effects upon criminal investigations. The judicial deregulation of the Rules gave comfort to officers who followed their own practices and set the pattern for a wider problem related to the actions of the Criminal Investigation Department (CID), a division of the police with a long and shadowy history.

The Origins of the CID

Despite early resistance to plain clothes policing,[32] a small contingent of detectives was appointed in the Metropolitan Police in 1842.[33] Concerns over public reaction to 'police spies'[34] and the difficulty controlling these officers held back expansion but moral panics over the possible increase in crime by convicts released on tickets-of-leave[35] led to the appointment in 1868 of a Departmental Committee to investigate policing. The Committee's recommendation for an increase in the strength of the detective force went unheeded until a decade later when the Met was convulsed by a great scandal.

In 1877 the three top Scotland Yard detectives were involved in a major bribery case.[36] Of the four Chief Inspectors of the Met, three (Clarke, Palmer, and

[31] Glanville Williams, 'Police Interrogation, Privileges and Limitations: England' (1961) 52 Journal of Criminal Law & Criminology and Police Science 50.

[32] This was to be expected since the police were created to *prevent* crime by patrolling in uniform.

[33] See Phillip Smith, *Policing Victorian London* (Greenwood Press 1985).

[34] This was founded in a distrust of 'Continental' spying methods and the example of William S Popay who secretly joined the Political Union of Camberwell and Walworth acting as a double agent and allegedly incited members against the government. See: HC Deb 27 June 1833, vol 18, cols 1254–63; HC Deb 27 June 1833, vol 20, cols 834–39.

[35] A parole document issued to convicted persons who had demonstrated that they could be entrusted with some freedoms.

[36] On this generally, see Ascoli David, *The Queen's Peace* (Hamish Hamilton 1979) (hereafter Ascoli, *Queen's Peace*) 143ff; Richard Stewart, *The Great Detective Case of 1877* (The Battered Silicon Dispatch

Druscovitch), together with Inspector Meiklejohn and a solicitor named Froggatt, faced trial on conspiracy to obstruct the course of justice.[37] Two fraudsters, William Kurr and Harry Benson, operated a series of racing scams and secured protection through tip-offs about police inquiries from Meiklejohn who soon roped in Clarke, Druscovitch, and Palmer. The scams netted large sums with, for example, the Countess de Goncourt in Paris being swindled out of £10,000 and the police officers receiving kick-backs of up to £2,000. The involvement of the police was unaccountably said to be unknown to the head of detectives, Superintendent Williamson, a pattern of ignorance that was to become a hallmark of future corruption cases.[38]

Following their convictions, Kurr and Benson turned King's evidence and convictions were obtained against Meiklejohn, Palmer, Druscovitch and the solicitor Froggatt.[39] As Clive Emsley put it:

> The case underlined all the concerns about detectives, particularly the fears that low-paid, unsupervised men, working in close proximity, even if ostensibly in opposition, to criminals, could easily be corrupted.

Forced into action, the Home Secretary appointed a Departmental Commission to inquire into 'the state, discipline and organization of the Detective Force of the Metropolitan Police'. The Report was presented in 1878. The Detective Division was to be reorganized under a Director of Criminal Investigations. Shortly afterwards, a twenty-nine-year-old barrister, Howard Vincent (later to become author of the seminal Police Code, 1881),[40] applied for and was appointed Director in March 1878. The CID was established a month later with twenty-four men supported by six office staff at Central Office with a total of 254 in Divisions.[41]

Box 2000); George Dilnot, *The Trial of the Detectives* (Charles Scribner's Sons 1928) (hereafter Dilnot, *Detectives*); Clive Emsley, *The English Police: A Political and Social History* (2nd edn, Longman 1996); Alan Doig, *Corruption and Misconduct in Contemporary British Politics* (Penguin Books 1984); Thomas Alan Critchley, *A History of Police in England and Wales* (2nd edn, Patterson Smith 1972) (hereafter Critchley, *History of Police*).

[37] Ascoli, *Queen's Peace* (n 36) states: '... it is arguable that only a sense of professional loyalty saved a number of other detectives from joining the defendants in the dock.' 146.

[38] Dilnot, *Detectives* (n 36).

[39] Clarke was acquitted at trial and retired to run a public house!

[40] The Commission had been influenced by a Memorandum submitted by Vincent who had studied the French centralized detective system.

[41] The CID branch expanded under Vincent rising to some 800 within six years. As Critchley wryly observes, despite the increase in size the Department 'does not seem to have been very efficient' (*History of Police* (n 36) 161), the Whitechapel murders (ascribed to a single perpetrator to be known as Jack the Ripper) leading to public panic and criticism of the CID for its failure to catch the culprit.

The establishment of the CID as a separate entity with its own line of command, special pay, and status, itself a source of jealousy among uniformed officers, put in place the systemic problem of 'the firm within a firm' that was to dog the police thereafter.[42] The Royal Commission on the Duties of the Metropolitan Police (1908), set up following allegations of harassment and corruption arising out of the dismissal of a case against Eva D'Angeley for alleged 'riotous and indecent behaviour' (prostitution), elicited a torrent of complaints alleging police corruption, bribery, and perjury. The inability of most complainants to frame cogent allegations or supply supporting evidence and a disposition towards the status quo led the Commission to acquit the Met of wrongdoing of any consequence. But that was far from the whole story. The Met's own historian, David Ascoli, concluded that:[43]

> It is impossible to know the extent of police corruption during the fifty years after the CID was formed; corruption is difficult to define. But it is beyond argument that by the summer of 1922 the CID had become a thoroughly venal private army.

The CID from then on became an elite divorced from the uniform branch, its plain clothes said to cover a multitude of sins.

The most publicized case of police corruption involved Sergeant Goddard based at Vine Street, London. Goddard's responsibilities involved the suppression of brothels and gambling dens. Far from suppressing these activities, Goddard received kick-backs for tipping off Kate Meyrick, a brothel-owner, over police raids. Following the receipt of anonymous letters, secret observations of his activities, and the evidence of Meyrick, Goddard was convicted and received eighteen months' hard labour and ordered to pay £2,000, a fraction of the monies he secured through dishonesty.[44] Goddard's superior officers, supposedly ignorant of Goddard's actions, were reprimanded and transferred to other Divisions.[45] The Commissioner did not report his actions to the Home Office.[46]

[42] As Ascoli observed '. . . a dangerous precedent had been set' *Queen's Peace* (n 36) 149.

[43] ibid 210.

[44] This was merely indicative of wider problems involving mistreatment of individuals, perjury, and organized corruption.

[45] HO 287/90.

[46] POL 225/1/31. In fact, the Met had been warned about Goddard as early as 1922 when a young officer, Josling, who had arrested a bookmaker, was told by Goddard to 'leave the betting boys alone'; in return, Goddard would 'see him all right'. Josling reported it to his superiors, was charged with making false statements about Goddard, and dismissed from the force. See James Morton, *Gangland* (Piatkus 2008) 246.

Had the Home Office been alert, it would have sensed the dangers from the Tribunal of Inquiry held in 1928 and the Report of the RCPPP in 1929. Both inquiries arose after the magistrate refused to accept sworn police evidence and dismissed the charges against Miss Irene Savidge and Sir Leo Chiozza Money, a former Liberal MP, (whose behaviour when sitting together under a tree in Hyde Park was thought to offend public decency) as well as awarding costs against the police.[47] The Tribunal appointed by the Home Secretary were split. The majority, comprising Sir John Eldon Bankes (a former Lord Justice of Appeal) and Mr Withers (a Conservative MP) exonerated the police of any wrongdoing. The Home Office would have done well to have looked with care at the minority view prepared by the Labour MP, Hastings Bernard Lees-Smith, who found Miss Savidge to be frank and a more credible witness than the two police officers involved:[48]

> The police officers did not give the impression that they were equally frank in their evidence, but denied both the probable and improbable with equal force. The mechanical precision with which the chief police witnesses corroborated every detail of each other's statements cast suspicion upon their evidence.

The Commission's Report in 1929 acquitted the police of any significant wrongdoing but contained a coded warning. The Commission stated that it had received 'a volume of responsible evidence which it is impossible to ignore suggesting that a number of voluntary statements now tended in Court are not "voluntary" in the strict sense of the word'. After listing various allegations of improper police conduct, the Commission indicated that, because of its inability to take evidence on oath, it was unable to investigate any of the individual allegations made to it, adding the following pointed comment:[49]

> Some of the C. I. D. (Scotland Yard) evidence, however, which we have heard in connection with this subject leaves a somewhat disquieting impression upon our minds. There is, we fear, a tendency amongst this branch of the service to regard itself as a thing above and apart, to which the restraints and limitations placed

[47] Whether the parties were innocently engaged is unclear. One of the officers involved at later stages of the Savidge case lied to a Tribunal established to investigate the matter: Lilian Wyles, *A Woman at Scotland Yard* (Faber 1952). However, soon after this case, Sir Leo was convicted of molesting a young woman in a railway carriage.

[48] See Harford Montgomery Hyde, *Norman Birkett* (Hamish Hamilton 1964) 244. Birkett had put the allegation in clear terms: 'The case, as presented is one that two police officers entered into a conspiracy to defeat the ends of justice at the expense of a girl . . . ' 242. For a more sympathetic account of the role of the police, see Douglas Browne, *The Rise of Scotland Yard* (George Harrap & Co 1956) 327–29.

[49] RCPPP, *Report* (1929) (n 8) para 269.

> upon the ordinary Police do not, or should not, apply. This error, if not checked, is bound to lead to abuses which may grow until they bring discredit upon the whole Police Force.

This prescient judgment was never attended to with any real sense of purpose despite the reform efforts in other areas undertaken by the Met Commissioner, Lord Trenchard.

Trenchard, who came out of retirement to take the office, had the capacity to identify and confront corruption but failed to do so. He had an excellent, probably unparalleled, personal relationship with the King, was well connected in political circles, with, as Chief of Staff of the Royal Air Force, vast experience in running a major national institution and with a formidable personality.[50] Although Trenchard's reforms raised the quality of life for police officers, improved training methods and facilities, he spoke about but did nothing to confront corruption.[51] David Ascoli described his handling of the CID as a failure remarking that Trenchard, a man of decision, showed an uncharacteristic irresolution:[52]

> Although constantly alive to the extent of CID corruption and his correspondence with Gilmour[53] during 1934 is a curious commentary on his intellectual cowardice. The man who could talk with kings seemed frightened of corrupt constables.

The result was summarized by James Morton:[54] 'Detectives played the game according to their own rules, confident that neither their superiors nor the courts would accept the word of known or convicted criminals.' The impact that this would have on the criminal justice system was about to be felt.

The 1950s: Cracks in the Foundations of Policing

After a post-War honeymoon period in which the police enjoyed the trust of the courts and approbation of the middle and upper classes,[55] doubts emerged because

[50] Andrew Boyle, *Trenchard—Man of Vision* (Collins 1962).

[51] See Ascoli, *Queen's Peace* (n 36) 226ff. Among his achievements may be listed the opening of the Police College and Police Forensic Laboratory at Hendon.

[52] ibid 240.

[53] Sir John Gilmour was Home Secretary.

[54] James Morton, *Bent Coppers: A survey of Police Corruption* (Warner Books 1993) 82.

[55] See Robert Roberts, *The Classic Slum: Salford Life in the First Quarter of the Century* (Penguin 1973). This, with its account of working class experiences of and resistance to policing, is a useful corrective to the view that the police had secured universal approval.

of instances of discreditable conduct. While most attention fell on evidence of corrupt activities, there were also concerns over 'detention for questioning'[56] and the veracity of police evidence at trials. The concerns were inflamed, on the one side, by growing public alarm over what was seen as a rise in crime,[57] reduced capacity and low morale in the police; and, on the other, by increasing disquiet over the death penalty and its irrevocable character, including cases where there were grave doubts as to guilt. As the 1950s wore on, there was more open questioning, if not yet a loss of faith.

Examples of corruption, proven and alleged, gathered around the police. In Leeds, for example, a sergeant and three police constables were convicted in 1952 of breaking into premises and stealing; another was convicted in 1953 of breaking and entering shops and being in possession of housebreaking instruments by night; and in 1953, a Superintendent and a Chief Inspector from the CID were required to resign in relation to the extraction of 'protection money' from city bookmakers; one CID sergeant was dismissed and two were reduced to constables and then, after appeal to the Home Office, required to resign for receiving kick-backs; and one constable was reduced in pay for one year.[58] The Home Secretary's recommendation to Cabinet that a Tribunal be set up to enquire into the administration of the Leeds Police was rejected because 'it would reflect gravely upon the Leeds City Council and that the unsatisfactory state of discipline in the Leeds Force could be said to be due largely, if not entirely to the present state of the betting laws . . . '[59] The Home Secretary instead ordered a special inspection of the force by HM Inspectors of Constabulary.

Back in London, apart from individual cases of dishonesty,[60] evidence began to emerge of more significant criminality. The occasion for this arose out of the burglary trial of Joseph Grech, a thief and brothel-keeper. A major plank of Grech's

[56] See, eg, the dropping of a murder charge against a deaf mute, George Roberts, where Devlin J referred to 'one matter that disturbs me'. The matter in question was that Roberts had been taken to the police station and detained there for three nights 'no charge of any sort being made against him during that time, although at that time he was questioned and questioned in a manner that was not designed merely to elicit facts but was in the nature of what we call cross-examination': *The Times* (25 March 1953). See also criticism by Cassells J: *The Times* (18 May 1957); Report of Commander Hatherill speech: *The Times* (19 February 1954). See also 'Youths Questioned in Stabbed P. C. Case' *The Times* (18 December 1958).

[57] See, eg, Home Office, *Penal Practice in a Changing Society* (1959) which opened: 'It is a disquieting feature of our society that, in the years since the war, rising standards in material prosperity, education and social welfare have brought no decrease in the high rate of crime reached during the war: on the contrary, crime has increased and is still increasing.' See also: HL Deb 8 April 1959, vol 215, cols 400–558 in which concern was expressed over indictable offences known to the police which, having stood at 283,000 in 1938 had risen to 548,000 in 1957 (the figures for the first nine months of 1958 showing a further 15 per cent increase).

[58] See HO 287/90, Pol 225/1/54; and 'More Reorganisation of Leeds CID' *Yorkshire Post* (23 November 1954).

[59] See HO 287/90, Pol 225/1/54.

[60] See, eg, the instances described in Donald Thomas, *Villain's Paradise* (John Murray 2005).

defence was that the key used in the burglary also fitted his own house, a fact confirmed by Detective Sergeant Robertson when he gave evidence. Grech was convicted and sent to prison for three years. From Maidstone Prison, Grech said that the idea of the duplicate key had been that of Detective Sergeant 'Jock' Robertson whose evidence was supposed to have led to an acquittal. At the subsequent trial of Robertson, Ben Canter (Grech's solicitor), and Morris Page (Canter's 'runner') for conspiracy to pervert the course of justice, Grech made a series of other allegations of police corruption in the West End. All three defendants were convicted and imprisoned.[61]

The balloon of police probity was more effectively punctured by the leakage of a confidential Report of Detective Superintendent Herbert 'Burt' Hannam to the Home Office.[62] Hannam's Report was given prominent coverage by the *Daily Mail* in November 1955 and revealed extensive corruption among West End police officers relating to owners of night clubs, brothels and gaming-houses, prostitutes and pimps. Some officers in Soho were said to be receiving up to £60 a week[63] in kickbacks for tipping off when a raid was about to take place and evidence was said to be 'cooked' or 'adjusted' by officers to benefit accused persons.[64] Predictably, the Commissioner denounced the Report as an unwarranted attack upon a fine body of men[65] but this did not stem the flow.

The decision in 1956 to take disciplinary action against the Chief Constable of Cardiganshire on the grounds of inefficiency was simply a minor prelude to what happened the next year. In 1957 two senior Sussex CID detectives received five years' imprisonment for receiving money in exchange for information from a nightclub owner with some evidence held back at trial as too sensitive to be aired.[66] While the prosecution was assisted by the evidence of

[61] Another detective, Inspector Jacobs, an officer with more than twenty commendations, was alleged by Grech to have blackmailed him.

[62] The existence of the file was disclosed when DS Hannam was giving evidence in the trial of Robertson, Canter, and Page. See 'West End Police Scandal' *Daily Mail* (17 November 1955) and 'Hannam of the Yard Guards Secret File'—'Confidential to the Home Office' *Daily Mail* (19 November 1955). Several Freedom of Information requests failed to gain access to this Report (correspondence on file with the authors).

[63] The equivalent of more than £1,500 today.

[64] Thus, officers would state that when raiding premises, fully clothed women were there when, in fact, they were naked. Prostitutes could, for a fee, postpone court appearances to a more convenient date.

[65] See *Daily Mail* (18 November 1955). In his Statement, Sir John Nott-Bower said that the reports were 'grossly unfair' and, on a visit to the West End Central Police Station he said that 'there was no truth whatever' that the Hannam Report contained allegations of corruption. The Under-Secretary of State for the Home Office (Sir Hugh Lucas-Tooth) supported the Commissioner: 'As the Commissioner made clear in a statement yesterday, the general accusations made in certain quarters against the police are unwarranted and unsubstantiated:' HC Deb 18 November 1955, vol 546, cols 913–14.

[66] HO 287/92. For an account of the trial see H Palmer, 'The Brighton Conspiracy Case' [1958] Criminal Law Review 422.

a constable and a detective sergeant, there is little doubt that other Brighton CID officers were involved but spared.[67] The Chief Constable, Charles Ridge, who was acquitted at trial,[68] was replaced soon afterwards[69] following scathing remarks from the trial judge, Donovan J,[70] who was concerned that the case would be used to discredit Brighton officers when they gave evidence in future prosecutions:

> This prospect and this risk will remain until a leader is given to that force who will be a new influence, and who will set a different example from that which has lately obtained.

In the same year, a Tribunal of Inquiry had to be established following an incident in which a youth had been assaulted by one of two police officers on duty in Thurso[71] and the Chief Constable of Worcester was sent to prison for embezzlement.

Such were the concerns over the management of the police that the issue boiled over in 1958 on a seemingly trivial matter. Brian Rix, a well-known actor famous for performing in Whitehall farces, was stopped by Constable Eastmond for allegedly speeding. Travelling behind the police car was a civil servant named Garratt who stopped his car and became involved in an argument with Eastmond, in the course of which Garratt said he was thrown over a hedge by Eastmond who, in turn, alleged that Garratt had assaulted him. Garratt was released from police custody when the Inspector refused to accept the charge. Garratt then brought an action for damages against Eastmond for assault and battery and against the police for false imprisonment. The action was settled out of court with payment of £300 from police funds. With no disciplinary action taken against Eastmond, the matter seemed settled but a year later the farce became a drama when the issue came before the House of Commons.

The Home Secretary, as Police Authority for the Met, faced a motion of censure for permitting public money to be used in an out-of-court settlement. Why pay if the constable had done nothing wrong; if he had, why was he not disciplined?

[67] Subsequent to his conviction, along with the CID detectives, the Brighton bookmaker Samuel Bellson's confession to a reporter from *The People* was such as to cause the reporter surprise that 'only three officers of the Brighton force were put in the dock'; 'New Bribery Case Sensation: Gaoled Bookie Confesses' *The People* (8 June 1958).

[68] The facts included that Ridge went to an admitted briber of police in private and alone and that he admitted to his private room a 'much-convicted and hectoring bookmaker and there [discussed] with him, almost as a colleague, the policy of the police in certain matters . . . ' (Donovan J).

[69] Ridge was dismissed by the Watch Committee, a decision he subsequently overturned because he had not been informed of the charges he was to face: *Ridge v Baldwin* [1964] AC 40. For an excellent review of the case see, Stephen Bailey, ' "Nuff said": Ridge v Baldwin' in Satvinder Juss and Maurice Sunkin (eds), *Landmark Cases in Public Law* (Hart Publishing 2017).

[70] These remarks did not escape criticism. See *Police Review* (7 March 1958).

[71] The John Waters Tribunal was established under the Tribunals of Inquiry (Evidence) Act 1921.

The public outcry forced the government to establish another Royal Commission (on the police) announced on 16 December 1959. The Terms of Reference were restrictive:[72]

> To review the constitutional position of the police throughout Great Britain, the arrangements for their control and administration and, in particular, to consider:
>
> 1. the constitution and functions of local police authorities;
> 2. the status and accountability of members of police forces, including chief officers of police;
> 3. the relationship of the police with the public and the means of ensuring that complaints by the public against the police are effectively dealt with; and
> 4. the broad principles which should govern the remuneration of the constable, having regard to the nature and extent of police duties and responsibilities and the need to attract and retain an adequate number of recruits with the proper qualifications.

In answer to a question as to whether the Commission would cover consideration of the taking of statements by the police from people who were detained but not charged, the Prime Minister said:

> I do not think that the terms of reference, although they are wide, actually cover what one might call police powers and procedure. These, of course, were the subject of the Royal Commission on Police Powers and Procedure, which reported in 1929. They are rather specialised subjects which I think these terms of reference, broad as they are, could hardly be expected to cover.

This was, at best, an evasion since, as we have seen, the RCPPP (1929) had found a great body of evidence contradicting the 'voluntary' nature of confessions and a 'disquieting impression' left by some of the CID evidence placed before it. The question posed to the Home Secretary came on the back of concerns that had started early in the decade around a possible miscarriage of justice and would soon escalate on the back of another.

Pressure for Reform

The first focus of concern was the case of Timothy Evans. Evans, with his wife, Beryl, and daughter, Geraldine, were living as tenants of John Reginald Christie

[72] HC Deb 16 December 1959, vol 615, cols 1452–55.

at 10 Rillington Place in London. In 1950, Evans, an impressionable man of below normal intelligence, was hanged for the alleged murder of his thirteen-month-old daughter.[73] Soon after there were serious misgivings that there had been a miscarriage of justice, his conviction being based on a garbled 'confession' extracted after prolonged custodial interrogation by CID officers at Notting Hill Police Station with details that Evans could not know seemingly having been supplied by the police; the police had failed to undertake a proper search of Christie's small garden where Christie had already buried the bodies of two other women he had murdered[74] and where a thigh bone of one of the victims, dug up by Christie's dog visibly propped up the wooden fence; the police had pressurized one workman to change a witness statement wholly inconsistent with Evans' confession; and a second workman who resisted police pressure to alter his statement, again inconsistent with Evans' confession, was never called for the prosecution.

Three years later, the principal prosecution witness at Evans' trial, Christie (described by the trial judge as 'this perfectly innocent man'), was arrested following the discovery of the bodies of four women walled up in the kitchen of his former flat at 10 Rillington Place, other bodies being found in the small garden after a proper search had been undertaken. All the women had been strangled with a ligature. Christie was found guilty of the murder of his wife Ethel and he admitted, whilst in custody, murdering six other women[75] including Beryl but he denied murdering Evans' daughter, Geraldine.

The case generated public concern once the bodies of Christie's wife and three other victims had been discovered in Christie's house. These circumstances raised the probability that the person who had murdered these individuals also murdered Evans' wife and baby; after all, the chance that there would be two serial murderers, unknown to each other, under the same roof, using the same methods to kill, was not thought to be high.

Efforts to secure an Inquiry into the conviction of Evans, however, were deflected. The strategy of the Home Office had twin aims. The first was to avoid the suggestion that Evans had been wrongfully convicted, thus threatening the reputation of the British legal system. The exposure of miscarriages of justice was then a relative rarity to which in future the Home Office would, unfortunately, get more accustomed. The second aim was to avoid any impact upon the death penalty, the preservation of which was actively contested by opponents.

[73] Evans was also charged with the murder of his wife, Beryl, but this charge was left to lie on the file.

[74] Christie murdered Ruth Fuerst in 1943 and Muriel Amelia Eady in 1944 both of whom he buried in the small garden.

[75] These included Ruth Fuerst, Muriel Eady, Kathleen Moloney, Rita Nelson, and Hectorina MacLennan.

However, following Christie's conviction, the Home Secretary was forced on 6 July 1953 to establish an Inquiry under John Scott Henderson QC, the Recorder of Portsmouth, to consider whether there may have been any miscarriage of justice in the conviction of Evans.[76] But the Home Office still seemed intent on digging the truth in rather than digging it up, Scott Henderson being required to conduct his Inquiry in semi-secret under restrictive conditions and to present his Report with unseemly haste. Indeed, the completion of the Report by 13 July 1953 was breathtaking[77] undermining rather than strengthening his conclusion that Christie's confession to having murdered Beryl was false and that there was no ground for thinking that there may have been any miscarriage of justice in the conviction of Evans for the murder of Geraldine.

The House of Commons Debate on the Inquiry was the scene of scathing criticism of its conclusions,[78] the thrust of these was set out by Geoffrey Bing MP in the following terms:[79]

> The inquiry arose because it subsequently turned out that in Evans's case the principal witness for the Crown was found to have murdered six women in exactly the same way as he had, in the witness box, by implication, accused Evans of murdering two female persons. Quite apart from any confession, or absence of confession, it would be a really extraordinary coincidence that there should be two killers, killing their victims in exactly the same way, hiding them, as it turned out, in exactly the same place, and acting completely independently of each other. That is what Mr. Scott Henderson found had taken place.
>
> This coincidence alone would be quite sufficient to justify looking into the case, but when one looks at the second coincidence one finds that it is the even more remarkable one that Evans, without knowing anything about any of the murders committed by Christie—not one word was said in the cross-examination—nevertheless chose to accuse, just by chance—and that is Mr. Scott Henderson's case—the one person, probably in the whole of London at that time, who was murdering people in exactly the same way.
>
> If it had been known at the trial of Evans that Christie, who was described by the prosecution as the principal witness, had in fact already murdered two women, hidden their bodies temporarily in the very washhouse where Evans was accused of hiding the bodies, and had subsequently buried them in the garden, Evans would have been bound to be acquitted.

[76] HC Deb 6 July 1953, vol 517, cols 863–67.
[77] Immediately afterwards, Christie was executed on 15 July 1953.
[78] HC Deb 29 July 1953, vol 518, cols 1435–85.
[79] ibid col 1437.

In calls for a public inquiry, the police were accused of engaging in 'grave irregularities' and suppressing evidence; Scott Henderson was accused of a cover up and carrying out 'a most deceptive and improper method of writing a report'; and his Report was said to be 'shot through with prejudice and evidence of irregularities playing down the evidence on the one hand, and playing it up on the other.' One Member put the accusation at its most sharp:[80]

> We are not attacking this Report merely because, in our view, this Report does not disclose the truth; we are attacking the Report because we say that it deliberately conceals the truth. We are attacking this Report not because it is mistaken, but because, we say, it is dishonest.

The Home Secretary was accused of establishing 'a secret or semi-secret inquiry, and an inquiry at which the case for Evans was not represented by a lawyer',[81] Lamely, the Home Secretary said that the Report was not a rushed job: 'I believed and still believe that in the time, say 12 days, or 11 days—I do not want to exaggerate for a moment—that Mr. Scott Henderson had, he had full time to examine the subject and the subject was of such a compass that it could be dealt with in that time.'[82]

A detailed critique is not of concern here and has been dealt with elsewhere.[83] What is of moment is that pressure on the Home Office was building up driven not only by external events but by the manner in which the Home Office responded. Not only did the Home Secretary push aside the concerns raised in the Debate but did so with an air of finality. This did not quell the disquiet. Year after year, MPs raised concerns focusing both on the inadequate nature of the Inquiry that had been undertaken and the shortcomings of the original police investigation.[84] The Home Office mindset was resolutely against any further action, Members being repeatedly told that a further inquiry would not serve any useful purpose.[85] Although the Home Office continued to block an inquiry into the Evans case[86] and concerns

[80] Mr Paget MP ibid col 1480.

[81] Michael Foot MP ibid col 1453.

[82] HC Deb 29 July 1953, vol 518, col 1468.

[83] See, eg, the classic account of Ludovic Kennedy, *10 Rillington Place* (Victor Gallancz 1961 and Panther Books 1971).

[84] See, eg, HC Deb 22 October 1953, vol 518, cols 288–94W; HC Deb 27 October 1955, vol 545, col 51W; HC Deb 17 April 1956, vol 551, col 65W; HC Deb 1 August 1957, vol 574, col 246W; HC Deb 26 January 1961, vol 633, col 49W.

[85] See, eg, HC Deb 1 August 1957, vol 574, col 246 where the Home Secretary stated: 'I have carefully considered this case, but I do not think that a further inquiry would serve any useful purpose. All the relevant facts are on record, and there is no reason to believe that any new information would be forthcoming.'

[86] Extraordinarily, in 1966, a second judicial inquiry, by Brabin J, concluded that on the balance of probabilities Timothy Evans did not kill his daughter, of whose murder he had been convicted, but that he probably did kill his wife, with whose murder he had not been charged. The Brabin Report was inconsistent with the Scott-Henderson Report. Its conclusion was also inconsistent with the prosecution case that both murders had been committed by the same person. Evans was granted a Free Pardon in

over police behaviour in other respects,[87] its hand was forced to allow further consideration of the rules governing police investigations by another contentious case, that of George Riley.[88]

The body of Adeline Mary Smith, a sixty-two-year-old widow, was discovered by her sister and neighbours in her bedroom at 10:00 am on Saturday 8 October 1960, the police arriving at the crime scene at 10:55 am. Adeline had been subjected to a vicious attack and her injuries were horrific. The details are relevant if distressing. The pathologist later stated that her mouth and nostrils were blocked by blood. A tooth was found on the bed, another on the floor and another was embedded in her chin and a fourth was found later to have been knocked down her windpipe. Her face had been deformed and flattened, her nose fractured and her eyelids were swollen and bruised. There were deep lacerations on her left cheek and chin. Her upper jaw was fractured and her lower jaw splintered. Professor Webster, a consultant pathologist, maintained unwaveringly at the trial that the condition of the widow's face and head indicated that blood must have spurted all over the assailant and the force of blows must have been considerable. The Report of the Home Office pathologist was consistent with blood staining of an extensive kind including on the blankets, an eiderdown, drawers of the dressing table, blood splashes on the wall to the left of the dressing table, on the wall beneath the electric fire, on the surface of a built-in cupboard, and on the walls between the dressing table and the built-in cupboard: 'The back of the head lay in a mass of clotted blood and there was a thick pool of clotted blood on either side of the neck. The carpet showed blood staining above the head and at the shoulders and left elbow … The face was a mass of clotted blood.'

Although they had *no* evidence, the police immediately went to George Riley's workplace and took him into custody before midday of the same day. Riley, a twenty-one-year-old trainee butcher, was known to the police having served a term of six months' imprisonment for 'Grievous bodily harm' after using a flick-knife in a fight.[89] After some seven hours in custody, Riley 'confessed' in a short

1966 immediately following the Brabin Report. Following a decision by the Home Office to make an ex gratia payment of compensation to Timothy Evans' personal representatives, the independent assessor, Lord Brennan QC, concluded that the conviction and execution of Timothy Evans for the murder of his child was wrongful and a miscarriage of justice and that there was no evidence to implicate Evans in the murder of his wife. The most probable outcome, he said, was that she was murdered by Christie. See *Westlake v Criminal Cases Review Commission* [2004] EWHC 2779 (Admin) in which the court accepted that Evans had been exonerated of the murders of his wife and child and that 'it is recognised that he committed neither murder' para 35.

[87] Including the John Waters case raised in House: HC Deb 3 February 1959, vol 599, cols 349–58W involving among other things police brutality, the rejection of police evidence, and the destruction of a police notebook.

[88] National Archives, DPP 3173.

[89] Riley's previous conviction occurred when he was in the Army Apprentices' School from which he was discharged as a result of his conviction. He then had various jobs as a labourer at a timber importers from which his services were dispensed with for poor timekeeping and continual absences; as a builder's labourer for a few days; as a warehouse man ('satisfactory, very polite and caused no internal

statement in his own handwriting. Riley was to say at his trial that the statement had been written under the suggestive promptings of a CID Inspector. The confession was, as commentators noted at the time, remarkable for its lucidity, containing the bare facts required for conviction with none of the irrelevant elaborations so frequently associated with such confessions. The links with the Evans case were readily made:[90]

> ... no evidence was produced that Riley's knuckles had been lacerated or that any weapon had been used. The prosecution relied instead upon the fact that Riley was wearing a ring upon which there was some blood—again unidentifiable.
>
> On the staircase there were two pieces of blood-spattered wallpaper which the police had removed. The widow's assailant had obviously left her dying in the bedroom and brushed his bloodstained jacket on the staircase wall as he descended. Yet these two pieces of vital evidence were missing at the trial.
>
> Was it that the pathological test on those two pieces of wallpaper did not fit with the police theory of the crime, just as the time sheets of the workmen in the washhouse of 10 Rillington Place were never available at the trial of Timothy Evans...
>
> As in Evans' case, Riley signed his death warrant with the confession; but in Riley's case it was made in his own handwriting at, Riley insisted throughout the criminal proceedings, the suggestive promptings of Detective-Inspector Brumpton of the C. I. D.

Extraordinarily, at Riley's trial, no fingerprint evidence was offered; though blood covered her bedroom, Riley was not bloodstained and no blood evidence was tendered; despite the obvious force of the blows, no evidence was produced that Riley's knuckles had been lacerated or that any weapon had been used, the prosecution relying instead upon the fact that Riley was wearing a ring upon which there was some small unidentifiable blood spots;[91] despite the alleged robbery motive, there was no disturbance in the house and Amelia's purse was left untouched; the police made no effort to check or verify anything, closing down the investigation once the confession had been obtained. No money had been taken but the words which ended the confession, 'I was short of money', under the law as it then stood, took the crime into the category of capital offences.[92]

troubles'); and then as a butcher's assistant ('a good worker, willing and a jovial type of person'). As a juvenile he had convictions for stealing a purse and a pedal cycle. He also had convictions for fighting in the street and causing wilful damage to a motor car and conduct likely to cause a breach of the peace when, with another, he lifted a small car off its wheels causing ten pounds worth of damage.

[90] See *Shrewsbury Chronicle and Advertiser* (4 February 1961).

[91] This was consistent with the known fact that Riley had the night before been involved in dance-hall fights.

[92] The brief for the prosecution warned that the defence might suggest that it was not capital murder 'particularly as nothing in the house appears to have been touched but in view of Riley's statement this

Although the Home Secretary did not relent, George Riley being hanged on 9 February 1961, the Home Office faced great pressure to take action with respect to police questioning of suspects. In January 1961, Ludovic Kennedy's book on the Evans case had excited widespread approval[93] and gave further ammunition to critics of police investigation methods. At the same time, the influential Council of JUSTICE, learning that police investigation methods might not be considered by the Royal Commission on the Police, wrote to the Home Secretary to urge a different approach since, it argued:[94]

> The majority of complaints arise from methods of questioning suspects, and detentions at police stations, and it was public uneasiness over a number of incidents which led to debates in Parliament and in part to the appointment of the Royal Commission.

The press stepped up the pressure. *The Daily Telegraph*, drawing together concerns voiced by lawyers, academics, and the general public,[95] said that the case of George Riley had again drawn attention to the need both to redefine and strictly enforce the Judges' Rules, stating, among other things: 'disregard of the Rules by the police has been encouraged by the laxity of many judges in admitting confessions or evidence so obtained'; 'in practice ambiguities in the wording of the Rules enable the police to continue questioning past the point at which it should stop'; 'the modern tendency is not only to ignore the Judges' Rules but also to obtain confessions by means which bear some resemblance to the techniques of brain-washing: midnight arrest, continuous questioning, and deprivation of sleep'.[96] Questions in the House of Commons soon followed.

The Home Secretary ('Rab' Butler) was asked whether he would review existing procedure in the light of growing concern about convictions in criminal cases,

will be difficult'. After reviewing exchanges between Riley and a police officer, the brief continued: 'Of course, if the statement were to be excluded the prosecution would be bound to fail . . . In view of the rather remarkable absence of blood on Riley, [the Home Office Senior Forensic Officer] was asked if the clothing had been washed but, apparently, there is no evidence of this.'

[93] The Home Secretary told Parliament that he was examining the book together with all other relevant information available: HC Deb 26 January 1961, vol 633, col 49W.

[94] Letter from the Chairman of Council, Lord Shawcross, dated 6 February 1961. Lord Shawcross pointed out that whilst it was true that the Royal Commission of 1929 considered these matters, 'they still cause active concern and there is a wide variety in the practice and standards of different police forces'. National Archives, HO 287/222: this file has been heavily weeded.

[95] Richard Yorke, 'Questioning by the Police' *The Daily Telegraph* (11 February 1961) which cited, among others, the views of Professor Glanville Williams, and Lord Devlin. See also 'Matters of Life and Death' *The Guardian* (Editorial) (17 February 1961), giving voice to 'misgivings' about the way in which the Judges' Rules were being used.

[96] An Editorial ('I did it') in *The Observer* (12 February 1961) was even more hard-hitting arguing that uncorroborated confessions should be excluded from evidence unless repeated by the accused before the court.

particularly murder trials, where convictions resulted from confessions made while in police custody without adequate corroboration of guilt.[97]

The instinct of the Home Office was to fend off these concerns.[98] Guidance to the Home Secretary provided by the permanent Under-Secretary, Sir Charles Cunningham,[99] was to the effect that 'you are not convinced that any alteration is called for in the present practice of the police in relation to the taking of statements; and if the point is pressed you will no doubt continue to take the line that you are not persuaded, on the evidence at present available, that there is any need for this issue to be reviewed'. If pressed hard, the Home Secretary was advised that it would be necessary to reiterate that police methods of investigation fell outside the terms of reference of the Royal Commission; that the Commission could consider how complaints against the police should be investigated without going into the general police methods out of which a particular complaint may have arisen; but that 'in deference to the views that have been expressed you are proposing to consult with the Chairman of the Royal Commission'.[100] The Home Secretary was advised to make clear, if pressed, that the question being discussed with the Royal Commission was whether it should look at police methods of investigation and not merely at the operation of the Judges' Rules; but since any review would involve the Judges' Rules 'you may think it right to state that you will be consulting the Lord Chief Justice as well as the Chairman of the Royal Commission'. The Home Secretary faithfully stuck to the brief.[101]

Despite Home Office resistance, the volume of concern over these interrelated issues was such that a new inquiry of some sort was inevitable. While the Members of the Royal Commission on the Police were of the view that the Commission ought not to look at the Judges' Rules and were concerned that a separate inquiry by the judges at the same time would result in overlap, at a meeting held in the Home Secretary's room on 21 February 1961, the Lord Chief Justice accepted that there was a case for overhauling the Judges' Rules. The Home Secretary was thus able to respond positively to further parliamentary questions on this matter:[102]

> I am glad to say that the Lord Chief Justice, with whom I have been in touch, has been good enough to agree that the time has come when it would be appropriate for the judges to carry out a review of the scope and operation of the Judges' Rules; and that he is making the necessary arrangements to do so. The Chairman of the Royal Commission on the Police, whom I have also consulted, has agreed to make

[97] HC Deb 16 February 1961, vol 634, cols 1746–47.

[98] File notes indicate that the Home Office officials struggled to find words which would respond to the concerns but at the same time deflect pressure for an inquiry.

[99] The Guidance Note was drafted by the deputy Under-Secretary, Philip Allen (later, Sir Philip Allen, Permanent Under-Secretary 1966--72), and approved by Sir Charles.

[100] This concession had already been made in reply to Lord Shawcross.

[101] HC Deb 16 February 1961, vol 634, cols 1746–47.

[102] HC Deb 16 February 1961, vol 634, col 145W.

available, for the purpose of this review, any relevant material that comes, or has come, to the Commission's notice.

Conclusion

The Judges' Rules were not in many ways the rules of the judges but rules of the Home Office. Often lauded for their so-called professionalism, Home Office officials, from clerks to permanent Under-Secretaries, exhibited technical ineptitude in the drafting of the Rules and stored up difficulties of interpretation of the Rules themselves and problems in the management of police encounters with suspects. A more cynical view is that the Home Office judged that its 'order maintenance' function was best served by allowing the police the latitude it wanted accepting that there would be little to protect the rights of suspects. Awareness of dubious or illicit police practices did nothing to encourage the Home Office to initiate a programme of reform. The establishment in 1961 of a formal reconsideration of the Judges' Rules was not, accordingly, a formality. The standing of the Rules as 'administrative directions' for the guidance of police officers rather than 'rules of law' combined with their ambiguous (if not illusory) nature, endorsed by Avory J and Hewart LCJ, had given the police some basis for more extended questioning than a strict interpretation might suggest and over the years they took rich advantage of this latitude. The plain clothes division, with its close links to the criminal fraternity and the opportunities for wrongdoing this presented, had done their bit but, by the 1950s, they were joined by officers at all levels. One consequence of the lax interpretation of the Rules was that it facilitated police misconduct in criminal investigations. Only after apparent miscarriages of justice came to light did the pressure for reform become unstoppable, the Home Office deflecting criticism for as long as it could manage.

5

The First Draft

The Judges and the Home Office

Introduction

Revising the Judges' Rules proved protracted and stressful, spanning the period from February 1961 to January 1964. It entailed delicate exchanges bearing upon the independence of the judiciary and the role of the Home Office in criminal justice administration.[1] In this chapter, we describe the initial phase in which the judges sought to draw up new Rules against the background of the changing climate of police–citizen relations and heightened public concern that the post-war period had inaugurated.

Taking Soundings

After exchanges of correspondence, a private meeting was held in the Home Secretary's room attended by the Home Secretary, Parker LCJ, Sir Henry Willink (Chairman of the Royal Commission on the Police), Sir Ian Jacob,[2] the deputy Under-Secretary Philip Allen, and two other Home Office Officials (T A Critchley; and A W Glanville). Two interrelated issues were under discussion: the role of uncorroborated confessions in criminal cases; and the Judges' Rules.

Uncorroborated Confessions

The Home Secretary raised the question 'which had arisen in the Riley case and was being revived in the Evans case' of whether there should be any change in the law to ensure that convictions could not be obtained solely on confession evidence.

Lord Parker said that it was his impression that the Director of Public Prosecutions (DPP) had undertaken 'in a private conversation' that he would ordinarily proceed 'only if there were ample outside evidence' and he wondered if a statement could be made 'in order to remove public disquiet' to say that the DPP

[1] A full picture is hampered by gaps in the files which are located in HO 287/222.
[2] Lieutenant-General Sir Ian Jacob had recently retired as Director-General of the BBC.

The Myth of Judicial Independence. Mike McConville and Luke Marsh, Oxford University Press (2020). © Mike McConville and Luke Marsh. DOI: 10.1093/oso/9780198822103.001.0001

and chief officers of police were alive to the dangers of prosecuting a person when the only evidence was contained in a confession to the police.

The Home Secretary said that this was 'a matter of acute public controversy' and that 'the question of making any such statement raised a number of problems'. Who should make any statement? When should it be made? The Home Secretary continued:

> More serious, would it not be read as meaning that proceedings should not have been taken against Riley? The plain fact was that Riley would not have been hanged if he had not made a confession.

The Home Secretary curtailed discussion saying that it could not be dealt with by amending the Judges' Rules and was well outside the terms of reference of the Royal Commission.

The Judges' Rules

At the suggestion of the Home Secretary, it was agreed that any revision of the Judges' Rules would be a question for the judges not the Royal Commission. Lord Parker readily accepted the need to overhaul the Rules:

> [I]n his view it ought to have been done more frequently in the past, and ought to be done from time to time in the future. The great advantage of the Judges' Rules was that they provided for a certain amount of elasticity, and left a good deal to the discretion of the Judges. He thought it important not to 'ham-string' the police in their work of detecting crime ... He saw no objection in principle to extending the Judges' Rules to cover the stage of enquiry before the police officer had made up his mind to make a charge.

The Procedure of Any Inquiry

Given the criticisms of the Scott Henderson Report and its 'semi-secret' character, the procedure for reviewing the Rules was of both technical and political importance. Lord Parker had already formed a view:

> The Lord Chief Justice said that the procedure he had in mind was that a small committee, consisting probably of himself, Mr. Justice Lawton and two other judges, should prepare a draft and should then consult the Home Office and the police. He thought it important that the police should be brought in to full consultation, and readily accepted the suggestion that this should be arranged by

> the Home Office. He said that he did not contemplate that any outside evidence should be taken; he thought that the representations already made, and the knowledge and collective experience of the Judges, provided ample material on which they could carry out their examination.

The proposed, essentially private, process was bound to raise suspicions and was hardly addressed by Parker's pledge to get in touch with the Home Office 'in due course' in order to ascertain 'their views and the views of the police about any provisional conclusions which the Judges reached'. The concerns of others outside were soon voiced.

Within weeks the Home Secretary faced parliamentary questions on the Riley case and on confessions obtained in police stations.[3] The Home Secretary's oblique answers suggested that some kind of inquiry would be forthcoming[4] exciting further press comment.[5] The Lord Chief Justice (LCJ) informed the Home Secretary by letter dated 6 March 1961 that he had appointed a small Committee of the Queen's Bench judges to consider the Judges' Rules with him so that the Home Secretary was able to formally announce to Parliament on 16 March 1961 that the 'scope and operation' of the Rules would be reviewed.[6] It was privately agreed that the police input would be arranged through the offices of the permanent Under-Secretary, Sir Charles Cunningham.[7] It appears that, at this stage, the Committee appointed by Lord Parker to assist him included Elwes J, Winn J, and Lawton J.[8]

The proposed procedure soon came up for consideration in Parliament. Members said that there was considerable public concern over removing consideration of the Rules from the purview of the Royal Commission, Mr Fletcher MP, asking the following question:[9]

> We all agree that this inquiry is very important, but can the [Secretary of State] assure us that the result will be made public, in the same way as would the result of an inquiry by a Royal Commission; and that people who wish to give evidence and make representations to the judges will have the same facilities for doing so as they would have if the investigation were conducted by the Royal Commission?

[3] HC Deb 2 March 1961, vol 635, cols 1745–46.

[4] Mr Butler said that when he was ready he would make a statement because 'it is quite reasonable that there should be an investigation'.

[5] *The Guardian* (3 March 1961) said that it 'seems tolerably clear that the Home Secretary will order an inquiry into police methods of questioning in the course of criminal investigations'; *The Daily Herald* (3 March 1961) thought that an imminent inquiry following the George Riley case might lead to a change in the law; and *The Times* (3 March 1961) noted the 'uneasiness at police interrogations'.

[6] HC Deb 16 March 1961, vol 636, col 145W.

[7] Letter of Lord Parker to the Home Secretary dated 20 March 1961 responding to the suggestion made in a letter of same date from Mr Butler.

[8] 'The Constable and the Law' *Police Review* (24 March 1961). All had been recently elevated to the Queen's Bench: Elwes J in 1958; Winn J in 1959; and Lawton J in 1961.

[9] HC Deb 30 March 1961, vol 637, cols 1512–14.

The Home Secretary said that he would get in touch with Lord Parker so that 'we can be sure that if people wish to make submissions there is a quarter where they can be received'. Further attempts to secure assurances that there would be an opportunity to make representations were rebuffed.

The semi-secret character of the inquiry is clearly underlined in Home Office notes following an approach from the Chief Constable of Bedfordshire, Mr Pratt. The Home Office deputy Under-Secretary, Philip Allen, recorded on 12 May 1961 that he had explained to Mr Pratt that there was no question of the judges receiving oral evidence 'or indeed of their inviting the submission of evidence', and that although it was theoretically open to the Chief Constables to volunteer a written statement, he expected Lord Parker to consult the Home Office who would then consult Chief Constables about the judges' provisional conclusions before any final decision. In consequence, he noted, the 'Chief Constables therefore were likely to be put in a privileged position'. Allen continued:

> I impressed on Mr. Pratt the importance of seeing that there was no publicity for the fact that the Chief Constables were likely to be consulted, since other sections of the community would be likely to take a poor view of this.

Influential voices continued to protest. Indeed, Lord Shawcross, founding member and Chairman of JUSTICE, was reported[10] in the context of the taking of statements by the police as follows:

> I confess that some of us do not care for secret procedures of this kind. We do not know what evidence is being received ... nor are we convinced that a committee of judges is by its nature the best sort of machinery to investigate a problem of this kind.

Although an influential and respected lawyer, having been, *inter alia*, Attorney-General and Chief British Prosecutor at the Nuremberg War Crimes Tribunal, the views of Lord Shawcross cut no ice and the review continued in secret.

The First Iteration

As a matter of fact, progress was inordinately slow. In November 1961, Lord Parker told Charles Cunningham that it 'had not been possible to make very much progress and asked whether the Home Office regarded this as a matter of great urgency, and Sir Charles Cunningham assured him that we did not'. On this basis,

[10] 'Study of the Rights of the Individual' *The Times* (28 June 1961).

Lord Parker said that if the Chief Constables enquired about progress, it would be 'perfectly proper to tell them that it would be some time yet before we were likely to hear anything from the judges'.[11] Indeed, it was some time; but when the *First Draft* was forwarded to the Home Office on 25 June 1962, it made an immediate, if unintended, impact.

The *First Draft* was in several ways a radical document. Instead of a regime marked by fudge and interpretative latitude, the new provision sought to establish brighter lines. Whereas in recent years judges, including Lord Parker,[12] had almost belittled the Rules, in response to public concern police officers were now to be subject to a tighter and more comprehensive regulatory framework.

Lord Parker's letter accompanying the *First Draft* disclosed that it had been prepared by 'three of us'. At this stage, it appears that the remaining Queen's Bench judges had not been consulted.[13] Lord Parker's letter set out their thinking and invited comments from the Met Commissioner:

> While anxious to meet public disquiet and criticism, we certainly do not wish to hamper the Police and to make their task more difficult. It is for this reason that we should welcome the views of the Commissioner in the first instance.

This tension between the 'interests of the police' and the 'interests of the public' came to be resolved by the judges in favour of greater regulation of the police.

The *First Draft* most nearly resembled the model eventually incorporated into the Police and Criminal Evidence Act 1984 (PACE). It sought to provide a comprehensive regulatory regime with an emphasis upon formality, the rights of the individual, and the necessity for full police record-keeping, as we describe below.

Investigation: General

Rule 1 provided that whenever a police officer is trying to find out whether, or by whom, an offence has been committed, he is entitled to question any person or persons, whether suspected or not, from whom he thinks that useful information may be obtained. It was further provided by Rule 1(2) that before questioning anyone, the investigating police officer 'should record in his official note book, and inform the person of, his reasons for thinking it desirable to question him ...'

[11] File Note (14 November 1961) by Philip Allen.

[12] Indeed, while judges were in the process of overhauling the Rules, *Hennell v Cuthbert*, QBD *The Times*, 8 December 1961 (hereafter *Hennell*) was decided. In that case, the lead judgment given by Lord Parker himself (sitting with Slade J and Widgery J) included the statement: '*The Judges' Rules were only rules of practice, and even if they were contravened the evidence could still be admissible*' (emphasis supplied).

[13] This was apparently disclosed in a confidential note by Sir Charles Cunningham (26 June 1962).

At each police station, a 'Station Officer' was charged with responsibilities for overseeing the actions of investigating officers and for the welfare of those being questioned in essentially the same way that PACE separates the responsibilities of 'Custody Officers' from those of investigating officers. Just as under PACE Custody Officers have responsibility over the *Custody Record*, Station Officers had charge of an '*Investigation Occurrence Book*' in which the actions of investigating officers were to be recorded. The *First Draft* also drew a distinction between (a) persons questioned at a police station prior to any arrest having been made and (b) persons who were detained in custody at the police station following formal arrest. We shall deal with the former (unarrested) group first.

Persons questioned at a police station without having been arrested

Before a police officer started to question a person at a police station he was required to enter into the *Investigation Occurrence Book* his reasons for thinking it desirable to do so and inform that person accordingly. Questioning, or the provision of a statement by those electing to do so, was subject to close and contemporaneous regulation, all occurrences to be recorded, 'so far as possible as the events happen'[14] in the *Investigation Occurrence Book* by the Station Officer. These events were detailed as follows:[15]

- The time of arrival at the police station;
- The times when the questioning or making of any statement took place and who was present;
- If the questioning or making of any statement was interrupted for any reason, the reason for the interruption and the times of stopping and starting;
- The time or times at which a caution was given;
- The time when a charge was made and/or the person arrested.

The *First Draft* also made specific provision regarding the conditions which should obtain during the questioning/taking of a statement, as follows:

- The person being questioned or making a statement should be told, if such is the case, that he is not under arrest and should be seated, as should be all the police officers present;
- The questioning or taking of any statement should not be continued for more than two hours at a time without a break of at least half-an-hour and reasonable

[14] Rule 1(4).
[15] Rule 1(4) (i).

arrangements should be made for the comfort and refreshment of the person concerned;

- As far as practicable children (whether suspected of crime or not) should not be interviewed save in the presence of some person who is not a police officer, and is of the same sex as the child;
- Reasonable facilities should be afforded to the person being questioned or making a statement to communicate with a solicitor if he asks to do so. If the solicitor can be telephoned the person being questioned or making a statement, upon paying for the call, should be allowed to speak privately to the solicitor by telephone;
- No entry in an Investigation Occurrence Book should be shown to any person other than a police officer acting in the course of duty or a barrister or solicitor acting on behalf of the prosecution without an order of the Court which is trying or will try any defendant to whom the entry refers.

Cautioning

Rule II of the *First Draft* made provision for the caution and when it should be given:

- The caution should be in the following terms:
  'You are not obliged to say anything unless you wish to do so, but whatever you say will be taken down in writing and may be given in evidence.'
  Care should be taken to avoid any suggestion that a person's answers can only be used in evidence against him.
- Whenever and as soon as a police officer knows of, or believes that there are, facts which, if not explained, point to the guilt of any person, he shall caution such person before putting to him any questions or further questions as the case may be.[16]

The cautioning regime set out here was a restatement of the position that had been made to the police in the process of revision of the Rules in 1918.

Provisions regarding persons in custody

Rule III of the *First Draft* sought to re-inforce the rule that prisoners (ie, arrested persons) should not be subject to cross-examination, a position that had been

[16] The provisions regarding entry of all events in the Investigation Occurrence Book applied to all such questioning.

ignored by the police. Under the new regime, as soon as it was decided to arrest a person or not to permit him to go freely, the police were required to tell the person that he had been arrested and caution him after which questioning was to be permitted only in prescribed circumstances, as follows:

(1) If a police officer thinks that it is proper to bring any supposed facts about the offence for which he is held to the notice of the person held, or to bring to his notice the contents of a written statement made by another person, a statement in writing of such facts or such statement should be handed to him but nothing should be said or done to invite a reply. If the person says that he would like to make a statement in reply or starts to say something he should at once be cautioned.[17]

(2) Exceptionally if a police officer thinks that it is expedient in the interests of justice or to prevent harm or further harm being suffered by the public or some other person, to question a person in custody, he may do so; but before doing so he should record his reasons and sign such record and should caution the person. If the person is to be questioned at some place other than a police station these reasons should be recorded in an official notebook. If the person is questioned at a police station these reasons should be recorded in the Investigation Occurrence Book. The caution must be written out and signed by the police officer and, if he agrees, the person to be questioned. Every question and answer should be written down before another question is put. (This Rule should only be relied upon in exceptional circumstances, as, for example, a case in which a person in custody has admitted abducting a child or injuring someone but has not said where the child or victim is to be found or has admitted disposing of property but has not said where or how or to whom.)

(3) If, after the person making any statement has finished writing or telling a police officer what he wants written down, it appears to the senior police officer present that what has been written is unintelligible or ambiguous he, or some other officer authorised by him, may question the person making the statement for the purpose of making it intelligible or unambiguous; but if he does so, he must write down each question as it is put and record the answer, if any.

This represented a clear determination that persons in custody under arrest, with very limited exceptions, should not be cross-examined by police officers and that any questioning should be carefully documented in official books.

[17] Thereafter, the formal procedure for taking of statements (*infra*) was to be followed.

Manner in Which Statements Are to Be Taken

Under Rule IV, the Judges also made detailed provision regarding the way in which any statement was to be taken from those in custody or those who had elected to make a statement, as follows:

(1) If such a person says that he wants to make a statement he should be told that it is intended to make a written record of what he says. It is highly desirable that the person making the statement should write it in his own hand and he must always be asked to write down himself what he wants to say; if he says that he cannot write or that he would like someone to write it for him, a police officer may offer to write the statement for him. If he accepts the offer the police officer should, before starting, write out and ask the person making the statement to sign, or make his mark to, the following: 'I want (state name of the police officer) to write down what I say.'
(2) Any person writing his own statement should be allowed to do so without prompting or questioning.
(3) Whenever a police officer writes the statement, he should take down, as far as possible, the words spoken by the person making the statement: he should not question him, or prompt him.
(4) When the statement is finished the person making it should be asked to read it and to make any corrections, alterations or additions he wishes and to initial them. When he has finished reading it he should be asked to write and sign the following Certificate at the end of the statement: 'I have read the above statement and I have been told that I can correct or alter or add anything I wish. This statement is true.'
(5) If the person who has made a statement refuses to read it or to write the above mentioned Certificate at the end of it or to sign it, the senior police officer present should record on the statement itself and in the presence of the person making it, what has happened. If the person making the statement cannot read, or refuses to read it, the officer who has taken it down should read it over to him and ask him whether he would like to correct, alter or add anything and to put his signature or make his mark at the end. The police officer should then certify on the statement itself what he has done.
(6) If Rule II or III applies, the person making the statement, if he is going to write it himself, should be asked to write out and sign before writing what he wants to say, the following: 'I make this statement of my own free will. I have been told that I need not say anything unless I wish to do so and that whatever I say may be used in evidence.'

As soon as practicable after a person had been told that they were to be arrested or charged with an offence, the judges required that the person be formally charged and cautioned as follows under Rule VI: 'Do you wish to say anything in answer to the charge? You are not obliged to say anything unless you wish to do so but whatever you say will be taken down in writing now and may be given in evidence.'[18]

The Principles Animating the Draft

It is clear from this *First Draft* that the judges intended that police interrogation be subjected to close regulation. But we can go further: at this point in history, the judges, whilst wanting to do nothing to 'ham-string' the police, continued to hold certain common law principles regarding the freedom of the individual as fundamental, and were watchful of any encroachment thereon. This much can be seen from the dialogue that took place soon after on a proposal to fundamentally alter the form of the caution.

In November 1963, the Solicitor-General and the Attorney-General suggested to Lord Parker and Winn J[19] that the right to silence be attenuated through amendment to the form of the first caution as set out in **Illustration 5.1**.

The key part of this proposal was to include in the caution a warning regarding the consequences of silence:

> You are not obliged to say anything unless you wish to do so but what you say may be put into writing and given in evidence. *If you choose not to answer any question your failure to do so may be commented on* (emphasis supplied).

While the Law Officers are recorded as thinking that the two judges had some sympathy for this radical suggestion, Lord Parker was said to have felt that this was such a fundamental departure from the Rules that he ought to consult his brother judges as well as the Law Society and the Bar Council before anything might be decided.[20] And it *was* a departure because it went to the very core of the common law principle regarding the right to remain silent.

[18] Whatever was said was to be taken down at once in an official note book, read over and the person invited to sign or make his mark etc.

[19] Letter (22 November 1963) from Sir John Hobson, Attorney-General to the Home Secretary.

[20] The Home Secretary, on pragmatic grounds, thought that such a proposal would be highly controversial and so adversely commented upon as to outweigh any possible benefit that other changes ('concessions' from the Judges) to the Rules might bring. The Lord Chancellor (and former Attorney-General), Sir Reginald Manningham-Buller, often seen as a hawk, was opposed to this suggestion on principle: 'I would not myself support the inclusion of the last sentence. A man is entitled to refuse to answer any question the answer to which may incriminate him and to have power to comment on the failure to answer a question is getting close to saying that a refusal to answer will tend to incriminate.'

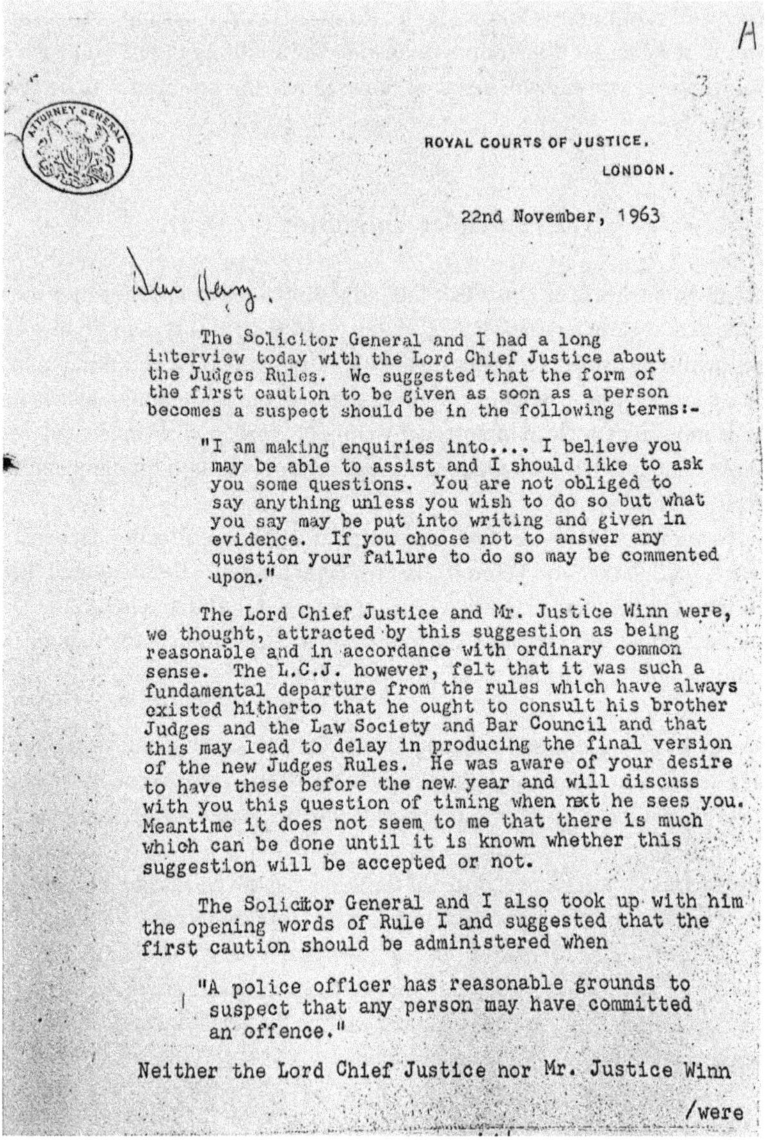

A

3

ATTORNEY GENERAL

ROYAL COURTS OF JUSTICE,
LONDON.

22nd November, 1963

Dear Harry.

The Solicitor General and I had a long interview today with the Lord Chief Justice about the Judges Rules. We suggested that the form of the first caution to be given as soon as a person becomes a suspect should be in the following terms:-

"I am making enquiries into.... I believe you may be able to assist and I should like to ask you some questions. You are not obliged to say anything unless you wish to do so but what you say may be put into writing and given in evidence. If you choose not to answer any question your failure to do so may be commented upon."

The Lord Chief Justice and Mr. Justice Winn were, we thought, attracted by this suggestion as being reasonable and in accordance with ordinary common sense. The L.C.J. however, felt that it was such a fundamental departure from the rules which have always existed hitherto that he ought to consult his brother Judges and the Law Society and Bar Council and that this may lead to delay in producing the final version of the new Judges Rules. He was aware of your desire to have these before the new year and will discuss with you this question of timing when next he sees you. Meantime it does not seem to me that there is much which can be done until it is known whether this suggestion will be accepted or not.

The Solicitor General and I also took up with him the opening words of Rule I and suggested that the first caution should be administered when

"A police officer has reasonable grounds to suspect that any person may have committed an offence."

Neither the Lord Chief Justice nor Mr. Justice Winn

/were

Illustration 5.1 Letter from the Attorney-General Concerning the Right to Silence (November 1963) (National Archives)

Once Lord Parker had consulted the other judges it became clear that there was 'very considerable opposition' to the suggestion. As outlined by Lord Parker and set out in **Illustration 5.2** the opposition took two forms.

The responses of the judges were compelling. Lawton J invoked the history of the common law going back to Sir Thomas More's defence to the charge of

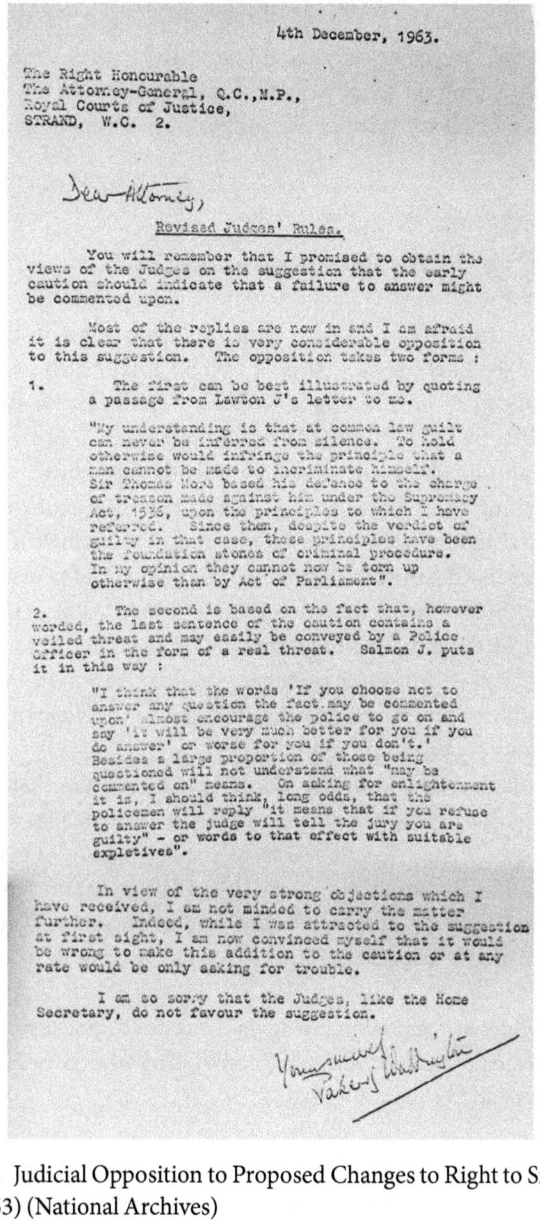

4th December, 1963.

The Right Honourable
The Attorney-General, Q.C., M.P.,
Royal Courts of Justice,
STRAND, W.C. 2.

Dear Attorney,

Revised Judges' Rules.

You will remember that I promised to obtain the views of the Judges on the suggestion that the early caution should indicate that a failure to answer might be commented upon.

Most of the replies are now in and I am afraid it is clear that there is very considerable opposition to this suggestion. The opposition takes two forms :

1. The first can be best illustrated by quoting a passage from Lawton J's letter to me.

"My understanding is that at common law guilt can never be inferred from silence. To hold otherwise would infringe the principle that a man cannot be made to incriminate himself. Sir Thomas More based his defence to the charge of treason made against him under the Supremacy Act, 1536, upon the principles to which I have referred. Since then, despite the verdict of guilty in that case, these principles have been the foundation stones of criminal procedure. In my opinion they cannot now be torn up otherwise than by Act of Parliament".

2. The second is based on the fact that, however worded, the last sentence of the caution contains a veiled threat and may easily be conveyed by a Police Officer in the form of a real threat. Salmon J. puts it in this way :

"I think that the words 'If you choose not to answer any question the fact may be commented upon' almost encourage the police to go on and say 'it will be very much better for you if you do answer' or worse for you if you don't.' Besides a large proportion of those being questioned will not understand what "may be commented on" means. On asking for enlightenment it is, I should think, long odds, that the policemen will reply "it means that if you refuse to answer the judge will tell the jury you are guilty" - or words to that effect with suitable expletives".

In view of the very strong objections which I have received, I am not minded to carry the matter further. Indeed, while I was attracted to the suggestion at first sight, I am now convinced myself that it would be wrong to make this addition to the caution or at any rate would be only asking for trouble.

I am so sorry that the Judges, like the Home Secretary, do not favour the suggestion.

Yours sincerely,
Parker of Waddington

Illustration 5.2 Judicial Opposition to Proposed Changes to Right to Silence (December 1963) (National Archives)

treason and subsequent principles which were 'the foundation stones' of criminal procedure which could not be 'torn up' other than by Act of Parliament. Salmon J set out the practical dangers of a change which contained a veiled threat which could 'easily be conveyed by a Police officer in the form of a real threat'. In the light of these (and other undisclosed) responses, Lord Parker stated that though 'attracted to the suggestion at first sight', he was now also convinced 'that it would be wrong to make this addition to the caution' or at any rate it would be 'only asking for trouble'.[21] Accordingly, revision of the Rules had to be undertaken in a context in which the judges were acting on grounds of firmly held[22] principle.

The Reception of the Draft

The *First Draft* ran into trouble at once against a background of strong objections from influential sections of the police as well as others such as the DPP[23] and the Commandant of Bramshill Police College.[24] Confidential comments made to the Home Office by the DPP, the Metropolitan Police Commissioner, and HM Inspectors of Constabulary were 'almost entirely disapproving'.

Before describing these objections, it is worth noting that the Home Office received a very different view from Commander William Willis, one of Her Majesty's Inspectors of Constabulary (1953–64), who had previously served as Chief Constable of Bedfordshire from 1940 to 1953. Willis set out his unambiguous opinion at the outset of his response:[25] 'Generally, if adopted, these recommendations will in no way hamper the police.' Although the internal files show no indication that any weight was attached to the view of Willis, we will note his comments at various points.

The line of attack reflected in the Home Office files was that the *First Draft* was not in line with the purpose of the existing Rules which, as expressed in the Home Office Consolidated Circular, was 'to ensure that any statement tendered in evidence should be a purely voluntary statement and therefore admissible in evidence'. Instead, the *First Draft* was said to lay down rules of procedure rather than giving guidance about admissibility.[26] As the DPP put it:

> The existing Rules are limited to giving guidance to the police as to how statements, that are to be tendered in evidence, should be taken in order to be prima facie voluntary and therefore admissible.

21 Letter to the Attorney-General (4 December 1963). It is likely that Lord Parker bowed to the weight of opinion of the other Judges. Parker was a deeply conservative judge. See Thomas Grant, *Jeremy Hutchinson's Case Histories* (John Murray 2015) (hereafter Grant, *Case Histories*) 54; Hyde, *Birkett* 588.

22 As we now know and, as we shall see, judicial 'firmness' melted all too quickly.

23 Sir Theobald Matthew.

24 Mr Lawrence.

25 Letter to Kenneth Parker of the Home Office (3 July 1962).

26 Since the First Draft did not include a statement that non-compliance risked the rejection of evidence obtained the Home Office felt that there was a suggestion that failure to comply with the Rules constituted in itself malpractice by the police.

> But the revised Rules have no such limitation. They purport to tell the police how when and where they should take statements from any person who may be able to assist in the investigation of a crime … I feel strongly that this attempt by the Judiciary to dictate to the police how they should conduct their criminal investigations is going miles outside their province, and can only lead to the complete frustration of the C. I. D. side of the police.

Against this objection, the Home Office itself recognized that there were two important points, as reflected in the following internal note:

> (a) The Rules may have begun, or may be very strictly interpreted, as a mere legal guide to admissibility; but they are generally taken also as a set of rules protecting suspects; and the Judge who, as Lord Parker says, are bound to take account of 'public disquiet and criticism', may argue that they cannot be absolutely bound by the narrower of these two views;
> (b) The consolidated Circular does contain some 'further recommendations' by Lord Goddard when Lord Chief Justice … which are reminiscent of many of the revised Rules in their particularity. This might afford the Judges some precedent.

In regard to the first point, the Home Office and the police were aware of the serious misgivings expressed over the years, and increasing in volume at precisely this point in history, in respect of dubious interrogation procedures and their impact upon the reliability of criminal convictions. In that context, the Judges' Rules, for all their deficiencies, had indeed come to be seen as, however ineffective and deficient, a set of rules protecting the rights of the individual.

In regard to the second point, as the Home Office well knew, the *First Draft* was in many respects simply a repetition and further elaboration of instructions already distributed to the police by the Home Office with the approval of the then LCJ, Lord Goddard.[27] Further, those instructions were directed precisely to the *procedures* that should be adopted so as to 'give no ground for challenge, either as to the content or as to the manner in which they were taken, in the event of their use in evidence' and set out in a Home Office Circular eponymously entitled, *Procedure in Taking Statements from Persons under Caution*,[28] and repeated in other documents, *Supplementary Rules on*

[27] Lord Goddard was Chief Justice over the period 1946–1958. A firm but fair judge, he is now, however, best-known for his biased summing-up in the Bentley and Craig trial: *R v Derek William Bentley (deceased)* [1998] EWCA Crim 2516.

[28] Home Office Circular No 238/1947.

Procedure in Taking Statements Contained in Home Office Circulars 238/1947 (26 November, 1947) and 27/1948 (3rd February, 1948) approved by the Lord Chief Justice.[29] Although these Circulars were not as comprehensive as the judges' *First Draft*, they did include detailed guidance on how the police should treat suspects questioned under caution, as the following illustrations from the 1947–48 Circulars demonstrate:

(1) The caution should not be printed at the top of the sheet on which the statement is taken down, but should be written out as given in each case and the person making the statement invited to write his signature immediately underneath.
(2) The statement should be written down as nearly as possible in the actual words used, provided that they are intelligible. They should not be translated into 'official vocabulary, a course which may create a misleading impression as to the genuineness of the statement (original emphasis).
(3) When a statement has been written down, the person making the statement should be invited to read it over and alter it if he wishes. The statement should in all cases be read over to him, and he should be asked to sign it, and to initial each page and any alterations. The police officer taking the statement should, immediately below the statement and the signature of the person making it, write and sign a note that the statement was taken by him, that he has read it over to the person making it and (if it be the fact) that it has been read over by that person. This note should also be signed by any other person who was present at the taking of the statement.
(4) If the person making the statement would prefer to write it out himself and his degree of education is enough to enable him to do so, he should be encouraged to do so and should be supplied with writing materials. The police officer should first write out the caution, as described above, and invite the person who is making the statement to write his signature immediately underneath. The procedure set out in paragraph (3) should then be followed as far as it is applicable; in particular, the police officer should append a note to the effect that the statement was written out in his presence and that he has read it over to the person who wrote the statement.
(5) … [omitted]
(6) … [omitted]
(7) A record should be kept by the police officer concerned in his notebook of the times at which the taking of the statement started and finished, and of any

[29] It is noteworthy also that an internal note prepared by Philip Allen and approved by Cunningham for the guidance of the Secretary of State on 15 February 1961 on the history and purpose of the Judges' Rules sets out, in addition to the nine Rules, the further recommendations in 1947 and 1948 as to the procedure in taking statements from persons under caution as approved by the LCJ.

intervals and refreshments. It is unnecessary to include these times as part of the statement.

(8) ... [Omitted][30]

Moreover, as the Home Office files documented,[31] while these procedural recommendations were not formally a part of the Judges' Rules, those Rules were themselves merely *administrative guidelines* and their relationship to police regulation was hardly different to other forms of guidance contained in official Circulars.

Even the *Investigation Occurrence Book* was not an innovation nor was it unfamiliar to the Home Office, the Met Commissioner, or the police themselves. Indeed, since the nineteenth century, a similar documentation system was provided for by the Metropolitan Police General Orders.[32] The so-called 'White Book' set out detailed regulations and orders to which the police were subject, the second edition of which in 1900 contained, as summarized by the Royal Commission Upon the Duties of the Metropolitan Police (1908), the following account:[33]

> There is to be kept at each Police Station, under the supervision of the inspector or other officer in charge of the station, a book called the Occurrence Book, in which there are entered the events happening during each day which the Orders and Regulations require to be entered therein.
>
> We do not find that any Regulation has been made giving a general description of the events or occurrences that ought to be entered in this book, but specific orders require that events of certain kinds shall be entered therein. For instance, when a divisional surgeon is called in to examine a prisoner alleged to be drunk he is required to make in the Occurrence Book an entry showing the result of his examination.[34]
>
> So again officers in charge of stations are to enter in the Occurrence Book at the expiration of their tour of duty a list of constables who have been taken from their beats for any purpose, and for however short a time.[35]
>
> So again a report of the particulars respecting accidents or occurrences entered by a constable on duty in his note book is to be made as early as practicable, and is to be entered in the Occurrence Book for information and reference.[36]

[30] Other recommendations covered 'the taking of statements to be given in evidence from foreigners who wish to make them in their native language.'

[31] Thus, the Home Office Files contain law reports on *Hennell* (n 12) and *R v Smith (John Ernest)* (1962) 46 CR App R 51 in which the Court of Criminal Appeal said that a Recorder had a discretion to admit confession evidence obtained in breach of Judges' Rules.

[32] See *Royal Commission Upon the Duties of the Metropolitan Police, Report* (Cd 4156, vol i, 1908).

[33] ibid 45.

[34] White Book 99.

[35] ibid 557.

[36] ibid 16.

> These are but examples of the events which ought to be chronicled in the Occurrence Book. The book may be looked upon as a diary of all the principal events which happen at the station or in connection with the work of the Police Station each day.

The real point, however, was not one of technicality[37] since those consulted by the Home Office had divergent views on detailed matters:[38] it was that the police, the DPP, and the Home Office were strongly against such detailed regulation. In particular, the police were adamantly against the *First Draft*, as set out in internal Home Office notes:

> It is quite clear ... that if anything like the draft Rules put forward by the L.C. J. is published, the C. I. D. throughout this country will regard themselves as hampered to an extent that they are not by the present rules and that the general police view will be that the revision has gone beyond what could reasonably be said to have become necessary because of the degree of public concern expressed in Parliament and elsewhere ...
>
> Unless substantial changes are made, there can be little doubt that the Association of Chief Police Officers, to whom they will presumably have to be shown at a later stage, will feel bound to criticise them severely; and it would of course create a disastrous situation if the Judges and the Police were known to be at odds in a matter of fundamental importance of this kind.

There were in the *First Draft*, without any question, administrative responsibilities imposed on the police, particularly the Station Sergeant, which would have been too onerous as framed and would have required further refinement but the *Draft* touched other nerves: the gap between legal understanding and the Met's view of

[37] As a *First Draft*, there were indeed technical objections, some of which were contained in a letter from the Commissioner, Sir Joseph Simpson (18 July 1962). For example, the Commissioner pointed out that in a complex case, such as murder, hundreds and sometimes thousands of people may be spoken to by the police and, he said, to go through the elaborate procedures laid down in the *First Draft* 'would place an intolerable burden on the investigating officers'. Similarly, it was argued that if the Station Officer had to carry out all that was proposed, the Officer would have to get much of it second-hand from the investigating officer 'which nullifies the intended purport' of the provisions. By contrast, Commander Willis was more positive: 'I think that the Investigation Occurrence Book would help the police officer considerably and enable him to answer many of the unfair charges that are levelled against him in court.'

[38] The principal differences between the respondents are set out in a Home Office Note, 'Summary of views expressed'. Thus, eg, differences are enumerated along the following lines: 'Although Commander Willis feels that this [Sub-Rule (1)] is already general practice, Sir William Johnson considers the Sub-Rule unnecessary ... '; 'Mr. Lawrence makes the point that [Sub-Rule (2)] is either meaningless or may force the police to disclose more information at the outset of a case than is desirable. Commander Willis sees no objection to the Sub-Rule'; 'Commander Willis welcomes [Sub-Rule (3)] and feels it would help the police officer to answer many of the unfair charges which are levelled against him. The Commissioner strongly disagrees.'

police practice; and police suspicion of defence lawyers. This is clearly shown in the Commissioner's letter[39] to the Home Office:

> As I see it the main interest of the Bench in this matter is to ensure that admissions and confessions are free and voluntary if they are to be admissible in evidence; and the existing rules are directed to this end. *What so many people fail to understand is that if a police officer is to do his duty he may have to take a line which would render the information he obtains from that course of action inadmissible.* When such action takes place such evidence is not tendered to the Court. In fact, in a high percentage of cases, after an admission has been obtained, there is a plea of guilty and no evidence is heard in Court.
>
> The effect of the detailed Rules proposed would be to make a police officer who is conscientiously attempting to solve a crime feel that it is he who will be in the dock and he whose malpractice is the issue before the Court, rather than the question as to whether or [not] evidence tendered is admissible (original emphasis).

Extraordinarily, in what would come to be a common police argument, the very concerns of the public—that the police were engaging in illicit off-the-record practices—were now advanced as *justifications* for shielding police interrogations from external regulation of any kind.

The Commissioner also addressed the question of access to legal advice without police presence and indicated police lack of trust in (some) defence lawyers saying that the proposal:[40]

> ... assumes that all solicitors and managing clerks whom criminals are likely to approach are models of propriety. This is by no means the case. We cannot afford not to be present, although I agree that access to his solicitor should be facilitated.[41]

[39] Letter to Sir Charles Cunningham (18 July 1962).

[40] The suspicion was widely held. Thus, Sir Charles Martin, one of Her Majesty's Inspectors of Constabulary and formerly Chief Constable of Liverpool between 1948 and 1958, wrote to Kenneth Parker of the Home Office (3 July 1962) with his view of the complaints made about the existing system: 'I imagine that most of the criticisms or complaints often come from small pockets of professional people who very largely depend on the acquittal of persons accused of crime and whose attitude seems to be "no matter how guilty you are of crime you must never in any circumstances admit it to the police."'

[41] This issue was also forcefully put in a letter from the Merseyside Police (4 July 1962): '[I]t must be remembered that prosecuting solicitors about the country are not confined to prosecutions but are also available for and used in connection with the defence, and it is quite certain that as the procedure became known the defence would demand the production of this book in Court, and so we have still further demands upon the Police and, in the station officer, a further witness to be called and to be subject to cross-examination.'

Given the reduced public confidence in the police that the last decade had witnessed, police opposition alone was not enough to sink the *First Draft* and a wider strategy was needed.

Killing it Softly: The Strategy

The Home Office was fully aware of the delicate nature of the problem that the *First Draft* presented. Although the *First Draft* had united the Metropolitan Police and Law Officers in opposition to it, the Home Secretary had, after all, requested Lord Parker to undertake a review.[42] Moreover, Charles Cunningham himself felt that the hostile responses were unjustified in fundamental respects. While he agreed that the proposals were open to 'strong criticism in detail', he did not agree that the judges had gone beyond their 'legitimate interests in framing the Rules on the lines of the draft',[43] adding the following observation:

> It is true that what the judges have to do is to indicate in the Rules what the courts are likely to accept in evidence. I do not see that they can do this effectively, however, in this particular context, unless they indicate the conditions under which statements obtained by the police will be regarded as admissible. The present Rules, amplified as they are by Lord Goddard's comments, do in fact proceed on these lines.

This more measured view was, however, overshadowed by the concerted opposition of the Met Commissioner and the DPP. While a detailed point-to-point written refutation of the *First Draft* was ruled out[44] in favour of a personal discussion,[45] to overcome the views of the judges, a strategy was designed to achieve agreement: (i) that the Rules were intended to govern only the admissibility of evidence; (ii) that the need to administer a caution was only meant to apply to a definite suspect and that questioning could continue beyond the stage at which a suspect was taken into custody; and (iii) that much of the detailed procedure suggested in the *First Draft* would be more appropriate in a Home Office Circular.[46] The process adopted to achieve these ends was one of personal persuasion.

[42] An internal Home Office note of guidance for Cunningham by Kenneth Parker (24 September 1962): 'Both the Director [of Public Prosecutions] and the Commissioner [of Police of the Metropolis] accept that the L. C. J. cannot simply be told that the Judges have gone too far in framing rules on the lines of the draft, particularly in view of the fact that S. of S. invited the L. C. J. to conduct the review.'

[43] File Note to Mr Drew (16 August 1962).

[44] Note (16 August 1962).

[45] 'The object of the meeting with the Lord Chief Justice is presumably to get him to think again (everybody agrees that his draft will not do as it stands) but this may be achieved more easily in a frank talk . . . '

[46] On this last point, the internal Home Office Note states that the 'prospect of ruling out evidence as admissible because one of the small points of procedure suggested for example in Rule I has been

A full account of what then happened cannot be given because documents remain secret and the notes of the various meetings are incomplete. We know that Lord Parker met privately with the Met Commissioner who, during informal discussions, expressed himself to the Home Office as 'quite confident that [Lord Parker] will be prepared to accept fundamental criticisms of the draft Rules, if it can be shown that they would seriously hamper the police'.[47] A more formal meeting then took place on 28 September 1962 attended by various parties including the DPP, the Commissioner of the Metropolitan Police, representatives of the Home Office, together with Lord Parker, Lawton J, and Howard J. Beforehand, the Home Office felt that much depended on the atmosphere of the discussion with the judges but:

> ... it would obviously be a very satisfactory conclusion if agreement could be reached on what it was intended to achieve and an informal working party, consisting some of the Judges, the Director [of Public Prosecutions] and Home Office representatives, could be set up to look at the drafting.

It is apparent from later documentation that the Home Office did not succeed in getting consent to a working party; but it is also clear that, against a background of police and coordinated executive opposition, pressure on the judges led to the abandonment of the *First Draft*.

The pressure in question was the view that the proposals would 'hamper the police' in their investigation of crime and it was on this point that Lord Parker repeatedly gave assurances and made concessions. In particular, the LCJ is said in a Home Office note to have agreed: that the first caution was not intended to cover 'potential, as opposed to identified suspects and that there was no intention of hampering the putting of questions at an early stage of the investigation'; that, 'if the stage at which the caution was to be given was brought forward, it was the intention that questions could be put subsequently to the suspect'; that a detailed record should be kept of the course of investigations but without going into detail as to how this should be done; that if an 'unfettered right to private discussion' with a solicitor was likely (as the police urged) to place 'an undue burden on the police it should be dropped'; that it was 'impracticable' to require that all questions and answers should be recorded; and that in respect of the stage of the caution, the Met Commissioner should produce a redraft of Rule II (2) for the judges' consideration.

ignored, is surely absurd.' This point is itself a nonsense since the courts had consistently ruled that a breach of the Rules did not automatically lead to statements being held inadmissible.

[47] Home Office Note (24 September 1962).

Conclusion

Following the end of the policing honeymoon period in the years after the Second World War, a variety of policing scandals at all ranks and the realization that investigative practices, particularly by the Criminal Investigations Department, had developed in ways which showed disrespect for individual rights and caused wider doubts as to the reliability of police evidence, reconsideration of the Judges' Rules had become unavoidable. The judges, although far from radical by disposition, had come to realize that much stricter regulation was required than had been originally provided. Initially, they came up with a set of proposals specifically intended to meet public disquiet bringing together a number of existing elements rather than being revolutionary in substance or form. Yet this proved too much for the police and the Home Office. Whereas the judges sought to accord weight to what they saw as the 'public interest' while not hampering the police, both the police and the Home Office were determined to give prominence instead to 'police interests' and it was this latter viewpoint which prevailed. While this episode casts doubt on the so-called 'independence of the judiciary', what was to follow gave a much clearer message about the constitutional arrangements between the executive and the judiciary. It is to that story that we now turn.

6
The War of Attrition and the Vanquishing of the Judges

Introduction

While the precise manner in which the death of the *First Draft* of the revised Judges' Rules was brought about cannot be told even today, we can tell a lot from what happened to subsequent drafts. In this process, the wishes of the judges were set aside in a manner which overwhelmed their resolve and exposed the fallacy of the claim of the 'Westminster Model' of a political separation between the executive and the judiciary.

The Executive and the Judiciary

The constitutional relationship between the executive and the judiciary commonly comes to the fore when there appears to be public disagreement affecting the two branches of the state. Lord Parker became entangled in such a controversy while in Canada shortly after becoming Lord Chief Justice (LCJ)[1] when he delivered a speech criticizing the Homicide Act 1957 and the Street Offences Act 1959. The Home Office considered that this seriously breached the principle that, while a LCJ was entitled to take part in the discussion of legislation passing through Parliament, he should exercise 'proper restraint' once legislation has been enacted. In making the views of the Home Office known to the Lord Chancellor,[2] as then head of the judiciary, the Home Secretary drew on the doctrine which was said to govern such matters as expressed by Sir John Anderson in 1931 when a Metropolitan magistrate made an attack on shops legislation:[3]

> The immunity of the Bench from interference by the Executive implies some measure of reciprocity. Inasmuch as it is important in the public interest that nothing should be said or done to shake confidence in the good sense and

[1] Speeches of Lord Parker LCJ, National Archives, LCO 2/8155.
[2] Such was the seriousness with which this was viewed that the Home Secretary informed the Prime Minister of the terms of his letter and mentioned the matter to the Cabinet.
[3] Letter of Mr RA Butler, Home Secretary (7 September 1959).

The Myth of Judicial Independence. Mike McConville and Luke Marsh, Oxford University Press (2020). © Mike McConville and Luke Marsh. DOI: 10.1093/oso/9780198822103.001.0001

> freedom from bias of those who have to administer justice, the Executive must of necessity exercise the greatest possible restraint in commenting publicly upon even the most ill-advised action by judges or magistrates. That consideration in itself should be recognised as imposing a corresponding degree of self-restraint upon them.

The Lord Chancellor, Viscount Kilmuir, while unable to give a definite response because available reports of the speech were 'incomplete and confused' nevertheless felt that the trouble had arisen 'from the fact that the relatively cloistered life of the Bench leaves its occupants inexperienced as to the pitfalls of public relations'. The issue was dealt with in a *private* setting: on Parker's return from Canada, Viscount Kilmuir 'took him along the delicate path between the holy grounds of judicial independence and the minefields of public controversy in which he had been trespassing'.[4]

These exchanges raise the broader question of the principles governing the relationship between the two branches of the State. In particular, the principle that 'nothing should be *said or done* to shake confidence in the good sense and freedom from bias of those who have to administer justice' is directly engaged by the way in which the executive coerced the judiciary into abandoning successive drafts of the Judges' Rules.

The Prelude to the Second Draft

Immediately following the meeting with the judges, the Home Office and Scotland Yard began to consider drafting a Rule acceptable to the police.[5] In the light of police feelings, the Home Office was persuaded that the police should be permitted to question after the caution when the person interrogated was in custody, until the time of charge. The Home Office recognized the hazardous nature of this concession to the police, Kenneth Parker's note to Charles Cunningham stating that, if these changes were made 'the new Rules will still be open to severe criticism from the newspapers and lawyers who have been criticising the existing Rules and the action taken under them'.

In his letter to Parker LCJ, Cunningham underlined the major points of the drafts as follows:[6] the requirement for the initial caution should come at the stage when the officer has facts/reasonable grounds for arresting the person on suspicion

[4] Letter to the Prime Minister (2 November 1959).

[5] The Met Commissioner, Sir Joseph Simpson, was asked by the Home Office to deal with this as quickly as possible and responded with initial drafting proposals by letter (1 October 1962). At the same time, the Home Office had also prepared a draft of Rule II (2) which was sent to the Commissioner for comment.

[6] Letter (22 October 1962), acknowledged by Lord Parker on 23 October 1962.

of committing the offence; questioning could continue until the suspect was actually under arrest; questioning after charge would be limited to clearing ambiguities about that offence but the police could still question about other offences; and, while records should be kept regarding questioning, this would apply to questions put after the initial caution only.

At the same time, the Law Society put forward its proposals. These would be regarded as modest by today's standards but solicitors then had little political influence and defence solicitors were not highly regarded within the legal profession itself.[7] The main recommendations[8] focused on securing access to a solicitor who should be able to consult the client in private.

The Second Draft

In March 1963, nine months after the *First Draft* had been thrown out by the executive and the police, the judges produced a *Second Draft*. The Rules were now preceded by a set of principles. The process of revision had reached this stage with drafting proposals supplied by the Home Office as described above.

The division between 'principles' prefatory to the Rules and the Rules themselves appears to have had its origin in a confidential Home Office Note of 9 August 1962 which looked for ways to bridge the gulf between the judges (who wanted wider regulation of the police) and the Director of Public Prosecutions (DPP) (who thought that much of the content of the *First Draft* was not a matter for the judges at all). The Note tentatively addressed this division of opinion as follows:

> The possibility might, therefore, be considered of the Home Office in consultation with the Judges putting out some procedural guidance—though this might be dangerous ground for the Home Office to tread.

Though initially considered 'dangerous' for the Home Office, this proved a key way in which the 'radical' views of the judges could be watered down.

The *Second Draft* began by stating that the Rules did not affect certain principles which were, in essence: that when a police officer knows or reasonably suspects a criminal offence has been committed he has a right to question any person in that regard whether or not the person has been arrested or otherwise taken into custody; that every person has a duty to help a police officer to discover and apprehend offenders; that police officers otherwise than by arrest cannot compel any person

[7] See, eg, Sir David Napley, *Not Without Prejudice* (Harrap 1982) (hereafter Napley, *Not Without Prejudice*) where he describes the lowly status of solicitors: 'Needless to say, solicitors, unlike barristers, cannot attend the judges' lunches . . . ' 172.

[8] The Memorandum was sent directly to the LCJ: Letter from Thomas Lund, Secretary of the Law Society (31 December 1962).

against his will to come to or remain in any police station; and that admissibility of any statement depends upon it being voluntary.

The letter from Lord Parker[9] accompanying the *Second Draft* expressed his belief that the new draft was on the whole satisfactory 'to the Commissioner of Metropolitan Police and to the Director [of Public Prosecutions] and to the Law Society which has been the most helpful body in making suggestions'.[10] The judges appear to have been influenced by the Law Society's view:

> A person suspected of a crime is, until arrest, a free man and in law has the same rights as any other person. In practice, however, the suspect will frequently be ignorant of this fact and its consequences, and a request by a police officer 'to accompany me to the police station' will convey the impression that he has no choice in the matter ... The Council are of the opinion that when a police officer makes a request of this nature, he should make it clear that it is a request and no more ...

This opinion, together with the recommendation that a standard form of words be prescribed for use by police officers when making such a 'request', underlay a key change now proposed that the time for giving the caution has been advanced, as Lord Parker said, 'to a very early date and the time when the curtain comes down and no further questions are to be put is postponed'. This requirement was set out in Rule II as follows:

> So soon as a Police Officer knows of allegations or other matters which if true or so long as unrefuted or unexplained point to the guilt of any person in respect of an offence, or suspected offence, he shall caution that person or cause him to be cautioned before any questions, or further questions, are put to him relating to that offence

Rule III addressed a continuing concern of the judges that the police were prone to delay the moment of charge and sought to provide a more 'objective' test, namely that once an officer 'knows of available and apparently credible evidence, including admissions, amounting to a prima facie case that the person is guilty of that offence'[11] no further questions relating to that offence were to be put until the person was charged, following which no other questions were permitted unless a further

[9] Letter to Cunningham (15 March 1963).

[10] The LCJ had held private talks with the Commissioner and the DPP.

[11] It is difficult to argue against a Home Office File Note (21 March 1963) which comments on the attempt to impose an objective test: 'If that is indeed the purpose of the new words, I doubt whether they achieve it.' The Note argues that the form of words actually offers the officer 'several attractive defences against attack' on the ground that the charge was delayed. For example, it was said, the officer could say: 'I know there was some evidence available but I did not think it was sufficient'; 'the available evidence did not seem to me to be apparently credible'.

caution was given and any such questions were to be limited to those intended to prevent or minimize harm or loss to some other person or the public. All such questions were required to be contemporaneously recorded in full and the record signed by that person or if he refused by the interrogating officer.[12]

The *Second Draft* is also noteworthy for what it did not contain. Although provision was made for the time and place of questioning to be recorded, a key regulatory instrument, the *Investigation Occurrence Book*, had disappeared as had the limitations (two hours) in regard to the length of interrogation before any break. However, under Rule I, 'reasonable facilities' were to be provided to enable the person questioned 'to communicate and consult *privately* with a solicitor if he asks to do so' (emphasis supplied).

Although the Commissioner set out various issues regarding the *Second Draft*, at this stage there was no sign of police hostility to this aspect of the proposal. The Commissioner pointed out that while the relationship between the proposed Rule II and Rule III was not clear there was:

> ... no doubt in my mind about it, appreciating that the intention of the judges is to ensure that some sort of caution is given at a very early stage, even though questioning may take place thereafter. At the same time they wish to find a much later stage at which there is no excuse for further interrogation and at which further interrogation therefore has to cease.

The issue was finding a formulation which would give effect to the intentions of the judges.

Before further consideration could be given to the Rules, however, a serious incident in Sheffield[13] suggested that concerns over police interrogation practices were not confined to persuasive techniques such as in the Timothy Evans and George Riley cases. Indeed, unlawful police practices might be systemic, of greater barbarity, and require far greater regulation, particularly of the Criminal Investigations Department (CID).

The Sheffield Incident

According to the official inquiry,[14] following a drop in the detection rate, the Chief Constable of Sheffield, Eric Staines, told Superintendent Carnill, head of the CID, to form a crime squad to address the issue. Inspector Rowley was chosen to lead

[12] Other detailed Rules made provisions regarding such matters as the taking of statements by an officer and the writing of a statement by the suspect.
[13] See Home Office, *Sheffield Police Appeal Inquiry* (HMSO 1963) (hereafter Home Office, *Sheffield Inquiry*).
[14] ibid.

it; other members included Detective Sergeant Hurd and Detective Constables Millicheap and Streets. On 14 March 1963 Superintendent Carnill and Detective Chief Inspector Wells told the squad that to achieve success they would have to 'take chances' and would have to 'stick together'. Sometimes the 'lie detector' would have to be used, a euphemism for using violence to obtain confessions.

The detectives picked up various locals (*not* suspected of a particular crime[15]) that same evening, including Patrick Bowman and the Hartley brothers who had been drinking heavily, were abusive and uncooperative. All three were charged with various breaking and entering offences.

At the Magistrates' Court the next day, Albert Hartley removed his shirt and showed weals and bruising on his back. A police officer told the magistrates that the injuries had been inflicted when the arrested men fought among themselves in the belief that one of them had 'grassed' (informed on the others); and that the police were themselves attacked when restoring order. The facts were found to be otherwise.

The men had been subjected to a sustained and savage beating by the police in the course of which truncheons and a 'rhino tail whip' were used and officers stripped to the waist and beat them with fists. At the same time, unidentified officers planted evidence in the Hartleys' van. However, on 13 May 1963, no evidence was offered in court.

After the violence was reported in the local newspaper, Millicheap and Streets were dismissed at a confidential disciplinary hearing. When they appealed, a Tribunal[16] heard detailed evidence that two senior officers were present,[17] one of whom instituted, and both of whom witnessed, the violence, DI Rowley telling the Tribunal: 'These things go off fairly frequently, don't they' and 'You can't have kid gloves on when detecting crime'. After the assaults, the squad spent five days 'in anxious deliberation' concocting versions that might answer the allegations, DI Rowley authoring a series of conflicting and concocted versions after sanctioning the violence in the belief that this type of prisoner would be unlikely to complain or to be believed if he did. The officers then made up their pocket books to accord with what had been decided would be the (false) version presented in court.[18]

[15] The officers believed that the men were habitual burglars who left no clues.

[16] The Tribunal was set up under the Police (Appeals) Acts 1927 and 1943.

[17] The Tribunal found that DI Rowley was present at and sanctioned assaults on both the Hartleys and probably Bowman and that DS Hurd saw and condoned 'a good deal more than he admitted, although he himself neither used nor actively instigated the use of violence' (Home Office, *Sheffield Inquiry* (n 13) 9). The Tribunal concluded that DC Rowlands, who had already resigned, was somewhat 'two-faced' and more deeply involved than he would admit; and that PCs Murphy and Jarvis had turned a blind eye to what had gone on, washed their hands of it, and eventually made statements to give support to a false version of what had happened.

[18] DCI Wells saw DI Rowley dozens of times in the days when the account was being concocted and was found by the Tribunal to have had 'a pretty shrewd notion of what was going on and was doing nothing to prevent it': Home Office, *Sheffield Inquiry* (n 13) 14.

As the Tribunal found, apart from the Chief Constable, no one within the Sheffield Police wanted to investigate the truth.

Although it became clear that Millicheap and Streets, who the Tribunal found[19] had committed the main assaults, had been singled out to take the whole blame and many police officers in Sheffield who claimed to have seen or heard nothing were driven by self-preservation and misplaced loyalty, the grim picture resulted in large-scale casualties including the suspension and resignation of the Chief Constable and the head of the CID.

These events should have made the case for regulating the police more closely along the lines proposed by the judges and weakened Home Office objections. The use of language within the squad, such as opaque references to the 'lie detector', the admissions of senior officers as to 'these things' taking place 'regularly', together with the planting of evidence, officers turning a blind eye to what had happened, the fabrication of police statements, and false entries in police note books showed a pattern of behaviour (to become appallingly familiar in decades that followed) that should have alerted the Home Office to practices widely at variance with the supposed regulatory regime; after all, setting aside all the other malpractices, under the Judges' Rules, the police were not even supposed to have questioned the individuals involved as they were not even 'suspects'. But, far from putting an end to institutional obstruction to reform, the Home Office sought to localize the problems,[20] the saga of opposition to wider police reform continued and the judges were forced into yet another revision.

Third Draft (27 May 1963)

Confidential consultations led the Home Office to send the judges further concerns prompting a *Third Draft* in May 1963 which, in structure, more closely resembled the Rules eventually agreed in 1964 with, however, the judges continuing to insist on a caution being administered at the earliest point in the investigation. The Rules were again prefaced by 'principles' which now included (downgraded from a Rule) the principle that every citizen at any stage of an investigation has the right to communicate and consult privately with a solicitor provided that no unreasonable delay or hindrance is caused to the processes of law or the administration of justice by his doing so. The principles also stated that the courts would not admit

[19] ibid 6–7.

[20] The Home Office response concentrated on ensuring that once the Tribunal's Report was made public, the press should be informed that the next step lay with the Sheffield Watch Committee, not the Home Secretary (Internal Note of Cunningham (30 October 1963) and endorsed by the Home Secretary, Henry Brooke) but that the Home Office should give private guidance to the Committee, which it did on 14 November 1963.

in evidence answers or statements obtained otherwise than in conformity with the Rules unless in the discretion of the court.

Rule 1 in the *Third Draft* began by stipulating that a caution should be administered at the earliest point in the investigation:[21]

> So soon as a Police Officer knows of allegations or other matters which if true or so long as unrefuted or unexplained point to the guilt of any person in respect of an offence, or suspected offence, he shall caution that person or cause him to be cautioned before any questions, or further questions, are put to him relating to that offence . . .

This reflected judicial concern for tighter regulation and because the major concerns of those consulted appeared to have been met. This much is evident from Home Office correspondence with Commander Willis, one of HM Inspectors of Police, who was informed that the new draft had been prepared in the light of comments made by HM Inspectors and of observations from the Commissioner and the DPP 'who now seem broadly content that these are the best we are likely to get'.[22] The *Draft* had some support from within police circles with the Chief Constable of Birmingham, Mr Dodd, telling the Home Office that, although 'a little doubtful' as to Rule 1 (it might well, he thought, prevent a perfectly innocent person from saying anything to clear himself 'because he is scared by the administration of a caution') there was 'very little in the revised proposals that is likely to cause any serious difficulty in police enquiry work'.[23] While the Home Office itself felt that the *Third Draft* was the best that was likely to be secured, the mood started to change once the views of the Association of Chief Police Officers (ACPO)[24] were received.

ACPO argued that while the Rules would 'not present serious difficulty to the skilled detective' the very 'legal nature of the draft Rules may lead to their unintentional breach by those [Uniformed] Police Officers who are not called upon to use them frequently, and this may result in some injustice'. It was accepted that objections to Rule 1 would lose some of their force if it was clearly to be read in conjunction with Principle 1.

In addition to its formal statement, the Chief Constable of Oxford who acted on ACPO's behalf, informed the Home Office that those Chief Constables who had been consulted were very concerned that 'the new Rules should be contemplated at this point in time when they are likely to hamper the police in this very

[21] Once again there was no reference to the *Investigation Occurrence Book* nor was there any attempt to regulate the documentation of police investigations with the thoroughness that marked the *First Draft*.

[22] Letter from Kenneth Parker to Commander Willis (14 June 1963).

[23] Letter to Kenneth Parker (22 June 1963).

[24] ACPO was replaced in 2015 by the National Police Chiefs' Council (NPCC).

critical period in the fight against crime'. The gravamen of concern was expressed as follows:[25]

> It is estimated that something in the region of 70 percent of all criminal prosecutions rely, to some extent, upon evidence of utterances and statements made by defendants. A high percentage of these cases without such evidence would never reach the Courts.

Once again, however, events on the ground suggested the need for tighter regulation of the police.

Police Malpractice and Doubts about Interrogations

As the Home Office had been aware from the 1950s, police officers in London were being accused not only of fabricating confessions but also of graft,[26] planting evidence on and assaulting suspects. An example was provided by the case of three young men, Patrick Tisdall, Thomas Kingston, and Sidney Hill-Burton, who found themselves charged on 6 August 1959 with possessing offensive weapons without lawful authority or excuse.[27] On leaving a pub in Finsbury Park on the evening of 5 August, the youths were asked by police officers, Tonge, Walden, and Young, to accompany them to the police station. The three officers were 'aides to CID', uniformed officers attached to the CID for experience and to see whether they would be suitable for transfer to the CID, an influential factor being the number of arrests they made. Walden had secured more arrests than any other aide to CID in his Division and in the last year had been involved in twelve of the twenty-one arrests for possessing offensive weapons.

The search at the police station took place in the presence of DS Bolongaro. According to Kingston, Walden purported to 'find' a razor in his pocket. When Kingston protested that Walden had 'planted' it, Walden struck him on his head and threatened him with a truncheon. Tisdall's story was similar, a razor having been 'found' in his jacket and, on his protest, being hit by Walden. On being asked to empty his jacket pockets in the presence of Walden, PC Tonge, and Bolongaro, Hill-Burton found a 'cosh' inside. When he protested, he said that he was threatened with a truncheon but not hit. Following their convictions and small fine, they entered appeals (against legal advice) where four further police officers (DS Bolongaro, Sergeant Cottam, DC Rust, and Inspector Ward) corroborated the

[25] *Memorandum from the Association of Chief Police Officers setting out its reactions to the draft Judges' Rules* (28 June 1963), accompanying the letter from the Chief Constable of Oxford.

[26] See, eg, the allegations of bribery and corruption among police in the West End of London arising out of large-scale prostitution: HC Deb 5 March 1956, vol 549, cols 1884–94.

[27] See Sir David Napley, *Not Without Prejudice* (n 7) 144ff.

accounts of the CID aides. The appeals were unsuccessful, the youths each sentenced to twenty-eight days' imprisonment.[28]

Following their release from the police station, the youths had kept to their detailed stories about their experiences under close interrogation by Edward Sorrell, a former police Inspector employed by their solicitor David Napley, and by Napley himself. Each became convinced that the accounts the youths gave were true. Accordingly, Napley wrote a long letter on 25 November 1959 to the Home Secretary expressing his 'concern and alarm at what had occurred, and demanding a public inquiry'. When the Home Secretary eventually replied, on 4 March 1960, Napley was informed that a full inquiry had been made and that no grounds had been disclosed justifying further action.

Evidence in other cases, however, began to emerge that could not be sidelined. It began on 6 July 1963 when a West Indian cricketer, Harold Padmore, went to the West End Central Police Station to arrange bail for his girlfriend. According to Padmore, he was put into a room with five to seven plain clothes officers including a DS Harold 'Tanky' Challenor,[29] who made a variety of racist remarks including 'We'll have some fun with this coon.' While being held by another officer, Padmore alleged that Challenor then proceeded to hit him, cutting his lip and breaking a tooth. When Padmore was charged with obtaining money by false pretences, the magistrate refused to grant his solicitor's application for a summons for assault against Challenor. However, the Home Office was forced to respond following Padmore's acquittal[30] and it did so by instituting a police inquiry which was practically assured to find little or nothing of concern.[31] That was not the worst, however, because Challenor's involvement in other incidents soon became a more major issue.

Challenor's problems began following the arrest of eighty-six individuals arising out of a demonstration against the visit of Queen Frederika of Greece. Eight were

[28] A later Inquiry (Mars-Jones QC) found that while no officer involved was dishonest, their evidence at the Inquiry was subject to significant shortcomings. Thus, Mars-Jones found that PC Walden 'gave the impression that he was prepared to say anything which he thought would favour his case;' that PC Taylor's account of his activities and his explanation for the inconsistencies between his own records and statements was 'unconvincing;' and that he 'could place no reliance on his testimony' of DS Bolongaro. While the bulk of the evidence tended to support the allegations of the three young men, in giving evidence as to what happened to them after the interrogations, their accounts were 'conflicting and confused.' Mars-Jones found that if the evidence disclosed in the Inquiry 'had been available at the Trial or the Appeal they would never have been convicted .... ' There is a full account, leading ultimately to free pardons for Tisdall, Kingston and Hill-Burton in Sir David Napley, *Not Without Prejudice* (n 7) 144–65, Napley having represented the three at the initial trial and subsequent Inquiry by Mars-Jones. There is also an account in James Morton, *Bent Coppers* (1993) at 108–13.

[29] Challenor had served with distinction in the Second World War and had been awarded the Military Medal.

[30] The other individuals charged by Challenor were also acquitted.

[31] The Police investigation of Padmore's complaint was undertaken by DI Oxford and set out in TS 58/791. By this stage, Challenor had been placed on sick leave on 6 September 1963 and admitted to and detained in the Netherne Hospital under the Mental Health Act on 27 October 1963. The officers present in the CID room all told DI Oxford that Padmore's account was untrue.

each said to have in their possession a piece of brick (to throw at the Queen) which they alleged had been 'planted' on them at the police station.[32] One of these was Donald Rooum, a talented political cartoonist and member of the National Council for Civil Liberties (NCCL), who had been heavily assaulted by DS Challenor. Mr Rooum was mistakenly denied police bail and so was able to hand over his clothes intact to his defence lawyer on his release from police custody. Rooum was acquitted after forensic examination demonstrated that he could not have had a brick in his pocket as alleged. In other cases,[33] the prosecution offered no evidence after Challenor was unable to be produced as a witness.

It emerged that the planting of half-bricks[34] was a strategy that Challenor used on large numbers of people, varying the evidence with his armoury of knives, hatchets, and iron bars. He had previously secured convictions against many people,[35] most prominently four individuals in December 1962 for conspiracy to demand money with menaces and possessing offensive weapons arising out of the activities of an alleged protection 'gang' operating in Soho,[36] their convictions being quashed only when Challenor's past delicts came to light.

While pressure groups and the media,[37] aided by parliamentary pressure,[38] were instrumental in bringing this systematic, long-term,[39] discreditable conduct to light, the Home Office itself did little beyond foot-dragging.[40] Thus, while Challenor's misconduct was first reported in September 1962 and its significance clear on Rooum's acquittal in August 1963, the first free pardons were

[32] All of those charged refused to sign the property register because each lot contained a piece of brick.

[33] On evidence identical with that in the Rooum case, another defendant, John Apostolou, was initially convicted but the prosecution did not challenge his appeal.

[34] The bricks appeared to have come from a pile of builders' waste in White Lion Yard which was used on the evening of 11 July by the Police Reserve to which police officers had ready access while civilians did not: National Archives, Crim 1/4242.

[35] The NCCL exposed some twenty-six cases where Challenor had framed or assaulted suspects.

[36] The individuals were Ricardo Pedrini, Joseph Oliva, Alan Cheeseman, and John Ford. At the police station, Pedrini was given an iron bar, Cheeseman a flick-knife, and Fraser a razor. A fifth individual, James Fraser, was acquitted of conspiracy at the initial trial but convicted of the possession offence. Two other police officers gave evidence that supported Challenor's account.

[37] The UK press was almost unanimous in labelling the government's handling of the Challenor case a 'whitewash': Barbara Smoker, 'The Challenor Case' (1966) 6(1) British Journal of Criminology 68 (hereafter Smoker, 'Challenor').

[38] See, eg, 'Four Questions for the Chanellor Inquiry' *The Times* (6 July 1964). See also the account in Mary Grigg, *The Challenor Case* (Penguin 1965) and that of Challenor himself: Harold Challenor and Alfred Draper, *Tanky Challenor* (Leo Cooper 1990). Eventually, in June 1964, three police colleagues of Challenor were tried and convicted of conspiring to pervert the course of justice by fabricating false evidence, Challenor himself being found unfit to plead.

[39] Pedrini and his co-defendants had been arrested in September 1962 and convicted in December of that year. Others granted a free pardon arising out of separate encounters with Challenor included Lionel King and David Silver who were convicted in June 1963 after two detonators were allegedly found in King's car. Free pardons were also granted to John Ryall, Ronald Ryall, and Colin Derwin who had been convicted in August 1963 of possessing bricks at a demonstration.

[40] Such was the official sloth, that several of Challenor's targets served their entire prison sentence (almost two years in some instances) before the convictions were quashed.

not announced until July 1964. Nor did the Home Office tie in these and other suggested policing malpractices with the ongoing discussion over revision of the Judges' Rules. Indeed, the Home Office took every precaution to ensure that the real state of policing would not emerge and add to pressures for reform.[41]

But there was more to come: added to the Report of the Sheffield Inquiry,[42] the so-called 'Profumo Affair' and trial of Stephen Ward[43]—arguably a catalyst for the social and sexual revolution of the 1960s—not only excited salacious media interest but also had a direct bearing upon police practices and the Judges' Rules.

Stephen Ward

Dr Stephen Ward was an osteopath with clients such as Winston Churchill, Mahatma Gandhi, and Frank Sinatra; and a talented portrait painter of such people as the Duke of Edinburgh, Peter Sellers, and Sir John Betjeman. Ward was a kind, if louche, individual, whose private life was in tune with, if not ahead of, the changing sexual mores.[44] His Bohemian, champagne lifestyle attracted young women who went to parties he gave in the grounds of Cliveden, the stately home of his friend Lord Astor. At some of these parties, he introduced one of these women, Christine Keeler, his live-in platonic girlfriend, to other guests, including John Profumo. Over a period of time, she began an affair with Profumo, the Secretary of State for War, whose responsibilities included highly sensitive areas such 'Polaris' (a submarine-based nuclear weapons missile system). An awkward relationship became potentially explosive when Keeler, on several occasions, met with Yevgeny Ivanov, a Russian spy under cover as a military attaché, with whom it was rumoured she also had an affair (although this was never established).

Toxic rumours of sex scandals and spies[45] added to the pressure on the deeply unpopular and crumbling government of Harold Macmillan. On 22 March 1963, Profumo falsely denied having an improper relationship with Keeler (rather uncharitably described by Tom Mangold as 'not quite a tart') in a personal statement

[41] For example, the inquiry in 1964 by Arthur James QC had its terms of reference restricted to discovering whether any senior officers were at fault in failing to detect that Challenor was suffering from the onset of paranoid schizophrenia, a condition that even experts found difficulty in diagnosing. James did find that Padmore had been struck by Challenor and that other officers had played down serious misconduct. For a critique of the inquiry, see Smoker, 'Challenor' (n 37) and Ben Whitaker, 'The Challenor Case Re-Examined' *The Spectator* (29 January 1965).

[42] The Report (Home Office, *Sheffield Inquiry* (n 13)) was published on 15 October 1963.

[43] See the excellent account of this in Geoffrey Robertson, *Stephen Ward Was Innocent, OK* (Biteback Publishing Ltd 2013) from which much of the foregoing is based. See also Phillip Knightley and Caroline Kennedy, *An Affair of State: The Profumo Case and the Framing of Stephen Ward* (Jonathan Cape 1987); Ian Crawford, *The Profumo Affair* (White Lodge 1963) (hereafter Crawford, *Profumo Affair*).

[44] See Tom Mangold, 'The Fall Guy for Profumo' *The Telegraph* (19 May 1963) (hereafter Mangold, 'Profumo'); Tom Mangold, *Profumo Confidential*, Archive 4 (BBC Radio 4, 25 May 2013).

[45] The satirical magazine *Private Eye* gave a coded account of this on 21 March 1963.

to Parliament which had, in breach of constitutional proprieties, been drafted by the Attorney-General and the Solicitor-General.[46] This failed to do the trick. A scapegoat was needed. Accordingly, the Home Secretary called in the Met Commissioner and the Head of MI5 with an order to get Ward. The police were reluctant to act since they had nothing on Ward (who, unknown to the police, was actually an MI5 informant). They were told to get it.

Under constant harassment from the police and with his osteopathy practice in tatters, Ward tried to protect himself by spilling the beans on Profumo who then apologized for lying to the House[47] and resigned on 4 June 1963.[48] Soon afterwards, Ward was charged with living off immoral earnings based on Keeler's account that she had sex with several men at Ward's flat and paid part of the money she received to Ward. To get this evidence, the police interviewed Keeler twenty-four times and went ahead with her as the prosecution's star witness fully aware that much of her account would be false.[49]

Ward's trial opened on 22 July 1963, immediately prior to which Keeler's account, written and embellished by reporters from the *News of the World* (not then in the ownership of Rupert Murdoch) was published. As Ward's trial was drawing to a close, the Court of Criminal Appeal was set to hear an appeal by a jazz singer, Aloysius 'Lucky' Gordon,[50] Keeler's former lover,[51] whose conviction for assault on her had been secured by Keeler's perjured evidence,[52] lies that she had repeated in Ward's trial. Had this been known to Ward's trial, he would almost certainly have been acquitted; but, in an extraordinary episode in legal history, the judges came to the aid of the government.

Contrary to all convention, the Court of Appeal (headed by Lord Parker and including Widgery J, the next LCJ) started the appeal an hour early at 9:00 am and concluded it within nine minutes. Shockingly, they decided not to hear the

46 Profumo's first *Personal Statement* is at HC Deb 22 March 1963, vol 674, cols 809–10809 in which he said that there was 'no impropriety whatsoever in my acquaintanceship with Miss Keeler'. In his resignation letter of 4 June 1963 to the Prime Minister he wrote that '... this was not true, and that I misled you and my colleagues and the House' *Daily Mail* (5 July 1963).

47 The Parliamentary Debates which ensued give a flavour of the febrile atmosphere that these events generated. The Leader of the Opposition, Harold Wilson, eg, said: 'This is a debate without precedent in the annals of this House. It arises from disclosures which have shocked the moral conscience of the nation. There is the clear evidence of a sordid underworld network...': HC Deb 17 June 1963, vol 679, cols 34–176. The Prime Minister, Harold Macmillan, described the revelations as 'wholly unprecedented' adding: 'A great shock has been given to Parliament, and, indeed, to the whole country. On me, as head of the Administration, what has happened has inflicted a deep, bitter, and lasting wound.'

48 Home Office officials sought to carry on as usual. On the day that Profumo resigned, Cunningham wrote to Colonel Arthur Young, Commissioner of Police of the City of London, requesting comments 'in the course of the month, because the Judges are anxious to complete the revision and have the rules promulgated in the autumn.'

49 In fact, Keeler had been living off Ward, not the other way around.

50 Lucky Gordon was a Jamaican hustler, singer, and occasional cook. Gordon died in March 2017. See Chris Salewicz, 'Lucky Gordon' *The Guardian* (24 March 2017). Keeler died in September 2017.

51 Keeler first met Gordon at the Rio Café in Notting Hill when she bought some marijuana from him with money given to her by Profumo.

52 Keeler had been assaulted by Johnny Edgecombe, an Antiguan illicit bar owner.

uncontested fresh evidence of two witnesses recounting Keeler's perjury or the ten hours of tapes in which Keeler's versions repeatedly changed; they gave no account of the evidence that was offered; they gave no reasons for the court's actions; and, extraordinarily, they delivered no judgment in upholding the appeal.[53] Instead, the scant remarks they sent to Ward's trial court were so couched that they were used not to destroy but to bolster Keeler's evidence. They pretended they were quashing Gordon's conviction not because of the lack of credibility of Keeler, but because two witnesses had not attended Gordon's trial. In despair, and following a highly adverse summing up,[54] Ward took a massive overdose. He was convicted in his absence and died a few days later never regaining consciousness. Parker then personally ordered that the transcript of Ward's trial be withheld.[55]

There was to be further pressure with the publication on 20 September 1963 of a Report by Lord Denning even though that seemed to have been crafted to assist the government.[56] Although Denning had been asked to undertake an inquiry on the security implications of the circumstances leading to Profumo's resignation, the Report switched the focus to Ward. The slapdash Report, completed in three months and published six weeks after Ward's suicide, fell far below the standards Denning had set elsewhere. In a naked exercise in self-aggrandizement,[57] Denning, a dimwit in sexual matters,[58] made Ward a scapegoat not only for Profumo but for the government.[59] Denning exhibited little familiarity with the trial and contented himself with denunciations of Ward describing him as 'utterly immoral', as seducing young girls, procuring them to be mistresses for his influential friends, catering 'for those of his friends who had perverted tastes' and ready to arrange 'whipping and other sadistic performances'.[60] As Tom Mangold said: 'It wasn't even

[53] See the comment in the [1963] Criminal Law Review 600ff.

[54] All transcripts of which have been unaccountably lost!

[55] Ludovic Kennedy, *On My Way to the Club* (Fontana 1989) (hereafter Kennedy, *Way to the Club*) 296.

[56] This was one example of what David Williams called the involvement of judges in 'extra-judicial activities carried on behalf of the executive': David Williams, 'Bias; the Judges and the Separation of Powers' [2000] Public Law 45, 48. While some such inquiries are formally constituted under legislative provisions, that by Lord Denning had no statutory basis at all. David Williams was surely right in stating that: 'Lord Denning's inquiry into the Profumo affair might today be exposed to challenge, if only on procedural grounds' 54. A file about the setting up of the Denning Inquiry is available at the National Archives but four documents have been removed. See Jack Malvern, 'National Archives: Dossier on Profumo affair Proved too Good to Miss' *The Times* 28 December 2018.

[57] This is clear from the *Introduction* to *The Denning Report* (1963, Pimlico reprint 1992): 'My report was published as a Blue Book on Thursday 26 September 1963. Nothing like it had ever been seen before. Nor since ... I wrote every word of the report myself in my own hand ... The report had much political impact ... It was a major influence in the fall of the Government.'

[58] As Ludovic Kennedy said, Denning was 'in sexual matters ... a simpleton', was singularly unfitted for this task with his authoritarian puritanical view of sex, and, as it transpired, a prurience that was too easily excited: *Way to the Club* (n 55) 295ff.

[59] When challenged on the evidential failings and contradictions with the trial itself, the Secretary to the Denning Inquiry, Thomas Critchley, a Home Office civil servant, told Ludovic Kennedy that they didn't have time to 'read all the details of the trial' ibid 296.

[60] Crawford, *Profumo Affair* (n 43) 11.

half true.'[61] On the back of this moralizing crusade, Denning found Ward guilty of procuring girls for sex with other men (a charge on which he had been found not guilty) and of arranging 'whipping parties and other sadistic performances' as to which no evidence had been offered at Ward's trial.[62] Despite Denning's efforts, the actions of the police in 'hounding' Ward and 'using' Keeler contributed to concern over the adequacy of police regulation.

Ward and the Judges' Rules

While the press frenzy naturally focused upon sex and espionage, the way in which the police had carried out the investigation into Ward attracted criticism as did the procedure for reviewing the Judges' Rules. A report in the *Sunday Telegraph*,[63] for example, concluded that the case of Stephen Ward had 'reawakened doubts about police methods of interrogation'. The article by 'a distinguished Harley Street' psychologist concluded that there were simple methods available that could make virtually 'all of us confess to our real, and sometimes, imaginary offences'. Police interrogation, the article asserted, had been withdrawn from the Royal Commission on the Police and placed in the hands of a secret committee of High Court judges.

While the process continued in the hands of the 'secret committee,' the increasing criticism of the police appeared to be having some impact, Cunningham, reporting a conversation that he had the previous day with the LCJ, noted that Lord Parker 'has had it very much in mind that the Judges will be criticised for framing Rules which do not provide sufficient protection to the public against improper behaviour by the police'.[64]

The Judges Submit the 'Final' Draft

Immediately following upheaval in the government, the Prime Minister Harold Macmillan having resigned on 19 October 1963 to be succeeded by Alec Douglas-Home,[65] on 21 October 1963, Lord Parker submitted what he hoped was the 'final draft as agreed by the Judges' which contained 'slight verbal alterations' to the previous version. A week later, Cunningham replied by sending a Draft Circular and

[61] Mangold, 'Profumo' (n 44).

[62] See Frances Gibb, 'Profumo Scapegoat's Conviction "Would not Stand Today"' *The Times* (9 September 2017).

[63] 'Anything you Say' *Sunday Telegraph* (11 August 1963).

[64] Minute to the assistant Under-Secretary of State of the Home Office, Francis Graham-Harrison (1 October 1963).

[65] In the Parliamentary Debate on the 'Profumo Affair' in June, 1963, the government had, in fact, secured a majority of sixty-nine votes but Macmillan was considerably weakened with twenty-seven Conservative Members abstaining.

administrative instructions and repeated, 'for the record', concerns over Rule 1 that were now[66] entertained by the Chief Inspector of Constabulary and the Commissioner of the Metropolis.[67] The concerns were threefold:[68]

(i) that when a preliminary caution is administered, many suspects will refuse to say anything more;
(ii) that many police officers, particularly inexperienced ones, will feel such difficulty over the preliminary caution that they will refrain from questioning at all; and
(iii) that the Rule will give great scope for the prolonged cross-examination of police officers by an otherwise unmeritorious defendant.[69]

As a matter of fact, the Home Office had already despaired of changing the views of the judges. Thus, an internal note to the deputy Under-Secretary of State, Francis Graham-Harrison, recorded police concerns and suggested that Charles Cunningham meet with the LCJ before the Draft Circular accompanying the Rules was sent[70] but concluded:

> Subject to anything which comes out of this discussion, I am afraid that the answer to police criticism expressed after the publication of the Rules can only be that the Judges took fully into account the views expressed to them but decided that the Rules as now drafted represented a fair balance between the conflicting interests of the police on the one side and persons being interrogated on the other.

This pessimism was shared by Graham-Harrison who appended a hand written note which read in part: 'I share the doubts that have been expressed about the effect of Rule I, but I agree that it will be difficult to press them further on the L. C. J. at this stage.' The response of the Lord Parker in his letter dated 1 November 1963, set out in **Illustration 6.1** merely added to the sense of gloom.

Nevertheless, the gathering strength of police opposition had already prompted officials to take the matter up with the Home Secretary.[71]

[66] 'Now' because when Rule I was discussed at a meeting in the Home Office in the early summer of 1963 the Commissioner of the Met and the DPP 'both accepted Rule I in substantially its present form; and Sir Charles Cunningham took the view that the Home Office could not press the Lord Chief Justice the dangers of a draft which was in substance acceptable to the Commissioner and the Director': Internal Home Office Note (23 October 1963).

[67] It was recognized within the Home Office that the views of the police had been 'slow to form on this'.

[68] These echoed precisely the views of the Commissioner set out in his letter to the Home Office (18 October 1963).

[69] It is clear that Sir Charles had sent a draft version of the Rule to Lord Parker on 22 October 1963 (not in the file) but that this had not been accepted.

[70] Internal Note of KAL Parker (28 October 1963) in which the meeting was suggested 'as this would be the last possible occasion for raising any points on the Rules themselves'.

[71] Memorandum, *The Judges' Rules* (29 October 1963).

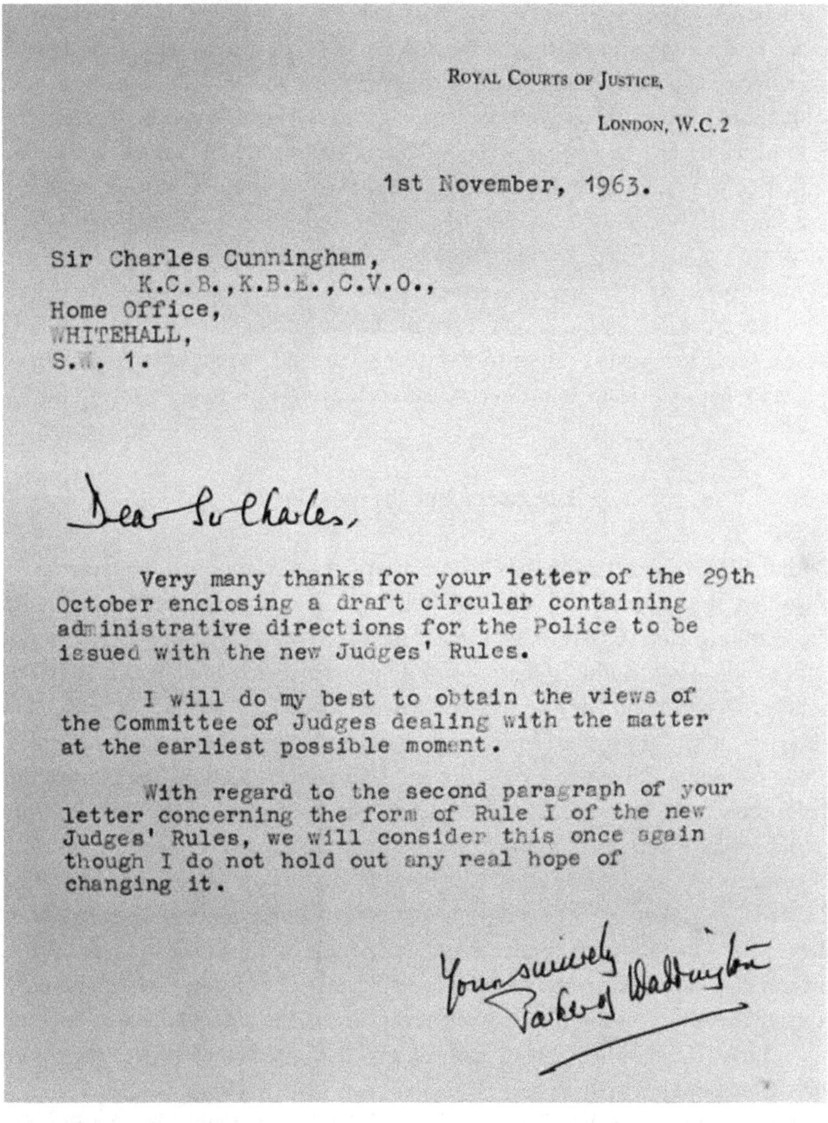

ROYAL COURTS OF JUSTICE,

LONDON, W.C. 2

1st November, 1963.

Sir Charles Cunningham,
K.C.B.,K.B.E.,C.V.O.,
Home Office,
WHITEHALL,
S.W. 1.

Dear Sir Charles,

Very many thanks for your letter of the 29th October enclosing a draft circular containing administrative directions for the Police to be issued with the new Judges' Rules.

I will do my best to obtain the views of the Committee of Judges dealing with the matter at the earliest possible moment.

With regard to the second paragraph of your letter concerning the form of Rule I of the new Judges' Rules, we will consider this once again though I do not hold out any real hope of changing it.

Yours sincerely
Parker of Waddington

Illustration 6.1 Letter from Lord Parker Restating Constancy in Judicial Thinking (November 1963) (National Archives)

Apart from copies of a Draft Circular and Draft Administrative Directions, the Home Secretary was also provided with a copy of the Rules 'in what is believed to be final form'. More significantly, Cunningham repeated ('realising that the judges are unlikely to change their view') the anxiety of the police that Rule 1 will hamper the investigation of crime. Against this was what appeared to the Home Office to be the *realpolitik* over this issue:

> I believe that the judges, on the other hand, take the view that this is the least that can be done by way of change in the Rules to meet the anxiety which has been expressed about the Rules in their existing form; and that they are apprehensive that they may be criticised for not having gone far enough. I do not, therefore, think it likely that they will be willing at this stage to reconsider the new Rule 1. If they adhere to it in its present form, there is, of course, nothing that we can do about it.

In his annotation, the Home Secretary considered it a 'tragedy' that the judges 'should act to lessen the likelihood of criminals being brought to justice' and looked forward to Lord Parker's response. Before any substantive reply, the Home Office began to shape a strategy to further pressurize the judges.

The Executive Strikes Back

With the Home Secretary in the Chair, a meeting took place on 8 November 1963 including the Attorney-General; the Solicitor-General; the Director of Public Prosecutions; Her Majesty's Chief Inspector of Constabulary; four senior Home Office officials (including Charles Cunningham); and a member of the Law Officers' Department. They were assembled for battle.

At the outset, 'grave concern' was expressed at the form of the new Rules which it was said seemed likely to hinder the police in crime detection. The reasons the Rules took this form were also recognized: 'The Judges had been under considerable pressure to tighten up the Rules in ways which would protect the interests of suspects and accused persons.' Nonetheless, it was stated that in the course of 'informal consultation'[72] the judges had been 'left in no doubt of the anxiety of the Home Office and of the police that the difficulties of the police in investigating the growing volume of crime should not be increased by the introduction of more restrictive Rules.' Despite these efforts, it continued, the judges appeared 'to have taken little account of the police interest, and had ignored alternative proposals which had been put to them.'

In discussion it was felt that it would be 'difficult to retrieve this situation' because 'the last word lay with the Judges' and because the judges were understood to feel that the changes they now proposed were 'the least that could be done to meet criticism of the present Rules, and even these might not go far enough. They would not be disposed, therefore, to modify their draft.'

The law enforcement dilemma created by police non-compliance with the Rules was also recognized:

[72] As to which no record exists in the files.

> The present Rules required the police to caution a man first at the point in the investigation where they decided to charge him. It was common ground for criticism of the Rules that the police could delay a caution well after that point, in order to get more evidence, and subsequently maintain under cross-examination that they had not then made up their minds to prefer a charge.

Nevertheless, the objections to the present draft were 'so serious' as to call for further action. The major concern centred on Rule 1 which stated that a caution should be administered when only 'allegations or other matters which if true or so long as unrefuted or unexplained' pointed to the guilt of a suspect. If there was to be a compromise, the first caution should be given where the police had 'reasonable cause' to suspect that a man was guilty 'though even this would give rise to some difficulty'. Accordingly, the Home Secretary undertook to write to Lord Parker because it was essential, '*in the interests of the police*', that the judges should be asked to think again about their proposals.

A further discussion was held in the Lord Chancellor's Office on 11 November. The Lord Chancellor said he shared the concern of the Home Secretary and the Law Officers about 'the attitude of the Judges in this matter'. He proposed to intervene, as head of the judiciary, and convene a meeting to which the LCJ (with other judges, if he wished) 'should be invited to discuss with Ministers the serious objections to the draft Rules'.

The Judges Remain Unmoved

The judges did not succumb to Home Office pressure. On 10 November 1963, Lord Parker wrote to Cunningham informing him that he had now consulted with the four judges working with him as a Drafting Committee. The reply was categorical:

> As I suspected, none of us are prepared to alter Rule 1. I think the Judges can be trusted not to permit the prolonged cross-examination of Police Officers which is feared.

In the event, the Home Secretary wrote again to Lord Parker who expressed himself 'extremely sorry' to hear of the Home Secretary's reaction. While welcoming a discussion with the Home Secretary, Lord Parker pointed out that under existing Rules, once a person is taken into custody, he should be questioned only in very exceptional circumstances and even then not as regards his complicity in the alleged offence.[73] Lord Parker sought to reassure by pointing out that the Rules are

[73] Citing the Home Office Circular (24 June 1930).

'by no means adverse to the police as compared to the existing Rules'. Whereas today (under existing Rules), Lord Parker said, if a man is held at the police station:

> . . . there is a complete bar even if a caution is given against his being questioned as to his complicity. Under the new Rules, however, custody is no bar to questioning. In other words, the Police can go on questioning him until they have a prima facie case against him. This, as it seems to me, is of enormous advantage to the Police and far outweighs any possible handicap resulting from the advance in the time when a caution should be given.

Lord Parker said that the handicap of the new Rules was limited to the case where a person is cautioned and not in custody; but, he said, he understood that in such cases the hardened criminal will not say anything whether the caution has been administered or not; and in other cases, 'a man will want to get it off his chest and will do so again whether the caution is administered or not'.[74]

The firmness of Lord Parker's thinking on this is clear from a 'long interview' he and Winn J had with the Attorney-General and the Solicitor-General on 22 November 1963 and as set out in a Note he sent to judges of the Queen's Bench Division on 25 November 1963. Following the 'interview', the Attorney-General told the Home Secretary that he and the Solicitor-General had suggested that the first caution should be administered when: 'A police officer has reasonable grounds to suspect that any person may have committed an offence' but that: 'Neither the Lord Chief Justice nor Mr. Justice Winn were at all anxious to adopt this simplified formula and we did not make much progress on this point.' In the Note to the Queen's Bench judges, Lord Parker stated that Rule 1 has given rise to 'a violent reaction among certain of the Police, who complain that they will be severely handicapped'. However, he added that from 'enquiries made at an earlier stage by the Sub-Committee, it seems clear that this suggested handicap has been grossly exaggerated'.

The Departmental Wrangle

From the beginning, management of the revision of the Judges' Rules had been the responsibility of the Home Office. More particularly, rather than involving the Secretary of State,[75] it was directed and driven by the permanent Under-Secretary, Charles Cunningham assisted by Philip Allen who was destined to succeed him.

74 Lord Parker said he would welcome a discussion and that he could bring along Winn J (the only other judge dealing with this who was in London).

75 It is, of course, well established that Ministers are often guided by officials.

It was Cunningham who held informal (unminuted) meetings with Lord Parker, guided discussions, and set the policy agenda. Thus, as late as 29 October 1963, an internal Minute by Cunningham updating the Home Secretary on progress demonstrated the understanding of the Home Office that this was a matter for them:

> I am sending a copy of this minute, and the enclosures, to the Attorney-General, who has not been consulted by the judges. *We understand that the Lord Chancellor has seen the Rules in their revised form, though he is not departmentally concerned with them* (emphasis supplied).

While the Home Office had achieved a significant measure of success, as it saw matters, in causing the judges to shelve 'radical' proposals, it had not persuaded them to modify Rules which continued to antagonize the police. That was to change when the Home Secretary informed the Lord Chancellor of the need to 'continue to press' the judges, as shown in **Illustration 6.2.**

The Lord Chancellor, Sir Reginald Manningham-Buller (later, Viscount Dilhorne), was a formidable individual known for his intimidating style, hence his nickname 'Bullying-Manner'.[76] Lord Devlin later described him thus:[77]

> He was a bully without a bullying manner. He could be downright rude but he did not shout or bluster. Yet his disagreeableness was so pervasive, his persistence so interminable, the obstructions he manned so far flung, his objectives apparently so insignificant, that sooner or later you would be tempted to ask yourself whether the game was worth the candle: if you asked yourself that, you were finished.

Though the Home Office had sought to keep him away, this was difficult to achieve because of Manningham-Buller's pugnacity and because the Lord Chancellor was the then head of the judiciary.

The Lord Chancellor's intervention started in the middle of November 1963 when he wrote to the Home Secretary and suggested that it would be 'useful' if he could be informed of the detailed criticisms of the Rules following which he could invite Lord Parker to a meeting.[78] He also said bluntly, cutting directly across the Home Office and police line, that he did not 'attach very much importance to the caution having to be given so early'. In the result, a Home Office

[76] Bernard Levin's sobriquet was widely regarded as entirely apposite. See, eg, Thomas Grant, *Jeremy Hutchinson's Case Histories* (John Murray 2015) where Hutchinson describes him as having 'wobbling crimson cheeks and … apoplectic, bulging eyes' 55.

[77] Patrick Devlin, *Easing the Passing* (The Bodley Head 1985) 39.

[78] Letter to Brooke (18 November 1963). By letter of the same date, the Home Secretary had informed Lord Parker of the criticisms of the Rules and, it seems, invited him to a discussion (which Lord Parker welcomed).

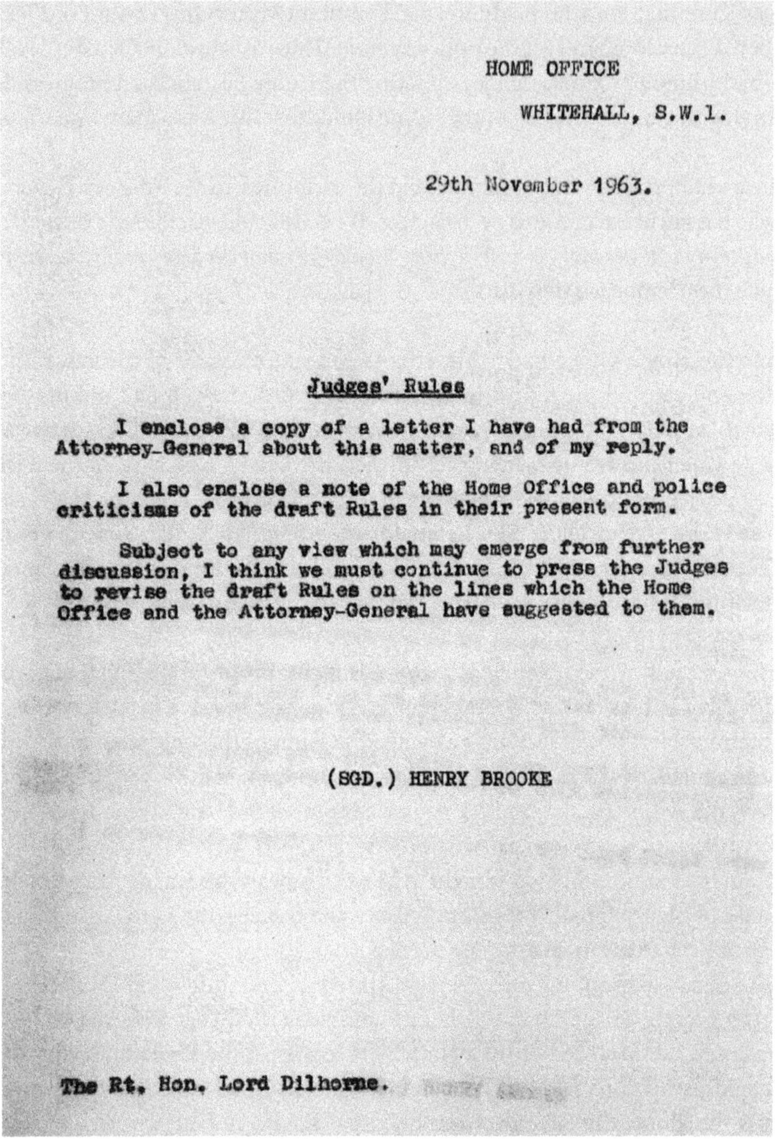

HOME OFFICE

WHITEHALL, S.W.1.

29th November 1963.

Judges' Rules

I enclose a copy of a letter I have had from the Attorney-General about this matter, and of my reply.

I also enclose a note of the Home Office and police criticisms of the draft Rules in their present form.

Subject to any view which may emerge from further discussion, I think we must continue to press the Judges to revise the draft Rules on the lines which the Home Office and the Attorney-General have suggested to them.

(SGD.) HENRY BROOKE

The Rt. Hon. Lord Dilhorne.

Illustration 6.2 Letter from Home Secretary Indicating Need to Press Judges (November 1963) (National Archives)

meeting with the Lord Chancellor had to be expedited after learning that Lord Parker had approached the other judges about the suggestion to attenuate the right to silence and without mentioning the real concerns of the Home Office and police regarding Rule 1. Once the Lord Chancellor was engaged, the whole issue moved on at pace.

A War Cabinet is Assembled

The first step was to assemble a war cabinet under the chairmanship of the Lord Chancellor on 11 December 1963.[79] It was acknowledged in the Notes of that Meeting that there would be 'great difficulty in persuading the Judges to modify their draft at this stage; they already regarded their proposals as a compromise in which *they had gone as far as they could to meet the interests of the police*' (emphasis supplied). With a focus upon Rule 1, it was recognized that the judges had tried to find an objective statement of the point in time at which the first caution became necessary 'in order to overcome the criticism that the present Rules left it open to the police to delay unduly the first caution in order to prolong questioning of a suspect'. It was felt that the formula proposed was too complex and at so early a stage that the task of the police in detecting crime would be seriously prejudiced. Since the judges 'appeared to insist' that the first caution should be administered earlier than at present, 'it should be suggested to them that the proper stage was when the police officer had reasonable grounds for suspecting that the person in question had committed the offence'.

The Meeting agreed that a revised version of the Rules should be prepared taking into account the points raised in the discussion and employing simpler language so that it could be better understood by the police. The revised draft, accompanied by a separate note indicating the particular amendments made, would then be sent by the Lord Chancellor to Lord Parker and inviting him to a meeting (with other judges if he wished) with the Lord Chancellor, the Home Secretary, the Law Officers, and Charles Cunningham. Nothing in the Notes hinted at the next step which had none of the Home Office diplomacy and instead bore the hallmark of Manningham-Buller's bludgeoning style.

The Killer Blow

Arising out of that meeting, the Lord Chancellor 'asked the Home Office to prepare a draft [of the Rules] which would be acceptable to them and to the police'.[80] On 2 January 1964 the revised version of the Rules was then sent to Lord Parker by the Lord Chancellor. The Letter began by referring to the meeting he had had before Christmas with 'the Home Secretary, the Law Officers and officials' with the implication that what followed, in terms, had their collective approval. Although

[79] Those present included: the Home Secretary; the Attorney-General; the Solicitor-General; the Commissioner of the Metropolitan Police; the DPP; four officials from the Home Office (including the permanent Under-Secretary); two officials from the Lord Chancellor's Department (including the Permanent Secretary); and a representative from the Law Officer's Department.

[80] Lord Chancellor's letter (2 January 1964). The drafting was undertaken by J K T Jones of the Home Office.

the Lord Chancellor's letter included explanations for certain amendments to the draft Rules[81] and repeated some points already urged on previous occasions,[82] the time for persuasive argument had passed. In advance of a planned meeting[83] with Lord Parker, it was now time to deliver a political and constitutional killer punch. Manningham-Buller did not mince his words as can be seen in the opening page of his letter, **Illustration 6.3**.

In terms, Manningham-Buller not only stated the obvious—that the Rules would arouse great interest and be debated in Parliament—but intimidated the judges with naked threats that are worth restating:

> *I think the judiciary would be placed in a very unfortunate position if the Home Secretary speaking for the Government was among the critics.* I think great efforts should be made to stop this happening ... *One of the difficulties is that the Judges' Rules once published cannot be withdrawn and amended in the light of criticism without some loss of judicial prestige* (emphasis supplied).

Such blunt language had its desired effect. Threats to drag judges into the political arena and to undermine their prestige proved a mixture sufficiently toxic to cause the judges to abandon their principled positions and bring them into line with executive thinking. In place of reasoned arguments,[84] these sentiments represented a direct political and constitutional threat to the judiciary whose proposals, repeatedly asserted to be in 'final form' and defended by argument, were now subject to an attack directed at undermining the judiciary's authority. It was threat enough: the resistance of the judges was broken.

The response of Lord Parker by letter dated 13 January 1964, having consulted the other members of his Sub-Committee, was not simply to express 'general agreement with the layout of the Home Office draft' but to accept, with minor amendments, its substance including the administration of the first caution to be conditional on the constable having evidence which would afford reasonable grounds for suspecting that the person has committed an offence.

[81] For example, the Lord Chancellor said that 'taken into custody' had replaced 'has been arrested or otherwise taken into custody' bearing in mind that one of the 'principles' makes it clear that the police cannot take into custody unless they arrest.

[82] Principally, the new requirement that the caution be administered not at the outset of inquiries but only as soon as a 'police officer has reasonable grounds for suspecting ... ' was justified, once again, on the basis that a caution administered earlier would lead to 'many offenders' remaining silent resulting in many criminals going free and the task of the police in detecting offenders would be 'gravely prejudiced'.

[83] This was to take place on 21 January 1964 in the Lord Chancellor's Office with the Home Secretary, Law Officers, and officials.

[84] Robert Stevens documents a few occasions on which the Lord Chancellor's Office sought to advise judges as to their conduct (such as publishing views about the law) or engaged in generalized 'lobbying' of the LCJ in the hope that the judges would not be lenient when sentencing armed 'bandits': Robert Stevens, *The Independence of the Judiciary* (OUP 1993) 94–96.

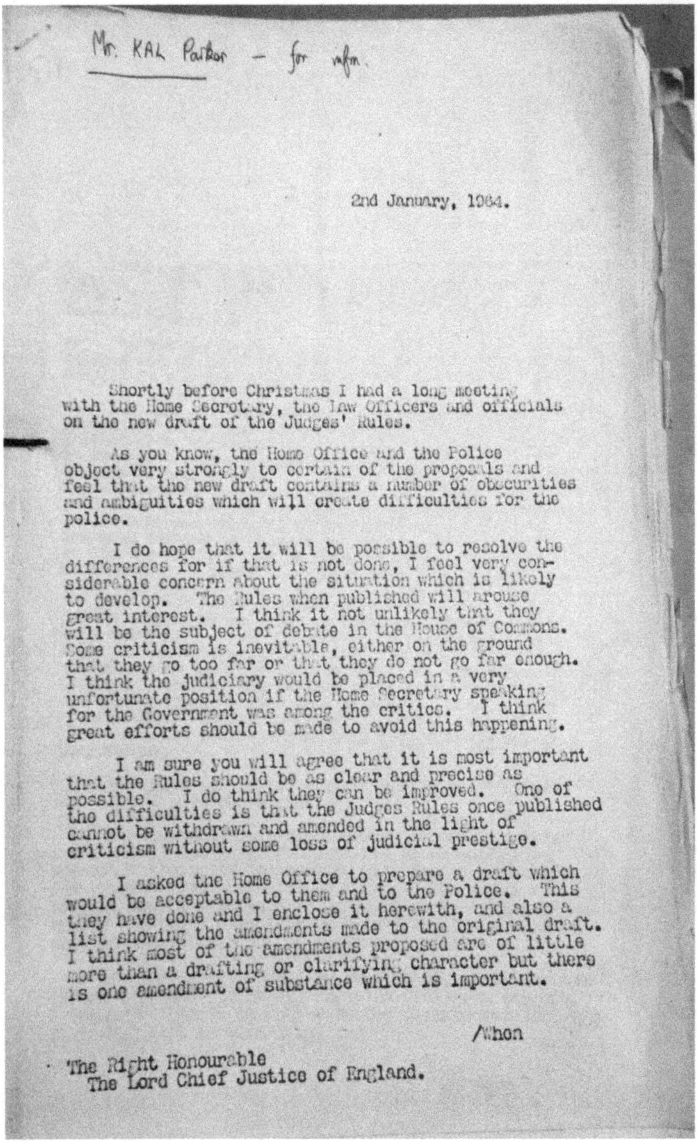

Mr. KAL Parker – for infm.

2nd January, 1964.

Shortly before Christmas I had a long meeting with the Home Secretary, the Law Officers and officials on the new draft of the Judges' Rules.

As you know, the Home Office and the Police object very strongly to certain of the proposals and feel that the new draft contains a number of obscurities and ambiguities which will create difficulties for the police.

I do hope that it will be possible to resolve the differences for if that is not done, I feel very considerable concern about the situation which is likely to develop. The Rules when published will arouse great interest. I think it not unlikely that they will be the subject of debate in the House of Commons. Some criticism is inevitable, either on the ground that they go too far or that they do not go far enough. I think the judiciary would be placed in a very unfortunate position if the Home Secretary speaking for the Government was among the critics. I think great efforts should be made to avoid this happening.

I am sure you will agree that it is most important that the Rules should be as clear and precise as possible. I do think they can be improved. One of the difficulties is that the Judges Rules once published cannot be withdrawn and amended in the light of criticism without some loss of judicial prestige.

I asked the Home Office to prepare a draft which would be acceptable to them and to the Police. This they have done and I enclose it herewith, and also a list showing the amendments made to the original draft. I think most of the amendments proposed are of little more than a drafting or clarifying character but there is one amendment of substance which is important.

/When

The Right Honourable
The Lord Chief Justice of England.

Illustration 6.3 Letter from Lord Chancellor to Lord Parker (January 1964) (National Archives)

Charles Cunningham wrote to the Commissioner of Police to let him know the good news, as set out in **Illustration 6.4**.

The Home Office assessment was accurate: the judges (under threat) had made 'substantial concessions to the Home Office and police point of view' with the Home Office accepting that the judges were 'unlikely to give way' over their

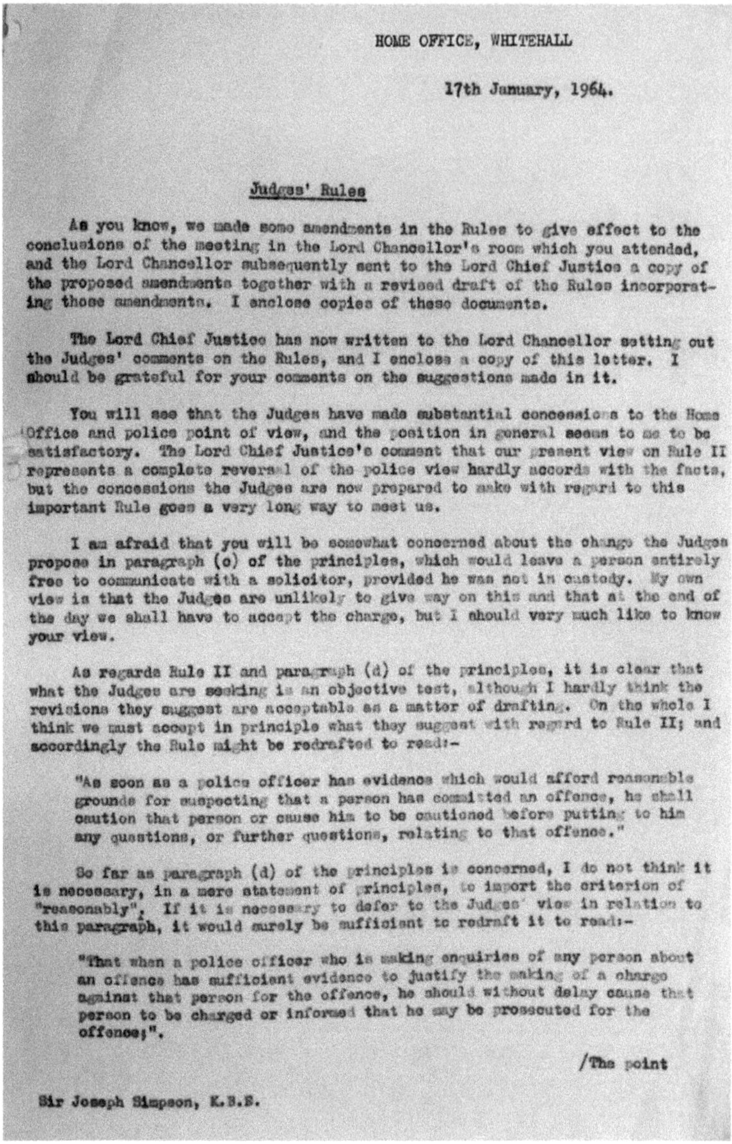

HOME OFFICE, WHITEHALL

17th January, 1964.

Judges' Rules

As you know, we made some amendments in the Rules to give effect to the conclusions of the meeting in the Lord Chancellor's room which you attended, and the Lord Chancellor subsequently sent to the Lord Chief Justice a copy of the proposed amendments together with a revised draft of the Rules incorporating those amendments. I enclose copies of these documents.

The Lord Chief Justice has now written to the Lord Chancellor setting out the Judges' comments on the Rules, and I enclose a copy of this letter. I should be grateful for your comments on the suggestions made in it.

You will see that the Judges have made substantial concessions to the Home Office and police point of view, and the position in general seems to me to be satisfactory. The Lord Chief Justice's comment that our present view on Rule II represents a complete reversal of the police view hardly accords with the facts, but the concessions the Judges are now prepared to make with regard to this important Rule goes a very long way to meet us.

I am afraid that you will be somewhat concerned about the change the Judges propose in paragraph (c) of the principles, which would leave a person entirely free to communicate with a solicitor, provided he was not in custody. My own view is that the Judges are unlikely to give way on this and that at the end of the day we shall have to accept the charge, but I should very much like to know your view.

As regards Rule II and paragraph (d) of the principles, it is clear that what the Judges are seeking is an objective test, although I hardly think the revisions they suggest are acceptable as a matter of drafting. On the whole I think we must accept in principle what they suggest with regard to Rule II; and accordingly the Rule might be redrafted to read:-

"As soon as a police officer has evidence which would afford reasonable grounds for suspecting that a person has committed an offence, he shall caution that person or cause him to be cautioned before putting to him any questions, or further questions, relating to that offence."

So far as paragraph (d) of the principles is concerned, I do not think it is necessary, in a mere statement of principles, to import the criterion of "reasonably". If it is necessary to defer to the Judges' view in relation to this paragraph, it would surely be sufficient to redraft it to read:-

"That when a police officer who is making enquiries of any person about an offence has sufficient evidence to justify the making of a charge against that person for the offence, he should without delay cause that person to be charged or informed that he may be prosecuted for the offence;".

/The point

Sir Joseph Simpson, K.B.E.

Illustration 6.4 Letter from Sir Charles Cunningham Indicating Concessions of Judges (January 1964) (National Archives)

insistence that a person should be free to consult a solicitor provided they were not in custody. In the result, with some other minor drafting comments made by the judges on the Home Office draft being accepted and some rejected, a political settlement had been made, in the terms used by the Home Office itself, in favour of the *police interest* rather than the *public interest*.

Indeed, the involvement (and acquiescence) of the Law Officers of the Crown (with Attorney-General as chief legal adviser) throughout the drafting negotiations to push the *police interest* in this way was—putting it mildly—constitutionally dubious. Not only are the Attorney- and Solicitor-General supposed to act as legal advisers to the Crown rather than the formulators of government policy,[85] but they are entrusted to act with complete independence from the executive[86] in their role as 'Guardian of *Public Interest*'.[87] As Lord Shawcross explained:[88]

> ... although the Attorney-General is a member of the government he has certain duties which he cannot abdicate in connection with the administration of the law, especially of the criminal law ... These duties are sometimes said to be of a quasi-judicial nature. The Attorney-General has to discharge them with complete independence of the government ... In these matters ... the Attorney General's duty (and it is his duty) is to concern himself, and to concern himself *only*, with the *representation and protection of the public interest.*

Rush to Publication

Immediately on securing approval of the judges, the Home Office proceeded to finalize matters with inexplicable haste. The demand for printing copies of the Home

[85] J Ll J Edwards, *The Law Officers of the Crown* (Sweet & Maxwell 1964) (hereafter Edwards, *Law Officers*) 159. Of course, this is not to suggest there is no involvement in policy for the Attorney-General is 'also called upon to advise on the legal implications of Government proposals and he is at liberty to tender such advice without waiting to be asked for it': Lord MacDermont, *Protection from Power under English Law* (Stevens 1957) (hereafter MacDermont, *Protection from Power*) 29. The central point being that the Law Officers' focus should be on *implications* of policy, in light of the *public interest*, rather than the formulation of it.

[86] 'Maintaining the principle of independence does not entail the Attorney-General discharging his responsibility in the atmosphere of an ivory tower; at the same time it does require that the Attorney-General should not be placed in a position of subservience to the executive': Edwards, *Law Officers* (ibid) 214–15. This 'segregation of powers ... springs from a widespread feeling that the administration of the law, and particularly that of the criminal law, ought to be altogether above party politics', MacDermont, *Protection from Power* (n 85) 32. This understanding was echoed elsewhere: 'whilst participation in party politics, and of course, a share in the collective responsibility of the Government for action that is taken, are normally incidental to the office of Attorney-General, it remains the clearest rule that in the discharge of this legal and discretionary duties the Attorney-General is completely divorced from party political considerations and from any kind of political control', Sir Hartley Shawcross, 'Address delivered at the Law Society's Hall' (18 February 1953) 12, quoted by MacDermont, *Protection from Power* (ibid) 33.

[87] As emphasized by Lord MacDermont in his Hamlyn Lecture (*Protection from Power*): 'He [the Attorney-General] represents the public interest where public rights are at stake and there is no one else charged with the duty of protecting them. There are no bounds to this important function ... ' 30; To his credit, Lord MacDermont was fully recognizant of the frailty of protection from the executive offered by the Law Officers: 'In the end, of course, everything turns on the training, character and capacity of those who, between them, administer our criminal law, be they judges, Law Officers, members of the legal professions, policemen, officials or gaolers. If personal standards fall, the best of systems cannot prevent a decline' 40–41.

[88] Edwards, *Law Officers* (n 85) 214–15, emphasis supplied.

Office Circular and Judges' Rules was issued on Wednesday 22 January 1964, with the Stationery Office requested to complete the order for special collection on Thursday 23 January 1964 so that copies could be placed in the Parliamentary Vote Office on Friday 24 January 1964 and distributed to police stations the same day, the Rules coming into operation on Monday 27 January 1964. The explanation given to the Stationery Office for the urgency was that it was 'because of a late Ministerial decision'.[89] Although this timetable was met, the drafting of the Circular had not in fact been agreed by Ministers until the early evening of 23 January.[90] The new Judges' Rules, fashioned by the Home Office in what it considered to be the interests of the police[91] were promulgated on Friday 24 January 1964.

A Delayed Inquiry

Two months after the Rules were promulgated and four years after David Napley had called for a public inquiry into the cases of Tisdall, Kingston, and Hill-Burton, against the background of the Challenor case the Home Office was forced into ordering a public inquiry under William Mars-Jones, QC.[92] It now emerged that, on receipt of Napley's complaint in November 1959, the Home Office, far from making a full inquiry, had merely asked the Met to conduct its own inquiry; and the officer charged with the investigation was, in fact, the officer in command of the very officers whose conduct was in issue.[93] The investigation reports, which, because of various mistakes and failings,[94] amounted to little more than a whitewash,

[89] Letter from KAL Parker of the Home Office to Mr Wolverson of the Stationery Office (24 January 1964).

[90] Note from KAL Parker of the Home Office to Mr Bunker, Principal Establishment Officer (27 January 1964). Sir Charles Cunningham later wrote a note to the Stationery Office thanking them for the 'exceptional efforts' in responding at such short notice explaining that the 'hurried timetable was not of our choosing . . . :' Letter (7 February 1964).

[91] In fact, it was a police viewpoint only from a high level. While the public were excluded from the process, there were complaints following promulgation from Chief Constables Association (CCA) and Police Federation that they had not been consulted: *The Times* (25 January 1964).

[92] The inquiry was prompted by assertions made by Eric Fletcher MP during the Committee stage of the Police Bill in February 1964, two of the individuals (Halloran and Cox) involved being his constituents. Fletcher's intervention after this very considerable lapse of time was fortified by statements given to him by a number of police superintendents and ex-superintendents that the internal police investigation in 1959 had been a whitewash. The Home Office was forced to order the inquiry because Mr Fletcher had made allegations against both the police and the Home Office: Letter from Cunningham to the Commissioner (18 March 1964).

[93] The investigating officer had failed to obtain a transcript of the court proceedings at which the appeals had been rejected. Without the transcript, no-one in the Metropolitan Police appreciated that the allegations were not confined to the three officers involved in the initial arrests (and mentioned by Mr Napley) but included a police Sergeant (Bolongaro) and another Detective Constable (Rust) which would have been evident from the transcript.

[94] This was as much to do with bureaucratic deficiencies as malpractice. Thus, eg, Commander Townsend realized that a transcript would be needed and wrote a Minute to this effect but, having passed it to the relevant police section, it was not acted upon because the officer involved was on holiday.

had been filed with the Home Office, as the Home Secretary confirmed, but no further action had been taken on them.[95]

Mars-Jones, reporting in December 1964, found that five police officers had lied about their encounter with the youths; that the weapons had been 'planted'; that the officer designated to undertake the initial inquiry requested by the Home Office had distorted his findings to lend support to the officers and had omitted the evidence of witnesses which would have confirmed the story of the youths; and that the Assistant Commissioner had prematurely halted the police inquiry without giving the matter proper consideration because of friction between the uniform and CID branches of the Metropolitan Police and under pressure to submit a report to the Home Office which had, as was its practice, required that the investigation be completed within a short time.[96]

Although the Home Secretary was forced to recommend the grant of free pardons to the youths, the sordid episode was put to bed when it was announced that the DPP had decided not to institute proceedings against any of the five police officers who gave false evidence and that no action could be taken against any serving officer in view of an undertaking by the Commissioner, given when the inquiry was set up, that disciplinary action would not be taken against any serving officer who gave evidence before the inquiry.[97]

Had the Home Office been alert or disposed to dispassionate judgment, the Report of Mars-Jones contained details that amounted to a damning indictment of police culture within London. In addition, any objective judgment would have seen that the Judges' Rules were not fit for the purpose of dealing with corruption within the police and the opportunities for deviance that work in the CID presented. The

[95] See HC Deb 26 March 1964, vol 692, cols 661–64.

[96] The extract from Hansard 3 December 1964 703 at para 752 reads: 'In the case of Tisdall, Kingston and Hill-Burton, which occurred in 1959, the allegation was that the facts disclosed by an investigation made in 1960 were deliberately covered up in order to avoid embarrassment to the police. Mr. Mars-Jones finds that no one connected with the investigation acted dishonestly; that there was no attempt to conceal from the Home Secretary information relevant to the guilt or innocence of the men; and that there was no breach of duty by any official in the Home Office. He does find, however, that five police officers of subordinate rank—three of whom have since resigned—lied about the time and place of their first encounter with the three accused men; that if the evidence disclosed in the course of his inquiry had been available at the trial or appeal the three men would not have been likely to be convicted; and that the investigation of the complaint was neither thorough nor impartial. Mr. Mars-Jones criticises three senior police officers—who have since retired; he attributes some part of the failure of the investigation to friction between a senior officer of the uniformed branch and the C.I.D. in the district concerned and at Scotland Yard; and he also criticises certain aspects of the arrangements for handling complaints against members of the Metropolitan Police. In the light of the Report I am recommending the grant of free pardons to the three men concerned. I have referred the Report to the Director of Public Prosecutions, but he informs me that he would not feel justified in instituting proceedings against the five officers, or former officers, who were found by Mr. Mars-Jones to have given false evidence. In view of an undertaking given by the Commissioner of Police—which was communicated to the House by my predecessor when he announced the setting up of the inquiry—that disciplinary action would not be taken against any serving officer who gave evidence before the inquiry the Commissioner is not free to take disciplinary action.'

[97] See HC Deb 3 December 1964, vol 703, cols 751–55. The undertaking had in fact been sought by Eric Fletcher MP, who had raised the matter with the Home Secretary.

Home Office, however, contented itself with assurances from the Commissioner that all was now well with the Metropolitan Police, the situation having developed 'from personal and local factors' which no longer obtained. Writing in 1982, Sir David Napley aptly summarized the outcome as follows:

> [O]ne would like to be able to write that as a result the safeguards would have been strengthened, the procedures revolutionized, and the Home Office practices reformed to such an extent that a dreadful thing like this could never happen again. Unhappily, it is not so; little if anything changed, other than a direction from the then Commissioner, Sir Joseph Simpson, that in future complaints against a CID officer must not be investigated by his own division.

Conclusion

The extraordinary episode of the revision of the Judges' Rules saw the executive confront the judges at a time when deference to the office of LCJ was stated to underpin the relationship. The judges had sought to act on what they saw as the public interest. It was understood by all that the judges would be open to criticism if they did not do so. Whereas they had stood on principle when invited to attenuate the right to silence, here their agreement was secured not by force of argument, or statistics, or other convincing evidence regarding the rise in crime, nor on blind trust in police integrity or general police practices. Instead, the judges (under the auspices of Lord Parker) were forced to abandon principle by political threats that went to the heart of British constitutional arrangements, the 'separation of powers', and the associated notion of 'judicial independence'.

The age of deference did not stand in the way of threats to publicly degrade and embarrass the judges and undermine their legitimacy. Despite increasing evidence of dubious or improper police practice occurring over the period when the reformulation of the Rules was being undertaken and to which they had determined to respond, the judges finally gave in to naked political pressure. In this dark but revealing episode of legal history, the unqualified principle of judicial independence was forfeited as the judges were pressed into setting aside the public interest in protecting citizens from overreach by the state in favour of a law and order perspective advanced by the executive on behalf of a policing system whose integrity was being eroded by actions that became a matter of public notoriety; and all this had occurred under the supposed watch of the Home Office.

7
The Legacy of the 1964 Rules

Introduction

The 1964 Rules held sway for the next twenty years in England and Wales with an even longer life in some other jurisdictions. Born at a time of increased public concern over detention and interrogation practices and a more general reduction in public trust of the police, the Rules were meant to provide reassurance in what was asserted to be the 'public interest'. The history of the previous fifty years showed the need to guard against a policing culture which favoured autonomous action and the related capacity for corrupt activity presented, in particular, by detective policing. Alongside this, there remained the question of the impact of executive interference with the judiciary following the rejection of the judges' preferred formulae for regulating the police. It is to the success (or otherwise) of the new Rules in these respects that we now turn.

Promulgation and Publication

While the presentation of the 1918 Rules as having been 'approved' by the judges was misleading, the promulgation of the 1964 Rules constituted active misrepresentation and a false prospectus. The Home Office Circular[1] accompanying the Rules, drafted by Sir Charles Cunningham, calculatedly sought to pass off work of the executive as that of the judges.

As **Illustration 7.1a** and **Illustration 7.1b** show, the original Circular stated correctly that the Rules had been 'approved' by the judges and had superseded those previously 'approved' by the judges. This was altered so that the Circular as distributed stated that the 'new Rules have been *made* by Her Majesty's Judges of the Queen's Bench Division'; that the Rules 'supersede the Rules previously *made* by the Judges'; and that the Rules had been '*made* by the Judges as a guide to police officers conducting investigations . . .' (emphasis supplied).

These misrepresentations are important because the very standing and authority of the Rules derived from the perception that they were *rules of the Judges*. That authority was all the more significant because the public (and MPs) had been

[1] Home Office Circular No 31/1964.

The Myth of Judicial Independence. Mike McConville and Luke Marsh, Oxford University Press (2020). © Mike McConville and Luke Marsh. DOI: 10.1093/oso/9780198822103.001.0001

(a)

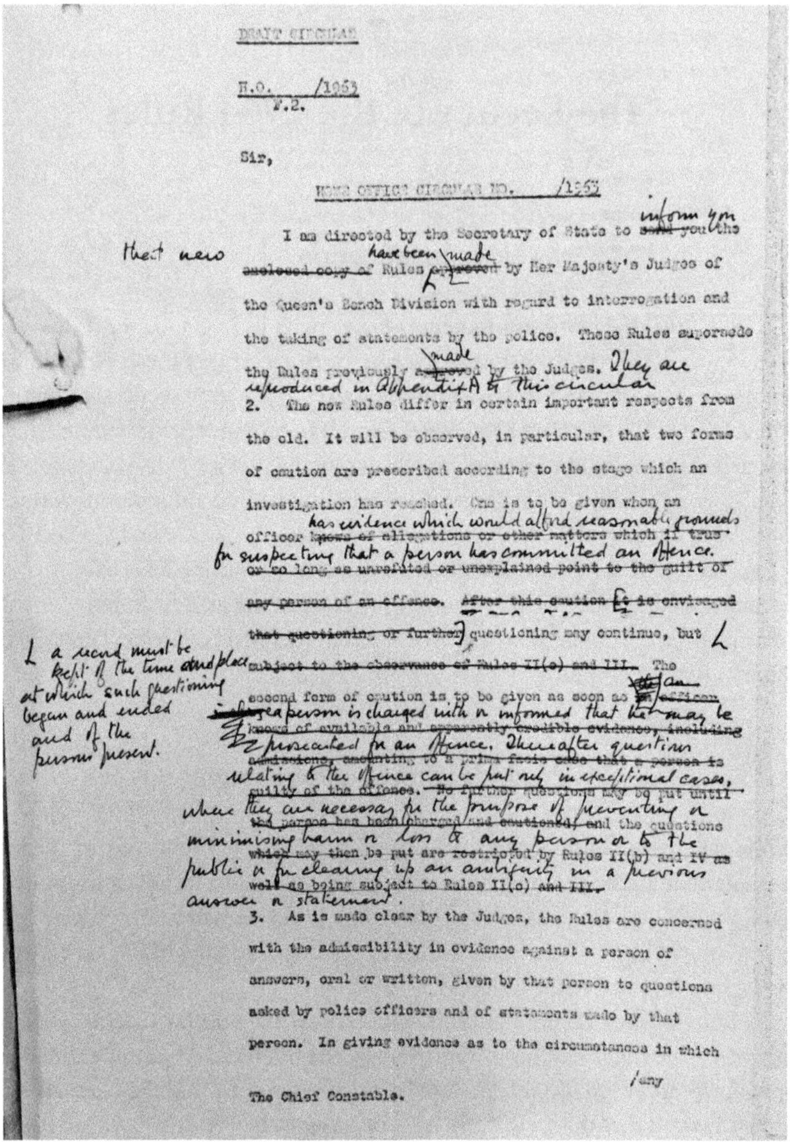

DRAFT CIRCULAR

H.O. /1963
F.2.

Sir,

HOME OFFICE CIRCULAR NO. /1963

I am directed by the Secretary of State to ~~send you the~~ inform you that new ~~enclosed copy of~~ Rules have been ~~approved~~ made by Her Majesty's Judges of the Queen's Bench Division with regard to interrogation and the taking of statements by the police. These Rules supersede the Rules previously ~~approved~~ made by the Judges. They are reproduced in Appendix A to this circular.

2. The new Rules differ in certain important respects from the old. It will be observed, in particular, that two forms of caution are prescribed according to the stage which an investigation has reached. One is to be given when an officer ~~knows of allegations or other matters which if true or so long as unrefuted or unexplained point to the guilt of any person of an offence.~~ has evidence which would afford reasonable grounds for suspecting that a person has committed an offence. ~~After this caution it is envisaged that questioning or further~~ questioning may continue, but ~~subject to the observance of Rules II(c) and III.~~ a record must be kept of the time and place at which such questioning began and ended and of the persons present. The second form of caution is to be given as soon as ~~an officer knows of available and apparently credible evidence, including admissions, amounting to a prima facie case that a person is guilty of the offence.~~ a person is charged with or informed that he may be prosecuted for an offence. Thereafter questions relating to the offence can be put only in exceptional cases, where they are necessary for the purpose of preventing or minimising harm or loss to any person or to the public or for clearing up an ambiguity in a previous answer or statement. ~~No further questions may be put until the person has been charged and cautioned, and the questions which may then be put are restricted by Rules II(b) and IV as well as being subject to Rules II(c) and III.~~

3. As is made clear by the Judges, the Rules are concerned with the admissibility in evidence against a person of answers, oral or written, given by that person to questions asked by police officers and of statements made by that person. In giving evidence as to the circumstances in which /any

The Chief Constable.

Illustration 7.1a 'Passing-Off' the Judges' Rules in the Home Office Circular (undated) (National Archives)

(b)

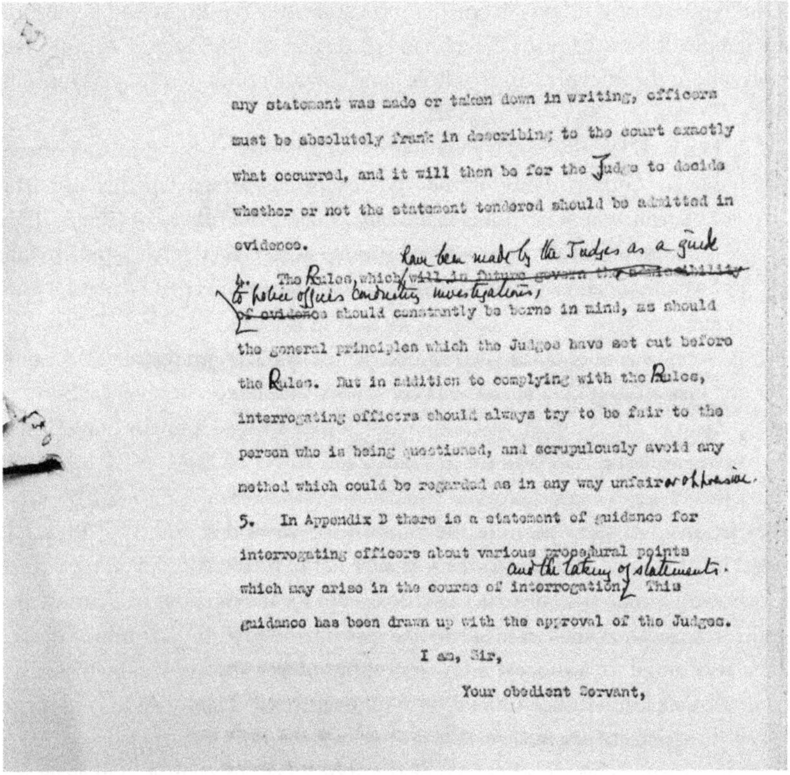

any statement was made or taken down in writing, officers must be absolutely frank in describing to the court exactly what occurred, and it will then be for the Judges to decide whether or not the statement tendered should be admitted in evidence.

4. The Rules, which [have been made by the Judges as a guide to police officers conducting investigations,] ~~will in future govern the admissibility of evidence~~ should constantly be borne in mind, as should the general principles which the Judges have set out before the Rules. But in addition to complying with the Rules, interrogating officers should always try to be fair to the person who is being questioned, and scrupulously avoid any method which could be regarded as in any way unfair [or oppressive].

5. In Appendix B there is a statement of guidance for interrogating officers about various procedural points which may arise in the course of interrogation [and the taking of statements]. This guidance has been drawn up with the approval of the Judges.

I am, Sir,

Your obedient Servant,

Illustration 7.1b 'Passing-Off' the Judges' Rules in the Home Office Circular (undated) (National Archives)

excluded from the deliberative process and were accordingly reliant upon official representations.

Confusion of Meaning

If the first drafting by Home Office officials resulted in unclear provisions, their efforts almost fifty years later fared no better. Indeed, there was already uncertainty as to their meaning *within* official circles as shown in correspondence between the Home Office (Kenneth Parker) and the Deputy Director of Public Prosecutions (DPP) (Maurice Crump) even though the DPP himself had attended key meetings[2] discussing revision of the Rules.

2 The DPP attended core meetings on 8 November 1963 and 11 December 1963.

The request for guidance from Crump came after the Rules had been in force for a couple of months prior to lecturing the police on the Rules. Crump was concerned about the interpretation of Rule I and II which provided (in part) as follows:

> I. When a police officer is trying to discover whether, or by whom, an offence has been committed he is entitled to question any person, whether suspected or not, from whom he thinks that useful information may be obtained. This is so whether or not the person in question has been taken into custody so long as he has not been charged with the offence or informed that he may be prosecuted for it.
>
> II. As soon as a police officer has evidence which would afford reasonable grounds for suspecting that a person has committed an offence, he shall caution that person or cause him to be cautioned before putting to him any questions, or further questions, relating to that offence ...

What troubled Crump was the meaning of the second sentence of Rule I since under the old Rules persons in custody were not to be questioned on the subject of the crime for which they were in custody except for the purpose of clearing up ambiguities, a view he believed the DPP had also passed to him.[3] It troubled the Home Office, too; and it took more than two months before they were ready to reply.

Initially, a Home Office official drafted an internal Memorandum to Kenneth Parker in which it was observed that it seemed 'quite clear that it was contemplated that custody was no bar to questioning'. As to the proposed answer, it now seemed 'fairly clear' that Rule II applied 'in practice when arrest may be justifiable for certain offence', that is to say, 'when the officer has evidence which would afford reasonable grounds for suspecting that the person concerned has committed the offence'. The official added: 'That, however, does not necessarily seem to be the moment when ... under Rule III, a charge must be preferred.' Further uncertainties in this Memorandum made Kenneth Parker wary, as is clear from his note to his colleague, Mr Jones:

> These are difficult matters when one gets down to detail, and although Mr. Crump (and the police!) wd no doubt like some expanded advice we cd hardly give it without consulting the L. C. J.: and he might well say that he wd prefer to deal with points as they arise in court.

With Parker and Jones in agreement that the reply should be restricted to the minimum necessary, Crump was told that it was:

[3] Letter from Crump (16 March 1964). The police, he said, argued that in some circumstances such questioning was permissible.

> … not really possible to go into detail about the circumstances in which questioning in custody can occur without infringement of the Rules without going back to the Judges, which seems premature until we have all had more experience of the way the rules work out in practice.

Parker restricted his substantive response by explaining that ('as we understand it') the intention of the Rules was that custody was not of itself a bar to questioning; that an officer could go on questioning a person about the offence for which he was in custody (as visualized by Rule I) until the officer had enough evidence to prefer a charge against the person (under Rule III).

As two months had passed since his initial inquiry, Crump had already acted and, after receiving the Home Office response, he wrote back:

> A strict reading of the Principles and the Rules does as you say indicate a right to question *under caution* a suspect in respect of the actual offence for which he is being held in custody.
>
> But as this was directly in conflict with decided cases it was clearly necessary for the Police to be advised at once and correctly as to the position.
>
> When therefore I did not hear from the one Parker[4] I wrote to the other[5] who on 6th April replied that what I described to you both as 'the Police view' is indeed the correct one.
>
> I therefore regard the matter as settled subject to any comments by constitutional lawyers! (emphasis supplied)

Thus, it appears that Parker LCJ (extraordinarily) gave *private* advice on the interpretation of the Rules; but that did not clear up the mess. While Crump concluded that the 'police view' was endorsed by Lord Parker, Crump misstated its effect because such questioning under Rule I was permitted *without caution*!

A detailed analysis of the new Rules is not our concern here but we illustrate the uncertainty they caused by reference to Rule I. In a penetrating analysis, Professor J C Smith, the leading authority on criminal law and procedure, heavily criticized the new Rules,[6] concluding that although they cleared up some points, they left others unresolved and raised new problems of their own.[7] On the issue that had troubled Crump, Professor Smith pointed out that the use of the word 'custody'

4 That is, Kenneth Parker of the Home Office.

5 That is, Parker LCJ.

6 As if this was not sufficient alarm, the then leading authority on English constitutional law, Geoffrey Marshall, was equally perplexed: 'Constables are now called upon under the Rules to draw some rather delicate distinctions, which at points might strain the capacities of moral philosophers' 'Comment' (1964) Public Law 97, 100.

7 John Cyril Smith, 'The New Judges' Rules—A Lawyer's View' [1964] Criminal Law Review 176 (hereafter *Smith*, 'A Lawyer's View').

in the Rules risked perpetuating the myth that 'there is some form of lawful restraint less than arrest',[8] a danger increased by the difficulty in interpreting Rule I. Professor Smith commented:

> This is difficult to understand . . . A person in custody must, if he is not unlawfully imprisoned, have been arrested. But if he has been arrested, how does it come about that he has not been charged or informed that he may be prosecuted?

The question arose because *Christie v Leachinsky*[9] provided that 'a citizen is entitled to know on what charge or suspicion of what crime he is seized'. It followed, Professor Smith said, that if a person is told the grounds of his arrest, he has been told that 'he may be prosecuted' for that offence; and, if so, the general right of questioning to obtain useful information under Rule I comes to an end.

> If he has been detained, but not told the grounds of his detention, it is unlawful. It can hardly be supposed that the judges have laid down a procedure for dealing with a man who is unlawfully arrested; but if the second sentence of Rule I does not do this, it is difficult to see what it does do.[10]

Leonard Hoffmann (later Lord Hoffmann)[11] sought to reconcile the provision with *Christie v Leachinsky* by venturing that the 'charge' contemplated by Rule I was not the informal on-the-spot notice required by the House of Lords but the formal decision to charge and the words 'informed that he may be prosecuted' in Rule I referred to the formal notification when the police intended to proceed by way of summons. On the other hand, a police officer[12] considered the meaning of Rule I by no means 'plain' because, among other things:[13]

[8] Gerald Abrahams, *Police Questioning and the Judges' Rules* (Oyez Publications 1964) (hereafter Abrahams, *Judges' Rules*) stated the accepted legal position as follows: ' . . . it is commonplace that the English law recognises no right of detention for questioning' citing *Tims v John Lewis & Co* [1951] 2 KB 459 adding: 'This assumption was discussed and accepted by the Royal Commissioners of 1929 (Cmd. 3297). It is the Home Office view.'

[9] [1947] AC 573.

[10] *Smith*, 'A Lawyer's View' (n 7) 180. David Arthur Thomas, 'The Revised Judges' Rules' (1963–64) British Journal of Criminology 383 sought to draw a distinction between arrest and charge by asserting that 'the law merely requires that an arrested person should be told for what act he has been arrested; he need not be told for what offence he will be prosecuted' citing *Christie* (n 9); and *Gelberg v Miller* [1961] 1 All ER 296. But the rule in *Christie* is clear: a citizen is entitled to know on what charge or suspicion of what crime he is seized. The explanation in *Gelberg* seems only that the reasons given need not be a specific charge and need not be the charge on which the arrested person is later held or arraigned.

[11] Leonard Hoffmann, 'The Judges' Rules' (1964) 7 The Lawyer 23.

[12] A Police Officer, 'The Judges' Rules and the Police' [1964] Criminal Law Review 173.

[13] ibid 174. The writer referred to the LCJ in *R v Buchan* (1964) *The Guardian* (28 January 1964). For another police viewpoint, see Thomas Eric St Johnston, 'Judges' Rules and Police Interrogation in England Today' (1966) 57(1) Journal of Criminal Law and Criminology 85.

> I would guess that most lawyers would maintain that this simply means that if a person is in custody for some offence he may be questioned about another offence, not that he may be taken into custody simply to be questioned.

Although the Court of Criminal Appeal subsequently controversially ruled that there was no difference between 'detaining' and 'arresting',[14] the distinction was not one that had been understood by the courts,[15] nor apparent to police officers nor to distinguished lawyers.

The broader issue over the status of 'detention for questioning'— the very practice which had given rise to concern—had in fact, unknown to commentators, already been voiced by others. Thus, the experienced Lord Chief Justice (LCJ) of Northern Ireland, John MacDermott, wrote to Lord Parker days before promulgation of the new Rules[16] distinguishing between '*de facto* custody' (when the person being questioned is not under arrest but 'held' for questioning or led to believe that he is so held) and 'lawful custody' (when the person is being questioned under arrest) and continued:

> On the whole, I am very doubtful about allowing the interrogation after caution of a person in custody of any kind. But if the revision [of the Rules] were to permit questioning in custody after caution, I think the custody would have to be limited to lawful custody and so as to exclude custody of the *de facto* type … (original emphasis).

Notwithstanding such concerns, the new Rules appeared to the police and some commentators to have given implied recognition to the practice of 'detaining for questioning' by means of an arrest on suspicion followed by a period of investigation before charge.[17] Much now depended on police practice and judicial regulation.

Police Malpractice (1)

With the image of the Metropolitan Police, and its showcase detective branch, tarnished, the catalogue of police wrongdoing laid out in the Mars-Jones Report should have triggered official action. Unfortunately, the Home Office—the then

[14] *R v Lemsatef* (1977) 2 All ER 835 *per* Lawton LJ. See also *R v Houghton and Franciosy* (1979) 68 Cr App R 197.

[15] See *R v Wattam* (1952) 36 Cr App R72.

[16] Letter (16 January 1964) in HO 287/222.

[17] See Abrahams, *Judges' Rules* (n 8) 26 44 to the same effect. See also 'The Constable and the Law: A Weekly Commentary' *Police Review* (31 January 1964): Referring to the new Rule I, the author says that this 'seems to usher in judicial recognition of something hitherto sternly (if ineffectually) forbidden—the status of being "detained for questioning"'.

police authority for London[18]—remained inert: although it had legal authority, it lacked political weight, insight, and competence to discharge its responsibilities in this regard. In reality, the Met had already acquired immense *political* power such that 'management' of it was, in practical terms, *self-management*. Home Office officials were dissociated from practical policing, lacked understanding of police culture, and were unwilling to confront the systemic problems created by the practice that all complaints of alleged crime within the Met were investigated by the Criminal Investigations Department (CID).

The appointment in December 1965 of Roy Jenkins as Home Secretary promised an era of reform. Jenkins encouraged the retirement of Charles Cunningham, who was seen as 'old guard' and as stultifying change, and secured Sir Philip Allen as his replacement. While his previous posts[19] (and, even, record[20]) did not immediately suggest that he was the right person to tackle policing problems, Allen set out to assist Jenkins in the task of modernization. And it soon became apparent what work there was to do.

Years of Home Office and judicial inaction had led to one certain outcome: the institutionalization of police corruption, the Mars-Jones Inquiry proving only the prelude to more startling revelations.[21] Once again, however, detachment from police work left the Home Office responding to events.[22] Although the then Commissioner, Sir Joseph Simpson, instituted various reforms, as by establishing the Drugs Squad and the Obscene Publications Squad (both of which, ironically, were to be the focus of future major scandals), the Met remained subject to interdepartmental rivalries and, most significantly, functioned on vertical lines of command which left the CID in 'a private world of its own'.[23] The relative isolation of the Home Office meant that it not only failed to see the problems coming but failed to see the problems at all. Once again, it was left to investigative journalists to lift the veil on police practices.

[18] In 2000 the Metropolitan Police Authority became the local police authority for London, its functions being transferred in turn to the Mayor's Office for Policing and Crime in 2012.

[19] Having joined the Home Office in 1934 Allen served in the War Cabinet from 1943 to 1944, was Deputy Chairman of the Prison Commission from 1950 to 1952, Deputy Secretary to the Ministry of Housing and Local Government between 1955 and 1960 before becoming Deputy Under-Secretary of State at the Home Office between1960 and 1962 under Charles Cunningham.

[20] During his time on the Prison Commission, Allen was guilty of misjudgement when he advised against a reprieve for Timothy Evans and, indeed, thought that Evans was guilty of the murder of his wife for which he was never prosecuted. Allen subsequently expressed his deep regret over these misjudgements: Obituary, 'Lord Allen of Abbeydale' *The Guardian* (11 December 2007).

[21] In the interim, the Chief Constable of Southend had been convicted of theft and false pretences and sentenced to two years' imprisonment.

[22] Yet, as Lord Allen himself has said, the methodology applied in areas such as prisons and factories, involved an application of the Benthamite philosophy of addressing social problems 'through inspection, enquiry and report': Lord Allen, 'State Service: Reflections of a Bureaucrat' in *The Home Office: Perspectives on Policy and Administration* (Royal Institute of Public Administration 1983) 25.

[23] David Ascoli, *The Queen's Peace* (Hamish Hamilton 1979) 292.

In November 1969, two reporters of *The Times*, Gary Lloyd and Julian Mounter, published an article, unprecedented for the newspaper, alleging CID corruption in London.[24] There was direct evidence that three Met detectives systematically blackmailed a petty thief (after tricking him into leaving his fingerprints on some gelignite), took money in exchange for dropping criminal charges, were 'going easy' on criminals in court, and allowing criminal activity to go unhindered. The petty thief was given advice by DS Symonds to put his profits into 'a little sweet shop with a bird running it. Then if a wheel comes off,[25] so what? You've got a home and a ******* business ... '[26] It was not just advice: it was intended to be a continuing relationship:

> ... don't forget always to let me know straight away if you need anything because I know people everywhere. Because I'm in a little firm in a firm. Don't matter where, anywhere in London I can get on the phone to someone I know I can trust, that talks the same as me. And if he's not the right person that can do it, he'll know the person that can. All right?'

There were clear suggestions that other detectives were similarly involved.[27]

The evidence in *The Times* shot the 'bad apples' defence[28] to pieces, with over thirty officers identified or identifiable: it *was* 'a firm within a firm'. Given this, it is hard to disagree with Sir Robert Mark's assessment[29] that the most appropriate course of action for the Home Office would have been to have ordered an investigation by an outside force.[30]

Instead, the Home Office, through plain incompetence or political calculation,[31] invited the Met, that is the CID of the Met, to investigate itself. Such was the scandal, however, that the Home Office was forced, after five days, to appoint Frank Williamson, HM Inspector of Constabulary (Crime), as an independent person 'associated' with the investigation. The delay, however, enabled the main police suspects to be tipped off by colleagues. What then followed resembled more of a

24 The Home Office files on this are sealed until 1 January 2047: National Archives, HO 287/2188.

25 Meaning, if something goes wrong.

26 See, John Alexander Symonds, *Romeo Spy* <www.romeospy.co.uk/Pages/fall_of_scotland_yard_1.htm> accessed 1 January 2020. Symonds was one of the officers identified in the newspaper scoop.

27 Gary Lloyd and Julian Mounter, 'London Policemen in Bribe Allegations: Tapes Reveal Planted Evidence' *The Times* (29 November 1969). See also Barry Cox, John Shirley, and Martin Short, *The Fall of Scotland Yard* (Penguin Books 1977) (hereafter Cox and others, *Scotland Yard*).

28 Clung onto unashamedly by the judges: 'It does seem that some of the present doctrines and principles have come down in our law from earlier times when the police of this country were not to be trusted, as they are *now to be trusted in almost every case*, to behave with *complete fairness* towards those who come into their hands or from whom they are seeking information' (*R v Northam* (1967) 52 Cr App R 97 *per* Winn LJ, emphasis supplied).

29 Sir Robert Mark, *In the Office of Constable* (William Collins & Sons 1978) (hereafter Mark, *Office of Constable*) 108.

30 Mark relied upon s 49(1) Police Act 1964.

31 There was a concern within the Home Office to limit the damage risked by a full-scale investigation.

cover-up than the 'stringent inquiry' that *The Times* leader had demanded as the destructive forces within the Met soon materialized.

In May 1970, barely six months after his investigation had started, Commander Virgo, the head of the Met's specialist crime squads, replaced the initial investigating officer, DCI Lambert,[32] by DCS Moody, Head of the Met's Obscene Publications Squad. Moody (together with Virgo),[33] was in fact corrupt, in the pay of Soho pornographers and himself destined in 1977 to receive twelve years' imprisonment for corruption.

Williamson, with a reputation for complete integrity after earlier securing the conviction of the Chief Constable of Southend for theft and false pretences,[34] was unable to effectively oversee the 'inquiry' given a lack of cooperation and internal obstruction.[35] The ensuing 'investigation' succeeded in limiting the damage to the conviction in March 1974 of two detectives—Robson and Harris—a third officer absconding before trial[36] with two others avoiding prosecution.[37]

Transformation in Senior Judicial Attitudes

Although evidence of the unreliability of police evidence was now rapidly accumulating in a very public fashion, within a very short time it became clear that (senior) judicial attitudes had undergone a remarkable change, if not flat reversal.

This transformation was driven by the disposition and actions of successive LCJs—the key policy-makers for the judiciary. It both anticipated and built upon the notorious Eleventh Report of the Criminal Law Revision Committee (1972) (CLRC),[38] headed by Edmund Davies LJ, which, out of concern over an alleged

[32] In a chilling insight into corruption and internecine warfare, Virgo told Lambert: 'You have backed the wrong horse. You have backed Frank Williamson against your own senior officers.'

[33] Although Commander Virgo (now deceased) was also convicted and sentenced to twelve years' imprisonment, his conviction was overturned on appeal on the basis that he did not have a fair trial. Despite this, there are detailed accounts of the corrupt practices in national newspapers (eg, Tony Rennell, 'King of the Corrupt Cops' *Daily Mail* (online) 24 May 2019; and see Chris Green, 'Ali Dizaei Most Senior Scotland Yard Officer to Be Convicted of Serious Crime since 1977' *The Independent* (8 February 2010). For general accounts of this period see Cox and others, *Scotland Yard* (n 27); James Morton, *Bent Coppers: A Survey of Police Corruption* (Warner Books 1993) (hereafter James Morton, *Bent Coppers*). See also Paul Bleakley, 'Cleaning up the Dirty Squad: Using the Obscene Publications Act as a Weapon of Social Control' (2019) 8(1) State Crime Journal 19; David I Woodland, *Crime and Corruption at Scotland Yard* (Pen & Sword Books 2016); Neil Root, *Crossing the Line of Duty* (The History Press 2019).

[34] The records relating to this remain sealed until 2041: National Archives, HO 242/8.

[35] See further Mark, *Office of Constable* (n 29). Investigation files were removed, telephones tapped, and prospective witnesses 'nobbled' by corrupt Met officers.

[36] Sergeant John Symonds fled to Morocco. See Sarah Hall, 'From the Yard to Shadow World' *The Guardian* (13 September 1999). Symonds returned after seven years and received two years' imprisonment.

[37] One was demoted and the other continued in service until a later resignation.

[38] See generally Colin Tapper 'Evidence (General) Eleventh Report of the Criminal Law Revision Committee' [1972] 35(6) Modern Law Review 4; Michael Zander 'The Criminal Law Revision

'large and increasing class of sophisticated professional criminals', (for which, whatever the reality on the ground, no evidence was advanced in the Report), proposed dispensing with the caution, permitting inferences to be drawn from the failure of an accused to mention to the police any fact subsequently relied upon in the defence, and allowing silence in court to amount to corroboration of other evidence.[39] There was no recognition that such changes might prejudice innocent defendants.[40]

The change in judicial thinking first became evident in the views of Parker LCJ. In 1963[41] Parker had delivered to the Home Office a principled rejection of the proposal to attenuate the right to silence. However, as already noted, the 'very considerable [judicial] opposition' fell away under threats from the executive. What followed was even more remarkable: judicial thinking soon became aligned with emerging government policies.

In a speech in April 1970 and in an interview in April 1971,[42] Lord Parker 'predicted' and thereby encouraged the view that a number of rules within the criminal justice system would soon be abolished:

> I am quite certain that within a year we shall see the caution abolished or modified and a number of anomalies removed which unduly help the [suspect]. I would hope, for instance, that a [defendant] could be called upon to go into the witness box, and it could be said to him that he need not do so but that comment might be made if he did not. This is something which is not allowed today.

Within months, the new LCJ, Widgery,[43] gave an even stronger message.[44] In his view, the attempt should be made to break out of the 'stranglehold' of 'inflexible rules' so that there should be fewer restrictions on police interrogation. Confessions were the best means of proof, he said, and so far as the caution was concerned, Widgery considered that this 'invitation to keep quiet' was one 'we could no longer afford'. To reinforce the new judicial theology, he even called into question access to legal advice: 'Any rule requiring the presence of the suspect's lawyer during police interrogation was quite unacceptable.'

Committee Report: A Survey of Reactions' *Law Society's Gazette* (2 October 1974) 953; Robert Thorseby, 'Is Due Process Fleeing Its English Home?' (1973) 59 American Bar Association Journal 1046.

[39] Criminal Law Revision Committee, *Eleventh Report: Evidence (General)* (HMSO 1972).

[40] See Diane Birch, 'Suffering in Silence: A Cost-Benefit Analysis of Section 34 of the Criminal Justice and Public Order Act 1994' [1997] Criminal Law Review 769.

[41] See ch 5.

[42] See 'Why Shouldn't We Kill?—The Mentality of the Criminal Classes as Seen by the Retiring Lord Chief Justice' *The Times* (8 April 1971).

[43] As Widgery J, he had been involved in the disgraceful misleading of the trial court in the Stephen Ward case. See generally, the compelling account of Geoffrey Robertson, *Stephen Ward Was Innocent, OK* (Biteback Publishing Ltd 2013).

[44] See Marcel Berlins, 'Call to Ease Police Questioning Methods' *The Times* (17 July 1971).

These sentiments are remarkable coming so soon after the Rules had been revised amid swirling instances of police corruption, yet they were in line with a secret judicial practice of pressurizing defendants to plead guilty.

'Plea Bargaining' or 'State-Induced Guilty Pleas'

The origins of 'plea bargaining' in England and Wales are not clear[45] but at least some practices were extant from the 1950s and depended in part upon 'mutual back-scratching'[46] arising from the close-knit relations between Bench and Bar.[47] The process by which a sentencing offer was made[48] or an outcome informally 'agreed', however, eventually transformed into one marked by coercion, first signalled in cases such as *R v Barnes*[49] and *R v Turner*.[50] Moreover, *Turner* proved to be another example of 'judicial legislation', Lord Parker for the Court of Appeal (including Widgery LJ) laying down a series of guidelines purporting to control or even prevent 'bargaining' but in fact authorizing it.[51] Yet over this period, as was known to the judges, more evidence now emerged of police wrongdoing.

Police Malpractice (2)

One of the few robust actions taken by the Home Secretary to address deep-seated police corruption was the appointment of the Deputy Commissioner, Robert Mark, as Commissioner of the Met on 17 April 1972. As a former Chief Constable of Leicester City Police, Mark brought with him contempt for the arrogance of the Met and deep distrust of their practices.[52] Mark found that his major task was to deal with what *he* described as the 'most routinely corrupt organisation in

[45] For one account of the early history, see John Parris, *Under My Wig* (Arthur Barker 1961) who described 'closed door' negotiations as 'not infrequent' 52–53.

[46] See Graham Parker, 'Copping a Plea' (1971) 135 Justice of the Peace and Local Government Review 408.

[47] *R v Peace* (1975) *The Times* (November 28) *per* Widgery LCJ 52–53. For a review of early practices, see Philip Thomas, 'An Exploration of Plea Bargaining' [1969] Criminal Law Review 68; Anthony Davies, 'Sentences for Sale: A New Look at Plea Bargaining in England and America' [1970] Criminal Law Review 150; John Baldwin and Mike McConville, *Negotiated Justice* (Martin Robertson 1977); Philip Thomas, 'Plea Bargaining in England' (1978) 69(2) Journal of Law and Criminology 169.

[48] For other examples see Thomas Grant, *Jeremy Hutchinson's Case Histories* (John Murray 2015) 281, 311.

[49] (1970) Cr App R 100.

[50] (1970) 54 Cr App R 352.

[51] See ch 8 and the discussion in Mike McConville and Luke Marsh, *Criminal Judges* (Edward Elgar 2014) 66–73.

[52] This distrust was widely shared by provincial forces: Robert Parker, *Rough Justice* (Fontana 1981); Maurice Punch, *Conduct Unbecoming: The Social Construction of Police Deviance* (Tavistock 1985). One source of disquiet was that provincial forces were open to investigation by another force which in serious cases meant the Met.

London'—the CID. Rather than taking the hazardous route of prosecuting 'bent' officers, Mark called them in and told them that they should resign or face disciplinary action. As Commissioner, his hands were soon full.[53]

The period began with another newspaper scoop, this time by the *Sunday People* which, in February 1972, revealed that Commander Drury, Head of the Met's elite Flying Squad, had gone on holiday with a leading Soho pornographer, James Humphreys.[54] Mark forced the suspension of Drury and appointed Gilbert Kelland, a Deputy Assistant Commissioner, to investigate allegations of bribery and corruption among West End detectives. After three years' investigation, during which time many suspect officers had retired after being tipped off by other corrupt officers, Humphrey's house was raided: his diary showed regular 'payoffs' to seventeen police officers, including Drury, Moody, and Virgo.[55] Activities of the so-called 'Dirty-Squad' were, however, more than matched by those of the Drugs Squad.

Although there had been persistent complaints about Drug Squad officers planting drugs on innocent people, 'licensing' certain drugs-dealers in return for information, and seizing drugs from others to recycle them back onto the streets,[56] their downfall was caused by the fact that the importation of drugs was also investigated by HM Customs & Excise. After Customs had intercepted drug transactions managed or overseen by the head of the Drugs Squad, DCI Victor Kelaher,[57] Kelaher was transferred to administrative duties but such was the autonomy of the Met that the Home Office could do little other than tell Scotland Yard that the methods employed by Drug Squad officers should not be encouraged. The conviction of a major drug smuggler, Basil Sands, set another milestone because Kelaher's evidence at court, that Sands was an informant rather than a dealer, was rejected and this made an outside inquiry into practices at the Met inevitable.[58]

In September 1972, Kelaher and five other detectives were tried for conspiring to pervert the course of justice and all except Kelaher with various counts of perjury. The prosecution case itself was seriously hampered by one of its own witnesses, Commander Virgo, whose evidence in effect was 'defence-evidence' supportive of the six officers. The jury was not to know that Virgo was corrupt and would later face trial himself. Three of the officers were convicted of perjury but all, including

[53] During his time in office, Mark got rid of some 500 officers through dismissal or required resignation.

[54] Extraordinarily, Drury signed the hotel register with his full police rank and gave 'Scotland Yard' as his address: Cox and others, *Scotland Yard* (n 27) 188. See also, Graeme McLagan, *Bent Coppers: The Inside Story of Scotland Yard's Battle Against Police Corruption* (Orion 2004) (hereafter *McLagan, Bent Coppers*). McLagan gives an extended account of corruption from the 1970s through to 2001.

[55] Internal DPP files on Virgo have been sealed until January 2047. See National Archives, DPP 2/5763.

[56] See also Maurice Punch, *Police Corruption* (Routledge 2009).

[57] Officers in the Drugs Squad said that involvement in such transactions was the best way to catch the big fish.

[58] Following the inquiry by Lancashire police detectives, no action was taken against Kelaher.

Kelaher, were acquitted of conspiracy. The Yard finessed the exit of Kelaher by giving him a medical discharge.[59]

Despite these events, the Met emerged with most of the dirt swept under the carpet. The Home Office detachment from operational policing left it reliant on 'intelligence' provided all too frequently by misinformation and lies supplied from senior sources within the Met[60] and ineffectual police-led investigations;[61] as it began to sense the depth of wrongdoing,[62] it lacked the resolve to confront the all-powerful Met.

Mark, who had established a new department (A10) to investigate all complaints against officers,[63] undermined from within, resigned after five years, with bad practice and allegations of corruption given a new lease of life and repeated internal investigations hitting the buffers. Most significant was the investigation ('Operation Countryman') set up by Mark's successor, David McNee, headed by Leonard Burt, then Assistant Chief Constable of Dorset, into allegations[64] involving both City of London officers and members of the Met's elite Flying Squad. In short, it was alleged that officers were deeply involved in major armed robberies (one in May 1978 in which a security guard was shot dead), receiving bribes from criminals, dropping charges against/not opposing bail in respect of known criminals, and fabricating evidence against innocent individuals. The investigation was treated with derision by the Met and actively obstructed, files being stolen and other evidence going missing.[65] The trials of the eight Met officers all ended in acquittals[66] although two other officers were convicted.[67]

As was clear from the Sheffield abuses, police wrongdoing was not confined to London and more was to follow. Indeed, not long after the new Rules came into force, equally startling revelations came to light with the Leeds Police being accurately described as having 'paraded a thoroughly unattractive collection of incidents

[59] The Minister of State at the Home Office, Alex Lyon, confirmed that he had been informed by the Commissioner that had Kelaher not resigned 'serious allegations would have been made against him in disciplinary proceedings': Hansard (14 May 1974) 1262.

[60] See Morton, *Bent Coppers* (n 33) 136.

[61] Among other inquiries at the time was that led by the Chief Constable of Kent.

[62] Cox and others make various references to the Home Office having a dossier on officers of the Drugs Squad: *Scotland Yard* (n 27) 108 145.

[63] Prior to this, although the Commissioner was responsible for force discipline, allegations of criminal conduct against officers were the responsibility of the CID: Dick Hobbs, *Doing the Business* (OUP 1988).

[64] Some of these allegations came from 'super-grasses' (usually serious professional criminals) who had been cultivated to inform on other criminals.

[65] A full picture is not available because Operation Countryman files are sealed until 2047: National Archives, HO 287/2970. A detailed account of the background to Operation Countryman is provided by Duncan Campbell and Rob Evans, 'Files Shed Light on Alleged Efforts to Hide 1970s Police Corruption' *The Guardian* (19 August 2018) (hereafter *Campbell and Evans*, 'Efforts to Hide 1970s Police Corruption'). See also *McLagan, Bent Coppers* (n 54)).

[66] Subsequently, however, three of the officers were dismissed following disciplinary hearings, one resigned, and four resumed duty. See, Morton, *Bent Coppers* (n 33) 150.

[67] For detailed accounts, see Morton, *Bent Coppers* (ibid) 150–53 and *Campbell and Evans*, 'Efforts to Hide 1970s Police Corruption' (n 65).

which virtually covered the spectrum of corruption a force could reasonably manage'.[68] These incidents included theft, forgery, burglary, and bribery. Following an outside investigation,[69] Inspector Ellerker[70] and Sergeant Kitching were convicted in 1971 of a series of assaults on David Oluwale, a homeless Nigerian immigrant, but acquitted of his manslaughter on the direction of the judge.[71]

Not to be outdone, in the 1970s and 80s, the West Midlands Serious Crime Squad embarked on a campaign of brutality towards suspects and persons detained[72] including beatings, placing plastic bags over their heads until they virtually lost consciousness, conducting mock executions, burning skin with cigarettes, taking them to roof tops and threatening to throw them off, and putting guns into their mouths with threats to shoot unless a confession was forthcoming.[73] All this occurred with startling repetition in the most serious offences, including terrorism and armed robbery. Other police forces showed similar disregard for the Judges' Rules, the improprieties becoming public only years later.[74]

Judicial Attitudes

Setting aside corruption, research showed that the police utilized their own 'working rules' making it difficult, as judges knew well, for suspects to see a solicitor.[75] Yet, despite these practices and the catalogue of proven police misconduct the CLRC proposals received support from judicial heavyweights such as Lords Diplock and Hailsham and judges at all levels shored up police evidence at trial.[76]

68 Morton, *Bent Coppers* (n 33) 129

69 In the course of the inquiry, over 1,000 members of the Leeds Police were traced and interviewed, over 1,500 statements taken, and 1,000 documentary exhibits checked: National Archives, MEPO 26/55; DPP 2/4910–12.

70 At the time, Ellerker was serving a prison sentence for his part in a conspiracy to prevent a charge of causing death by dangerous driving being brought against a Superintendent of the Leeds City Police.

71 See further Kester Aspden, *The Hounding of David Oluwale* (Vintage 2008).

72 In some cases innocent people were simply 'fitted up'.

73 Chris Mullin, *Error of Judgement: Truth About the Birmingham Bombings* (Chatto & Windus 1986) (hereafter Mullin, *Error of Judgement*); Gareth Peirce, 'The Birmingham Six: Have We Learned from Our Disgraceful Past?' *The Guardian* (12 March 2011).

74 See, eg, *R v Alan Richardson* [2004] EWCA Crim 1784, a case involving Nottinghamshire Police in 1986 prior to PACE coming into force. See also the West Yorkshire Police in the case of Stefan Kiszko, convicted in 1976 of a murder he could not have committed. See also Satish Sekar, *The Cardiff Five* (Waterside Press 2012); Jon Robbins, *The First Miscarriage of Justice* (Waterside Press 2014); Richard Horwell, *Mouncher Investigation Report* (HC 292, 2017).

75 See John Baldwin and Mike McConville, *Jury Trials* (Clarendon Press 1979); Paul Softley, *Police Interrogation: An Observational Study in Four Police Stations* (HMSO 1990); Carole Willis, *The Tape-Recording of Police Interviews with Suspects: An Interim Report*, Home Office Research Study No 82 (HMSO 1984); Anthony Bottomley and others, *The Impact of PACE: Policing in a Northern Force* (Hull Centre for Criminology and Criminal Justice (1991)); David Brown, *Investigating Burglary: The Effects of PACE*, Home Office Research Study No 123 (Home Office 1989).

76 Pre-PACE, the police practice of 'verballing' was facilitated by a refusal to exclude evidence, despite flagrant breaches of the Judges' Rules.

Thus, when cases rested primarily upon police evidence, some trial judges fell over backwards to negate defence challenges. In the Birmingham Six case (1975), for example, Bridge J told the jury that, if the defendants were telling the truth, the police had been involved in a conspiracy 'unprecedented in the annals of criminal history'. The allegations involved, he said:[77]

> ... giving perjured evidence in which the police must have spent many hours ... trying to ensure that their various lies would accord with each other ... Consider the scale of the conspiracy in terms of those involved, it ranges does it not, from detective constables and police constables right up through the police hierarchy ... Consider, lastly, the subtle artistry that has gone into the preparation of these statements, if indeed they are works of fiction. If the evidence of the defendants is true, it shows the police not only to be masters of the vile techniques of cruelty and brutality to suspects. It shows them to have a lively and inventive imagination.

Bridge was quite right—but it was a description of what the police *actually did*. When the Six appealed, Widgery LCJ said, shamefully, (referring to one of the men's black eye inflicted during police custody) that this was nothing 'beyond the ordinary'. When the Home Secretary sent the case back to the Appeal Court in 1987, the new LCJ, Lord Lane, outdid Bridge saying that defence expert witnesses (who destroyed prosecution 'scientific' evidence) were either lying or mistaken. And in an ancillary civil case, Lord Denning, notoriously denied the Birmingham Six legal aid on the grounds that if they won it would be an 'appalling vista' that could not be allowed to happen. This disposition towards the police, while simply examples of judicial bias in summing up cases to the jury[78] and on appeal,[79] sustained the Judges' Rules well beyond their shelf life.

Moreover, senior judges did more than the police could reasonably expect of them by maintaining the Judges' Rules in form while depriving them of substance in, for example, the practices of 'detaining' individuals to carry out further inquiries, preventing a suspect from securing bail at court, or denying access to a solicitor. Thus, in *Lemsatef*,[80] the Court of Appeal provided recipe answers that

[77] See Mullin, *Error of Judgement* (n 73) 201.

[78] See, eg, *R v Berrada (Rachid)* (1990) 91 Cr App R 131.

[79] See, eg, the summing up of Cusack J in the *Cooper and McMahon* murder trial (1969) who told the jury that to believe, as the defence asserted, that the key prosecution witness, Mathews, had falsely implicated three innocent men would be 'wicked beyond belief'. In fact, Mathews was a professional criminal, had committed the crime himself (with others unknown because of police complicity), was in the pay of a corrupt police officer, Commander Drury of Scotland Yard's Flying Squad, who was later sent to prison for corruption. See also the Bridgewater Four case (1979) in which Drake J commented to the jury about a prosecution witness with convictions totalling 34 offences with 139 others having been 'taken into consideration' and having been sentenced to a total of nine years in prison: 'Perhaps you found his evidence unusually convincing for a man of his background': Paul Foot, *Murder at the Farm* (Sidgwick & Jackson 1986) 164, 177.

[80] (1977) 2 All ER 835.

officers could give *irrespective of the facts* to cover non-compliance with the Rules. In *Stephen King*,[81] where the police admitted not informing the suspect of his right to consult a solicitor, the Court of Appeal perversely ruled that the police were under no such obligation in the absence of the suspect himself first raising the matter. Given this background, it is hardly surprising that as the judges mocked their own Rules the police regarded them with contempt.

End of the Rules

Despite the efforts of judges, reform was eventually precipitated by a single case. This arose out of the death of Maxwell Confait in April 1972. As a result of alleged confessions, Ronald Leighton (aged 15) and Colin Lattimore (aged 18) were charged with Confait's murder and, with Ahmet Salih (aged 14), with arson of the premises where Confait's body was found. After years of lobbying by the families and their MP, Christopher Price, the Court of Appeal found the lynch-pin of the prosecution case destroyed by new medical evidence and, accordingly, the admissions relied upon by the Crown could not be true. The resulting public clamour forced the establishment of an inquiry by a former High Court judge, Sir Henry Fisher.

Fisher concluded that the Judges' Rules and police actions were deficient in fundamental respects.[82] Key elements of the Rules were (apparently) not known to police officers, others were misunderstood. Fisher identified deficiencies which, for example, permitted officers to extend the period of questioning by delaying a charge; and in enforcement procedures which were neither certain nor regularly applied. Although Fisher diluted the findings by concluding (erroneously) that the boys were *probably guilty* (the civil standard) of various offences,[83] the government was forced to establish a Royal Commission on Criminal Procedure (RCCP) whose Report ultimately led to the Police and Criminal Evidence Act 1984 (PACE) and the replacement of the Judges' Rules with statutory rules and Codes of Practice.

The regime introduced by PACE contained elements which resembled the Judges' Rules as first proposed by the judges (see Chapter 5) before they buckled to 'police interests'. Thus, under PACE, a 'Custody Officer' is responsible for overseeing the actions of investigating officers and for the welfare of detainees in broadly the same way, as in 1962, the judges envisaged the role of the 'Station Officer'. Likewise, whereas the judges had proposed that Station Officers should have charge of an *Investigation*

[81] [1978] Crim L R 632.

[82] The Fisher Inquiry heard evidence of prosecution wrongdoing, including police breaches of the Rules, alteration of police records, unreliable 'expert' evidence, and improper conduct by prosecuting counsel.

[83] See the devastating critique by Doreen McBarnet, 'The Fisher Report on the Confait Case; Four Issues' [1978] 41(4) Modern Law Review 455.

Occurrence Book in which the actions of investigating officers were to be recorded, under PACE Custody Officers have similar responsibilities over the *Custody Record*.[84] In place of an indeterminate right, section 58 PACE also granted suspects a right to consult a solicitor privately at any time. Although there were caveats which did not make this right unqualified and police practices could easily undercut it,[85] the PACE provision was clearly a significant advance on the Judges' Rules.

Police Lobbying

PACE was not a charter for individual rights. Instead, it was influenced by a police campaign that had started with the 1973 Dimbleby Lecture of Sir Robert Mark[86] and with political responses (primed again by police lobbying) following major street disorders in 1981.

In a highly polemical and one-sided[87] assault, Mark argued, without supporting evidence, that the rate of acquittals ('*whom experienced police officers believe to be guilty*') was unacceptably high in a system of trial 'so inefficient that it lets [criminals] go free';[88] and one constantly and 'ruthlessly exploited by the knowledgeable criminal and his advisers' with some lawyers labelled 'more harmful to society than the clients they represent'.[89] Mark's cynicism extended to the jury which, he argued,

[84] In the pre-Custody Record era, an occurrence book would be kept, but was filled in at random, with no pro forma columns and no time stamp requirement, or rule that it had to be filled in contemporaneously, giving it limited evidential value. In short, the occurrence book bore the trademark of the Judges' Rules regime: police were not properly regulated, facilitating if not encouraging abuse of their power, and they presented suspect evidence, which was generally approved and protected by the judiciary.

[85] Research studies showed that, following PACE, access to a solicitor increased significantly: David Brown, *Detention at the Police Station under the Police and Criminal Evidence Act 1984* (HMSO 1989); Andrew Sanders and others, *Advice and Assistance at Police Stations under the 24-Hour Duty Solicitor Scheme* (Lord Chancellor's Department 1989). Where they felt it helpful, officers continued to use 'ploys' to avoid the presence of a solicitor and many of those who attended in the early years were not legally qualified advisers: John Baldwin, 'Legal Advice in the Police Station' (1992) 142 New Law Journal 1762; David Dixon, 'Common Sense, Legal Advice and the Right to Silence' [1991] 7 Public Law 233 (hereafter Dixon, *Right to Silence*); and Mike McConville and Jacqueline Hodgson, *Custodial Legal Advice and the Right to Silence* (HMSO 1993). For research data on the practices of solicitors, see Mike McConville and others, *Standing Accused: The Organisation and Practices of Criminal Defence Lawyers in Britain* (OUP 1994) (hereafter McConville and others, *Standing Accused*); Daniel Newman, *Legal Aid Lawyers and the Quest for Justice* (Hart 2013); Hannah Quirk, *The Rise and Fall of the Right of Silence: Principle, Politics and Policy* (Routledge 2016) (hereafter Quirk, *Right of Silence*).

[86] Robert Mark, *Minority Verdict*, BBC Dimbleby Lecture (1973).

[87] Mark prefaced his lecture with the claim that '[t]he fact that the British police are answerable to the law, that we act on behalf of the community and not under the mantle of Government, makes us the least powerful, the most accountable and therefore the most acceptable police in the world.' While Mark conceded some blame lay with police, he was quick to mitigate: '... the criminal trial has come to be regarded as a game of skill and chance in which the rules are binding on one side only. It is hardly surprising that a policeman's belief in its fairness should decline as he gathers experience, or that he should be tempted to depart from the rules' ibid 4.

[88] ibid 5.

[89] ibid 10

was acquitting too many guilty people. Other, newly empowered, police chiefs joined Mark in lobbying for greater powers and reduced individual rights,[90] his successor, David McNee, admitting that police officers (whom, he took the view, lacked adequate powers) had manipulated the law with methods that bordered on 'trickery and stealth'.[91] He did not explain why they could be trusted to comply with any wider powers that they might be granted.

PACE came on the back of widespread public uprisings involving street disorders against heavy-handed and discriminatory police practices particularly involving members of the black community.[92] Indicative of concern in London were the activities of the Special Patrol Group (SPG) consisting of mobile units deployed to deal with demonstrations or potential public disorder. Following the killing of Blair Peach in 1979 by a Met police officer's truncheon, a raid on the police lockers of the SPG unit believed responsible found a stockpile of 'weapons' including a rhino whip, leather-encased truncheons, and a lead-weighted leather stick.[93]

Concerns about policing in London (and elsewhere) were not confined to the SPG or to individual cases: there had been a build-up in tension,[94] particularly with the black community, arising out of differential stop and search[95] tactics and other discriminatory policies. Major street disorders broke out in Brixton, London in April 1981 following saturation policing ('Operation Swamp 81') under which, within a few days, almost 1,000 people were stopped by officers (plain clothes and

[90] The enhanced power of police chiefs resulted from the reorganization of police forces following the Police Act 1964 which reduced the number of police forces from 117 to 49, with further reductions to 43.

[91] See Michael Freeman, 'Law and Order in 1984' (1984) Current Legal Problems 175.

[92] See, eg, John Brown, *Policing by Multi-Racial Consent* (Bedford Square Press 1982).

[93] Conor Foley, 'Police Violence and Death: An Old Story' *The Guardian* (26 April 2009); Paul Lewis, 'Blair Peach Killed by Police at 1979 Protest, Met Report Finds' *The Guardian* (27 April 2010). An investigation, withheld for more than twenty years and available only in redacted form, found that the SPG had lied to investigating officers: FOI Request by David Cinzano and can be accessed here: by following this link <https://www.whatdotheyknow.com/request/193807/response/474577/attach/3/report%20 23aug1999%20pseudonyms.pdf> accessed 1 January 2020.

[94] Major street disorders broke out in 1958 following prolonged racist attacks by white gangs on West Indian people in Notting Hill in London and Nottingham. See Martin Kettle and Lucy Hodges *Uprising!* (Pan Books 1982); and David Cowell and others, *Policing the Riots* (Junction Books 1982). The police covered over the racism involved by depicting the Notting Hill disorders as the work of 'ruffians, both coloured and white' when they were overwhelmingly the work of white racists. See Alan Travis, 'After 44 Years Secret Papers Reveal Truth about Five Nights of Violence in Notting Hill' *The Guardian* (24 August 2002).

[95] Under so-called 'sus' laws based on the Metropolitan Police Act 1839. Research showed that most stops were disproportionately on black people: Policy Studies Institute, *Police and People in London* (1983); Carole Willis, *The Use, Effectiveness and Impact of Police Stop and Search Powers*, Home Office Research and Planning Unit Paper No 15 (1983). The position is deteriorating. The latest figures for England and Wales for 2017–18 show that black people are nine and a half times more likely to be stopped and searched than their white counterparts, more than double the rate for the year 2014–15: <ethnicity-facts-figures.service.gov.uk/crime-justice-and-the-law/policing/stop-and-search/latest> accessed 1 January 2020. This is despite the fact that drugs were less likely to be found on black people than on white people: Her Majesty's Inspectorate of Constabulary and Fire and Rescue Services, *Annual Report* (2017).

SPG) and over eighty arrested.[96] The scale of disorders led to an inquiry by Lord Scarman whose Report was published in November 1981.[97] The relatively modest proposals, involving such things as a greater emphasis upon community policing and greater police accountability to local communities, were, however, quickly overwhelmed by a concerted police lobby for more police powers.

The extended powers in PACE came directly out of the informal 'police handbook' which depicted crime as escalating out of control with a heavy emphasis (contradicted by official research[98]) upon inner-city black youths as responsible particularly for street robberies. Led by police briefings, saturation press coverage created a moral panic around street crime and black people.[99] On the back of this, David McNee produced a 'Shopping List' to the Royal Commission. The success of the campaign is seen in new powers in PACE[100] which included extended powers of stop and search which then provided the platform for further discriminatory police interventions.

Demands for Change Continued

Although the Judges' Rules were jettisoned, they still influenced law reform debate. Police lobbying[101] continued and in this they were joined by the government and the judges. Collectively, they worked to undermine the protective elements of PACE, in particular, the right to silence. Indeed, the starting gun was set in 1987 when the Home Secretary announced a re-examination of the right to silence only a year after the coming into effect of PACE (on 1 January 1986) and established a Home Office Working Group not to examine but to consider how best to curtail the right to silence.[102] It was open season on individual rights.

The judges now formally entered the fray. In *Alladice*,[103] where the suspect had been improperly denied access to a solicitor, Lane LCJ added to the decision a rider

[96] Evidence of broader dissatisfaction with policing came in July 1981 with major street disorders in other cities including Birmingham, Bristol, Leeds, Leicester, Liverpool, Manchester, and Nottingham.

[97] Lord Scarman, *The Brixton Disorders 1–12 April 1981* (HMSO 1981).

[98] Philip Stevens and Carole Willis, *Race Crime and Arrests* Home Office Research Study No 48 (HMSO 1979) demonstrated that black people were not disproportionately involved in street crime.

[99] See, eg, Peter Burden, 'More and More Muggers: But the Police Fight Back' *Daily Mail* (21 January 1982); 'Muggings of Women Double' *Daily Telegraph* (4 February 1982); 'The Menace of the Muggers' *The Sun* (18 February 1982). The Police Federation took out advertisements in national newspapers attacking Labour politicians and siding with Conservatives and the 'rule of law': Robert Reiner, *The Politics of the Police* (3rd edn, OUP 1985). See also the excellent account in Joe Sim, 'Scarman: The Police Counter-Attack' (1982) Socialist Register 57.

[100] Others included taking bodily samples from persons suspected of involvement in serious arrestable offences (s 63 PACE), subsequently extended by the Criminal Justice Act 2003 and modified by the Crime and Security Act 2010.

[101] See, Paul Keel, 'Senior Police to Call for End of Right to Silence' *The Guardian* (22 September 1987).

[102] Home Office, *Report of the Working Group on the Right to Silence* (HMSO 1989).

[103] (1988) 87 Cr App R 380. See further Steven Greer, 'The Right to Silence: A Review of the Current Debate' (1990) 53(6) Modern Law Review 22 (hereafter Greer, 'Right to Silence').

on behalf of the whole Court ['*per curiam*'] in relation to the relevant provision (PACE section 58(1): 'A person arrested and held in custody in a police station or other premises shall be entitled, if he so requests, to consult a solicitor privately at any time') that:

> It was high time that a proper comment was permitted on the silence of a detainee when interviewed by police but who produced at his trial an explanation of or defence to the charge which the police had had no chance to verify. The effect of section 58 of the 1984 Act was such that the balance of fairness between prosecution and defence could not be maintained unless such comment was permitted...

This high-level intervention,[104] however, soon appeared to be a cry in the dark as the criminal justice system was rocked by miscarriages of justice on a scale and seriousness greater than ever. The ignominious collapse of the corrupt West Midlands Serious Crime Squad[105] and overturning of the convictions arising out of bombings in the Guildford Four (1989), Maguire Seven, Birmingham Six (1991) cases and cases dealt with by the West Midlands Drug Squad[106] laid bare police practices (involving torture, brutality, coerced confessions, denial of legal advice, and perjury[107]) which set the protective regime of the Judges' Rules and PACE to nought. The establishment of another inquiry was inevitable.

The resulting Royal Commission on Criminal Justice (RCCJ)[108] established in 1991 was itself soon surrounded by an avalanche of similar miscarriages of justice[109]

[104] Lane reinforced his opposition to the right to silence in a speech to the Bar Council in 1987. Subsequently, Lane had to recuse himself from hearing the appeals in the Winchester Three case because of comments he had previously made advocating attenuating the right to silence. See Clare Dyer, 'Lane "Ruled Himself out of Appeal"' *The Guardian* (28 April 1990).

[105] See Tim Kaye, *Unsafe and Unsatisfactory? Report of the Independent Inquiry into the Working Practices of the West Midlands Police Serious Crime Squad* (Civil Liberties Trust 1991).

[106] See *R v Fraser* [2003] EWCA Crim 3180.

[107] See, eg, the material contained in the following sample of cases dealt with on appeal: *R v Twitchell* [2000] 1 Cr App R 373; *R v Dunne, Dunne, Brown and Gaughan* [2001] EWCA Crim 169; *R v Irvine* [2002] EWCA Crim 29; *R v Hagans and Wilson* [2003] EWCA Crim 3358; *R v O'Toole and Murphy* [2006] EWCA Crim 951; *R v Brown* [2006] EWCA Crim 141; *R v McCloy* [2007] EWCA Crim 1263; *R v Foran* [2013] EWCA Crim 437 and [2014] EWCA Crim 2047.

[108] The RCCJ (hereafter RCCJ) (1993)) was set up on the day the Birmingham Six convictions were quashed and reported in 1993 as required by its remit. For an excellent review of the background and surrounding debates see Quirk, *Right of Silence* (n 85).

[109] The Maguire Seven (1991); Tottenham Three (1991); Stefan Kiszko (1992); Darvell Brothers (1992); Taylor Sisters (1993); Ivan Fergus (1993); Cardiff Three (1993); Judith Ward (1993); and the cascade of cases arising out of activities of the West Midlands Serious Crime Squad (beginning with the case of Paul Dandy, HC Deb 25 January 1989, vol 145, cols 155–60 (hereafter *Paul Dandy*), and now numbering over thirty-four quashed by the Court of Appeal as well as others discontinued once the bad practices had come to light). Other miscarriages may come to light only by accident, as with Stephen Simmons convicted of mail bag thefts in 1975 on the false evidence of a Detective Sergeant Derek Ridgewell who was the real thief and who framed a number of innocent people for thefts he himself had perpetrated. See Duncan Campbell, 'Man Convicted of Theft in 1976 Cleared after Googling his Arresting Officer' *The Guardian* (17 January 2018) . Ridgewell was also responsible for notorious cases in which young black people were falsely accused of 'mugging' offences. See Winston Trew, *Black*

which appeared to demand a strengthening of the protections for suspects.[110] Many illegal police practices continued despite legislative 'reform' in PACE. Thus, in the Met, Winston Silcott, Engin Raghip, and Mark Braithwaite were convicted in 1987 of the murder of PC Blakelock on statements to which key incriminating passages were later added by police officers. Furthermore, a corruption inquiry, 'Operation Jackpot', centred on Stoke Newington police station, unearthed evidence of widespread planting of evidence resulting in more than ten individuals having their convictions quashed for serious offences including manslaughter and drugs offences.[111] In the West Midlands, discreditable tactics continued to be applied as normal: an original interview record 'disappeared' after evidence showed that the 'confession' had been forged by the police;[112] interview records were falsified and forensic evidence fabricated;[113] interview notes disappeared from court files[114] as did statements; off-the-record interviews were conducted; and officers intimidated suspects to obtain confessions and falsified custody records.[115]

However, another significant intervention came as the RCCJ was deliberating which helped undercut the right to silence; and, once again, it was from the senior judiciary. Taylor LCJ argued that the biggest inducement to police investigative malpractices was the alleged tilting of the rules in the defendant's favour. In particular, because the suspect had a right to silence and the police ('not always intelligent chaps') were exposed to cross-examination, Taylor argued that the police 'try and make up for it by other means' which would not happen if the suspect's right was attenuated.[116] Once again, police contempt for the law was held as a justification for greater police powers.

Against this background, and without examining cases of miscarriages of justice,[117] the RCCJ proposed shoring up 'plea bargaining' and, while equivocal

for a Cause. Not Just Because: The Case of the 'Oval 4' and the Story It Tells of Black Power in 1970s Britain (Black for a Cause 2015).

[110] The RCCJ (1993) (n 108) did not, however, analyse the miscarriages of justice. See Mike McConville and Lee Bridges, *Criminal Justice in Crisis* (Edward Elgar 1994); Mike Maguire and Clive Norris, 'Police Investigations: Practice and Malpractice' (1994) 21 Journal of Law and Society 72.

[111] See, eg, Terry Kirby, 'Two Cleared over "Tainted Police Evidence": Convictions Quashed after Court of Appeal Told Officers Could Not Be Relied Upon' *The Independent* (15 December 1993). See further Matthew Brace, 'PC Gets 10 years for Drug Smuggling' *The Independent* (25 February 1997); 'Malicious Officer Caught out by Bad Spelling' *The Times* (29 July 2017).

[112] *Paul Dandy* (n 109).

[113] The case of Ronald Bolden (1989) acquitted of bank robberies in Birmingham.

[114] The case of Michael Bromwell.

[115] See, eg, Mike McConville, 'Videotaping Interrogations: Police Behaviour on and off Camera' [1992] Criminal Law Review 552.

[116] See Hugo Young 'In Tune with the Times' *Guardian Weekly* (2 August 1992).

[117] In fairness, the files would have been sealed by the Home Office. Space precludes a full record of miscarriages of justice arising from police failures, which abound: for example, Stephen Downing, a seventeen-year-old with learning difficulties was wrongly convicted and imprisoned for twenty-seven years for the murder of a female office worker, following 'substantial and significant breaches of the Judges' rules' including being questioned without his lawyer (or guardian) and pressured into signing a confession: *R v Stephen Downing* [2002] EWCA Crim 263; Eddie Browning, wrongly convicted for the

about the right to silence, failed to support it in terms of principle as set out by the RCCP only ten years earlier.[118] Meanwhile, the government laid the foundations for future changes in England and Wales by pushing ahead with Northern Ireland legislation which curtailed the right to silence in cases of terrorism and other serious violence.[119] Back in the United Kingdom, the Home Secretary announced that the right would be limited.[120]

The Immediate Legacy

The process of the establishment and revision of the Judges' Rules reinforced the retreat from individual rights and left clear marks on the legal regime that followed. While PACE in general[121] had a greater effect upon police compliance with investigative procedures[122] than was the case with the Judges' Rules (though violations continue to occur with worrying frequency) and newly acquired police pragmatism[123] in this respect has helped in routine cases,[124] this is in large measure attributable to the weakening of the position of both suspects and defence lawyers. These changes, documented elsewhere,[125] include:

- Attenuation of the right to silence[126]

murder of a pregnant mother in 1989, was released from prison in 1994 by the Court of Appeal, which was critical of the police for withholding vital evidence from the trial: *R v Browning* NLJ 661; *The Times* 14 May 1994.

[118] See Greer, 'Right to Silence' (n 103) 709.

[119] Criminal Evidence (Northern Ireland) Order 1988, No 1987 N I 20. On this, see John Jackson, 'Recent Developments in Criminal Evidence' (1989) 40 Northern Ireland Legal Quarterly 26; John Jackson, 'Curtailing the Right To Silence: Lessons from Northern Ireland' [1991] Criminal Law Review 404; John Jackson, 'Silence Legislation in Northern Ireland: The Impact after Ten Years' (2010) 6(2) Journal of Civil Liberties 134.

[120] See Anthony Scrivener, 'Tough Justice on the Cheap' *The Independent* (7 October 1993).

[121] See the detailed evidence in Quirk, *Right of Silence* (n 85).

[122] See David Kyle, 'Correcting Miscarriages of Justice: The Role of the Criminal Cases Review Commission' (2004) Drake Law Review 52 657; Layla Skinns, *Police Custody: Governance, Legitimacy and Reform in the Criminal Justice Process* (Willan 2011).

[123] As experience with PACE increased, the police have come to a more realistic appreciation of the investigative value of interrogation without the need for breaches of the rules.

[124] See Dixon, 'Right to Silence' (n 85); Rachel Halliburton, 'When the Law Attacks the Lawyers' *New Statesman* (23 August 1999).

[125] See, eg, McConville and others (1994) *Standing Accused* (n 85); Roger Leng, 'Losing Sight of the Defendant. The Government's Proposals on Pre-Trial Disclosure' (1995) Criminal Law Review 704; Jenny McEwan, 'From Adversarialism to Managerialism: Criminal Justice in Transition' (2011) 31(3) Legal Studies: 519; Jenny McEwan, 'Truth, Efficiency and Co-operation in Modern Criminal Justice' (2013) 66(1) Current Legal Problems 203; and Quirk, *Right of Silence* (n 85). There is an excellent account of the process, in what is styled the 'New Regime', in Ed Johnston, 'The Adversarial Defence Lawyer: Myths, Disclosure and Efficiency—A Contemporary Analysis of the Role in the Era of the Criminal Procedure Rules' (2020) 24(1) The International Journal of Evidence & Proof 35–38 (hereafter Johnston '*Adversarial Defence*').

[126] By virtue of the Criminal Justice and Public Order Act 1994 (CJPOA) subsequently replaced by the Criminal Justice Act 2003; for an excellent review of the Northern Ireland legislation and the debate: John

- Strengthening of the state-induced guilty plea system[127]
- Broadening of rules requiring defence disclosure[128]
- Initiation of rules requiring a statement outlining the defence to be run at trial[129]
- Weakening of the position of defence representatives[130]
- Constructing trial judges as managers[131]

These changes, some crucially supported by,[132] some sponsored by,[133] and others unopposed[134] by judges themselves, have collectively acted to decentre the interrogation process (and the trial itself) by weakening the position of suspects, defendants, and their lawyers and to restructure trial judges as enforcers of an

Jackson, 'Inferences from Silence: From Common Law to Common Sense' (1993) 44 Northern Ireland Legal Quarterly 44 103. See also the foundational study of Roger Leng, *The Right to Silence in Police Interrogation: A Study of some of the Issues Underlying the Debate*, The Royal Commission on Criminal Justice Research Study No 10 (1993). See also Greer, 'Right to Silence' (n 103) 709; and Michael Zander, 'Abandoning an Ancient Right to Please the Police' *The Independent* (6 October 1993).

[127] See *R v Goodyear* (2005) EWCA Crim 888. In practice, however, the formalities of *Goodyear* may be bypassed as where a general inquiry led to the trial judge wrongly giving a sentence indication in ignorance of the exact nature of any pleas and without inviting prosecuting counsel to make any submission or to contribute one way or the other: see *R v Parish and Redford* [2017] EWCA Crim 2064.

[128] Defence statement provisions began by reference to the need for the defence to justify disclosure requests, and the consequent need to give notice of relevant issues for that purpose. Now, the defence statement is commonly treated as evidence in itself, often incriminatory (eg, discrepancies, omissions etc) and it often creeps into trials as the equivalent of a signed statement. The real point of concern therefore is not the initiation of a rule requiring a defence statement, but scope for unfounded, adverse comment as to content. The defendant does not draft the defence statement. It is often compiled in a background of drip feed prosecution disclosure, and ordered to be served before the reality of the prosecution case is known to the defence. The growing need for defendants (some with intellectual limitations) to explain the content, language, and constraints of a legal document is unjustified and unfair. The case law is far from easy to reconcile. See *Firth v Epping Magistrates' Court* [2011] EWHC 388 (Admin) and *R v Newell* [2012] EWCA Crim 650. See also *Phillips v R* [2007] EWCA Crim 1042. Indeed, the seeds of this cultural shift have germinated farther afield. Citing *R v Chaaban* [2003] EWCA Crim 1012 (hereafter *Chaaban*), the Court of Appeal in Hong Kong argued that a 'change in criminal procedure culture' was 'long overdue' in Hong Kong itself: *HKSAR v Hon Ming Kong* [2014] HKEC 538. See also, *HKSAR v Law Hoi Fu* [2016] 1 HKLRD 504 citing *R v Jisl* [2004] EWCA Crim 696 (hereafter *Jisl*).

[129] See *Rochford* [2010] EWCA Crim 1928. For empirical evidence of the contradictory response of defence lawyers to these new obligations, see Johnston, 'Adversarial Defence' (n 125).

[130] The defence lawyer has been constructed as the carrier of coercive state messages to the defendant. For a comprehensive review of the literature and original empirical data, see Quirk, *Right of Silence* (n 85) 98ff.

[131] See *Chaaban* and *Jisl* (n 128).

[132] The Debate on the Criminal Justice and Public Order Bill was transformed by the artful intervention of Taylor LCJ ('While they are my personal views, I know that they are shared by very many judges') who expressed support for the attenuation of the right to silence. He explained away the many miscarriages of justice that had recently occurred with breathtaking contempt for the facts: 'First [PACE] has introduced a regime of controls over police investigations and questioning which gives much greater protection to a suspect than existed in 1972 [the date of the CLRC's Eleventh Report]. As the noble Viscount [Lord Runciman] said, there have been instances where even that Act has not protected the defendant. We are dealing with human institutions': HL Deb 23 May 1994, vol 555, cols 482–537, 519.

[133] Sir Robin Auld, *The Criminal Courts Review* (Royal Courts of Justice 2001) (hereafter Auld, *Review*) was pivotal in the formalization of the modern procedural regime.

[134] For example, there was no judicial opposition to CJPOA. See the excellent review of the legislation and its context in Quirk, *Right of Silence* (n 85).

increasingly non-adversarial process. At the same time, judicial policy-makers (albeit somewhat constrained by European Court of Human Rights jurisprudence)[135] have pushed forward an agenda that has advanced the power of the state and diminished the rights of the individual;[136] not least with the steady development of the Criminal Procedure Rules (CrimPR), through which, in synchronization with executive thinking, the senior judiciary (under the guise of austerity) uncoupled reliance on traditional understandings of adversarial justice and oversaw the weakening of the independent Bar.[137]

The Judicial–Executive Agenda

Synchronization with the executive on measures directed towards a root-and-branch remaking of the criminal justice system is evidenced through the tenor of statutory instruments,[138] and various legislation including those pre-figured or buttressed by programmes,[139] policy papers,[140] reports,[141] reviews,[142] judgments,[143] initiatives,[144] judicial literature,[145] and speeches.[146]

[135] See, eg, *Murray v United Kingdom* A/593 (1996) 22 EHRR 29 holding that convictions must not be based solely or mainly on silence; and *Condron v UK* (2001) 31 EHRR 1 that juries should be specifically directed to take legal advice to remain silent into account.

[136] See Quirk, *Right of Silence* (n 85) 114 on role of the Court of Appeal in interpreting CJPOA.

[137] The defence is undermined by threats of punitive measures including contempt of court and wasted costs orders towards lawyers who simply seek to put the prosecution to proof. Sir Bill Jeffrey, *Independent Criminal Advocacy in England and Wales* (Ministry of Justice 2014). Ed Johnston (2020) in his empirical study of defence lawyers found that there has been a distinct change in adversarial culture and that while a small group of his sample sought to be adversarial these few represented 'a dying, rather than extinct, breed of lawyers in England and Wales' Johnston, 'Adversarial Defence' (n 125) 20.

[138] An example of which is the (now repealed) Prosecution of Offences Act 1985 (Criminal Courts Charge) Regulations 2015 (SI 2015/796) which unashamedly placed pressure on a defendant's plea by charging them a mandatory higher 'administrative' fee for a not-guilty plea than a guilty plea.

[139] The key principles underpinning projects under the Ministry of Justice's *Modernising the Criminal Justice System, The CJS Efficiency Programme* (21 December 2011) (hereafter MoJ, *Efficiency Programme*) were those that 'act as a catalyst for cultural change' and reduce 'waste' 2.

[140] The Home Office's *Way Ahead* (2001) and *Justice for All* (2002) fell in the footsteps of the Auld Review (n 133), borrowing liberally from it.

[141] For example, the Narey Report of 1997 on *Delay in the Criminal Justice System.*

[142] Auld, *Review* (n 133) and Sir Brian Leveson, *Review of Efficiency in Criminal Proceedings* (Judiciary of England & Wales January 2015) (hereafter Leveson, *Review*) represent major staging posts.

[143] For example, in an imitation of the language of the government's report *Delivering Simple, Speedy, Summary* Justice (2006), the President of the Queen's Bench Division, Sir John Thomas (as he was then) in *R (Drinkwater) v Solihull Magistrates' Court* [2012] EWHC 765 (Admin) commented that 'it is self-evident that proceedings in the Magistrates' Courts ought to be simple, speedy and summary'.

[144] Including Magistrate, *Stop Delaying Justice!* (2011) and Ministry of Justice, *Swift and Sure Justice* (2012).

[145] Roderick Denyer, *Case Management in the Crown Court* (Hart 2008).

[146] Sir Igor Judge (shortly before he became LCJ), 'The Criminal Justice System in England and Wales—Greater Efficiency in the Criminal Justice System, Time for Change?' Speech given at University of Sydney in August 2007; The Rt Hon Sir Stanley Burnton, *Delivering Justice in an Age of Austerity* (JUSTICE 2015).

In this new narrative, the system needs to be 'rebalanced',[147] 'reshaped',[148] 'transformed',[149] and endure 'significant retrenchment'.[150] A near perfect alignment of these judicial–executive pronouncements—be it the need for justice which is 'swift',[151] 'sure', 'simple', speedy', or 'streamlined'[152]—reflects a preoccupation with prioritizing both 'cost-efficiency' in the 'business' and 'redistribution' of the criminal courts[153] rather than principled engagement with it. Located within the government discourse of 'austerity'[154] the assertion of judicial figures laying claim to a 'sea-change'[155] or 'new landscape'[156] goes beyond the merely descriptive and is held up to legitimate 'evolutionary'[157] reconfigurations to the blueprint of the system.[158]

Underpinning the judicial–executive strategy are key ideological assumptions as to where system 'failure' is located. Thus, according to Auld, procedural protections are held to offer an unfair advantage to defendants (presumptively guilty and undeserving who seek to exploit the 'weak spots')[159] and their legal representatives,

[147] Rebalancing-the-system rhetoric first arose in *Justice for All* (n 140), framed 'rebalancing the criminal justice system in favour of the victim' as its 'single clear priority' 14.

[148] Thomas LCJ, 'Reshaping Justice' Speech delivered to JUSTICE (3 March 2014) (hereafter Thomas, 'Reshaping Justice').

[149] See, eg, Ministry of Justice, *Transforming Legal Aid: Delivering a more Credible and Efficient System* (2013); Ministry of Justice, *Transforming Summary Justice Initiative* and *Transforming Our Justice System* (2016) (hereafter *ToJS*).

[150] Thomas, 'Reshaping Justice' (n 148).

[151] A phrase that surfaces repeatedly, see, eg, *ToJS* (n 149). cf The account of seasoned criminal lawyer, Michael Proctor: 'Criminals are Not Getting Swift Justice' *CambridgeshireLive* (23 August 2019).

[152] Major streamlining initiatives include *Modernising Charging, Streamlined Process* and *Criminal Justice: Simple, Speedy, Summary*. See MoJ, *Efficiency Programme* (n 139).

[153] While reducing costs is a laudable objective, the evidence, at least in lower courts, suggests the reverse is occurring: Laurence Cawley, 'Magistrate Court Cases Take a Week Longer to Complete' (*BBC News Online*, 17 November 2016).

[154] Involving decreased public funding affecting, *inter alia*, the courts system, police, CPS, the National Offender Management Service, and Legal Aid Agency. See National Audit Office, *Efficiency in the Criminal Justice System* (2016) <https://www.nao.org.uk/wp-content/uploads/2016/03/Efficiency-in-the-criminal-justice-system.pdf> accessed 1 January 2020.

[155] Thomas LJ in *R (on the application of the DPP) v Chorley Justices* [2006] EWHC 1795, 24–25.

[156] Thomas, 'Reshaping Justice' (n 148) 3.

[157] The accompanying notes to the CrimPR, state: 'The Rules promote a culture change in the management of criminal cases, but that change is evolutionary.' However '[the] rules will help the courts to promote the culture change in criminal case management that *the Committee wants*' (emphasis supplied) <www.justice.gov.uk/courts/procedure-rules/criminal/notes> accessed 1 January 2020. In support of this, *Disclosure: A Protocol for the Control and Management of Unused Material in the Crown Court* reads, 'The new regime under the ... Criminal Procedure Rules gives judges the power to change the culture in which such cases are tried.' para 63 <www.judiciary.gov.uk/wp-content/uploads/JCO/Documents/Protocols/crown_courts_disclosure.pdf> accessed 1 January 2020. This is concerning considering the almost unlimited powers judges have been given in codified form: 'the court may give *any* direction and take *any* step actively to manage a case unless that direction or step would be inconsistent with legislation, including these Rules' (CrimPR 3.5(1), emphasis supplied).

[158] 'Culture change' was to prove instrumental in the formal disempowerment of the defence under the CrimPR, as recognized in the government *Justice for All* (n 140): 'These proposals ... are far-reaching, often radical and require a culture shift' 160. Following this, Judge LJ in *Chaaban* (n 128) took the opportunity to 'highlight a significant recent change' which he explained away as 'less heralded than it might have been' 37.

[159] *Justice for All* (n 140) encapsulates this process: it sought 'reduced chances of the accused "playing the system" and escaping justice if guilty' 14; a central contention was that 'the system should not become a game where delay and obstruction can be used as a tactic to avoid a rightful conviction'.

causing 'cracked trials' and other negative features, a line of argument flatly contradicted by the Crown Court Study[160] and Official Statistics[161] and anchored instead in the (pseudo-empirical) premise that '*many in the system believe* that defendants' delayed guilty pleas are a tactic employed in the hope that witnesses will lose patience and decide not to testify'.[162]

Similarly, the traditional role of the defence[163] is held to compromise both the integrity and efficiency of the system. In this regard, Auld LJ cemented the paradigm shift in judicial attitudes with his claim that:

> the 'adversarial dialectic' and the 'principle of orality' have been elevated to ends in themselves rather than means to get at the truth and also, as a result, *discourage modern* and *more efficient ways* of putting evidence before the courts.[164]

This anti-adversarial stance was soon codified with the CrimPR in 2005 and its accompanying Overriding Objective of 'dealing with cases justly' which includes 'acquitting the innocent and convicting the guilty'[165] and 'dealing with the case efficiently and expeditiously' (Rule 1.1(2)(a) and (e)).

Although the robust case management culture demanded by the CrimPR has now concretized itself among a dispirited legal profession,[166] strengthening the underlying message (that the system no longer organizes along lines of intrinsic needs,

[160] Michael Zander and Paul Henderson, *Crown Court Study*, Research Study No 19, The Royal Commission on Criminal Justice (HMSO 1993).

[161] Unlike the Crown Court Study, the Official Statistics do not enable a discrete breakdown of the categories of cracked cases. What the current statistics show clearly is that 15.0 per cent result from the prosecution ending its case and 18.0 per cent from the defendant pleading guilty to an alternative new charge. While the great majority result from a 'late plea' by the defendant, this category includes cases in which the guilty plea had been previously rejected by the prosecution. The reasons for other late pleas, which may include inefficiencies in both the prosecution and defence services, are not identifiable: *Criminal Court Statistics Quarterly* Q1 2019. Similarly, the current statistics (Q1 2019) show that, for the category most disruptive to the court and the parties, 'ineffective trials' (because, unlike 'cracked cases' they are not completed on the day but are subject to adjournment), the majority are caused by dislocations in court administration and prosecution readiness (53 per cent): *Criminal Court Statistics: January to March 2019*, Table AC3. See more generally *Criminal Court Statistics Quarterly*: January–March 2016, Table C Key reasons for cracked Crown Court trials in England and Wales, annually 2007–2015, quarterly Q1 2009–Q1-2016. The point is that arrangements for serious cases are complex and will inevitably malfunction from time to time and this provides no rational basis for distorting the whole system on ideologically attributed 'blame' to one party.

[162] Auld, *Review* (n 133) 4.41. For a powerful critique see Michael Zander, *Lord Justice Auld's Review of the Criminal Courts: A Response* (2001) <www.lse.ac.uk/collections/law/staff%20publications%20full%20text/zander/auld_response_web.pdf> accessed 1 January 2020.

[163] Encompassed in the duty to make every honest endeavour to succeed: Lord Denning, *Tombling v Universal Bulb Co. Ltd* (1951) 2 TLR 289.

[164] Auld, *Review* (n 133) ch 11, para 9.

[165] A conundrum for most adversarial lawyers, as explicitly underscored by Lady Hale in *R (on the application of Adams) (FC) (Appellant) v Secretary of State for Justice (Respondent)* [2011] UKSC 18 (at 116): 'Innocence as such is not a concept known to our criminal justice system'.

[166] In 2015, a research survey for the Bar Council found that over half of the self-employed Bar were 'disengaged', suffering from a 'lack of autonomy', and 'reduced status' <www.barcouncil.org.uk/media/348371/wellbeing_at_the_bar_report_april_2015__final_.pdf> accessed 1 January 2020.

rather by reference to external economic constraints) remains a central function of judges. The 2015 *Review of Efficiency in Criminal Proceedings*, by Leveson LJ (The Leveson Review) is a milestone in this regard.[167]

A primary aim of Leveson was to locate areas of the criminal process where further compression could occur,[168] with emphasis on reducing the presence of the defence at preliminary stages or eliminating it entirely.[169] The senior judiciary's concession that the 'resolution of cases has *historically* revolved around advocacy before a judge in a physical courtroom'[170] should be viewed against the 'virtual' direction in which lawyers are being pulled.[171] 'Video hearings' are flaunted in a digital vision[172] of even 'swifter justice'[173]—one reinforced by a judicial duty to implement technology where viable[174]—which is at odds with the reality of the client–lawyer relationship, and the dwindling capacity of defence representatives to foster an environment of trust and confidence.[175] Leveson's involvement is critical because of the way he sought to inculcate the 'virtual' and 'efficient' approach to case disposal, requiring 'maximum efficiency' from every system participant

[167] At the time Leveson published his *Review* (n 142), he noted that the powers afforded to judges under the CrimPR '... are rarely exercised, doubtless because of the general culture of the adversarial process practised in this country that Judges are arbiters or umpires. Active case management both before and during a trial necessarily involves greater participation' 74.

[168] Leveson, *Review* (n 142) Terms of Reference (1a): 'recommend ways in which ... procedures could be further reduced or streamlined'.

[169] Leveson's Terms of Reference focused on technology solutions which could lead to preliminary hearings 'without requiring the attendance of advocates' (1b).

[170] *ToJS* (n 149) 5 emphasis supplied.

[171] In a conference speech, Leveson presented a 'solution' to the problem of inefficiency in the system where '... much of the preliminary work will be done by everyone in their ... *living room* or remote video suite'. Hearings will be 'conducted on line (either by *rapid exchange of text* or ... using video conferencing tools *we can all access from home*)' 'Modernising Justice Through Technology' (24 June 2015) 4–5 <www.judiciary.gov.uk/announcements/speech-by-president-of-the-queens-bench-division-modernising-justice-through-technology/> accessed 1 January 2020. Subsequently a joint statement of the Lord Chancellor and LCJ declared: 'In many cases, attending hearings in person will only be needed where there is no other alternative; parties will be able to engage virtually or online rather than have to take time to attend hearings in person': *ToJS* (n 149) 6–7.

[172] A research study investigating the use of virtual technology in criminal courts explained that it 'inevitably degrades the quality of human interaction. Nuances may be undetected, misunderstandings may go unnoticed more easily. Empathy may be lost. Defence counsel may find it harder to support their clients effectively, and there are some indications that the technology may actually affect court outcomes. In other words, there is no guarantee at present that virtual hearings will not damage the quality of justice.... it would be naïve to ignore the fact that a hearing is an occasion, not simply a transaction. And it seems very likely that the quality of the occasion is thinned by the technologies of virtual reality': Penelope Gibbs, *Defendants on Video—Conveyor Belt Justice or a Revolution in Access?* (Transform Justice 2017) 1 <www.transformjustice.org.uk/reports/> accessed 1 December 2017. See also Nicola Padfield and Tom Hawker, 'Sentencing via Video Link' (2017) Criminal Law Review 585.

[173] See Ministry of Justice, 'Virtual Courts Brings Swifter Justice' (28 November 2011) <www.gov.uk/government/news/virtual-courts-brings-swifter-justice> accessed 1 January 2020.

[174] It is the duty of the court to make use of technology actively to manage the case: CrimPR 3.2(1), (2)(h). For arguments as to why this IT panacea is misconceived, see Luke Marsh, 'Leveson's Narrow Pursuit of Justice: Efficiency and Outcomes in the Criminal Process' (2016) 45(1) Common Law World Review 51.

[175] See, eg, Monidipa Fouzder, 'Virtual Court Pilot Is 'Not Fit for Purpose' *The Law Society Gazette* (26 September 2016).

alongside 'reduced tolerance'[176] towards those non-compliant with any aspect of the CrimPR[177] or those marked out as resistant to the supremacy of its case management powers.[178]

As with Auld, Leveson's 'efficiency' proposals were unchastened by empirical findings.[179] The respective disregard for empirical data reveals an impoverished conception of judicial reasoning that has become a hallmark of system-change.[180]

Not only did Auld's attack on 'calculating' defendants as the cause of substantial wasted resources rest on a false representation of system waste and the cause of waste[181] but Leveson, too, perpetuated that line of thinking by asserting, albeit

[176] *Review* (n 142) para 199. For examples of how 'reduced tolerance' manifests itself, see *R v Cordingley* [2007] EWCA Crim 2174, [2008] EWCA Crim 2043; *R v SVS Solicitors* [2012] EWCA Crim 319.

[177] Some of which are plainly counter-intuitive eg, defence lawyers now have a duty to help convict their clients notwithstanding, eg, the prosecution's inability to prove its case because of the absence of witnesses or its reliance upon inadmissible evidence.

[178] The barrister Ian West is held up by the Leveson *Review* (n 142) as an example in this vein (see footnote 94). *West, Re* [2014] EWCA Crim 1480: '… [his conduct], if it was to become the norm, will cause our present system to collapse for want of sufficient funding with the risk causing enormous damage and *replacement by a process that imperils many of the hard gained improvements designed with the interests of justice in mind*' 55 (emphasis supplied). See Mike McConville and Luke Marsh, 'Adversarialism goes West: Case Management in Criminal Courts' (2015) 19(3) International Journal of Evidence & Proof 172.

[179] On the issue of evidence, see 'The starting point is data. Information. Evidence. When those responsible for leading and administering the justice system have previously concluded that it has or is failing to deliver justice effectively, they have not done so on any concrete data' (Sir Ernest Ryder, Senior President of Tribunals, 'Implementation and Application of the Law: The Governance of Justice' Speech given at the Society of Legal Scholars Conference in Preston (4 September 2019) para. 10.

[180] Leveson's remark also disregards a 'root and branch' shift in the operation of criminal justice. In other areas of the law, the usual principle is that the losing side pays the successful party's reasonable costs. In criminal law, that no longer applies following the enactment of s 31 of the Legal Aid, Sentencing and Punishment of Offenders Act 2012 (LASPO) and s 18 of the Criminal Legal Aid (Financial Resources) Regulations 2013. A grave consequence of this legislation is its resulting discrimination against a sizeable proportion of defendants who earn more than the threshold. In sum, full funding of the cost of legal representation is only likely available to those with an adjusted income of £12,475 or less. Even if an accused is adjudged innocent of the crime(s) alleged, a substantial part (if not all) of those costs incurred in fighting the charge will not be returned to him/her, even where the state agencies have demonstrated gross incompetence which led to the case going to trial. Concerns of victimization under the 'innocence tax' provisions under LASPO have since manifested (see, eg, Richard Holden, 'Months of Hell, 15 Minutes for my Name to Be Cleared' *The Sunday Times* (8 July 2018)). Nor can the resulting pressure on the voluntariness of an accused's plea be understated: see further Rebecca Helm, 'Conviction by Consent? Vulnerability, Autonomy and Conviction by Guilty Plea' (2019) 83(2) Journal of Criminal Law, 161.

[181] In fact, evidence demonstrated that 'waste' was exaggerated to the point of being fictitious; that a substantial proportion of trials 'cracked' because of decision-making by the prosecution; and that in only 6 per cent of cases did the trial 'crack' because the defendant changed his mind. See Michael Zander and Paul Henderson, *Crown Court Study*, RCCJ Research Study No 19 (HMSO 1993) Table 5.1. Despite the backlog of cases endemic to the system (see eg, Jonathan Ames, 'Fraud Trial Delayed by Ten Months as Court "Crisis" Deepens' *The Times* (24 September 2019)), criminal courts (that have not been sold off) sit empty: 'Home Office figures show that last year only 8.2 per cent of reported crimes in England and Wales resulted in a suspect being charged or appearing in court. That was the lowest level since 2015, when the present system for recording crimes was introduced. For some crimes, the clear-up rates were even lower: 3.8 per cent for sexual offences, 5.4 per cent for criminal damage and 6 per cent for theft', 'Justice Denied' *The Times* (28 June 2019). See also a recent research survey covering thirty-four Crown Court centres (approximately half of the criminal justice estate), which found 127 courtrooms

without any empirical studies being carried out, that 'some' defendants 'have no interest in improving the efficiency of the system or saving public money'.[182]

Without any evidence-based recommendations to existing practices on offer,[183] we contend that a judicial–executive ideology has commandeered the direction in which the justice system is headed.[184] How else could one explain Leveson disregarding his Terms of Reference to go off-piste with 'Further Observations' which were 'Out of Scope' and which, intended or not, provide a platform for future governmental attempts (pre-figured by James 1975, Roskill 1986, and Narey 1997) to attenuate the right to jury trial?[185] And, not to be outdone by Auld (whose Report he fully endorsed) Leveson buttressed his concerns over the jury without empirical support[186] using the passive voice:

out of 260 were 'sitting idle': Owen Bowcott, 'Criminal Cases Delayed across England and Wales as Courts Lie Idle' *The Guardian* (19 August 2019).

[182] Leveson, *Review* (n 142) 158, echoing Auld's *Review* (n 133) (at ch 10, para 1): 'Guilty defendants seeking to avoid conviction have not the same urgency as the public about the need for an efficient criminal justice system. Some innocent defendants, advised by their lawyers to keep their cards close to their chests, are equally unenthusiastic.' This comment is doubly ironic in light of the serious problems that have accompanied the programme of system reform rolled out under Leveson's watch. For example, the growth in the number of unqualified third parties seeking to advise or represent applicants (as a result of reduced funding) which has led to multiple hidden costs, not least the spate of expensive appellate proceedings to manage them. See, eg, *R v Conaghan (Terence)* [2017] EWCA Crim 597; [2017] 2 Cr App R 19 (CA (Crim Div)) and commentary on this case by Peter Hungerford-Welch who points out: 'Some might say that it is false economy to restrict public funding of legal representation to the extent it has been restricted in England and Wales': 'Unrepresented Defendants: R. v Conaghan (Terence)' (2017) 12 Criminal Law Review 1009. What should have been emphasized by Leveson is that, to put it at its lowest, and as the Official Statistics show, thousands of people charged with serious crime before the Crown Court *do* have an interest in efficient disposal if only because they are acquitted following withdrawal of the prosecution or collapse of the prosecution case on the direction of the trial judge or are acquitted by verdict of the jury at trial. See also George Greenwood and Frances Gibb, 'Thousands Cleared by Evidence Failures' *The Times* (17 December 2018).

[183] While Leveson is to be applauded for recognizing in his *Review* (n 142) some of its limitations, his concession that there was 'no time or little opportunity for evidence gathering' (at 9) nor any 'quantitative analysis of the effect of the changes' proposed (at 10) undermines the value of his conclusions and is remarkable considering '[t]he Home Office's research, development and statistics department is the largest and most sophisticated agency of its type in the world': Michael Tonry, *Punishment and Politics—Evidence and Emulation in the Making of English Penal Policy* (Willan 2004) 25. Further, even a close examination of the official *Criminal Statistics* would have taken a matter of minutes.

[184] In an instance of judicial candour, the Australian judge Sir Anthony Mason revealed the early driving-force behind this ideology: 'It must be recognised that the main push for case management comes from governments anxious to reduce the cost of the court system to government. The push does not come so much from the judiciary or the legal profession. Indeed, the judiciary and the profession *have reservations about case management, its impact upon judicial work and the interests of justice.*' Sir A Mason, 'The Judiciary in the Modern World' (13 November 1998) 8 emphasis supplied <www.hkcfa.hk/filemanager/speech/en/upload/119/Mason%20-%20The%20Judiciary%20in%20the%20Modern%20World.pdf> accessed 1 January 2020.

[185] His analysis begins revealingly under the heading '*Changes* to the right to elect trial by jury' (emphasis supplied).

[186] Where empirical evidence does exist in the form of the experience of judges who try serious fraud cases, Leveson simply sets it aside on the bizarre ground that it was 'not implausible' to suggest that greater focus on the real issues would result: *Review* (n 142) 357. Removal of juries in fraud cases is perceived as a possible inroad and has judicial support at the highest level: 'Juries Ill-Equipped for Fraud Trials, Supreme Court Judge Says' *The Times* (26 October 2018).

> Although expressed views were not unanimous, *the Review has heard the voices of many involved in the criminal justice system* calling for a change to the right to elect trial by jury. A court, not a defendant, *it is said*, should decide how he is to be tried (emphasis supplied).[187]

In similar fashion, invoking the opinion of one contributor as to choice of forum,[188] the view of the accused is displaced by a so-called 'objective' assessment to be made by an 'independent judiciary', a task made easier in a context in which society's interests, *as represented by victims and witnesses*, are set against those of the accused who, by this sleight of hand, are already removed from society.

This reanimated judicial narrative, in which defence rights are reduced or eliminated, coerced guilty pleas favoured, and trials positively disparaged as a costly impediment to justice,[189] is further evidence of symbolic policies espoused without or in contradistinction to available data.[190]

With governmental reliance on the 'legitimacy' which senior judges impart through reviews,[191] claims to 'evidence-based' policy that traditionally anchored reform are abandoned[192] and politically expedient proposals become available for cherry-picking. The continuation of this agenda is guaranteed under the aegis of senior judges,[193] bolstered through repetitive efficiency

[187] *Review* (n 142) 336.

[188] Lord Hardie, as set out at ibid 342.

[189] In his final weeks in office, Thomas LCJ backed a government proposal to give magistrates the power to jail offenders for twelve months rather than six, shifting more than 10,000 cases from the Crown Court to magistrates' courts, with financial savings touted as a principal justification: Frances Gibb, 'Toughen Sentencing Powers of Magistrates, Says Law Chief' *The Times* (19 September 2017). For a contemporary account of magistrates' courts, see Jennifer Ward, *Transforming Summary Justice—Modernisation in the Lower Criminal Courts* (Routledge 2017); for evidence of de-skilling that has undermined the quality of determinations in modern magistrates' courts, see Laurène Soubise, 'Prosecuting in the Magistrates' Courts in a Time of Austerity' (2017) 11 Criminal Law Review 847. See also the House of Commons Justice Committee report (17 October 2017), 'The Role of the Magistracy' paras 100–05 <www.publications.parliament.uk/pa/cm201617/cmselect/cmjust/165/16502.htm> accessed 1 January 2020; and s 154 of the Criminal Justice Act 2003 (not yet in force).

[190] Black, Asian and, Minority Ethnic (BAME) defendants are left especially vulnerable by the undercutting of jury trial. *The Lammy Review* (September 2017) analysed close to 400,000 criminal cases, and found that juries were consistent in their decision-making, irrespective of the ethnicity of the defendant. Conversely, judges exhibited a racial bias, with BAME offenders being significantly more likely to receive a custodial sentence than white offenders for comparable crimes <www.gov.uk/government/publications/lammy-review-final-report> accessed 1 January 2020.

[191] As exemplified by the former Lord Chancellor: 'It is my intention to do everything I can to support the Lord Chief Justice, Sir Brian and his colleagues in their work. Not for the first time in our history, it is our judges who see most clearly what needs to be done to help the vulnerable, the overlooked and the victimised in our society': Rt Hon Michael Gove MP, 'What Does a One Nation Justice Policy Look Like?' Speech given at the *Legatum* Institute (23 June 2015) (hereafter Gove, *Legatum*).

[192] On publication of the Leveson *Review* (n 142), the then Lord Chancellor wrote to him (on 11 March 2015): 'I welcome your recommendations and *accept them all in principle* as they will lead to more efficient criminal courts' (emphasis supplied).

[193] In fact, this support is no longer masked: 'The vision is to modernise and upgrade our justice system … The Government and the judiciary have a shared commitment to make this a reality' *ToJS* (n 149). One manifestation of this, following the Leveson *Review* (n 142), was the 'Better Case Management' project which is a judicial cross-agency initiative pursued, in large part, to encourage early guilty pleas: see HMCPSI, *Better Case Management—A Snapshot* (November 2016).

initiatives[194] and a circularity of validation.[195] Now, through its various arms, the state requires *all* parties to sign up[196] to a cost-efficiency system[197] driven by trial-avoidance mechanisms, including, but not limited to, sentence discounts.[198]

All of this has been constructed notwithstanding the failure to confront police malpractice and corruption in any serious way.[199] Police distortion of evidence on an industrial scale relating to the Miners' Strike[200] and the Hillsborough Disaster remain obscured and largely uncondemned[201] as do the activities of the

[194] The cascade of efficiency initiatives post-Leveson is ongoing: see, eg, *Transforming Summary Justice Initiative* <www.cps.gov.uk/publications/agencies/transforming_summary_justice_may_2015.html> and *Better Case Management Initiative* (ibid.).

[195] '[The judiciary] have commissioned work which makes the case for quite radical change. Should anyone doubt the need for dramatic steps, Sir Brian Leveson's report on the need for change in our criminal justice system makes the case compellingly. He argues with great authority and makes a series of wise recommendations. They need to be implemented with all speed:' Gove, *Legatum* (n 191).

[196] For the defence, this means away from the client—towards the state. *R v Rochford* [2010] EWCA Crim 1928 *per* Hughes LJ, para 25, typifies this understanding: 'The lawyer's duty is not to give the advice on what to do. The lawyer's duty is to explain the statutory obligation that he has and to explain the consequences which follow from disobedience of it.'

[197] On which see Mike McConville and Luke Marsh, 'Factory Farming and State-Induced Pleas' in Hunter and others (eds), *The Integrity of Criminal Process* (Hart 2016) 99–116.

[198] The *Reduction in Sentence for a Guilty Plea Definitive Guideline* (June 2017) has both fettered discretion of trial judges and heightened levels of cooperation expected from defendants by shifting the point at which a defendant can receive maximum credit for their guilty plea from the 'first available moment' to the 'first stage of proceedings', defined as the point where a plea or indication is sought (usually the first appearance at the Magistrates' Court). See <www.sentencingcouncil.org.uk/wp-content/uploads/Reduction-in-Sentence-for-Guilty-plea-Definitive-Guide_FINAL_WEB.pdf> accessed 1 January 2020. This regime disregards the woeful state of prosecution disclosure that has plagued criminal courts for decades (see HMCPS Inspectorate, *Transforming Summary Justice: An Early Perspective of the CPS Contribution* (February 2016)) with lower courts particularly affected (see the Interim Criminal Law Solicitors' Association disclosure survey results of 2017 which indicate disclosure failings by the CPS in the magistrates court are rife, in part stemming from a lack of accountability in court). For a case exemplifying the dangers inherent to the system, see comment on *R v on the application of the DPP) v Leicester Magistrates' Court* (unreported, 9 February 2016): Ed Johnston and Tom Smith, 'The Early Guilty Plea Scheme and the Rising Wave of Managerialism' (2017) 181(13) Criminal Law & Justice Weekly 210.

[199] There is, however, increasing judicial recognition that the integrity of this 'new landscape' of criminal justice is not impervious to austerity measures: 'Forensic Budget Cuts Risk Wrongful Convictions, Says Lord Chief' *The Times* (21 November 2018). Indeed, upon his retirement from the bench on 23 June 2019, Leveson appeared to concede the recommendations in his *Review*, are unlikely to bear fruit: '... I would have loved to say that I was leaving the system and, in particular, the criminal justice system in a better place than it was ... In many ways, it is. Consider the enormous strides in procedure, in PACE, in disclosure, in dealing with vulnerable complainants, victims, witnesses and, indeed defendants. Consider also the efforts made to deal with the challenges of technology and ensuring consistency of approach to sentencing. But in other ways it is not. The truth is that many facets of the system are struggling. Crime is not being detected; volumes through the court are decreasing. The police, forensics, the CPS, the fabric of the court, the prison and probation service, all are struggling.' See <https://www.judiciary.uk/wp-content/uploads/2019/06/Sir-Brian-Levesons-valedictory-speech-June-2019.pdf> accessed 1 January 2020.

[200] The wholesale perjury in this case, in which the cases against fifty-six miners collapsed, remains a bleak monument to official venality, a promise of an inquiry undertaken by Theresa May as Home Secretary overturned in 2016 by the then Home Secretary Amber Rudd on the extraordinary basis that no one had died!

[201] Some miscarriages are uncovered by accident, as in the case of Stephen Simmons who had been framed in the 1970s by a British Transport Police officer who had stolen Royal Mail bags, resold them, and framed others for the crimes. This all came to light when an internet search found that the arresting officer had himself been subsequently convicted of these crimes and, with the support of the Criminal

Special Demonstration Squad.[202] Although there have been minimal efforts to address police corruption and to stimulate a desire for internal reform among the police,[203] officers who are the subject of investigation for misconduct are routinely allowed to retire or resign.[204] The review by Mark Ellison relating to the murder of Stephen Lawrence uncovered evidence of corruption against a key detective in the investigation, inadequate reviews of the murder and its investigation by the Independent Police Complaints Commission (IPCC) in 2006, and by the Metropolitan Police itself in 2012, mass shredding of evidence and the likelihood that other evidence relating to corruption was 'lost' or destroyed.[205] There remains clear evidence that should police officers decide to contravene the existing rules, they may do so with relative[206] impunity: *R v Maxwell*

Cases Review Commission, the CA quashed the conviction of Simmons: 'Surrey "Mailbag Thief" Jailed in 1976 Overturns Conviction' (*BBC News Online*, 17 January 2018).

[202] The SDS and the National Public Order Intelligence Unit were secret squads established by the Met to collect 'intelligence' rather than evidence. These undercover squads are the subject of investigation by Operation Herne.

[203] See Maurice Punch, *Police Corruption* (Routledge 2009) for an overview. See also Denis O'Connor, *Closing the Gap* (HMIC 2005); Eugene McLaughlin, 'Forcing the Issue: New Labour, New Localism and the Democratic Renewal of Police Accountability' (2005) 44(5) Howard Journal 473.

[204] Thus, in *R v Joof and Ors* [2012] EWCA Crim 1475, a case involving the murder of Kevin Nunes, following an IPCC investigation ('Operation Kalmia'), recommended disciplinary action was not undertaken by the forces involved, with one officer allowed to retire on grounds of 'ill health' before disciplinary charges could be preferred. See also on the *Maxwell case*, Operation Walhorn in redacted form <www.whatdotheyknow.com/request/183457/response/470284/attach/6/Waldhorn%20Redacted.pdf> accessed 1 January 2020.

[205] Oral Statement by the Home Secretary (6 March 2014) Hansard, vol 576, col 1061. See further, *Rees and Ors v Commissioner of Police for the Metropolis* [2017] EWHC 273 and (on appeal) [2018] EWCA Civ 1587 detailing some of the activities of a corrupt police officer, DCS Cook, in the investigation and prosecution of individuals for the murder of Daniel Morgan. In 2018 it emerged that the Independent Office of Police Conduct is examining allegations of 'serious corruption and malpractice' within the Metropolitan Police involving alleged interference in, and curtailment of, investigations by potentially conflicted senior officers, failure to investigate allegations of wrongdoing, systemic removal of the restrictions of officers under investigation, and racial discrimination. Among the serious allegations are that officers within the Directorate of Professional Standards are shielding officers from a wide range of allegations. See Tom Harper, 'Elite London Met Police Shielded from Corruption' *The Times* (22 July 2018).

[206] Although the plain clothes divisions remain difficult to penetrate, there are notable disciplinary successes by the police themselves. Thus, eg, Nottinghamshire Police successfully rooted out corrupt officers who had assisted Colin Gunn and his gang to turn the city into what the media was able to portray as 'Shottingham' over the period 2002–05. See Jamie Doward and Carl Felstrom, 'Brutal Ganglord who Fell Victim to His Own Drugs' *The Guardian* (5 August 2007). Indeed, figures show that more than 189 officers have been convicted of grave and serious crime since 2013: see Camilla Tominey, 'Revealed: The 189 Police Officers Convicted of Crimes Including Murder, Child Pornography and Drug Dealing since 2013' *The Telegraph* (20 January 2019). See also 'Essex Police Child Abuse Officers Jailed for Misconduct' (*BBC News*, 10 May 2019); 'Julian Cole: Three Bedfordshire Police Officers Sacked' (*BBC News Online*, 22 October 2018), reporting on a case in which three officers were found to have lied in statements about Julian Cole at the time of his arrest. Added to this, Chief Constables continue to fall on personal grounds as, eg, following findings of misconduct (Nick Gargan, Avon and Somerset Police in 2015: Emma Griffiths, 'Nick Gargan Profile: Troubled End for High-Flying Police Chief' (*BBC News Online*, 16 October 2015); and following complaints by two female officers of inappropriate behaviour (Mike Veale, Cleveland Police in 2019: Martin Evans and Robert Mendick, 'Police Chief Resigns after Two Female Officers Make Accusations of Inappropriate Behaviour Against Him' *The Telegraph* (21 January 2019).

(2010);[207] *Joof and Ors* (2012);[208] *Grant & Ors* (2015)[209] being cases which, considered together, show how procedural and legal rules can be set aside, non-disclosure to prosecution and defence lawyers is pernicious, the Crown Prosecution Service deliberately deceived, courts (including the Court of Appeal) given perjured evidence by police officers, police notes corrupted, the custody record falsified, with violent offences winked at.[210]

One ready-made escape hatch for corrupt officers is illustrated in *Maxwell*. There Supreme Court Justices heard that West Yorkshire detectives allowed a key witness in a murder trial, a serving prisoner in their temporary custody, to visit brothels, consume hard drugs, enjoy periods of unsupervised freedom and to not proceed against him for the vicious stabbing of another prisoner, the alleged rape

207 Involving officers from the West Yorkshire Police.

208 Involving officers from the Staffordshire Police.

209 Involving officers from the Metropolitan Police.

210 In *Grant* (ibid), police officers (ex DI Horsley and DS Wright) improperly concealed evidence from both prosecution counsel and the trial court in a murder trial in such a manner, said the Court of Appeal, as to justify the view of prosecution counsel on appeal that the misconduct 'may well have led to disciplinary procedure if DI Horsley remained in office' (para 19); in *Maxwell* (n 207), a case involving murder and two robberies in which the prosecution relied upon the evidence of a major criminal, Karl Chapman, Lord Brown in the Supreme Court summarized the wrongdoing as follows: 'A large number of police officers involved in the investigation and prosecution of the … robbery and murder case, including several of very high rank, engaged in a prolonged, persistent and pervasive conspiracy to pervert the course of justice. They colluded in conferring on Chapman a variety of wholly inappropriate benefits to secure his continuing cooperation in the appellant's prosecution and trial. They then colluded in Chapman's perjury at that trial, intending him throughout his evidence to lie as to how he had been treated and as to what promises he had received. They ensured that Chapman's police custody records and various other official documents presented a false picture of the facts, on one occasion actually forging a custody record when its enforced disclosure to the defence would otherwise have revealed the truth. They lied in their responses to enquiries made of the CPS after the appellant's conviction and, in the case of the two senior officers who gave evidence to the Court of Appeal, perjured themselves so as to ensure that the appellant's application for leave to appeal against his conviction got nowhere.'; and in *Joof* (n 204), a case involving five defendants convicted of murder in what appeared to the Court of Appeal to be 'a serious perversion of the course of justice', relevant information concerning the way in which police officers managed a key informant was not disclosed to the defence or the trial court, internal police documentation was falsified and, had the defence been aware of this, they could, said the Court of Appeal, have shown that the relevant police department (the Sensitive Policing Unit) was a dysfunctional organization fractured by infighting, containing officers whose honesty and integrity were open to question and whose documentation in respect of the key prosecution witness could not be trusted. While the subsequent IPCC investigation into the *Joof* case found no evidence of a cover up or of wilful omission by any of the fourteen officers involved, it found that there had been significant and serious collective failings within Staffordshire Police, in relation both to the management of a protected witness, and ensuring disclosure of all relevant material to the CPS and the courts. Of the officers still then serving, the investigation found that a number of officers had a case to answer for gross misconduct and the IPCC considered that there were indications that criminal offences may have been committed by officers under investigation. However, the CPS concluded that there was insufficient evidence to justify any prosecution. The IPCC issued its findings to the appropriate authorities which, in turn, rejected the case to answer findings in relation to the senior officers. Two serving Staffordshire Police constables were found to have a case to answer for misconduct, which their appropriate authority accepted, in respect of one matter. One was given management advice; the other retired on health grounds. Although the IPCC considered that all four senior officers should still face disciplinary hearings over some matters, its recommendations were not accepted. The redacted Final Report of the IPCC is available at <https://policeconduct.gov.uk/sites/default/files/Documents/investigation_reports/IPCC_inv_reports/OpKalmia_%20RedactedFinalReport.pdf> accessed 1 January 2020.

of another, and assault on a WPC with whom he had been permitted to have sexual relations; all relevant information omitted from the custody records, not disclosed to the CPS and concealed through police perjury from the trial court and Court of Appeal. The Supreme Court Justices were astonished that none of the eighteen officers allegedly involved had been charged or disciplined. But they had overlooked the escape hatch. In fact, having allowed senior officers involved in *Maxwell* to retire, the West Yorkshire Force considered that it would be unfair to discipline the more junior officers who remained! And a Freedom of Information request made in 2017[211] elicited that since 2014, some 309 officers in the Metropolitan Police alone resigned/retired whilst under investigation for public complaints and internal misconduct.

Conclusion

A number of enduring themes emerge from the post Judges' Rules era of law 'reform' with continuing impact today. The inept drafting of the Rules significantly left unmediated discretion in the hands of judges who used it to shore up police evidence. Alongside this, the senior judiciary quickly filled the lacunae in policy-making. Where once they appeared to be the guardians of individual rights, within a few years they became the architects of state power. This abrupt reversal first manifested in 1970 was unanchored in empirical evidence of any kind and, indeed, was contradicted by available data. Judicial thought became founded instead upon presuppositions about defendants as both guilty and unworthy and undisguised suspicion of criminal defence lawyers.[212] At critical moments the intervention of judges imported and indeed promoted the executive agenda which had lain dormant since the early 1960s to a trial-impoverished future. For its part, the police had become a powerful political arm of the state, its subterranean influence in the 1960–64 period being replaced by active public campaigning which drove executive policy as police malpractice continued to bubble under the surface.

[211] FOI Request Reference No: 2016090001051. Reversing a key reform proposal of Theresa May as Home Secretary, the Policing and Crime Act 2017 allows officers under investigation for misconduct to resign or retire. Misconduct hearings will continue in the absence of such an officer and, in limited circumstances, gross misconduct proceedings could also be brought against officers in the twelve months after they have resigned or retired.

[212] See, eg, Auld, *Review* (n 133) ch 10, paras 5 and 154.

8

Rule of Law and Common Law

Introduction

While the Judges' Rules and associated judicial decision-making in such areas as plea bargaining and trial management may be of shadowy pedigree there can be little doubt as to their impact on the criminal justice system. In this chapter, we consider how this form of 'judicial' decision-making accords with foundational precepts of the common law, the bedrock of judicial claims regarding the role of judges in the constitution. We begin by addressing a related question that commentators posed when the 1964 Rules were promulgated and is still live today: what kind of regulation do the Rules represent and what is their significance.[1]

The Status of the Judges' Rules

Little regard was paid to the status of the Judges' Rules when they first appeared in 1918, nor was detailed consideration given when the Home Office told the Royal Commission into Police Powers and Procedures (RCPPP) (1929) that the Rules 'introduced no new principle' and 'merely formulated in terms the rules which for many years had guided His Majesty's Judges in deciding whether statements submitted as evidence were admissible or not'.[2] Nevertheless, the perceptive Chief Inspector of Police, Sir Leonard Dunning, had already seen the issue and had written to the Head of the Home Office Police Department, Sir Arthur Dixon, as follows:[3]

> The Rules approved by H. M. Judges in 1918 will be embodied in the Instruction Book which is now being prepared for the guidance of the County and Borough Police Forces as recommended by the Desborough Committee, *but they more nearly resemble statements of the law than an instruction by superior officers of police* and in some particulars will require amplification by instruction (emphasis supplied).

[1] This remains a live issue in jurisdictions which have imported the Rules as we discuss in ch 11.

[2] *Report of the Royal Commission on Police Powers and Procedure* (HMSO 1929) (hereafter RCPPP, *Report* (1929)) para 184.

[3] Recorded in File A52, 392/22 and File A52, 392/30 (2 February 1924).

The Myth of Judicial Independence. Mike McConville and Luke Marsh, Oxford University Press (2020). © Mike McConville and Luke Marsh. DOI: 10.1093/oso/9780198822103.001.0001

The Rules came under greater scrutiny in the 1960s when political review of and academic interest in criminal law and procedure intensified.

The status of the Rules was questioned immediately following their promulgation.[4] In Parliament, the Home Secretary was asked by Reginald Paget QC the following question:

> I ask the right hon. Gentleman whether he is aware that I, at any rate, have always been brought up to believe that it was for us to make laws and for the judges to interpret them? *This appears to be an act of legislation by the judges.* Will the right hon. Gentleman tell us from where they get their authority to do this? (emphasis supplied)

The Home Secretary sought to allay concerns:

> This is not an act of legislation. This is an indication by the judges of what they will take into account when they are hearing evidence in court as to the admissibility of that evidence.

Others were far from persuaded. The doyen of criminal law, Professor J C Smith, for example, stated that while it was not unusual for a judge to exclude evidence which in strict law is admissible:[5]

> What is unusual is to have a declaration of a new policy in the exercise of this discretion, made by all the judges, not from the bench, but extra-judicially.[6]

He concluded his analysis as follows:[7]

> It is thought that there is much force in the criticisms that have been made in Parliament and elsewhere as to the manner in which the Rules have been made—*for they are, in substance, legislation* ... (emphasis supplied).

An Editorial in the leading criminal law journal was of the same view:[8]

> [T]he judges' function is to decide particular cases in court not to lay down out of court rules for the guidance of themselves or others. The framing of a code of police practice is properly the work of the legislature after public debate.

[4] HC Deb 28 January 1964, vol 688, cols 209–12.
[5] John Cyril Smith, 'The New Judges' Rules—A Lawyer's View' [1964] Criminal Law Review 176.
[6] ibid 177.
[7] ibid 182.
[8] 'The Judges' Rules' [1964] (March) Criminal Law Review 161.

Judges themselves added to the opaque status of the Rules. Thus, the Privy Council in *Shabadine Peart v The Queen*[9] began with the words: 'The Judges' Rules constitute a striking example of *judge-made law*. Although classed formally as administrative directions for the guidance of police officers interviewing suspects, they were afforded over time a *higher status* ... ' and continued: 'The Judges' Rules are *administrative directions, not rules of law* ... '[10] (emphasis supplied).

It hardly needs saying that the three descriptors ('judge-made law'; 'administrative directions'; and 'higher status') simply serve to underline the ambiguous nature of the Rules and their close affinity to legislation. If these various judicial initiatives are 'law', it is necessary to first address the question whether judges possess a law-making power.

Judges and the Law-Making Power

The involvement of judges in law-making has been a source of controversy in England and Wales as well as in other jurisdictions[11] primarily because it is argued by some to involve 'social reordering' or 'politics'.[12] Concerned by this, judges have counselled against the idea that they are active law-makers. Thus, Lord Bingham has insisted that judges have no warrant to vary, add to, or subtract from the effect of what Parliament has enacted, nor to give effect to what they consider Parliament may have intended and otherwise to declare what the common law is and, by implication, always has been.[13] In the same vein, before taking up office in the UK Supreme Court, (Lord) Sumption warned of the dangers of judges straying into the political arena,[14] a view he subsequently repeated.[15] Despite this, Sumption recognized that 'some degree of judicial lawmaking is unavoidable, especially

[9] *Shabadine Peart v The Queen* (Jamaica) [2006] UKPC 5 (see ch 11).

[10] ibid para 24.

[11] See, eg, the competing views of the role of the US Supreme Court in Alexander Bickel, *The Least Dangerous Branch: The Supreme Court at the Bar of Politics* (2nd edn, Yale University Press 1986) and Robert Bork, *The Tempting of America: The Political Seduction of the Law* (Sinclair-Stevenson 1990) discussed in Martin Loughlin, 'Sumption's Assumptions' (hereafter Loughlin, 'Sumption's Assumptions') in Nicholas Barber, Richard Ekins, and Paul Yowell (eds), *Lord Sumption and the Limits of the Law* (Hart 2016) (hereafter Barber and others, *Limits of the Law*).

[12] For a general discussion of the issue see Sir John Laws 'Law and Democracy' [1995] Public Law 72 (hereafter Laws, 'Democracy'); JAG Griffith, 'The Brave New World of Sir John Laws' (2000) 63(2) Modern Law Review 159 (hereafter Griffith, 'Brave New World').

[13] Lord Bingham, 'The Judges: Active or Passive?' in Peter James Marshall (ed), *Proceedings of the British Academy, 2005 Lectures* (OUP 2007) 139.

[14] Jonathan Sumption, 'Judicial and Political Decision-Making: The Uncertain Boundary' FA Mann Lecture (2011).

[15] See Lord Sumption, 'The Limits of the Law' in Barber and others, *Limits of the Law* (n 11). A composite of Sumption's views on this issue is found within his book *Trials of the State: Law and the Decline of Politics* (Profile 2019) which pools together and expands upon the contents of his Reith Lectures delivered in 2019 (transcripts available via the BBC website). For a stimulating discussion of both, see Stephen Sedley, 'A Boundary where there Is None' (12 September 2019) 41(17) London Review of Books.

in an uncodified common law system'.[16] Indeed, it is now widely agreed that the common law changes as a result of judicial decisions and that judges 'make' law[17] in some areas whether the 'declaratory theory' of law (that previous decisions overruled by judges in later cases must always have been 'wrong')[18] is considered as a 'fairy tale'[19] or whether it is considered valid as a statement of the judge's vocation and responsibility to clarify past rulings in terms of what can reasonably be said to have been the law that, all things now considered, was properly applicable at the time.[20] In this context, we discuss below three principal justifications for judicial law-making.

Force majeure

The mere fact that a case is before the court places judges in a position in which they have to determine the outcome; they cannot abjure from making a decision and, in doing so, they will in certain circumstances effectively be 'making' law[21] albeit subject to limitations. Thus, in the area of criminal law, while the court cannot create new criminal offences,[22] the judgment may[23] adapt existing law to accommodate new issues, such as rape within marriage.[24] Likewise, the area of law

[16] See also *Re Spectrum Plus Ltd* [2005] 2 AC 680 where Lord Nicholls said: 'The common law is judge-made law. For centuries judges have been charged with the responsibility of keeping this law abreast of current social conditions and expectations. That is still the position. Continuing but limited development of the common law in this fashion is an integral part of the constitutional function of the judiciary.'32. See also Lord Radcliffe: '[t]here was never a more sterile controversy than that upon the question whether a judge makes laws. Of course he does. How can he help it? . . . Judicial law is always a reinterpretation of *principles* in the light new combinations of *facts*' Lord Radcliffe, *Not in Feather Beds* (Hamish Hamilton 1968) 216, emphasis supplied.

[17] We recognize the problem of distinguishing between the 'law' and 'politics'. For a judicial view of how the common law operates, see Sir Philip Scales, 'The Common Law: Context and Method' (2019) 135 (Jan) Law Quarterly Review 47.

[18] See Lord Goff in *Kleinwort Benson v Lincoln County Council* [1998] UKHL 38.

[19] Lord Reid, 'The Judge as Law-Maker' (1972) The Journal of Public Teachers of Law 22. Lord Reid said that the idea that in some Aladdin's Cave there is hidden the common law which descends on a judge on his or her appointment is no longer tenable: '[W]e do not believe in fairy tales anymore.' See also, Lord Reid's judgment in *West Midland Baptist Association v Birmingham Corp* [1970] AC 874.

[20] See John Finnis, 'Judicial Law-Making and the "Living" Instrumentalisation of the ECHR' in Barber and others, *Limits of the Law* (n 11).

[21] Thus, in *Airedale NHS v Bland* [1993] AC 789, against a background of Parliamentary inaction, the House of Lords had to decide whether to allow Tony Bland, who was in a persistent vegetative state, to die with dignity through the withdrawal of life-prolonging treatment.

[22] Judges may not develop the law to create new criminal offences or widen existing offences so as to make punishable conduct of a type hitherto not subject to punishment: *R v Withers* [1975] AC 842 in which the House of Lords ruled that the judges have no power to create new offences. cf earlier determinations of *Shaw v DPP* [1962] AC 220; *Knuller v DPP* [1973] 435.

[23] Courts accept that there are limitations on their role even where it might be considered 'corrective' of a set of problems arising out of legislation as in *Roberts & Ors* [2016] EWCA Crim 71.

[24] See, eg, *R v R* [1992] 1AC 599 where, earlier in the CA, Lord Lane CJ said: 'This is not the creation of a new offence, it is the removal of a common law fiction which has become anachronistic and offensive and we consider that it is our duty having reached that conclusion to act upon it.'

covered by judicial review has been ripe with controversy where judges have expanded the scope of review of administrative actions by public bodies. Even in such cases, however, it can be argued that judges are not 'making' law but are, as Ronald Dworkin elaborates,[25] engaged in the difficult task of finding the best answer.

Whatever its merits, the defence of force majeure is not available to judges in the present context. Indeed, *all* the essential decisions judges took were *elective not required* courses of action. The judges were not obliged to create the Judges' Rules, a ready mechanism being available through the Court of Appeal to clarify contradictory determinations by different courts. Nor were the judges required to invent plea bargaining or construct trial judges as case managers both of which were atypical acts of expediency outside the trial arena.

Human rights

At the heart of another justification is a claim that judges have been accorded a duty to intervene on moral grounds[26] or to protect rights which are in some way 'fundamental'. The debate around judicial law-making and the separation of powers has been most intense in the area of judicial review.[27] The background concern has been the rise in political significance of the judiciary particularly over the past fifty years spurred on by the incorporation into English law of the European Convention on Human Rights by the Human Rights Act 1998 which transferred part of an essentially legislative power to the judiciary. For some, the effect has been to expand the judicial function from 'interpretation and enforcement' of the law to involvement in policy questions regarding determination of where the 'public interests' lie.[28] Other scholars argue that the nature, purpose, and method of constitutional law has been transformed over the last fifty years through a 'rights revolution' shifting the focus from the role of constitutions in conferring powers on public institutions towards that of protecting the rights of citizens.[29]

This justification has no relevance to the Judges' Rules which antedated the 'rights revolution' by almost a hundred years. In criminal matters, moreover, the

[25] Ronald Dworkin, *Law's Empire* (Harvard University Press 1986).

[26] Sir John Laws for example argues that the control of power by unelected judges is underpinned by moral force (Laws, 'Democracy' (n 12)).

[27] In a penetrating analysis of tort law, Paul Craig demonstrates that many of the same issues also arise in private law: 'Limits of law: Reflections from Private and Public Law' in Barber and others, *Limits of the Law* (n 11).

[28] See, eg, Lord Sumption: 'The Limits of the Law' the 27th Sultan Azlan Shah Lecture, Kuala Lumpur <www.supremecourt.uk/docs/speech-131120.pdf> accessed 1 January 2020.

[29] See Loughlin, 'Sumption's Assumptions' (n 11). Loughlin's critique explains clearly how, in the development of judicial review, although it is impossible to draw a bright line between law and politics, judges operated a clear set of doctrines, rules, and practices that had evolved through the common law reasoning process and sought to enforce a strict conception of legality. See also Kate Malleson, 'The Evolving Role of the Supreme Court' [2011] Public Law 754.

Court of Appeal can hardly be said to have constituted itself as 'a legitimating force in society' searching for the fundamental presuppositions of an evolving political morality consonant with the British tradition. The Judges' Rules were not laid down to protect the rights of citizens and the courts have not been consciously involved in the determination of some notion of 'fundamental law'. Likewise, in the more modern era, the introduction of plea bargaining (state-induced guilty pleas) and the 'changed culture' which is said to have inspired the Criminal Procedure Rules (CrimPR) have been openly founded in cost-efficiency claims (albeit now reconfigured to be in the 'interests of justice') rather than in terms of the rights of citizens.

Accountability

Echoing a common criticism which tells against judicial law-making, John Griffith said of judges:[30] '[T]hey are not accountable and not dismissible.' Against this, it has been argued that one of the distinguishing features of courts has been the expatiatory power of judges who by common law tradition offer reasoned arguments in support of their determinations[31] and do so on a public and individual basis.[32] As Sir Stephen Sedley pointed out in discussing a related issue:[33]

> When critics of the bench describe judges as unaccountable, they cannot mean that judges do not account for their decisions, for judges uniquely have to give full reasons in public for everything they do.

Lord Brown made a similar observation in contrasting the judiciary with the legislature arguing that judges were 'rather more so ... than government decision-makers':[34]

> First, subject to very few exceptions ... , judges reach their decisions in open court, based entirely upon evidence and arguments openly placed before the court, giving full reasons which are then open to scrutiny by all ... Secondly,

[30] Griffith, 'Brave New World' (n 12) 174.

[31] There is debate as to the meaning of 'accountability' in any broader assessment of the judicial role but at its core it simply involves 'the giving of reasons or explanations for decisions or conduct': Graham Gee and others, *The Politics of Judicial Independence in the UK's Changing Constitution* (CUP 2015) 17.

[32] The Court of Appeal (Criminal Division) traditionally gives a single judgment although there is provision for separate judgments to be given in exceptional cases: Supreme Court Act, 1981, s 59.

[33] Stephen Sedley, *Lions Under the Throne: Essays on the History of English Public Law* (CUP 2015) (hereafter Sedley, *Lions Under the Throne*) 279. See also Stephen Sedley, 'Judicial Independence is a Fragile Thing' *Financial Times* (22 January 2017).

[34] Lord Brown, 'The Unaccountability of Judges: Surely their Strength not their Weakness' in Christopher Forsyth and others (eds), *Effective Judicial Review: A Cornerstone of Good Governance* (OUP 2010) 213.

> judges ... reach their decisions in their own names, putting their own individual reputations at stake, dissenting where they feel compelled to do so. Thirdly, there is a judicial appeal structure, generally with the opportunity at least to apply for a second tier appeal.

This justification is not, however, applicable to the areas that we are considering. No reasons were ever advanced for promulgating the Judges' Rules, the Court of Criminal Appeal simply revealing them belatedly years later at the end of the judgment in *Voisin*.[35] The *post hoc* reasons offered to justify plea bargaining have been recognized by judges themselves to be spurious and are no longer seriously advanced.[36] The rationale offered for making trial judges 'case managers' (leading to the CrimPR)—that this was a response to a change in culture that had already taken place—was a naked inversion of events and nothing to do with 'accountability' in any meaningful sense.

It is clear then that none of the traditional justifications for judicial law-making apply to the formulation of the Judges' Rules, state-induced guilty pleas, or the CrimPR. While it has been an indelible part of our Constitution that judges can make law, governing by rules differs in significant ways from governing by law, however made, and in this there is a clue as to the real issue which requires a larger analysis of the meaning of the rule of law[37] and the common law in this context. It is to these that we now turn in that order.

Rule of Law

The rule of law is to be taken seriously if only because the Constitutional Reform Act 2005 in its first section[38] provides that the Act does not adversely affect—

35 *R v Voisin* [1918] 1 KB 531. Counsel had not been made aware of the Rules beforehand and they were not, accordingly, subjected to forensic scrutiny. Indeed, throughout the process, all the parties, including Lush J who intervened at various points, conducted the argument on the basis of authorities (the Criminal Evidence Act 1898 and a plethora of common law cases) which predated the coming into existence of the Rules. In effect, counsel had been misled as to the basis on which the appeal would be decided.

36 The 'justifications' put forward, now no longer tenable, include that a reduction in sentence was to reward remorseful defendants.

37 In his first Reith Lecture (2019) Sumption takes the view that '[t]he rule of law is one of the clichés of modern life which tends to be invoked, even by lawyers, without much reflection on what it actually means.' For a survey on how the term has developed since the twentieth century across prominent UK legal textbooks, see Brian Christopher Jones, 'The Rule of Law in UK Public Law Textbooks: From Critique to Acceptance?' [2018] Public Law 594.

38 Lord Hodge held this provision to be the 'first pillar' of ten, of which he argued, support judicial independence: 'Upholding the Rule of Law: How we Preserve Judicial Independence in the United Kingdom' Speech given to Lincoln's Inn Denning Society (7 November 2016). Further judicial speeches and writings on this and related topics are in copious supply. See, eg, the 2017 Atkin Lecture delivered by The Rt Hon Lord Justice Beatson FBA, 'Judicial Independence: Internal and External Challenges and Opportunities', especially footnote 10. For a scholarly perspective of the position of the judiciary as it

(a) the existing constitutional principle of the rule of law, or
(b) the Lord Chancellor's existing constitutional role in relation to that principle.

The reference to 'existing' principle is not to any earlier statutory enactment but to the *idea* and constitutional convention[39] that there is such a thing as the 'Rule of Law'. Under section 17 of the Constitutional Reform Act 2005, the Lord Chancellor is required to swear to 'respect the rule of law' and to 'defend the independence of the judiciary'.[40] Despite its uncertain origins,[41] the idea that the rule of law (although, of course, referenced elsewhere[42]) is a cornerstone of the Constitution of England and Wales,[43] long associated with Professor Dicey,[44] has been assiduously promoted by judges[45] and even embraced by some of the criminal justice system's strongest critics.[46]

While it remains an elusive and protean concept[47] and a matter of dispute as to whether it is formal or substantive,[48] the most influential attempt at giving

has developed since 2005, see further Graham Gee and others, *The Politics of Judicial Independence in the UK's Changing Constitution* (CUP 2015).

[39] As Geoffrey Wilson put it: 'The Rule of Law is not in fact a rule of law. It is a conventional obligation which lies in the first instance on government and the legislature, since it is up to them what powers they bestow in the statutes which give public bodies their powers in the first place' 'Postscript: The Courts, Law and Convention', in Rt Hon Lord Nolan and Sir Stephen Sedley, *The Making & Remaking of the British Constitution*, (Blackstone Press Ltd 1997) .

[40] Constitutional Reform Act 2005, s 17(1).

[41] The common assumption that the inspiration for the term was Professor Albert Venn Dicey in his book *An Introduction to the Study of the Law of the Constitution* (Macmillan and co 1885) (hereafter Dicey, *Law of the Constitution*) needs to be qualified by later scholarship. See John Allison, *The English Historical Constitution* (CUP 2007). The phrase goes back in English law at least to 1636 where in a Ship Money case (*Bromfield v Chambers*, 1636), the court is reported to have said: 'There is a rule of law and a rule of government, and things that may not be done by the rule of law may be done by the rule of government': James S Hart Jnr, *The Rule of Law 1603–1660* (Routledge 2003).

[42] The 'rule of law' has a prominent place in other settings, as, eg, in the preamble to the Universal Declaration of Human Rights (proclaimed by the United Nations General Assembly in Paris in 1948: General Assembly Resolution 217A).

[43] The House of Lords Constitution Committee, *The Process of Constitutional Change—Constitution Committee* (2011) identifies the rule of law as one of the 'five basic tenets of the UK constitution': para 10 <www.publications.parliament.uk/pa/ld201012/ldselect/ldconst/177/17707.htm> accessed 1 January 2020.

[44] See Dicey, *Law of the Constitution* (n 41) in which Dicey described the rule of law as comprising three components: (i) that no person can be punished or lawfully made to suffer a penalty except for a distinct breach of the law established in the ordinary legal manner before the ordinary courts; (ii) that everyone is subject to the same law administered in the ordinary courts; and (iii) that these principles derive from the decisions of the judges and not from any fixed constitution.

[45] An example is *Guardian News and Media Ltd v AB CD* [2014] EWCA Crim (B1) where Gross LJ said: 'The Rule of Law is a priceless asset of our country and a foundation of our Constitution': para 2.

[46] Most notably Edward Palmer Thompson, *Whigs and Hunters* (Pantheon Books 1975): 'I am insisting only on the obvious point ... that there is a difference between arbitrary power and the rule of law. We ought to expose the shams and inequities which may be concealed beneath this law. But the rule of law itself, the imposing of effective inhibitions upon power and the defence of the citizen from power's all-intrusive claims, seems to me to be an unqualified human good' 266.

[47] Sedley, *Lions Under the Throne* (n 33) 280.

[48] See Paul Craig, 'Formal and Substantive Conceptions of the Rule of Law: An Analytical Framework' [1997] Public Law 467. Those who favour the formal conception look to how the law is constructed and applied rather than to its values and substance.

meaning to the rule of law has been made by Lord Bingham.[49] Bingham set out its core meaning in these terms:[50]

> That all persons and authorities within the state, whether public or private, should be bound by and entitled to the benefit of laws publicly made, taking effect (generally) in the future and publicly administered in the courts.

The ingredients of the rule of law he listed are as follows:[51]

- Accessible, intelligible, clear and predictable
- Rights and liabilities determined by law not discretion
- Laws should apply equally (except where objective differences justify differentiation)
- Public powers must be exercised in good faith, fairly, for the purpose for which the powers were conferred and not unreasonably
- The law must adequately protect fundamental human rights
- Courts must be available and accessible
- Adjudicative procedures must be fair
- The state must comply with its obligations in international law

So that the importance of the rule of law was not underestimated, Bingham concluded that it was the difference between Good and Bad Government and that, while its concept was not fixed for all time, in a world divided by differences of such things as nationality, race, colour, religion, and wealth:[52]

> ... it is one of the greatest unifying factors, perhaps the greatest, the nearest we are likely to approach to a universal secular religion. It remains an ideal, but an ideal worth striving for, in the interests of good government and peace, at home and in the world at large.

On the rare occasions on which Bingham directly engages with criminal justice, he gives little or no attention to some of the central issues that have preoccupied the judges (and their critics) over the past fifty years and which we briefly note here. The Judges' Rules are a case in point.

[49] Tom Bingham, *The Rule of Law* (Penguin Books 2010) (hereafter Bingham, *Rule of Law*).

[50] ibid 37.

[51] Sir Stephen Sedley observed that the list was interesting for what it did not contain: '... a democratic polity; separation of the state's powers; an independent judiciary. All of these, it is manifest from his commentary, he takes for granted. But not everybody does' Sedley, *Lions Under the Throne* (n 33) 273.

[52] Bingham, *Rule of Law* (n 49) 174.

No serious observer could argue that the Rules meet the criterion of being 'accessible, intelligible, clear and predictable' or the related criterion that rights and liabilities should be determined 'by law not discretion'.[53] Indeed, the 'elasticity' which Parker LCJ claimed as their virtue, left the regulation of police investigation, the rights of suspects and defendants, and the rights and responsibilities of defence lawyers unclear, unpredictable, and inaccessible, entirely determined by judicial discretion.[54] Moreover, the judicial introduction of 'plea bargaining' and the placing of defendants under pressure to plead guilty without legislative or common law support[55] through threats of substantial differential sentencing, warrant no discussion by Bingham although clearly relevant to such matters as the right to a fair trial and the determination of rights and responsibilities by law not discretion. Similarly, while Bingham does discuss the issue of disclosure, this is confined to situations in which the matter comes before the trial judge to determine whether disclosure would jeopardize the public interest or compromise the defendant's right to a fair trial.[56] This is extraordinary because, apart from a disconnected glancing reference,[57] no serious attention is given to the notorious fact that underlying many miscarriages of justice and quashed convictions[58] has been prosecution non-disclosure of material that would have helped the defence and furthered the public interest.

[53] The case against discretion rather than law was compellingly made by Hewart LCJ in his book, *The New Despotism* (Ernest Benn Ltd 1929) whose principal target was the increase in quasi-judicial powers being given to bureaucrats and the growth of delegated legislation allowing Ministers to amend Acts of Parliament. In response, the British government formed a committee including Sir John Anderson (Lord Waverley) to investigate whether an improper trespassing on Parliament's legislative power or upon the domain of judicial authority by the executive had occurred. The report that followed, in 1932, was a whitewash: '... there is nothing to justify any lowering of the country's high opinion of civil servants or any grounds for believing that our constitutional machinery is developing in directions which are fundamentally wrong' (quoted in Robert Jackson, The *Chief—The Biography of Gordon Hewart, Lord Chief Justice of England (1922–40)* (Harrap & Co Ltd 1959) 215).

[54] Key decisions in related criminal cases fall short, we argue, of meeting the Dworkinian requirements of a proper interpretive approach as analysed by Trevor Allan: 'the judge's duty of fidelity to law combines with his conviction that legal principle always dictates a determinative answer to guarantee that legal and moral obligation perfectly coincide': 'Interpretation, Injustice, and Integrity' (2016) 36(1) Oxford Journal of Legal Studies 58, 59.

[55] Even the (*ex post facto*) statutory provision bearing upon the issue simply requires a court in determining sentence to have account of the stage at which the offender indicated an intention to plead guilty and the circumstances in which this indication was given. See, Criminal Justice Act 2003, s 144(1) replacing the Criminal Justice and Public Order Act 1994, s 48.

[56] Bingham was personally involved in the leading case of *R v H* (2004) UKHL 3.

[57] The reference in question, in the company of an equally slight and 'historical' reference to judges summing up in favour of conviction in highly tendentious terms, arises in a paragraph dealing, in the context of adjudicative procedures provided by the state, with the notion that 'fairness is a constantly evolving concept': Bingham, *Rule of Law* (n 49) 91–92.

[58] See, eg, *R v Pendleton* [2001] UKHL 66; *R v H and Ors* [2004] UKHL 3; *Mushtaq Ahmed v The Queen* [2010] EWCA Crim 2899; *R v Burridge* [2010] EWCA Crim 2847; *Jones v R* [2014] EWCA Crim 1337; *R v Jason Garland* [2016] EWCA Crim 1743; *Embleton v R* [2016] EWCA Crim 1968. See Mike Redmayne 'Disclosure and its Discontents' (2004) Criminal Law Review 441. See also Laurie Elks, *Righting Miscarriages of Justice? Ten Years of the Criminal Cases Review Commission* (JUSTICE 2010).

In a real sense, however, the problem with Bingham's analysis is not located merely in picking apart its individual components; the fatal flaw is found instead in the disjuncture between the elements of the rule of law in their totality and the core characteristics which constitute the common law in which, in England and Wales, the rule of law is to be ultimately located.

The Common Law

The common law is vital to an understanding of the English criminal justice system. One of the reasons that it has taken such hold is that its roots are deep in the social organization and the structure of rights in British history. The common law is nothing less than the outgrowth of a political settlement between the rulers and the ruled in which *the ruled* played a vital part. To take an early example: in 1649, a Leveller, John Lilburne, asserted the right not to incriminate and to be tried by jury, telling the court: 'By the laws of England I am not to answer questions against or concerning my selfe',[59] as well as the right to see the charges set out in English (not Latin or French). Similarly, the role of the jury in English criminal procedure was effectively secured in 1670 in *Bushell's Case*[60] in which a jury (under the leadership of Edward Bushell[61]) refused to be bullied by the trial judge[62] into returning a verdict against its conscience by convicting two Quakers, William Penn[63] and William Mead, of causing a tumultuous assembly by preaching to a crowd of several hundred in Gracechurch Street in London. And the right of a jury to return a general verdict, as opposed to a special verdict (in which the jury's role was restricted to answering specific questions set out by the trial judge who would then decide the effect of those answers in law), was effectively settled[64] in *R v Shipley*[65] when the

[59] Lilburne also asserted other rights including the right to know the charges, the right to counsel, and the right to call witnesses. For an account see Michael Braddick, *The Common Freedom of the People: John Lilburne and The English Revolution* (OUP 2018).

[60] (1670) 124 ER 1006. *Bushell's Case* is cited by Bingham (*Rule of Law* (n 49) 14) but only in relation to its endorsement of the writ of habeas corpus. Yet, it was in Chief Justice Vaughan's judgment in *Bushell's Case* that there appeared affirmation of the independence of the jury or what Plucknett termed 'a declaration of the irresponsibility of the jury' (Theodore Plucknett, *A Concise History of the Common Law* (Liberty Fund 1929, 1956 edn) (hereafter Plucknett, *Common Law*) 134, that is the right to return a verdict in accordance with their conscience without the shadow of punishment hanging over them. In an earlier show of independence, a London jury acquitted Sir Nicholas Throckmorton of high treason, eight of the jurors being fined considerable sums of money in consequence, the other four having 'confessed' to not considering the truth of the matter: Throckmorton's Case (1554) in Holinshed's *Chronicles of England, Scotland and Ireland*.

[61] Bushell is spelled as 'Bushel' in some instances.

[62] The trial was presided over by the Recorder, Thomas Howel J, together with two other judges, Thomas Bloodsworth and John Robinson, and one observer, the Lord Mayor of London (Samuel Stirling).

[63] William Penn was an individual of formidable intellect who later went on to found Pennsylvania.

[64] The issue was settled by Fox's Libel Act 1792, an Act promoted by Erskine's friend, Charles James Fox.

[65] (1784) 21 St Tr 847. See Lloyd Paul Stryker, *For the Defence* (Staples Press 1949).

jury, fortified by the impassioned arguments of Thomas Erskine, returned a verdict of 'Guilty of publishing only' as opposed to 'Guilty of sedition'.[66] Lord Bingham's formalistic analysis overlooks such cases[67] and their importance in demonstrating that the rule of law, like the common law itself, is and should be regarded as much more than a professional project.

The common law is distinctively home-grown, pragmatic, fact-based, and unscientific.[68] While the common law is an independent source of law, its importance goes much wider. The distribution of power, responsibility, and authority rests upon an unlegislated division between judges and counsel (and, indeed, the jury). At common law, judges do not play an active part in the dispute.[69] Historically, the role of the judge has been to *preside* and to ensure that the lawyers observe the rules. Under the principle of party autonomy, it is for the parties to collect evidence, determine which, if any, witnesses to call,[70] to examine witnesses[71] and present arguments on both the facts and the law.

The common law process[72] begins with a *factual matrix* which underpins a case; in criminal cases the basic 'facts' are initially contained in the allegations of the prosecution.[73] These basic facts are then subject to forensic examination by the defence which may, in turn, dispute facts advanced by the prosecution or propose alternative 'facts'.[74] It is in this context that rules of evidence seek to ensure that the parties do not distort the process by overly selective use of material. It is from among these competing theories of the case and the fact scenarios

[66] Erskine triumphed through the sheer power of persuasion against a mass of legal authority. See Plucknett, *Common Law* (n 60) 500 and Stephen James Fitzjames, *A History of the Criminal Law of England*, vol iii (Macmillan 1883) 330ff.

[67] Other champions of the common law might include: John Wilkes; John Horne Tooke; Thomas Hardy; and John Thelwell. To any such list would be added advocates such as Thomas Erskine and William Garrow.

[68] This section has benefitted from discussions with the late Professor Geoffrey Wilson and his unpublished notes.

[69] This was not always the case. See John Langbein, 'The Criminal Trial Before Lawyers' (1978) 45 University of Chicago Law Review 263.

[70] Exceptionally, in the interests of justice, a judge may call a witness who has not been produced by either side.

[71] The judge has, however, an overall responsibility to ensure that the trial is fair. The judge is accordingly entitled to ask supplementary questions or questions designed to clarify answers already given and to clear up ambiguities. Extraordinarily, the Court of Appeal has upheld convictions notwithstanding extensive judicial questioning such that the judge at times assumed the role of prosecutor: *R v Webb and Simpson* [2000] EWCA Crim 56.

[72] According to Plucknett, the common law was originally merely the custom of the King's Court; the regular routine which they developed in the administration of justice became settled and known, and therefore served as the basis upon which people could forecast with some certainty the future decisions of the courts: Plucknett, *Common Law* (n 60) 342.

[73] Historically, the defendant was under no obligation to contribute to the facts and, even though in serious cases today there must be a written defence statement if there is to be a not guilty plea, the statutory requirement may be satisfied by a mere denial of the truth of the prosecution allegations.

[74] It should be noted that 'facts' are the outcome of a social process and are in reality 'constructed'. On this, see Malcolm Spector and John Kitsuse, *Constructing Social Problems* (Transaction Publishers 2001); Mike McConville, Andrew Sanders, and Roger Leng, *The Case for the Prosecution* (Routledge 1991).

underpinning them that the facts material to the decision are drawn. The importance of these material 'facts' cannot be underestimated:[75] they constrain the parties; more than this, they constrain the trial judge in summing up to the jury; and more than this, they constrain future courts which seek to utilize the principle underlying the decision as a precedent. It is because of this that it has been the practice and culture of the common law that legal arguments in court, legal advice out of court, and judgments of the court are conducted in terms of the factual matrix and in terms of the decisions of past cases and not only the decisions but the *judgments* in past cases.

The quality of the system accordingly is dependent not only on the quality of the trial judges[76] but even more on the quality and integrity of the barristers[77] who present the cases before them.[78] Independent and fearless advocates ensure that the facts are explored and arguments tested even in the face of an overbearing or dim-witted judge. The close relationship that has existed between judges and the Bar[79] is accordingly of great constitutional and practical importance.

At the heart of the criminal trial is the jury before whom the competing theories and arguments are presented.[80] Trial by jury, though now forming a statistically small fraction of determinations,[81] is at the core of criminal cases whose proponents claim as the embodiment of the principle of participatory democracy, however imperfect that has been in the past.[82] More than this, the legitimacy of the verdict is claimed to be enhanced, at least in 'serious' cases, by entrusting the defendant's fate to his or her 'peers' rather than to professional

[75] This is one of the messages of the famous article: Arthur Goodhart, 'Determining the Ratio Decidendi of a Case' (1930) 40 Yale Law Journal 161. Goodhart summarized the central points as follows: 'The principle of the case is found by taking account (a) of the facts treated by the judge as material, and (b) his decision based on them ... In finding the principle it is also necessary to establish what facts were held to be immaterial by the judge, for the principle may depend as much on exclusion as it does on inclusion' 182.

[76] Of course, judges themselves may fall into error: *R v Waters* [2015] EWCA Crim 402; *R v Uddin & Ors* [2015] EWCA Crim 1918; *R v Clark* [2015] EWCA Crim 2192.

[77] For a history of the Bar see Barnett Hollander, *The English Bar: A Priesthood* (Bowes 1956). In England and Wales, barristers no longer have a monopoly on advocacy in the higher courts with a large number of solicitor-advocates active in criminal cases.

[78] That confidence which judges must have in counsel may be compromised in individual cases by what appears to be a fall from the standards. See *Ekaireb v R* [2015] EWCA Crim 1936; *R v Ali Shabani* [2015] EWCA Crim 1924; and *R v Dodd* [2013] EWCA Crim 660.

[79] Whenever judges speak in public lectures they pay tribute to the legal profession, usually calling them 'independent' and 'fearless' (eg, Bingham, *Rule of Law* (n 49) 92).

[80] See Patrick Devlin, *Trial by Jury* (Stevens 1956); Mark Findlay and Peter Duff (eds), *The Jury Under Attack* (Butterworths 1988).

[81] Whereas magistrates' courts dispose of approximately 1.5 million cases each year. By contrast, in the Crown Court where jury trial is available (some 60 per cent of those committed to the Crown Court actually plead guilty), the latest figures show that 85,620 defendants were dealt with in trial cases, of whom 57,457 (67.1 per cent) pleaded guilty to all counts, 16,508 (19.3 per cent) were acquitted, and 11,655 (13.6 per cent) convicted: Ministry of Justice, *Criminal Court Statistics* (2017).

[82] Notoriously, the property qualification for jury service was not abolished until the Criminal Justice Act 1972, ss 25–26.

judges who may have a more limited insight into the community from which the defendant is drawn.[83]

In the event of an appeal, the outcome is a judgment at the heart of which is the doctrine of precedent. Judges do not simply announce the result but discuss the legal conclusions in the light of relevant judicial decisions in the past. It is the responsibility of judges to show where and how the decision fits into the general pattern of past decisions. Judgments are discursive precisely because the route by which the decision is reached and the underlying principles are an expected part of the common law.

This arrangement is not simply a formal allocation of responsibilities: it is a celebration of *values* that the system holds dear. The adversary system manifests the significance of independent decision-making, the autonomy of the individual, and the maintenance of personal freedoms, so that no one arm of the state has carriage of the affairs of its citizens. In this way the common law not only privileges transparency but importantly reasoned argument—appeal to principle and regard to facts—tested both in the forensic arena of the trial and also before a number of tiers of the judiciary.[84]

In its ideal form, the common law process is thus both 'democratic' and 'developmental'. Democratic because rulings on law and verdicts at trial arise from argument tested openly in a participatory process.[85] Developmental because appellate judgments founded in the factual matrix ensures that the law, excepting statutory intervention, evolves *only incrementally* as and when new factual (or social) situations arise.[86] The common law is accordingly fluid because it begins with and is driven by a factual matrix which is unique but which may yield a more generalized rule or principle which in turn is then tested and refined in the light of other similar factual situations which may abrogate or confine the rule or make it more expansive.

The common law ideally yields not only theoretical benefits but *practical* dividends. Public confidence in the verdict derives not only from the burden of proof which requires the prosecution to establish guilt beyond reasonable doubt[87]

[83] Sean Doran, 'Trial by Jury' in Mike McConville and Geoffrey Wilson (eds), *The Handbook of The Criminal Justice Process* (OUP 2002).

[84] See Thomas LCJ, 'Developing Commercial Law through the Courts: Rebalancing the Relationship between the Courts and Arbitration' Bailii Lecture (9 March 2016).

[85] cf references in the internal Home Office files to 'private assurances' about the prosecution of capital offences said to have been offered by the DPP. See also examples of private exchanges given in Thomas Grant, *Jeremy Hutchinson's Case Histories* (John Murray 2015): a plea bargain offered by a civil servant at a private dinner party in the *ABC Case* at 311; and 'an accommodation' offered to the defendants in *R v Cairns & Ors* (1971) *unreported* whereby, in return for guilty pleas, the prosecution would not press for the case to go to the higher court but remain in the magistrates' court, at 281.

[86] This is not a defence of judicial law-making but a statement as to the limits to which it can legitimately go in its ideal justification.

[87] The defence never have to establish innocence and thus, as John Mortimer put it, the defence barrister 'is not a kind of professional hypocrite': Edward Majoribanks, 'Introduction to *Famous Trials of Marshall Hall*' (Advanpress Ltd 1989) xii.

but also from determination by an independent tribunal of fact. In this way the system offers some protection against innocent people being wrongly convicted (because the common law deems it a greater outrage that innocent people are punished than that the guilty go free) even at some expense to itself.[88] And experience has shown that, with notable exceptions, a properly conducted trial[89] can produce a correct result, sometimes to the surprise of the defence advocate[90] or the judge.[91] The practical result is important as Sir Stephen Sedley acutely observes:[92]

> Outcome is important because it is through outcome that we judge the principle which gave rise to it; if the principle is worth fighting for, it must be because of the capacity to produce acceptable outcomes. Principles, like rights, are not simply abstractions: their concrete outcomes are their justifications. The argument about principles and rights cannot be conducted purely or even principally in legal terms.

[88] We require the state to establish the accused's guilt. If the result is the occasional trial lasting for days (when they used to be measured in hours or less), and if as a result some guilty people walk free, 'it is not necessarily an excessive price to pay for trying to ensure that people are not convicted unless a fair trial has made a jury sure of their guilt': Stephen Sedley, *Ashes and Sparks* (CUP 2011) (hereafter Sedley, *Ashes and Sparks*) 32.

[89] Or, indeed, full argument as the UK Supreme Court acknowledged in *R v Jogee and Ruddock v The Queen* (Jamaica) [2016] UKSC 8 (hereafter *Jogee and Ruddock*) where in correcting the law on secondary party liability which had been misstated for thirty years, the Supreme Court explained: '… we have had the benefit of a much fuller analysis than on previous occasions when the topic has been considered' 80.

[90] See, eg, Harford Montgomery Hyde, *Norman Birkett* (Hamish Hamilton 1964) 362 describing a murder case at Nottingham assizes in 1933 in which Norman Birkett informed the judge (Finlay J) beforehand in fixing a trial date that he did not think it would take up much time 'as the facts were clear and the only possible defence seemed to be insanity'. However, following the cross-examination of the doctor who had performed the post mortem examination and an unexpected answer to one question, Birkett realized that there was a chance of an acquittal. In fact, the jury acquitted of all charges (murder, manslaughter, and attempted murder); and (ibid 174) an acquittal was secured in a murder case where an undisputed act (wife smoking as the doctor came to the house after she had shot dead—accidentally she claimed—her husband) portrayed by the prosecution as 'callously indifferent to the shooting' was nullified by a simple question from Birkett and simple answer: 'Why did you light a cigarette?' 'Because I was so shaken. I wanted to steady my nerves.' Again, in the case of Annie Dyer, charged with murder of her newborn child, the prosecution rested substantially on the fact that she said: 'How can anyone get rid of a baby?' just before the baby must have died and an apparent admission to a police officer. Yet the very words relied upon by the prosecution, by a slight change of emphasis and punctuation, constituted a conclusive defence. 'How *can* anyone get rid of a baby like this!' together with an admission that when she said this she was kissing and feeding the child contradicted the sense suggested by the prosecution. As to the admission: 'I killed it. I did not know what to do with it. I put it in a box.' The whole meaning of the statement is changed by making the middle sentence go with the last and not with the first, as illustrated by Marshall Hall and then fully agreed by Wills J. See Edward Majoribanks, *For the Defence: The Life of Sir Edward Marshall Hall* (Macmillan 1930) 110–11.

[91] See, eg, Majoribanks (ibid) describing the Camden murder trial in which Grantham J's summing up started heavily against the prisoner Robert Wood but, as the judge reviewed the evidence, suddenly it changed: 'I do not think the prosecution have brought the case home against him clearly enough' ibid 246. See also Majoribanks' accounts of other judicial changes of mind at 22, 115–17.

[92] Sedley, *Ashes and Sparks* (n 88) 355.

Foundation Stone of the Rule of Law

With an understanding of the common law it becomes possible to see more clearly the basic flaws in Lord Bingham's conception of the rule of law and of its significance for such 'inventions' as the Judges' Rules, state-induced guilty pleas, and the CrimPR. The essence of both the common law and the rule of law rest not only upon their ultimate purpose—that government itself has limited powers, challenges to which are determined by the courts—but additionally upon compliance with a particular *form*, and it is this form or process that is absent from Bingham's consideration. This is a critical restraining influence on judicial law-making which is a refining, not revolutionary, process.[93]

The setting should also, with rare exceptions be open, as stated by Lady Hale:[94]

> The principle of open justice is one of the most precious in our law. It is there to reassure the public and the parties that our courts are indeed doing justice according to law. In fact, there are two aspects to this principle. The first is that justice should be done in open court, so that the people interested in the case, the wider public and the media can know what is going on. The court should not hear and take into account evidence and arguments that they have not heard or seen. The second is that the names of the people whose cases are being decided, and others involved in the hearing, should be public knowledge.

A related aspect of this was identified by Lord Hoffmann, in commenting on the 1964 version of the Judges' Rules, when, noting that the judges clearly considered that it was absolutely essential to the fair administration of justice that suspects should be reminded at regular intervals that they are not obliged to say anything, added that the Rules 'being simply a bald statement of judicial policy, we are left in ignorance of the reasons why the judges placed such great faith in the giving of cautions'.[95]

Openness, the basis in and forensic testing of factual matrices, individualism, personal responsibility, and the duty to give reasons are simply aspects of the form that constitutes the foundations of the common law process and of the rule of law itself. Without this understanding, while each of the criteria Bingham enumerates has some bearing upon criminal justice, in the absence of locating them within the bedrock of the common law, they simply become part of an ideology about the

[93] Thus, in tort law, while the principle derived from earlier cases and set out by Lord Atkin in *Donoghue v Stevenson* [1932] AC 562 namely, that persons must avoid acts or omissions which can reasonably be foreseen would be likely to injure their neighbour, became the source of an expanded law of negligence, its application to such matters as psychiatric injury (*Alcock v Chief Constable of South Yorkshire* [1992] 1 AC 310) and pure economic loss (*Caparao Industries plc v Dickman* [1990] 2 AC 605) had to be worked out by the judges incrementally as new factual circumstances arose.

[94] *R (on the application of C) v Secretary of State for Justice* [2016] UKSC 2.

[95] Leonard Hoffmann, 'The Judges' Rules' (1964) 7 *The Lawyer* 23, 24.

office of the judge rather than *about the conduct and practices of courts*. In this articulation, so often repeated, judges become merchants of conformity[96] and integrity, and the rule of law simply a tool of impression management.

Whereas form and process are at the heart of the common law, they are absent from the Judges' Rules, as they are from the evolution of plea bargaining rules and the CrimPR. Cultivated in secret,[97] not underpinned by a specific factual matrix,[98] without cause assigned,[99] absent forensic scrutiny,[100] subject to unknown influence,[101] and lacking a justification in articulated reasons,[102] they contradict the very foundations of the rule of law and the form and process of the common law. And the importance of this is that form has not simply been a process but rather a *protection* for everyone involved against secret decision-making, arbitrariness, differential treatment, partiality, and corruption.

Law, Policy, and Guidelines

There is broad, though not universal, agreement that the constitutional separation of powers assigns primary responsibility for policy to Parliament and the executive, while questions concerning legality are primarily reserved for the courts.[103] Policy in this context may be regarded as the promotion of some general notion

[96] Subject always to 'let downs' (as when an errant judge, such as Judge Pickles, spills the beans on plea bargaining practices to the RCCP (reporting in 1981)) or 'ill-considered gestures' (such as Widgery LCJ's outburst in *Cain* [1976] Criminal Law Review 464 which had to be rectified by a Practice Direction of 26 July 1976) or 'plain wrongdoing' as when judges are caught in criminal violations, eg, Keith Shaw (a Deputy District Judge in the magistrates' who was sentenced to twenty weeks' prison for fraud offences, suspended for two years on condition of undertaking 200 hours unpaid work); and Constance Briscoe (a Recorder, convicted of three offences of perverting the course of justice and sentenced to sixteen weeks' imprisonment.)

[97] Lord Parker did not want the public to be involved when the Judges' Rules were being considered in 1961–64 and they were not in any way consulted in 1912 or 1918.

[98] At no stage in their various incarnations did the Rules address any factual foundation.

[99] Even when a full court in *R v Goodyear* (2005) EWCA Crim 888 set out new state-induced guilty plea rules under the rubric of 'advanced indications of sentence', it rested its justification on the basis of an alleged 'very different culture' to that which obtained when the earlier decision of *R v Turner* (1970) 54 Cr App R 352 institutionalized plea bargaining under the guise of banning it. See Mike McConville and Luke Marsh, *Criminal Judges* (Edward Elgar 2014) 94ff.

[100] While the courts have amended the state-induced guilty plea rules from time to time, this has resulted in large measure from the fact that the initial 'policy' or 'guidelines' were drafted outside the litigation crucible. The continued ambivalence in the guilty plea structure is further empirically demonstrated by Juliet Horne, 'A Plea of Convenience' (PhD thesis, University of Warwick) <warwick.ac.uk/lib-publications>).

[101] The role of Home Office officials as well as the police lobby on the development of the Judges' Rules is only now coming to light. The involvement, if any, of the executive in drafting or proposing the *Turner Rules* and *Goodyear Guidelines* is not known at present.

[102] The judicial or pseudo-judicial initiatives that we are examining have been entirely without reasoned defence (Judges' Rules) or with justifications abandoned as soon as proffered (plea bargaining) or with explanations that defy legal (as opposed to political) reason (CrimPR).

[103] An absolute division in terms of function cannot be sustained and there is a large literature, not relevant for present purposes, exploring the viability of the division.

of the 'public welfare' rather than determining issues of principle which arise in individual cases[104] (appealing to the rights of individuals).[105] Under the generally accepted division, government responsibility for policy is secured through ministerial responsibility to Parliament while the legality of acts and decisions of Ministers and officials is determined by the courts. Since the rule of law requires the strictest political neutrality of the judges, even the giving of advice in public to Ministers in respect of proposed policy formulation may be considered objectionable,[106] the more so if the advice is undisclosed.

While this would seem at first sight to take us to policy, we hesitate to call the Judges' Rules acts of policy. Policy requires a measure of consistency not a prescription or formula so infused with discretion that its application in any given case is unpredictable and arbitrary. As Sir Stephen Sedley observed, 'Policy has virtues of flexibility which rules lack and *virtues of consistency* which discretion lacks' (emphasis supplied).[107] Policy requires an element of public disclosure as to its provenance and purpose. Not only were the Judges' Rules formulated in a confidential private setting, the full records of which remain concealed from the public, but they were shaped by civil servants rather than the judges themselves with their authorship misrepresented. Setting aside such issues, the formulation of 'policy' in this way, even if it had been undertaken by the judiciary alone, is objectionable for a number of reasons which we outline below.

In the first place, even if they were considered qualified to do so, judges ordinarily lack the information necessary to engage in policy determination. The limitations of evidence production,[108] which under adversary procedures are largely in the hands of the parties and presented in a bivalent form, are such as to preclude any wide-ranging examination of public policy.[109] This is even clearer in the case of the Judges' Rules because there was no external input in 1912 and 1918 and, when the major revision took place between 1961 and 1964, there was no opportunity for forensic discussion in a trial setting,[110] public consultation was deliberately excluded, Members of Parliament side-lined at the outset and subsequently prevented from debating drafts, and even large sections of the police were not consulted. Similarly, plea bargaining was introduced without any consultation, public or otherwise, and

[104] Even law-making is, for courts, a piecemeal exercise, limited by the chance of litigation. See Lord Devlin, 'Judges and Lawmakers' (1976) 39 Modern Law Review 1.

[105] This overall division is, of course, open to various qualifications since, eg, judges often have to take account of the public interest, especially in civil cases but the broad distinction is useable in the present context. See further Ronald Dworkin, *Taking Rights Seriously* (Harvard University Press 1972) and the voluminous literature to which this has given rise.

[106] See the discussion in Bingham, *Rule of Law* (n 49) 93–95.

[107] Sedley, *Lions Under the Throne* (n 33) 153.

[108] In the ordinary case, there are also limitations imposed by procedure.

[109] Timothy Endicott, 'The Impossibility of the Rule of Law' (1999) 19 Oxford Journal of Legal Studies 1.

[110] The Law Society made various suggestions as to what might or might not be included as did JUSTICE but these were not directed to the drafts actually under discussion.

with no known input from outside the judiciary. While the CrimPR were eventually accorded a form of Parliamentary delegated authority, this came after they had been in essence and in disposition[111] unilaterally introduced as a judicial revelation[112] with a distinctive managerial philosophy.[113]

In the second place, the traditional function of courts involves the sifting of evidence and analysis of legal argument, independently of matters of public interest in order to ascertain and delineate the scope of legal rights and duties. Judges are not generally considered qualified by reason of training or experience to weigh the competing facets of public interest that are concerned in policy-making.[114] This is particularly so where, as here, the interests in question involve the right of citizens to go about their business freely on the one hand and, on the other, the interest of the state in order maintenance and the use of force to secure this.

[111] As will be clear, the design and philosophy of the CrimPR reflects all too well the perspectives of senior judges previously evidenced under the Judges' Rules.

[112] An explanatory memorandum accompanying the first version of the CrimPR stated, under the heading 'Policy objectives': 'These Rules bring together in one place—for the first time—the various rules of court that presently govern the practice and procedure to be followed in the criminal courts. The new rules, in Parts 1 and 3 of the Criminal Procedure Rules, are *intended to bring about a culture change* in the management of criminal cases by the courts' (emphasis supplied <http://www.legislation.gov.uk/uksi/2005/384/pdfs/uksiem_20050384_en.pdf>). However, the change in judicial approach was heralded by the review of Auld LJ (Sir Robin Auld, *The Criminal Courts Review* (Royal Courts of Justice 2001)) which advocated both codified procedural rules (ch 10, para 277) and more robust court control over cases and parties with the unsubstantiated claims: 'There is now *wide acceptance* that there is scope for greater intervention by the court … for more … co-operation by the parties … in the preparation of cases for hearing' (ch 10, para 2, emphasis supplied); '*For many*, the sooner the court takes hold of the case at an early preliminary stage, the better' (ch 10, para 203, emphasis supplied). Auld's underlying philosophy is ultimately seen in his view that 'where there is a need for a pre-trial hearing the court and the parties should take full advantage of it to resolve all outstanding issues as to the conduct of the trial and to deal with any preliminary issues of law or fact that will assist that resolution. This calls for the court to adopt a more interventionist and authoritative role than has been traditional in identifying the issues for trial and in securing the proper preparation by both parties to deal efficiently with them' (ch 10, para 7).

[113] Auld's recommendation and, importantly, *the underlying philosophy*, was enthusiastically adopted by the key cases of *Chaaban* [2003] EWCA Crim 1012 and *Jisl* [2004] EWCA Crim 696 in which, under its own steam, the Court of Appeal held that courts have a duty to manage criminal cases effectively. As it was put in *Jisl*: 'Active, hands on, case management, both pre-trial and throughout the trial itself, is *now regarded* as an essential part of the judge's duty. The profession must understand that *this has become and will remain part of the normal trial process*, and that cases must be prepared and conducted accordingly' (emphasis supplied). Even after the CrimPR came into force (on 15 April 2005), strengthening these earlier pronouncements, their collective impact was slow-setting cement amongst the legal profession. See, eg, Thomas LJ in *R (on the application of the DPP) v Chorley Justices* [2006] EWHC 1795 at [24] who stated: '[The CrimPR] effected a sea change in the way in which cases should be conducted, but it appears from what has happened in this case that not everyone has appreciated the fundamental change to the conduct of cases … that has been brought about by the rules'. See, further Jenny McEwan, 'From Adversarialism to Managerialism: Criminal Justice in Transition' (2011) 31(4) Legal Studies 519; Roderick Denyer, 'The Changing Role of the Judge in the Criminal Process' (2010) 14 International Journal of Evidence & Proof 96; Andrew Hall, 'Where Do the Advocates Stand when the Goalposts Have Been Moved' (2010) 14 International Journal of Evidence & Proof 107.

[114] The legislature may be better placed to secure popular support for proposed reforms and, ultimately, to determine what is an acceptable compromise in the face of conflicting interests and opinions. See Jonathan Sumption, 'Judicial and Political Decision-Making: The Uncertain Boundary' (2011) 16 Judicial Review 301. See also Dimitrios Kyritsis, 'Constitutional Review in Representative Democracy' (2012) 22 Oxford Journal of Legal Studies 297.

In the third place, even if they were trained and even if supplied with relevant information, by reason of their composition and culture, judges are ill-suited to set policy in areas as sensitive as police–public coercive relations and the pressurizing of defendants to plead guilty.[115] This is not about the character of individual judges but about the homogeneous character of the judiciary as a whole, its lack of diversity, and a particular orientation in respect of criminal justice. This is a sensitive area but it has not gone unremarked by distinguished lawyers. Thus, Serjeant Sullivan, writing in 1952 said this:[116]

> The Bench is exclusively composed of men who have grown up in the artificial atmosphere of the ruling class, the public school, the university, the well-provided apprenticeships to the Inns of Court, lucrative practice and the accumulation of wealth. None have ever suffered that excellent corrective to theoretical opinion, hunger for the want of the price of a meal.

These sentiments were echoed more recently by Sir Stephen Sedley[117]:

> The real problem with judges is that they come very largely from a tranche of society whose values, culture, données and attitudes are homogenous because they are socially and educationally inbred.

Additionally, arising out of decisions in the area of judicial review, some have questioned why judges, rather than Parliament, have the right to make policy determinations at all.[118] A major (but not sole) concern is lack of diversity.

The outcry over remarks of Lord Sumption in regard to gender inequality in the judiciary[119] elicited a set of official statistics which were presented as showing that more than half of judges under forty years of age in England and Wales are women.[120] As Professor Kate Malleson pointed out, the official response gave a

[115] See also Griffith, 'Brave New World' (n 12).

[116] Serjeant Alexander Martin Sullivan, QC, *The Last Serjeant* (Macdonald 1952) 276.

[117] Sedley, *Ashes and Sparks* (n 88) 22. See also Griffith, 'Brave New World' (n 12): 'In the performance of their judicial duties they seek to be honest, unprejudiced, and understanding. But, like the rest of us, they are limited by their background, their class, their status, and the narrowing of their experience which leads to their areas of ignorance' 174.

[118] See Griffith ibid.

[119] In an interview for the London *Evening Standard*, Sumption, speaking of the dearth of women in senior judicial positions, is reported to have said that while the lack of diversity is a significant problem, it is not the only one and: 'It takes time. You've got to be patient. The change in the status and achievements of women in our society, not just in the law but generally, is an enormous cultural change that has happened over the last 50 years or so. It has to happen naturally. It will happen naturally. But in the history of a society like ours, 50 years is a very short time.'

[120] See, eg, Owen Bowcott, 'More than Half of Judges under 40 in England and Wales are Women' *The Guardian* (30 July 2015). The Judicial Diversity statistics (2018) reveal 29 per cent of court judges were female and around half of court judges aged under fifty were female (the picture improved at magistrate level, with 55 per cent being female but there were very few magistrates aged under 40 (4 per cent)).

wholly misleading picture of the progress towards gender balance in the judiciary since, at the time, judges under forty made up only sixty out of 3,238 judges in post, adding:[121]

> Moreover, almost all of these younger female judges are clustered at the lower ranks of the judiciary. The picture at the top has barely changed at all. Of the 38 court of appeal judges, eight are women compared with seven in 2014. In the high court, 21 out of 108 judges are women, unchanged from last year. Lady Hale remains the only woman in the supreme court. Nor are younger female judges moving up the judicial hierarchy. Senior judges are generally appointed from a pool of fee-paid part-time judges such as recorders. This group has the lowest proportion of women of all the ranks, at 16%. Further, only 44% of the Judicial Appointments Commission's recommendations for legal posts in the courts and tribunals in 2014–15 were women, down from 52% in 2012–13. Lord Sumption's claim that it may take 50 years to achieve a diverse judiciary is starting to look extremely optimistic.

If the overall picture is one of homogeneity,[122] the position at the top in criminal justice is even more dramatic.[123] Thus, of the nineteen Chief Justices since the office

[121] 'Little Progress towards a Diverse Judiciary on either Gender or Race' *The Guardian* (3 August 2015). Professor Malleson added: 'The prospects for more solicitors or BAME (black, Asian and minority ethnic) lawyers being appointed—whether women or men—is particularly bleak. The senior judiciary remains dominated by white, male barristers from wealthy backgrounds.' In total, 7 per cent of court judges identified as black, Asian, and minority ethnic (BAME) (this increased to 12 per cent at magistrate level), whilst a third of court judges were from non-barrister backgrounds for court judges (a 3 per cent fall since 2014): Judicial Diversity statistics (ibid). At the senior end of the Bar, the number of ethnic minority candidates applying to become Queen's Counsel has reduced. The number of successful female applicants has also decreased: 'Fewer Women Advocates Make QC Grade' *The Times* (11 January 2019).

[122] 'Top judges and QCs ten times more likely to be privately educated' Sutton Trust and Prime (November 2015). A recent report shows that this is not untypical of the power structures in Britain. The study, Elitist Britain, by the Sutton Trust and Social Mobility Commission (25 June 2019) paints a picture of a country whose power structures remain dominated by a narrow section of the population: the 7 per cent who attend independent schools, and the roughly 1 per cent who graduate from just two universities, Oxford and Cambridge. Among the findings: two-fifths (39 per cent) of the elite group as a whole were privately educated, more than five times as many as the population at large, while a quarter (24 per cent) had graduated from Oxbridge. Politics, the media, and public service all show high proportions of privately educated in their number, including 65 per cent of senior judges, 59 per cent of Civil Service permanent secretaries, and 57 per cent of the House of Lords. Significantly, the senior judiciary top the league tables both of those drawn from independent schools and those Oxbridge educated <https://www.suttontrust.com/research-paper/elitist-britain-2019/>. For a judicial view of the efforts to change, see Lord Burnett, LCJ, 'A Changing Judiciary for a Modern Age' (2019) <https://www.judiciary.uk/wp-content/uploads/2019/02/mt-treasurers-lecture-final-for-publishing.pdf>.

[123] For a review of diversity in the High Court, see Michael Blackwell, 'Old Boys' Networks, Family Connections and the English Legal Profession' [2012] Public Law 425. Blackwell's survey concludes: 'The evidence presented . . . indicates that the English judiciary is still predominantly composed of men from a narrow range of educational backgrounds often with family connections to the legal profession' 442. See further Brenda Hale, 'Equality and the Judiciary: Why Should we Want more Women Judges?' [2001] Public Law 489; Terence Etherton, 'Liberty, the Archetype and Diversity: A Philosophy of Judging' [2010] Public Law 727. According to a recent survey for *The Times*, judicial harassment

was established in 1875, excluding the two who did not attend university at all and the one who was educated in Ireland, ten went to Cambridge (62.5 per cent), five to Oxford (31.25 per cent); one to UCL (6.25 per cent).[124] All were white; all were male, as Table 8.1 shows:

Table 8.1 Composition of Lord Chief Justices 1859–

Lord Chief Justices	Date	Gender	Ethnicity	Education
Alexander Cockburn	1859–1880	Male	White	Cambridge
John Coleridge	1880–1894	Male	White	Oxford
Charles Russell	1894–1900	Male	White	*Ireland*
Richard Webster	1900–1913	Male	White	Cambridge
Rufus Isaacs[1]	1913–1921	Male	White	*No University*
Alfred Lawrence	1921–1922	Male	White	Cambridge
Gordon Hewart	1922–1940	Male	White	Oxford
Thomas Inskip	1940–1946	Male	White	Cambridge
Rayner Goddard	1946–1958	Male	White	Oxford
Hubert Parker	1958–1971	Male	White	Cambridge
John Widgery	1971–1980	Male	White	*No University*
Geoffrey Lane	1980–1992	Male	White	Cambridge
Peter Taylor	1992–1996	Male	White	Cambridge
Tom Bingham	1996–2000	Male	White	Oxford
Harry Woolf	2000–2005	Male	White	UCL
Nicolas Phillips	2005–2008	Male	White	Cambridge
Igor Judge	2005–2013	Male	White	Cambridge
John Thomas	2013–2017	Male	White	Cambridge
Ian Burnett	2017–	Male	White	Oxford

[1] Rufus Isaacs had an eventful life before joining the Bar which included working in his father's trading firm; working his passage on a ship to Rio and back; working at the Stock Exchange by means of a false statement regarding his age and being 'hammered' for inability to meet his debts and being embroiled later as a judge in share dealing scandal.

(in various guises) in particular of women junior counsel is an unwelcome feature of the current legal landscape: Frances Gibb and Jonathan Ames, 'Judges Guilty of Bullying in Legal World that "Stinks of Testosterone"' (1 January 2019). See also 'Bullying Judges "Driving Women to Quit Bar"' *The Times* (12 February 2019) and 'Male Barristers Get the Big Cases Says Top Judge' *The Times* (8 March 2019).

[124] Harry Woolf LCJ was destined for Cambridge but his parents moved to London.

In the result, judges lack the breadth of experience to engage in policy formulation, certainly not of the radical kind involved in regulating the police or pressurizing defendants over plea. Determinations of the kind the judges have made present difficulties precisely because they are made outside the formal and intended structures by unrepresentative individuals or groups acting without appropriate information in settings where preformed notions and prejudices may thrive. The highly unrepresentative character of judges (and, incidentally, civil servants) is worrying for England and Wales; it is deeply disturbing for the rest of the world where they have secured such influence (see Chapter 11).

Conclusion

The Judges' Rules, state-induced guilty pleas, and the CrimPR all fail the basic tests associated with the rule of law and the common law in terms of both form and substance. Bingham's flawed analysis of the rule of law overlooks the heart of the common law—the adversary process itself—which manifests the significance of independent decision-making, the autonomy of the individual, and the maintenance of personal freedoms. In contrast to these judicially created stratagems, the common law, in the development of which the people have played a vital part, privileges transparency and reasoned argument tested forensically at trial and on appeal. These judicial innovations not only contradict the essence of the common law but, being made outside the formal structures by unrepresentative individuals without appropriate information in settings where preformed notions and prejudices may thrive, additionally cannot meet the tests of legitimate policy-making.

9

Constitutionalism and the Westminster Model

Introduction

In this chapter, we address the issue of judges and constitutionalism within a framework that is commonly expressed as a separation of powers involving a tripartite arrangement between Parliament, the executive and the judiciary. Although our principal focus has been upon the evolution of the Judges' Rules, we attach weight to other elements that we regard as of vital importance, including, but not limited to, the creation of state-induced guilty pleas ('plea bargaining') and of the Criminal Procedure Rules (CrimPR).

The means by which the Judges' Rules were drafted and redrafted has important implications for issues regarding constitutionalism and for the politics of the judiciary. In this process, there is, on the one hand, direct evidence of the ways in which the Civil Service orchestrated and/or authored the drafting of the Rules themselves and, on the other hand, the coercive, improper, and hence 'unconstitutional' influence that the executive was able to exercise when the judiciary sought to stick to principles.

Constitutionalism

The interrelationship between the executive and the judiciary has implications for our appreciation of the locus of power within the different arms of the state. Certain understandings must be qualified because, given the largely unwritten constitution of the UK,[1] it is difficult if not impossible to locate definitive guidance on the core issues of the 'separation of powers',[2] the 'independence of the

[1] With such provisions as the Constitutional Reform Act 2005, the Constitutional Reform and Governance Act 2010, and the Human Rights Act 1998, elements of the constitution are now incorporated into written form.

[2] Thus, for some, the proposal for a new Supreme Court in the United Kingdom was little more than 'superficial Americanisation' (Sir Christopher Foster, Letter to *The Times* (10 November 2003)) whereas to Professor Jeffrey Jowell the separation of the judiciary was essential because the judges were 'the ultimate arbiters of the actions of the other branches of government from which they should both be, and be seen to be, demonstrably independent' (Letter to *The Times* (13 November 2003)). The writings on this issue have given rise, with some justification, to the idea that the separation of powers is 'the

The Myth of Judicial Independence. Mike McConville and Luke Marsh, Oxford University Press (2020). DOI: 10.1093/oso/9780198822103.001.0001

judges',[3] and of 'constitutionalism' itself.[4] And the absence of a written constitution is not the only barrier. The meaning of concepts, such as 'independence', 'accountability', and 'political', are open to divergent interpretations.[5] Moreover, the relationship between the different arms of the state is not static but has changed throughout history.[6] In the following account, while sensitive to these concerns, we attempt to distil the core issues to which our account has given rise.[7]

The Westminster Model

Lord Neuberger, then President of the Supreme Court, set out his understanding of the constitutional framework of the United Kingdom as follows:[8]

> First, there are three branches of government, the legislature (the House of Commons and House of Lords) the executive (ministers, civil service, local

favourite vehicle of writers on political science and constitutional law for the conveyance of fallacious ideas': William Alexander Robson, *Justice and Administrative Law* (3rd edn, Stevens 1951) 16.

[3] Robert Stevens has shown how the judges in the nineteenth century utilized the concept of 'judicial independence' to exempt themselves from the general reform of institutions undertaken by the Victorians. See Robert Stevens, *The Independence of the Judiciary* (OUP 1993) (hereafter Stevens, *The Independence of the Judiciary*); Robert Stevens, 'Judicial Independence: The Case of England' (1999) 72 Southern California Law Review 101; Robert Stevens, 'The Act of Settlement and the Questionable History of Judicial Independence' (2001) 1 Oxford University Commonwealth Law Journal 253.

[4] Owen Hood Phillips was of the view that the separation of powers was not part of the constitution: 'A Constitutional Myth: Separation of Powers' (1977) 93 Law Quarterly Review 11.

[5] Helpful guides to unpacking the notions of 'judicial independence' and 'judicial accountability' are provided by Roger Masterman and Se-shauna Wheatle, 'Unpacking Separation of Powers: Judicial Independence, Sovereignty and Conceptual Flexibility in the UK Constitution' (2017) (July) Public Law 469; Graham Gee and others, *The Politics of Judicial Independence in the UK's Changing Constitution* (CUP 2015); Geoffrey Marshall, *Constitutional Theory* (OUP 1971); Shimon Shetreet and Sophie Turenne, *Judges on Trial: A Study in the Appointment and Accountability of the English Judiciary* (CUP 2013); Lord Hoffmann, 'Separation of Powers' (2002) 7 Judicial Review 137; David Williams, 'Bias; the Judges and the Separation of Powers' [2000] Public Law 45 (hereafter Williams, 'Bias'); Eric Barendt, 'The Separation of Powers and Constitutional Government' [1995] Public Law 599; Mark Bovens, 'Analyzing and Assessing Accountability: A Conceptual Framework' (2007) 13 European Law Journal 447; Andrew Le Sueur, 'Developing Mechanisms for Judicial Accountability in the UK' (2004) Legal Studies 73; Robert Stevens, 'A Loss of Innocence? Judicial Independence and the Separation of Powers' (1999) 19(3) Oxford Journal of Legal Studies 365.

[6] See, eg, Stephen Sedley, *Lions Under the Throne: Essays on the History of English Public Law* (CUP 2015) (hereafter Sedley, *Lions Under the Throne*); Stevens, *The Independence of the Judiciary* (n 3). See also John Parris, *Under My Wig* (Arthur Baker Ltd 1961). See generally, Richard Heffernan and others (eds), *Developments in British Politics* (Palgrave 2016) (hereafter Heffernan, *Developments in British Politics*).

[7] Any historical examination will show that the relationships between the three arms of the state have repeatedly changed.

[8] Lord Neuberger, 'Reflections on Significant Moments in the Role of the Judiciary' Personal Support Unit Fundraising Breakfast (16 March 2017) <https://www.supremecourt.uk/docs/speech-170316.pdf> accessed 1 January 2020. See to the same effect: Lord Templeman in *M* [1994] 1 AC 377: 'Parliament makes the law, the executive carry the law into effect and the judiciary enforce the law.' See also: *Duport Steel* [1980] 1 WLR 142; *Hinds v The Queen* [1977] AC 195.

> government) and the judiciary (the courts and judges). In summary terms, the legislature makes the law, the executive carries the law into effect, and the judiciary interprets and enforces the law. And it is fundamental to a modern civilised society that these three branches of government are independent of each other and respect each other's territory.

Although there are three branches of the state, according to general understanding of this 'Westminster Model',[9] in the absence of a codified constitution,[10] the core of the constitution and the rule of law rest upon twin foundations:[11] the sovereignty of the Queen in Parliament in making the law and the sovereignty of the Queen's courts in interpreting and applying the law.[12] Under this theory, only these two entities are sovereign: the actions of the executive (the departments of state over which Ministers preside together with various executive agencies and local government) are subject to review by the judges in respect of legality and fairness, the subject of public law.[13]

[9] See *DPP v Mollison (Jamaica)* [2003] UKPC 6 in which Lord Bingham said: 'Whatever overlap there may be under constitutions on the Westminster model between the exercise of executive and legislative powers, the separation between the exercise of judicial powers on the one hand and legislative and executive powers on the other is total or effectively so. Such separation, based on the rule of law, was recently described by Lord Steyn as 'a characteristic feature of democracies:' *R (Anderson) v Secretary of State for the Home Department* [2002] 3 WLR 1800, at 1821–1822, para 50.' Similar observations were made in *Ahnee v DPP of Mauritius* [1999] 2 AC 294; and *The State v Khoyratty* [2006] UKPC 13. See also Anthony King, *Who Governs Britain?* (Pelican 2015). The Westminster Model is also followed in jurisdictions, like Hong Kong, where political and constitutional arrangements diverge significantly from those of the United Kingdom. See *Yau Kwong Man* [2002] 3 HKC 457, *per* Hartmann J at 4701. cf Danny Gittings, 'Separation of Powers in Hong Kong: Inching Towards a More Flexible Judicial Interpretation' (2019) 49 Hong Kong Law Journal 187.

[10] The Constitution Committee of the House of Lords offered its own working definition of the constitution as being: 'the set of laws, rules and practices that create the basic institutions of the state, and its component and related parts, and stipulate the powers of those institutions and the relationship between the different institutions and between those institutions and the individual' Constitution Committee, 1st Report (2001–02): *Reviewing the Constitution: Terms of Reference and Method of Working* (HL Paper 11) para 20 <www.parliament.uk/business/committees/committees-a-z/lords-select/constitution-committee/> accessed 1 January 2020.

[11] This we take to be the correct position, as set out by Sir Stephen Sedley in commenting on Lord Sumption's FA Mann Lecture (2011) 'Judicial and Political Decision-Making: The Uncertain Boundary'. Sedley convincingly took Sumption to task for conflating 'government' and 'legislature': Stephen Sedley, 'Judicial Politics' *London Review of Books* (23 February 2012).

[12] Lord Bridge in *X v Morgan-Grampian Ltd* (1991) 1 AC 1, 'In our society the rule of law rests upon twin foundations: the sovereignty of the Queen in Parliament and the sovereignty of the Queen's courts in interpreting and applying the law' 48. See also Sir Stephen Sedley, *Ashes and Sparks* (CUP 2011) (hereafter Sedley, *Ashes and Sparks*) and *Lions Under the Throne* (n 6).

[13] See also *Miller* [2017]. We are not concerned here with the contentious constitutional question: can the judges hold an Act of Parliament to be invalid on the grounds that it is in violation of fundamental or natural law? This issue has been insightfully addressed by others including: Tom Bingham, *The Rule of Law* (Penguin Books 2010) 160ff; Sedley, *Lions Under the Throne* (n 6) 143ff; Professor Sir Francis Jacobs, *The Sovereignty of Law: The European Way*, The Hamlyn Lectures (CUP 2007); Trevor Allan, 'Parliamentary Sovereignty: Law, Politics and Revolution' (1997) 113 Law Quarterly Review 443; Vernon Bogdanor, *Politics and the Constitution: Essays on British Government* (Dartmouth 1996).

The principle of constitutionalism thus advanced requires not only having a constitutional framework but a willingness to respect its rules, values, conventions, and traditions. It also means that *the primary responsibility for observing the foundational principles lies with the major participants themselves*. The responsibilities are intended to safeguard two basic principles: 'independence' and 'freedom'. Independence is the *grundnorm*, the foundational norm that governs and legitimates the entire constitutional settlement providing assurance that the legislature and the judiciary can operate both independently and independently of each other.[14] The second element, freedom, is protected in theory by both Parliament and the courts being centres of freedom not only in the sense that they are forums in which issues can be debated but also as centres of institutionalized freedom which provide a ring fence around those working within them.

Within this context, while there is no settled understanding of the 'mystique'[15] of judicial independence, the concept still thrives. Our concern here is with the issue of *institutional* autonomy rather than with that of the personal independence of individual judges.[16] Moreover, we are less concerned with formal arrangements brought in by the Constitutional Reform Act 2005, to which we will return later, and more with the extent to which the judiciary is free from improper influence by the other arms of the state[17] in particular the executive.

The Civil Service

The Civil Service has importance because although political power rests in theory with Ministers, the use of this power has been to a large extent conditioned by 'the advice and assistance, even the direction, of the permanent officials'.[18] The basis of the 'Westminster Model' also has an importance for understanding the philosophy

[14] Thus, eg, it has been recognized, since *Entick v Carrington* (1765) 19 Howell's St Tr 1029 that the prerogative power of the Crown cannot be exercised so as to encroach on the judicial function.

[15] See Stevens, *The Independence of the Judiciary* (n 3) 3.

[16] The question of individual independence was notoriously raised in *R v Bartle and the Commissioner of Police for the Metropolis and others, ex parte Pinochet Ugarte* [1998] UKHL 41 in which Lord Hoffmann (who gave the deciding vote, without offering reasons) was subsequently adjudged to have been heavily involved with Amnesty International (as was his wife), an intervening party to the extradition case. On personal independence, see Stevens, *The Independence of the Judiciary* (n 3); Williams, 'Bias' (n 5).

[17] In addition to the problems of today, its history is obscure. The first major assertion of judicial independence is commonly linked to the declaration by Coke CJ in the *Prohibitions del Roy* (1607) 12 Coke Rep 63 that '... the King in his own person cannot adjudge any case ... according to the law and custom of England; ... [because] His Majesty was not learned in the laws of his realm of England' and granting judges security of tenure (subject only to dismissal by an address of both Houses of Parliament) by the Act of Settlement of 1700.

[18] John Kingsley, *Representative Bureaucracy: An Interpretation of the British Civil Service* (Yellow Springs 1994) 5. See also Catherine Haddon, 'Developments in the Civil Service' in Heffernan, *Developments in British Politics* (n 6).

that is supposed to imbue the lives of those involved in the day-to-day routines of political and bureaucratic life: it is a synonym for the constitution to which they are all pledged. As Rod Rhodes put it:[19]

> It is integral to the anonymity and political impartiality of civil servants and to the minister's understanding of his or her relationship to parliament and the cabinet. They believe in a public service ethos, and its values of integrity, honesty, impartiality, objectivity, and loyalty to the minister. They stick fast to the Westminster model's constitutional conventions.

Of course, no one knows the extent to which this group of unelected and unaccountable officials influence policy, for which the Minister is ultimately responsible,[20] because of the practices of not recording meetings and weeding of files (or, worse still, destruction) but it is safe to say that it was and is, at least on occasions, greater than publicly revealed[21] despite the increasing involvement of special advisers, consultants, and think tanks.[22] There is a hint of this in the observation of the permanent Under-Secretary, Sir MacKenzie Chalmers, in regard to public revelation of evidence to the Beck Inquiry, namely that 'many points of Home Office practice and the confidential relations with judges had much better not be discussed in public'.[23] It follows, accordingly, that any account of the fidelity to constitutional conventions or compliance with the Westminster Model's principles is compromised by the lack of public information which access to material deposited in the National Archives cannot wholly repair.[24]

[19] Rod Rhodes, *Everyday Life in British Government* (OUP 2011) (hereafter Rhodes, *British Government*) 306.

[20] William Wade and Christopher Forsyth, *Administrative Law* (11th edn, OUP 2014): 'The high degree of detachment and anonymity in which the civil service works is largely a consequence of the principle of ministerial responsibility. Where civil servants carry out the minister's orders, or act in accordance with his policy, it is for him and not for them to take any blame' 24–25. See also Rod Rhodes, John Wanna, and Patrick Weller, *Comparing Westminster* (OUP 2009).

[21] The qualification is important because ultimately officials have to carry out policies determined by their Minister even where they entertain doubts as to its efficacy though in many other instances they may shape the policy in various ways. The introduction of the Imprisonment for Public Protection (IPP) sentence by the Criminal Justice Act 2003 is an example where research has uncovered concerns of officials over the wisdom of the policy: Harry Annison 'Weeding the Garden: The Third Way, the Westminster Tradition and Imprisonment for Public Protection' (2014) 18(1) Theoretical Criminology 38.

[22] See, eg, Better Government Initiative, *Good Government: Reforming Parliament and the Executive* (Institute for Government 2010): 'The idea that the civil service has a monopoly of policy advice is a thing of the past. There is, rightly, an increased role for other sources of advice, whether think tanks, consultants, specialist academics and other experts, or special advisers' 37.

[23] Chalmers to Akers Douglas (14 October 1904), Chilston papers, U564/C119/2 cited in Jill Pellew, *The Home Office 1848–1914* (Fairleigh Dickinson University Press 1982 (hereafter Pellew, *Home Office*) 68.

[24] The addiction to secrecy can be seen in the Reports of the Advisory Council on National Records and Archives, the latest of which indicated that civil servants had not given enough thought to applications to retain records and that 'there was a noticeable trend for departments to withdraw their

The Gladstonian reforms introduced following the Northcote-Trevelyan Report of 1853[25] and the establishment of the Civil Service Commission in 1855[26] (charged with approving the appointment of the most senior civil servants) were intended to lead over time to the replacement of time-serving bureaucrats[27] appointed under patronage and the 'philosophy of the amateur' culture[28] by a modern, professional Civil Service staffed by individuals of outstanding ability, carrying out their duties on the basis of honesty, integrity, objectivity, and impartiality.[29] As Colin Matthew put it, those recruited would come from an existing elite marked by ability and high moral standards:[30]

> A Civil Service hitherto appointed by patronage and influence would give way to a non-political administrative class educated in the moral values of a liberal education further developed by a reformed Oxford and Cambridge. It was a means of extending, confirming, cleansing, and legitimizing and existing elite. Whereas, Gladstone thought, the seventeenth century had been an age of rule by prerogative, and the eighteenth by patronage, the nineteenth would become rule by virtue. For a liberal education attempted, above all, to produce citizens who were morally good, and such it was that would succeed in examinations.

The ethos of service was defined by the obligations undertaken:[31]

> Working commitment to the state, maintenance of professional secrecy, impartial loyalty towards the policies of the government in power, abrogation of direct political activity, and general integrity…

applications when challenged': Advisory Council on National Records and Archives, *14th Annual Report 2016–17*.

[25] The report was prepared by Sir Stafford Northcote and Sir Charles Trevelyan and is reprinted in the Fulton Report (1968). Subsequently the Haldane Report, *Report of the Machinery of Government Committee* (HMSO 1918) though unimplemented by Parliament, influenced the organization of the Civil Service in later years. For a detailed assessment of the importance of the Report, see John Greenaway, 'Celebrating Northcote/Trevelyan: Dispelling the Myths' (2004) 19(1) Public Policy and Administration 1.

[26] Initially constituted under the Royal Prerogative, the Commission was placed on a statutory footing by the Constitutional Reform and Governance Act 2010.

[27] The Northcote-Trevelyan Report characterized the unreformed Civil Service as desired by the unambitious, the indolent, or incapable.

[28] As Roger Keith Kelsall notes: 'Appointment to permanent posts was … a matter of patronage, much of which was … vested in the Treasury. Political influence was therefore necessary in order to secure appointment to a vacancy; the posts were virtually permanent; there were no tests of fitness, the only safeguard being dismissal for incompetence during the probationary year or so': *Higher Civil Servants in Britain* (Routledge 1955) (hereafter Kelsall, *Civil Servants*) 1.

[29] See further Peter Hennessey, *Whitehall* (Secker & Warburg 1989) (hereafter Hennessey, *Whitehall*).

[30] Henry Colin Gray Matthew, *Gladstone 1809–1874* (OUP 1986) 85 (hereafter Matthew, *Gladstone*).

[31] Pellew, *Home Office* (n 23) 190. The core requirements are now found in the Civil Service Code, the statutory basis for the management of which is set out in the Constitutional Reform and Governance Act 2010; the Code sets out the basis of appointment <www.gov.uk/government/publications/civil-service-code/the-civil-service-code> accessed 1 January 2020.

Those eventually destined to lead the Home Office were recruited as 'generalists' immediately following graduation: Troup[32] at the age of twenty-three; Anderson aged twenty-two; Cunningham aged twenty-three; and Allen aged twenty-two. These men were seen as incorruptible, loyal to any politician in charge of their department, able to view issues impartially, always acting with a strong sense of public duty and moral purpose.[33] For many years thereafter, senior members of the Civil Service, abounding with the same attributes as judges in terms of class and educational background, assumed a dominant role in the running of the country, the judiciary (generally)[34] content to allow this to happen.[35]

As is evident from earlier chapters, the commanding influence of the Civil Service was more than exemplified in the Home Office itself. Alongside, if not displacing, the undoubted deference to the judiciary displayed by officials in evidence to the Beck Inquiry, came a self-confidence born of intellectual excellence and self-belief. In the result, the proclaimed 'separation of powers', by which the judiciary is said to be insulated from inappropriate executive influence, was destined to fracture. As the records make clear, this occurred within a context in which senior state officials expressed fidelity to the doctrine of separation of powers and judicial independence.

From his appointment as permanent Secretary in 1908 at the age of fifty-one, Edward Troup not only dominated his department but rapidly gained influence over the judiciary such that the Judges' Rules were for more than forty years thereafter to bear his hallmark and carry the stamp of approval of his successor John Anderson (made permanent Secretary in 1922 at the age of forty).[36] Similarly, although the *coup de grace* on one point of issue (the time of the first caution) was delivered by the Lord Chancellor, the revisions of the Rules over the period 1961–64, were less the work of the judges and more the work of Home Office officials

[32] Although the Northcote-Trevelyan reforms began to shape the Civil Service soon after the Civil Service Commission was established, implementation did not occur properly until after 1870 and later still in the Foreign Office and the Home Office. Troup was not recruited into the Home Office until 1880 and did not become permanent Secretary until 1908, the Home Office having delayed response to the reforms on the pretext that it was a Department dealing with confidential material. See Lord Allen, 'State Service: Reflections of a Bureaucrat' in *The Home Office: Perspectives on Policy and Administration* (Royal Institute of Public Administration 1983).

[33] See Kelsall, *Civil Servants* (n 28). Writing of those who claimed to know something about the temper and outlook of these civil servants, Kelsall said that there was a high degree of unanimity as to their virtues: 'They are praised for their incorruptibility, their willingness to subordinate personal interest to that of the Service, their loyalty to Ministers, their conscientiousness and industry, their tact, personal charm and literary facility' 189. As to their alleged failings, Kelsall wrote: 'They are criticized for being cautious, for lack of drive and personal vitality, for having a negative attitude of mind, for smugness and complacency, for being out of touch with working-class problems …' 189–90.

[34] There were occasional voices of discontent at the delegation of power to administrative officials, most notably by Lord Hewart, *The New Despotism* (Ernest Benn Ltd 1929) in which he described the growth of administrative power as a 'new despotism' that was 'to subordinate Parliament, to evade the Courts, and to render the will, or the caprice, of the Executive unfettered and supreme' 17.

[35] See Stevens, *The Independence of the Judiciary* (n 3); Sedley, *Ashes and Sparks* (n 12).

[36] Sir John Anderson became Viscount Waverley in 1952.

superintended by Charles Cunningham (appointed permanent Secretary in 1957 at the age of fifty-one),[37] not only through managing meetings and overseeing correspondence but through direct confidential meetings with the Lord Chief Justice (LCJ) and with little involvement of the Secretary of State[38] until the goose was practically cooked.

Although the new recruitment policy was said to be so successful that, by the start of the twentieth century, 'the country's first true meritocracy, a genuine aristocracy of talent' had been established,[39] as Peter Hennessey observes,[40] there was at the heart of the Northcote-Trevelyan Report a basic flaw—near exclusive reliance on training the young rather than recruiting those with experience, expressed in the Report as follows:[41]

> Our opinion is that, as a general rule, it is decidedly best to train young men. Without laying too much stress on the experience which a long official life necessarily brings with it, we cannot but regard it as an advantage of some importance. In many offices ... the superior docility of young men renders it much easier to make valuable public servants of them, than of those more advanced in life ... The maintenance of discipline is also easier under such circumstances, and regular habits may be enforced, which it would be difficult to impose for the first time upon older men. To these advantages must be added the important one of being able, by proper regulations, to secure the services of fit persons on much more economical terms.

There were other core weaknesses in this corporatist bureaucracy theory[42] which gravely impacted upon the administration of the law. In part the problems cannot be dissociated from the background and life experience of the senior officials. Pellew, for example, in taking a sample of higher officials from Troup onwards found they had 'predominantly public school, Oxford and Cambridge, middle class backgrounds ... more or less typical of the first division as a whole at least until the second world war'.[43] Aside from an unthinking and unreflective commitment

[37] Cunningham was in the early stages assisted by Philip Allen who was to succeed him in 1966 at the age of fifty-four, although Allen was not involved in the later critical stages of reformulation of the Rules having been transferred to the Treasury.

[38] There were two Home Secretaries over the crucial period of the 1961–64 reforms, R A Butler being followed in July 1962 by Henry Brooke.

[39] Hennessey, *Whitehall* (n 29) 31.

[40] ibid 40.

[41] Extracted from the Northcote-Trevelyan Report where, as can be seen, cost-effectiveness was also a major consideration.

[42] The Northcote-Trevelyan Report distinguished between the lower, executive civil service grade for whom on-the-job training would be appropriate and the higher positions which might be filled by more 'mature' individuals.

[43] Pellew, *Home Office* (n 23) 201 citing Kelsall, *Civil Servants* (n 28).

to secrecy which degrades the concept of public interest and history itself,[44] the three basic flaws in the new bureaucrats most clearly displayed in the history of the Judges' Rules were: (i) the lack of life experience or relevant life experience; (ii) an inadequate grasp of ethical behaviour; and (iii) a misconception of the public interest. We briefly outline these below.

Civil Servants and Life Experience

The appointment of individuals immediately on graduation explains in some measure shortcomings in their later performance as permanent secretaries. Putting to one side the palpable lack of diversity in recruitment and consequent failure to make use of available human capital in society, in-house training[45] proved no substitute for exposure to the challenges of life in the real world.[46] Although Troup had a paper qualification as a barrister, he never practised and spent his whole career in the Home Office which proved a poor foundation for his decision to assume responsibility for drafting the Judges' Rules in 1918. Having taken over from Harry Simpson, he failed to appreciate the contradictions in the Rules which had been pointed out and his further efforts only added to the internal confusions. Afterwards, John Anderson, a brilliant intellect[47] but without any legal training whatsoever, felt able to disregard the clear advice of Home Office legal advisers regarding the deficiencies of the Rules[48] and instead left them unchanged in reliance,

[44] As we have noted, the over-zealous purging of records distorts accounts that can be constructed from official sources. The blind commitment to secrecy goes back to the establishment of the modern Civil Service during the Northcote-Trevelyan reforms. Those who resisted the reforms sought to argue that 'honourable secrecy' was a character trait of the aristocrats, protected by the prevailing system of patronage and threatened by appointing people through an examination system which could not measure character. Hence, the Northcote-Trevelyan reforms set out to instil in officials a secretive state of mind. See Christopher Moran, *Classified: Secrecy and the State in Modern Britain* (CUP 2013) 33ff. Although there are unauthorized leaks from time to time, the official files are testimony to the general commitment to secrecy within the civil service. See also Leslie Chapman, *Your Disobedient Servant* (Chatto & Windus 1978); Clive Ponting, *The Right to Know* (Sphere Books 1985); Peter Preston, 'A Source of Great Regret' (2005) 16(3) British Journalism Review 47; Alasdair Roberts, *Blacked Out: Government Secrecy in the Information Age* (CUP 2006). The farcical levels to which civil servants descended were ruthlessly exposed when the hapless Cabinet Secretary, Sir Robert Armstrong, gave evidence in the *Spycatcher Trial*. See Colin Pilkington, *The Civil Service in Britain Today* (MUP 1999).

[45] According to Sir Harold Scott, *Your Obedient Servant* (Andre Deutsch 1959) (hereafter Scott, *Obedient Servant*), who entered the Home Office in 1911, there was at that time no formal training and new recruits were expected to 'pick it up as you go along' 29.

[46] See to the same effect, Hennessey, *Whitehall* (n 29) 40.

[47] Scott, *Obedient Servant* (n 45) described him as '... the all wise, the all knowing, the all powerful' 63. For an account of Anderson's life, see John Wheeler-Bennett, *John Anderson: Viscount Waverley* (Macmillan 1962) (hereafter Wheeler-Bennett, *Waverley*).

[48] This is no moral aspersion upon a man described by his biographer in the following terms: 'Everything he did was backed by an unshakeable moral certainty, wholly constructive ... impelled by an instinctive sense of what was the moral centre of a given situation or problem:' Wheeler-Bennett, *Waverley* (n 47) 406. A possible explanation for Anderson's treatment of the Judges' Rules

it appears, upon a palpably aberrant if not bizarre note from Avory J written in his declining years.

In the 1960s, Charles Cunningham, another gifted official with no legal training, ran the process of reformulating the Rules and, although he did in fairness utilize Home Office legal advisers to finalize drafting proposals, driven, it must be said, by a focus on police concerns, he was unable to identify let alone correct manifest deficiencies built into the 1964 Rules.

Overall, reliance on in-house training through slavish adherence to precedents[49] and a related lack of professional practical experience resulted in all three major Civil Service actors failing, in the critical matter of police regulation, to reach the level of competence that the recruitment reforms had promised.[50]

Civil Servants and Integrity

The Northcote-Trevelyan reforms were not only directed towards professional competence: they were also designed to create a cadre of state officials imbued with integrity and an ethical commitment deserving of the reliance that would be placed in them. As Pellew notes:[51]

> Working commitment to the state, maintenance of professional secrecy, impartial loyalty towards the policies of the government in power, abrogation of direct political activity, and general integrity: these were the obligations, some of which the Treasury had codified, which had developed for civil servants.

It is, however, far from clear whether the 'non-political administrative class educated in the moral values of a liberal education further developed by a reformed Oxford and Cambridge' was sufficient to guarantee what Colin Matthew described as 'rule by virtue'.[52]

The collective failure of officials to intervene following Adolf Beck's second arrest and the risible explanation offered to the Beck Inquiry by Troup—that no one in the Home Office knew what the whole country knew—suggests at the least a loose grip on moral values. It can hardly be argued that the bureaucratic mind had

may be found in Wheeler-Bennett's assessment that Anderson had 'no special interest in Home Office subjects—apart from its fundamental responsibilities for law and order. He was interested more in the art of administering than in the subjects administered' 85 (footnote omitted).

[49] Hennessey, *Whitehall* (n 29) correctly describes the Home Office as a 'precedent-laden, casework-driven institution' 458.

[50] In the modern era, officials are said to be trapped into their own specialisms and unable to see the broader picture. See Rhodes, *British Government* (n 19).

[51] Pellew, *Home Office* (n 23) 190.

[52] Matthew, *Gladstone* (n 30) 85.

created such a distance as to create moral blindness since Beck's case had not only dominated the files of officials for years but had become a matter of public notoriety thanks to the splash coverage of a sensationalist press.

In the handling of the Judges' Rules themselves the moral line of virtue was again clearly crossed. Troup was himself centrally involved in drafting and introducing the 1918 Rules which were incompletely described as having been 'approved' by the judges, a disingenuous presentation perpetuated under Sir John Anderson in 1930 on their re-issue. Topping all this, the promulgation of the 1964 Rules as 'made' by the judges constituted active misrepresentation and a false prospectus by Sir Charles Cunningham. It is hard to see in these events the strong sense of moral purpose which was said to have imbued this elite band of bureaucrats.

Civil Servants and the Public Interest

The generalized concern that the higher Civil Service was 'out of touch' by reason of its lack of life experience and narrow class background[53] manifested itself in a particular understanding of where the 'public interest' lay. In setting out to reform the original Judges' Rules, Troup exhibited no appreciation of policing even though its parlous state should have been obvious, if only from the mass of evidence supplied to the Royal Commission Upon the Duties of the Metropolitan Police in 1908, press reports, dissatisfaction within the police, and widespread strikes over pay and conditions. And by 1929, John Anderson could hardly have acted in a state of ignorance since he had been informed by the distinguished Inspector of Constabulary that the police were not acting in accordance with the Judges' Rules; and, further, concerns regarding integrity within the Criminal Investigations Department (CID) in particular had been singled out for comment by the Royal Commission into Police Powers and Procedures (1929).

The situation Charles Cunningham and Philip Allen faced in the context of the 1960–64 reforms was different in important ways and of more enduring influence involving both a background rise in crime and a rise in police influence. Towards the end of the Second World War, a broad-party consensus dedicated to the creation of a post-war 'welfare state'[54] operated in a period in which crime began to rise[55] incrementally at first but more rapidly after the mid-1950s[56] with notable

[53] Kelsall, *Civil Servants* (n 28) refers to a commonly held criticism that they were out of touch with 'working class problems' 190. Certainly, they were unlikely to have ever had any experience with the kind of policing that was familiar to working class neighbourhoods.

[54] See, eg, Anthony Bottoms and Simon Stevenson, '"What Went Wrong?": Criminal Justice Policy in England and Wales, 1945–70' in David Downes (ed), *Unravelling Criminal Justice* (Macmillan 1992) 2.

[55] While statistics are notoriously difficult to interpret, it is generally agreed that the overall crime rates increased a little between the late 1940s and early 1950s, particularly in crimes of violence and sexual offences.

[56] See Frederick Hemming McClintock and Neville Howard Avison, *Crime in England and Wales* (Heinemann Educational Books 1968); Steve Chibnall, *Law and Order News* (Tavistock 1977). See

instances of street disorder associated with racial violence against members of the black community.[57] Significantly in this early period, beyond the traditional focus of the police upon working-class and ethnic minority communities, 'crime' became associated with alternative youth culture, both objects of press interest which led to the creation of 'folk devils' and 'moral panics'[58] associated in the 1950s with 'Teddy Boys' and in the 1960s with 'Mods' and 'Rockers'.[59] Outside the interest of the press, working-class street crime, including black market rackets, theft, and burglary continued to rise and, in the cities (especially London), organized crime became established through gambling, prostitution, and various forms of protection rackets.[60] But police corruption was also of central importance and Cunningham and Allen showed little grasp of the public interest in regulating the police, putting, as we shall see, 'police interests' ahead of rational reform.

The Police and Politics

The backcloth of the rise in crime had a major impact upon the politics of policing. Although insulated from direct political control through answerability to local Watch Committees and, in London, the Home Office itself, the police were necessarily a central part of the state's coercive apparatus in the maintenance of social order,[61] and combatting crime including the policing and even suppression of marches and demonstrations.[62] Crime was not only a fact that the police had

also Critchley Thomas Alan, *A History of Police in England and Wales* (2nd edn, Patterson Smith 1972) (hereafter Critchley, *History of Police*) 252 ff.

[57] The major street disorders in Notting Hill, London between the end of August and 5 September 1958 were preceded by a similar but smaller-scale riot caused by a racially motivated attack in the St Ann's district of Nottingham on 23 August 1958. See more generally Stuart Hall and others, *Policing the Crisis: Mugging, the State, and Law and Order* (Macmillan 1978); Phil Scraton, *The State of the Police* (Pluto Press 1985); Phil Scraton (ed), *Law, Order and the Authoritarian State* (Open University Press 1987).

[58] See the classic account of Stanley Cohen, *Folk Devils and Moral Panics* (Paladin 1972). See also Geoff Pearson, *Hooligan: A History of Respectable Fears* (Macmillan 1983); John Muncie, *The Trouble with Kids Today* (Hutchinson 1984); and John Davis, *Youth and the Condition of Britain* (Athlone Press 1990).

[59] On youth subcultures, see Stuart Hall and Tony Jefferson, *Resistance through Rituals* (Hutchinson 1998); Stanley Cohen, *Images of Deviance* (Penguin 1970); Howard Parker, *View from the Boys* (David & Charles 1974); David Downes, 'The Gang Myth' *The Listener* (14 April 1966).

[60] See: James Morton, *Gangland* (Piatkus 2008); Donald Thomas, *Villains' Paradise* (John Murray 2005).

[61] At an earlier stage in history, this included in the nineteenth century the suppression of working-class traditions and recreational practices: John Stevenson, *Popular Disturbances in England* (Longman 1979); Robert Storch, 'The Plague of Blue Locusts' (1975) International Review of Social History 20; Phil Cohen, 'Policing the Working Class City' in Bob Fine and others (eds), *Capitalism and the Rule of Law* (Hutchinson 1979).

[62] For example, marches by the National Unemployed Workers' Movement in 1932 were brutally dealt with resulting in days of serious violence across London and the formation after 1934 of the National Council for Civil Liberties. See John Stevenson and Chris Cook, *The Slump: Britain in the Great Depression* (Cape 1977).

to confront on the streets but a weapon they could use in the fight for resources through the Police Federation[63] and the Association of Chief Constables of England and Wales (ACPO).[64] While increases in crime inevitably placed burdens on police officers, for the police, crime became the door into politics.

Although the police were unable to act openly as a political force, their relationship with the Home Office provided them with leverage over policy. Indeed, internal Home Office files make clear that senior police, in particular the Metropolitan Police Commissioner, were closely consulted on the detailed formulation of the Judges' Rules. Not only were they consulted at every turn, their views, on the back of claims that the proposals could only lead to a 'complete frustration of the CID side of the police' and that '70% of criminal cases' would be lost, proved dispositive. By way of example, the Commissioner told the Home Office in October 1963 that the proposals would 'seriously jeopardise the detection rate of crime'; the Home Office as late as January 1964 told the judges that the 'efficient investigation of crime would be impeded' by their (Third) Draft Rules; and, near the end of the 'reform' process, the judges, it was said, had 'made substantial concessions to the Home Office and police point of view'.

Although, therefore, formal negotiations with the judges were undertaken by the Home Office assisted, at the eleventh hour, by the Lord Chancellor's Department, this was essentially a *police narrative*. While the police did not have the standing to be represented in Home Office meetings with the judges, it was *their* arguments, *their* claims, *their* insistence, and *their* demands which ultimately drove the dialogue. And certainly the files disclose that the LCJ did have private meetings with the Commissioner on the revision programme. In matters of order maintenance and crime control, therefore, the much-trumpeted tripartite constitutional narrative did not reflect the lived reality. Home Office civil servants, led by Cunningham and Allen, acted as surrogates for and mouthpieces of the police in formal discussions with the judges, organizing, distilling, and faithfully transmitting their concerns, fears, and prejudices. At the very least, the police became a covert constitutional force. And it was not long before the police gained enough confidence to come out of the closet and operate openly as a political force.

While the Commissioner and ACPO continued to have the ear of the Home Office, the lower ranks rapidly found their voice through their 'union',[65] the

63 The Federation came into existence by virtue of the Police Act 1919. Under the Act, the Federation could bring to the notice of police authorities and the Secretary of State 'all matters affecting their welfare and efficiency other than questions of discipline and promotion affecting individuals'.

64 ACPO came into existence in 1948 with the amalgamation of the Chief Constables Association founded in 1896 for the chief constables of cities and boroughs and the County Chief Constables Conference set up in 1920. See Critchley, *History of Police* (n 56) 195. In April 2015, ACPO was replaced by the National Police Chiefs' Council (NPCC) following a review by General Sir Nick Parker, *Independent Review of ACPO* (2013).

65 Strictly speaking, it is a staff association for those at the level of constable, sergeant, and inspector (up to chief inspector), the police being prohibited from establishing an ordinary trade union because of fears to public safety that a strike would pose. See now the Police Act 1996.

Police Federation, and became increasingly identified with agitation for more police powers. In this they had champions from above. As Commissioner, Robert Mark laid the foundation for political agitation, soon joined by his successor, David McNee arguing that police work could not be conducted according to then existing rules and attacking for good measure the institution of jury trial and the bona fides of defence solicitors.[66] The intervention into the political arena by Robert Mark in his famous attack on unscrupulous defence lawyers and perverse juries in 1973 was the first public indication of the power and influence of the police, in particular, the Metropolitan Police. The police thereafter became an effective political lobby whose influence was found in supporting a Conservative Party 'law and order' campaign in the 1980s and in bringing pressure on the Royal Commission on Criminal Justice set up in the wake of a string of high-profile miscarriages of justice. Police influence, now unconcealed, was influential in securing restrictions on the right to silence and placing the defence under wider disclosure obligations.[67]

The Lord Chancellor and the Law Officers

As civil servants charted the direction of the Judges' Rules, at various points over the reforms of 1960–64 they needed heavyweight intervention when they encountered major stumbling blocks. The assistance, as we have seen, was supplied by the Law Officers of the Crown (the Attorney-General and Solicitor-General) and the Lord Chancellor, then both a government Minister and Head of the Judiciary. While these officials had a perfect right to be informed of what was happening in the discussions with the judiciary, there were also clear breaches of the 'separation of powers' rule, once again driven by police interests.

As we have seen, the Attorney-General and Solicitor-General sought to influence the judges (at a private meeting with Lord Parker CJ and Winn J) to adopt a proposal under which, contrary to the thrust of the earlier Rules and to Home Office-led discussions that were then under way, was designed to amend the caution so that a suspect or accused who exercised the right to silence would be exposed to adverse comment at trial.

Perhaps more extraordinary was the threat contained in a letter from the Lord Chancellor to Lord Parker CJ that failure to conform to the representations made by the Home Office would lead to the judges being subjected to denunciation in

[66] See, eg, Robert Mark, *Minority Verdict* (BBC 1973); Robert Mark, *Policing a Perplexed Society* (Allen & Unwin 1977); Robert Mark, *In the Office of Constable* (Collins 1978); Sir David McNee, *McNee's Law* (Collins 1983).

[67] See Rod Morgan, 'The Process is the Rule and the Punishment is the Process' (1996) 59 Modern Law Review: 306; Criminal Justice and Public Order Act 1994; Criminal Procedure and Investigations Act 1996.

the House of Commons by the Home Secretary. The Lord Chancellor's intervention, too, was little more than speaking to a police brief as can be seen in the trace of correspondence around the question of the caution. On 18 November 1963, writing to the Home Secretary (Henry Brooke), he set out his own position on the issue of a caution being administered at the outset of investigations in the following terms:[68]

> I myself do not attach very much importance to the caution having to be given so early... I feel myself, that far too much importance is attached to the giving of the caution. To the old lags it makes no difference. The new offender may perhaps be deterred from making admissions by the caution but I would not think that very likely these days.

This stance caused alarm in the Home Office, Charles Cunningham stating in an internal Note[69] that it was 'essential, in view of the line which the Lord Chancellor has been taking, that there should be a preliminary meeting with him (as he has himself proposed) in the hope that we can form a united front'. That Meeting became 'a matter of the utmost urgency'[70] after the Law Officers had muddied the waters in their meeting with the LCJ. At the Lord Chancellor's request, the Home Office then sent a 'Note of Criticism' of the Draft Rules. This did little more than state that the criticisms were the views of 'experienced police officers', asserting that 'professional police opinion is unanimous in considering that draft Rule I in its present form will affect adversely the detection rate', and, directly confronting the Lord Chancellor's expressed opinion, reiterating that: 'The police do not subscribe to the view that the giving of a caution makes little or no difference to the course of the interrogation.' Recognizing that there was a need to 'avoid crossing the threads', the Lord Chancellor agreed to an urgent meeting, which he chaired, with Home Office officials and others. By 2 January 1964, as a result of that meeting, where he would have had the police view hammered home by Home Office representatives, he reversed direction. In a letter to the LCJ,[71] he now said:

> ... professional criminals are not likely to say anything no matter when the caution is given but in the view of the police, there will be many offenders upon whom the effect of giving a caution will be to stop them saying anything more, with the result that evidence which is now obtained and admitted would not be secured and many criminals would escape conviction. I must say I feel there is great force in this...

68 Letter to Henry Brooke (18 November 1963).
69 The Note was addressed to Mr Otton of the Home Office.
70 Note from Charles Cunningham to the Home Secretary (29 November 1963).
71 Letter to Lord Parker (2 January 1964).

In the result, the Lord Chancellor's intervention, like that of the Law Officers and the civil servants, was driven by *police interests*. Moreover, his stance was not a confusion of roles but a clear violation of the doctrine of the separation of powers and an infringement of the principle of judicial independence. The Lord Chancellor was not acting as Head of the Judiciary (which would, in and of itself, have been questionable) but as a government Minister conveying a blunt political threat to the LCJ.

The constitutional significance of the actions of the executive in these several respects should now be clear. In examining the notion of judicial independence Geoffrey Wilson pointed out[72] that while the Act of Settlement of 1701 and its protection of judges against dismissal so long as they behaved themselves (*quamdiu se bene gesserint*) was a traditional starting point of discussion, a fuller understanding required resort to constitutional conventions:[73]

> It is convention which imposes an obligation on governments not to attempt to interfere with the judges in the exercise of their functions and which imposes a duty on the judges to be independent (supported by the oath they swear on appointment) as one can see more clearly if one imagines not a situation in which a government is attempting to pressurise an unwilling judiciary but one in which there is a risk of the judiciary willingly colluding with those attempts.

This is precisely the way in which the basis of the constitution has been undermined: a willing judiciary joining together with the executive in drafting what were supposed to be the Judges' Rules in 1918; and the executive in 1963–64 pressurizing a most unwilling judiciary to accept its demands and succeeding in imposing its will.

Conclusion

The willingness of the senior judiciary to have involved themselves in off-the-record policy-making with members of the Civil Service and the higher echelons of the executive not only undercuts the 'Westminster Model', according to which the judiciary and the executive operate in 'independent' spheres, but also evinced a

[72] Geoffrey Wilson, 'Postscript: The Courts, Law and Convention' in Rt Hon Lord Nolan and Sir Stephen Sedley, *The Making & Remaking of the British Constitution* (Blackstone Press Ltd 1997).

[73] ibid 107. See to the same effect, Lord Thomas LCJ: 'No branch [of the State] should interfere in the proper working of the functions and responsibilities which the constitution has assigned to another branch; each must show a proper and mutual respect for the role of the other branches': 'The Judiciary within the State—The Relationship between the Branches of the State' Michael Ryle Memorial Lecture (15 June 2017) <www.judiciary.gov.uk/announcements/michael-ryle-memorial-lecture-by-the-lord-chief-justice-the-judiciary-within-the-state-the-relationship-between-the-branches-of-the-state/> accessed 1 January 2020.

readiness to depart from traditional notions of accountability. What was to follow, as we have charted in Chapter 8, put in issue the idea that the interests sponsored by judges were distinct from those advanced by government. This in itself raised the more fundamental question of the relationship of judges to politics, to which we now turn.

10
The Politics of the Judiciary

Introduction

In this chapter, we explore the contested question whether English judges can be said to be 'political'. We concentrate upon the modern criminal justice system rather than the position before the nineteenth century where examples of the close relationship of the judiciary and government can be readily identified. We confront the major theories which have been advanced in this regard and explain why another approach is not only more profitable but essential.

Politics and the Judiciary

We begin by restating that our concern is only with the criminal justice system. In some other areas the judiciary has developed a jurisprudence which evinces a willingness to stand between the citizen and government, as in judicial review where Sir Stephen Sedley accurately observed[1] that: '. . . [T]he judiciary is not consistently or homogeneously on the side of the state or the government.'[2] Despite a mixture of lassitude and obeisance to authority in the nineteenth century[3] and first half of the twentieth, exemplified by the notoriously craven opinion of the majority in *Liversidge v Anderson*,[4] the judiciary found the will, through developing judicial

[1] Stephen Sedley, 'Law and State Power: A Time for Reconstruction' (1990) 17 Journal of Law & Society 234, 239. In advocating that law should be taken seriously, Sedley rightly states: 'It can create or restore confidence in the vulnerability of state authority; it can sometimes bridge the gap between the rhetoric of justice, which courts cannot jettison at will, and the exercise of state power; and it can on occasion deflect the Orwellian boot as it descends on the upturned face' 238.

[2] Dawn Oliver makes a similar observation in relation to occasions on which judges have opposed either prevailing political and economic forces or the institutions of government, citing as illustrations the *Case of Prohibitions*, the *Case of Proclamations, Entick v Carrington, Ridge v Baldwin* and *Anisminic*: 'Book Review of *The Politics of the Judiciary* (by JAG Griffith) (3rd edn, Fontana Books 1985)' (1986) 6 (July) Legal Studies (hereafter Oliver, 'Review') 232.

[3] The nineteenth century marked the beginning of the state regulated through law made by Parliament rather than by the judges. Virtually no area of life was untouched from transportation (with the spread of railways and canals), industry (with the growth of factories), urban development (with the massive expansion of towns), and the incidents of industrialization (environmental impact, health and, education). See JAG Griffith, *Judicial Politics since 1920: A Chronicle* (Blackwell 1993).

[4] [1942] 2 AC 6 where the House of Lords decided that a Regulation requiring that the Home Secretary must have 'reasonable cause to believe' was to be interpreted to mean whether the Home Secretary considered that he had reasonable cause to believe rather than whether there were objectively reasonable grounds. See also Luke Marsh, 'All the King's Men, Police Powers and the Reining in of Liberty' (2014) 78 Journal of Criminal Law 4.

The Myth of Judicial Independence. Mike McConville and Luke Marsh, Oxford University Press (2020). © Mike McConville and Luke Marsh. DOI: 10.1093/oso/9780198822103.001.0001

review, to stand up to government where it was found to act illegally or unfairly, with added authority through the Human Rights Act 1998.[5] Similarly, the new constitutional arrangements ushered in by the Constitutional Reform Act 2005 cleared one string of argument about politics and the judiciary[6] by removing the Lord Chancellor as head of the judiciary.[7] And, in its 2019 landmark judgment, the UK Supreme Court unanimously ruled that the Prime Minister's advice to the Queen to prorogue Parliament was unlawful which led:[8]

> to the Order in Council which, being founded on unlawful advice, was likewise unlawful, null and of no effect and should be quashed. This led to the actual prorogation, which was as if the Commissioners had walked into Parliament with a blank piece of paper. It too was unlawful, null and of no effect.

Judicial politics, like judicial independence, is not a trackless subject but it certainly lacks firm foundations. What is not in doubt is that the broad terms of the debate were laid down in the United Kingdom by Professor John Griffith in his seminal work, *The Politics of the Judiciary*.[9] Although other commentators have entered the fray subsequently, it is with the thesis of Griffith that it is first necessary to engage.

John Griffith and Judicial Politics

From his survey of areas of law including industrial relations, individual rights, education, social services, crime, immigration law, and prisoners, the central proposition of Griffith, that judges do not mechanically apply neutral principles of law but act 'politically', is set out as follows:[10]

[5] Adam Geary, Wayne Morrison, and Robert Jago, *The Politics of the Common Law* (Routledge-Cavendish, 2009) argue that with certain members of the senior judiciary championing human rights in a way that has brought them into conflict with the executive, the judges are inherently political but these 'politics are now articulated over the meaning of human rights within a democratic polity' 126.

[6] For a discussion of the role of the Lord Chancellor prior to the Act, see Diana Woodhouse, *The Lord Chancellor* (Hart 2001).

[7] See the speech of Thomas LCJ, 'Judicial Independence in a Changing Landscape' 17 September 2015 <www.judiciary.gov.uk/announcements/speech-by-the-lord-chief-justice-judicial-independence-in-a-changing-constitutional-landscape/> accessed 1 January 2020: '... Under the new system, which has produced a clear and formal separation of powers, judicial independence is best served by more, not less, day-to-day engagement with government and Parliament. It has also necessitated a much more proactive stance by the judiciary in promoting an understanding of the importance of justice and in taking more proactive steps in many areas it might traditionally have left to others ...'

[8] *R (on the Application of Miller) (Appellant) v The Prime Minister (Respondent)* [2019] UKSC 41, para 69. Despite the judgment's obvious constitutional significance as an assertion of parliamentary sovereignty by delineating new legal limits on the exercise of the prerogative powers over prorogation, note that the court emphasized this case was a 'one off' in circumstances which had 'never arisen before and are unlikely to arise ever again' [1].

[9] JAG Griffith, *The Politics of the Judiciary* (5th edn, Fontana Press 1997) (hereafter Griffith, *Politics of the Judiciary*).

[10] ibid 336.

> . . . judges in the UK cannot be politically neutral because they are placed in positions where they are required to make political choices which are sometimes presented to them, and often presented by them, as determinations of where the public interest lies; and their interpretation of what is in the public interest and therefore politically desirable is determined by the kind of people they are and the position they hold in society; that this position is part of an established authority and so is necessarily conservative, not liberal. From all this flows that view of the public interest which is shown in judicial attitudes such as tenderness towards private property and dislike of trade unions, strong adherence to the maintenance of order, distaste for minority opinions, demonstrations and protests, support of governmental secrecy, concern for the preservation of the moral and social behaviour to which it is accustomed and the rest.

The argument is not that judges must sometimes, *force majeure*, take decisions which involve political choices but that, by reason of their class background and position in established society, the choices they make are essentially conservative and their understanding of and hence application of the test of 'public interest' is conditioned by a desire to uphold the *status quo*.

There are a number of preliminary problems with this argument. One is in fixing Griffith's exact position. The difficulty is shown in his analysis of the 'fares fair' policy in the Greater London Council (GLC) case. Having stated that the legal answer is sometimes clear, as when a public authority has exceeded its powers, he continues:[11]

> But sometimes the answer is much more doubtful, and here the general philosophy of the courts—*a philosophy which may change from time to time, and vary according to circumstances*—determines what the judges will do (emphasis supplied).

Statements of this kind make it impossible to know what 'philosophy' is being objected to, how and in what way it changes, what drives change, and what are the circumstances which cause it to vary.[12] The problem of indeterminacy is further seen when this is set against Griffith's observation, when the GLC case came to the House of Lords,[13] that there were consequences to judges entering more and more deeply into political battlegrounds:[14]

[11] JAG Griffith, 'Lord Denning Rolls the Dice against London' *New Society* (19 November 1981) 311, 312.

[12] As Stevens points out, the function of the judiciary has been subject to dramatic changes if a longer time-frame is used. See Robert Stevens, *The Independence of the Judiciary* (OUP 1993) (hereafter Stevens, *Independence of the Judiciary*).

[13] *Bromley LBC v Greater London Council* [1981] UKHL 7.

[14] JAG Griffith, 'The Law Lords and the GLC' *Marxism Today* (February 1982) 29, 31.

> And because, by their education, training and class, *they exercise their powers of interpretation in accordance with a particular code and a particular set of values*, they are becoming more and more distrusted by those having other codes and values (emphasis supplied).

Here there is a conclusion that, arising from their education, training, and class, there is a *constant* not changing judicial philosophy exercised in accordance with a particular, and presumably unchanging, set of values.[15]

Another problem is inconsistency in interpretation. Thus, judges are sometimes criticized by Griffith for giving effect to the will of Parliament where it is difficult for the courts to control the exercise of wide powers[16] but in the context of the judges 'drawing and re-drawing the lines of what they consider to be permissible and impermissible conduct'.[17] Added to this is the fact that his thesis does not account for dissenting judgments (which may eventually prevail in subsequent cases) or conflicts between the Court of Appeal and the House of Lords/Supreme Court.[18]

Added to this is the question of the persuasiveness of inferential reasoning from decided court judgments. Thus, the fact that the judiciary tends to be drawn from a narrow class background[19] does not give rise to a *necessary* inference that judicial decisions result from their class composition,[20] although it may be tempting to reach that conclusion[21] especially in criminal justice matters given the extraordinarily homogenous lineage of Lord Chief Justices, as set out in Chapter 8, Table 8.1.[22]

Another problem is that it unconvincingly accounts for shifts in the trajectories of decisions over time.[23] Thus, in the short span between the first edition of his

[15] See in this regard Griffith's observation that: 'It is idle to criticize institutions for performing the task they were created to perform and have performed for centuries': Griffith, *Politics of the Judiciary* (n 9) 343. As Dawn Oliver points out in respect of that remark: 'But this statement does not square with the thrust of the thesis. There is very strong criticism of the judges in Griffith's treatment of police powers, race relations, industrial relations and public law cases. And in any event it is not true that they have performed the same task for centuries ... [T]he tasks that the law, and therefore the judges, are expected to perform are multifarious, incompatible, and constantly changing' Oliver, 'Review' (n 2) 233.

[16] Griffith, *Politics of the Judiciary* (n 9) 160.

[17] ibid 158. On this see Oliver, 'Review' (n 2) and Stevens, *Independence of the Judiciary* (n 12) 179ff.

[18] As Lord Devlin put it, the difficulty is 'the lack of discipline among the judges; they do not always toe what Professor Griffith declares to be their party line. The law lords are sometimes divided: more frequently they quarrel with the court of Appeal': 'Judges, Government and Politics' (1978) 41(5) Modern Law Review 501 (hereafter Devlin, 'Judges, Government and Politics') 506.

[19] See Griffith, *Politics of the Judiciary* (n 9) 19–22 and Ch 8, *supra*.

[20] In reviewing Griffith's book, Lord Devlin writes: 'To my mind none of the evidence, general or specific, adds much to the inherent probability that men and women of a certain age will be inclined by nature to favour the *status quo*' Devlin, 'Judges, Government and Politics' (n 18) 509.

[21] See Oliver, 'Review' (n 2) who, after setting out several concerns writes: 'These points of criticism do not however detract from Griffith's point that the judges do tend, especially when their own values or the interests of their own sections of society (for judges like others belong to several not always overlapping interests groups) are threatened, to prefer their own values and interests to others' 234; and Geoffrey Bindman, 'Keep an Eye on the Judges' (2010) 160 New Law Journal 880.

[22] The lack of diversity is not confined to class but is seen across the spectrum. See Michael Blackwell, 'Old Boys' Networks, Family Connections and the English Legal Profession' [2012] Public Law 426.

[23] On this see Robert Stevens, *The English Judges: Their Role in a Changing Constitution* (Hart 2002).

book in 1977 and the fifth edition in 1997 Griffith detected a more robust, interventionist, and assertive attitude on the part of judges in challenging governmental power.[24] He accounts for this as follows:[25]

> The increased robustness of the judiciary in its attitude to the executive, together with the more extravagant challenges to the sovereignty of Parliament, may be seen as an attempt to regain lost ground and to establish or re-establish the judiciary as an important and influential constitutional force.

While the development of judicial review over the past thirty years suggests a more interventionist attitude on the part of judges,[26] it is not easy to reconcile this with Griffith's central claim that the judiciary's understanding of public interest is driven by the kind of people they are and the position they hold in society unless one adds a claim that they are no longer class-bound or captive to their backgrounds (a proposition that is not advanced) or that their determinations are also influenced by internal power struggles with other arms of the state[27] which, if valid, would undercut the alleged influence of background.

Alternative Approaches

Other commentators have explored the general issue in different and interesting ways. Alan Patterson, for example, examined House of Lords cases alongside extensive interviews with the judges themselves and access to some judicial notebooks.[28] Robert Stevens, in tracing the judiciary from the Act of Settlement 1700 onwards, sees law and politics intertwined with judges at the higher levels engaged in thoughtful creativity.[29] In an examination of human rights cases in the House of Lords, Poole and Shah conclude that opinions of individual Law Lords cannot be explained by differences in ideology.[30] By contrast, David Robertson subjected just

[24] Among the cases Griffith had in mind were: *R v Secretary of State for Social Security ex parte JCW1* [1997] 1 WLR 275 and *Akinbolu v Hackney LBC, The Times*, 13 May 1996.

[25] *Prologue* to Griffith, *Politics of the Judiciary* (n 9) xvii.

[26] Although it is unclear in what sense this may be said to have been an 'attempt to gain lost ground'.

[27] See on this Adrian Hunt, 'Review of Politics of the Judiciary' (1988) Civil Justice Quarterly 346.

[28] Alan Paterson, *The Law Lords* (Macmillan 1982). See now Alan Paterson, *Final Judgment* (Hart 2013) which also draws on extensive interviews with Law Lords and access to some judicial notebooks. The emphasis in Paterson's rich account is on decision-making as a collective or social process. For criticism of this approach, see Tamas Gyorfi, 'Review of Final Judgment: The Last Law Lords and the Supreme Court (by Alan Paterson)' (2015) 19(2) Edinburgh Law Review 289. See also Alan Paterson, '*Final Judgment* Revisited' (2015) 21(1) European Journal of Current Legal Issues 1.

[29] The vast collection of writings by Robert Stevens is sympathetically reviewed in Alan Paterson, 'The Judges, the House of Lords and Politics' (2009) 16(1) International Journal of the Legal Profession 43.

[30] Thomas Poole and Sangeeta Shah, 'The Law Lords and Human Rights' (2011) Modern Law Review 79.

over sixty decisions of the House of Lords to content and statistical analysis from the point of view of a political scientist.[31]

Whereas Paterson sees decision-making in the final court as a 'collective' or 'social' process best understood through analysis of principled dialogues in which the 'printed speeches are but the end product of a complex series of exchanges between Bar and Bench and between the Law Lords themselves',[32] Robertson prefers an explanation which revolves around the ideological preferences of individual judges in a highly discretionary setting which, by reason of the nature of cases presented, allows for choice as to outcome[33] while providing at the same time formulae or codes in which to express the end-choice.[34] Others seek to account for decisions (and differences between judges) on a nuanced interpretation of '*doctrine*'—the rules and principles derived from legislation and case law[35]– or as a response to shifts in understandings of the role of judges in relation to political changes within the administration of justice.[36] In his useful case study of Imprisonment for Public Protection (IPP), Harry Annison[37] draws upon case law, extra-judicial speeches, and interviews with five senior serving or retired judges in applying an interpretive politics model to the issue of judicial decision-making.[38] On the basis of his analysis, Annison argues that senior judges are 'thoughtful participants in British politics, seeking to affect the course taken by criminal justice and sentencing policy'.[39] The data he collected suggested to him that the senior judiciary were able to use the interpretive tradition[40] to mitigate the excesses of a law that was disproportionate

[31] David Robertson, *Judicial Discretion in the House of Lords* (Clarendon Press 1998) (hereafter Robertson, *Judicial Discretion*). Robertson's data base comprised twenty-nine tax appeals and thirty-three criminal appeals as well as interviews with the judges themselves.

[32] Paterson, *Law Lords* (n 28) 8.

[33] Robertson, *Judicial Discretion* (n 31).

[34] ibid 239. See in this context the book reviews of Robertson, *Judicial Discretion* (n 31) by Sir Stephen Sedley (1999) 58(3) Cambridge Law Journal 627 and John Baldwin (1999) 19 Legal Studies 580. Sedley argues that Robertson overlooked the importance of the judges repeatedly telling him that they tried 'not to cheat' and comments: 'An aversion to cheating is, I would have thought, neither inchoate nor evidence of unfettered discretion: it suggests an uncomfortable awareness of the tension that can exist between principle and outcome and of the need not to sacrifice the former on the altar of the latter. What it does not suggest is a bunch of power-drunk decision-makers with nothing to restrain them except the occasional piece of unambiguous legislation' 628.

[35] See the account of TT Arvind and Lindsay Stirton, 'Legal Ideology, Legal Doctrine and the UK's Top Judges' [2016] Public Law 418.

[36] See, eg, Diana Woodhouse 'Politicians and the Judiciary: A Changing Relationship' (1995) 483(1) Parliamentary Affairs 401, where it is argued that developments in judicial and political relations in the 1990s suggest an active role of the courts in the political process as the British government strived for efficiency.

[37] Harry Annison, 'Interpreting the Politics of the Judiciary: The British Senior Judicial Tradition and the Pre-emptive Turn in Criminal Justice' [2014] 41(3) Journal of Law and Society 339. See also Harry Annison, *Dangerous Politics: Risk, Political Vulnerability and Penal Policy* (OUP 2015).

[38] Annison draws on the theoretical model proposed by Mark Bevir and Rod Rhodes according to which relevant actors are able to respond to new situations through a reasoning process that is embedded in the tradition they inherit: Mark Bevir and Roderick Rhodes, *Governance Stories* (Routledge 2006).

[39] ibid 340.

[40] The interpretive tradition is exemplified by the views of Lord Bingham that the task of the judges is only to give effect to the will of Parliament and to declare what the common law is and by

and liable to individual injustice but that they remained within strict and largely self-defined boundaries. While recognizing the contributions of these various approaches, our analysis is primarily structural.

Judges, Politics, and Independence

Our analysis focuses upon the higher echelons of the criminal judiciary, in particular the Court of Appeal (Criminal Division) *as a court* and the Lord Chief Justice (LCJ) who generally provides the direction for judicial policy. In the area of criminal justice, many determinations of policy[41] are made by the LCJ[42] or at the level of the Court of Appeal where, by convention, decision-making is collective.

In this setting, our analysis leads to the conclusion that judges are not simply part of the machinery of state authority and as such cannot avoid taking political decisions;[43] rather, when initiating policy decisions, *senior judges may be considered 'political' actors at real risk of exhibiting bias in favour of state interests as against the interests of the individual citizen*. So that it is clear, we mean by 'political' the authoritative allocation of values,[44] 'the process through which competing choices over public policy are made and which legitimate the exercise of state power to enforce those choices'.[45] While this does indeed act to shore up the overall governance system, it is not simply identifying public interest with institutions of government as established by law[46] but rather a *dynamic* involvement in building state institutions.

We seek to instantiate our view not through appeal to those periods in history when there was no real separation between the judicial and political, or upon anecdotal or attitudinal evidence[47] or inferential reasoning based upon the 'attitudes' of particular judges or groups of judges[48] or on analyses of individual cases (though

implication always has been: Lord Bingham, 'The Judges: Active or Passive?' in Peter James Marshall (ed), *Proceedings of the British Academy, 2005 Lectures* (OUP 2007) 139.

[41] The cases that reach the House of Lords/Supreme Court almost always involve technical points of law.

[42] The LCJ, we argue, became an increasingly influential, probably determinative, figure in framing judicial policy after the hostile encounter with the executive in 1963–64.

[43] See Griffith, *Politics of the Judiciary* (n 9): 'Judges are part of the machinery of authority within the State and as such cannot avoid the making of political decisions' 292–93.

[44] David Easton, 'An Approach to the Analysis of Political Systems' (1956–7) 9 World Politics 383.

[45] See Richard Hodder-Williams, 'Six Notions of "Political" and the United States Supreme Court' (1992) 22(1) British Journal of Political Science 1, 2.

[46] cf Griffiths, *Politics of the Judiciary* (n 9) 343.

[47] It is difficult to know what store to place on narratives given by judges about how they approach their role; at the end of the day, what counts is what is in the judgments. See Lord Neuberger, 'Some Thoughts on Judicial Reasoning across Jurisdictions' 2016 Mitchell Lecture, Edinburgh (11 November 2016) <www.supremecourt.uk/docs/speech-161111.pdf> accessed 1 January 2020.

[48] For an alternative perspective, see Diana Woodhouse, 'The Judiciary in the 1990s: Guardian of the Welfare State?' (1998) 26(4) Policy & Politics 457. Woodhouse argued that British judges in the 1990s

there are many such which align with our theory) or upon singular acts of interference (successful or otherwise) by politicians in the judicial process,[49] or upon the vicissitudes in their relationship with one or more political parties at points in history.[50] We do so by demonstrating that *the judges, often in association with the executive, have fundamentally restructured the criminal justice system so that what they define as the 'public interest' merges with 'state-interest' and is expressed in the architecture of its institutions*. In this institutional-design process, therefore, not only are the judges political actors but by altering the architecture of the system they have reinforced its essentially 'political' character. We trace below the key components of this political system.

Design by Discretion

Although the rise of the regulatory state in Victorian times led to the proliferation of delegated legislation under which the executive acquired quasi-legislative powers thereby attracting the displeasure of one Chief Justice,[51] which in turn caused public controversy and governmental concern,[52] what was less noticed and less remarked upon was the rise of *judicial discretion* in criminal justice. While judges had always enjoyed a measure of latitude when implementing principles or interpreting statutes, the inauguration of the Judges' Rules proved to be the first step by which senior judges, sometimes in collaboration with the executive, dramatically transformed the very structure of the process itself. From then on, critical case-by-case determinations arbitrating between individual rights and state

assumed a more interventionist stance in relation to government than at any other time during the twentieth century: 458.

[49] A notorious attempt to interfere with the sentencing of offenders occurred in 1947 when the Lord Chancellor, Lord Jowitt, wrote to Lord Goddard LCJ expressing the hope that the judges would not be lenient towards 'those bandits [who] carry arms [to] shoot at the police' as described in Stevens, *Independence of the Judiciary* (n 12) 95.

[50] We accept that governmental policies occasionally excite a public response from the judges and that these may be portrayed as 'political' interventions, as, eg, the lecture by Lord Taylor 'Continuity and Change in the Criminal Law', at King's College London, 6 March 1996, in which Lord Taylor attacked government policy on minimum sentences, mandatory life sentences, and the ethos of management consultancy that was taking over the criminal justice system. On this: Diana Woodhouse, 'Politicians and the Judges: A Conflict of Interest' (1996) 49 July 3(1) Parliamentary Affairs 423.

[51] Lord Hewart, *The New Despotism* (Ernest Benn Ltd 1929). In explaining why he had written the book, Hewart wrote: 'A mass of evidence establishes the fact that there is in existence a persistent and well-contrived system, intended to produce, and in practice producing, a despotic power which at one and the same time places Government departments above the Sovereignty of Parliament and beyond the jurisdiction of the courts . . . ' 14.

[52] The government was pushed into establishing a Committee chaired by Lord Donoghmore (with Sir John Anderson as a member) whose deliberations produced an indecisive report (Committee on Minister's Powers, *Donoghmore Committee Report* (1932)) which thereafter never troubled governmental processes.

interests were of less long-term significance than alterations to the structure of the system realized outside the parliamentary process.

The first design change was the inauguration in 1912 of a practice that, uncontested, has become a principle, namely that judges can, outside of, and in contradiction to traditionally understood norms of the adversary process, alter the system itself.[53] By default, and in alliance with the executive, the senior judiciary escheated to itself the power to move the criminal justice system away from its foundational principles into something quite different; not an open forum in which the confrontation between the state and the individual may be litigated but one in which the rules of engagement are tilted heavily in the direction of the state without the opportunity for challenge and with the prospect of further disempowerment should cost-effectiveness (or some other to-be-found 'value') so require.

The second major design innovation took place at the pre-charge stage. Through the Judges' Rules, the judges, in collaboration with the executive, authorized detention for questioning. Prior to this, the detention of individual citizens in order to subject them to questioning was a matter of police practice not sanctioned by law. Indeed, this was not formally ruled to be lawful until a (civil) case in 1983[54] in which the appellate judges were unable to cite *any* prior supporting authority (statutory or common law), an opinion endorsed by the House of Lords with a similar lack of authority.[55]

The third design change flowed from the second. On its face, the power of police detention clashed not only with the principle that individuals, short of arrest, should be free to go about their business but with the further principle that, unless arrested, citizens should be free to decide whether to answer police questions and have the advice of a lawyer in this regard. The Judges' Rules changed the system so that, following detention, access to a lawyer could be secured only with the consent of the police and, to remove any doubt, judges devised recipe rules[56] that police officers could offer at court as plausible (if fictitious) reasons for denial of access. In this way, the principles of individual freedom and the interests of the state were politically inverted so that the latter took priority over the former.

The fourth design innovation came as a result of addressing the consequences of allowing the police to detain citizens and to deny them access to a solicitor. In such circumstances, it was inevitable that, without any objective record, occasions would arise when the police account would be at variance with that of the citizen.

[53] This much was acknowledged in 1914 by civil servants when a suggestion within the Home Office for reformulating the Rules was rejected. See Chapter 3 and Illustration 3.1.

[54] *Mohammed-Holgate v Duke* (1983) 3 WLR 598.

[55] *Holgate-Mohammed v Duke* [1984] AC 437 in which the opinion of Lord Diplock (agreed to by the other judges) rested on the meagre assertion that such detention 'had been given implicit recognition in rule 1 of successive editions of the Judges' Rules'.

[56] See *R v Lemsatef* (1977) 2 All ER 835. See also *R v Houghton and Franciosy* (1979) 68 Cr App R 197.

The police response was generally to buttress their account by producing several officers said to have been present all of whom would offer similar, often identical, testimony irrespective of the duration or complexity of the period of questioning. This exposed the officers to challenge since the testimony of every witness was at common law supposed to be independent. To avoid exposure, officers denied, in the teeth of the evidence, that they had collaborated. Since juries might see through this façade and conclude that the officers had not only collaborated but were committing perjury and that 'admissions' and 'confessions' had been fabricated, the judges reversed the common law rule that the evidence of each witness must be independent and endorsed the practice of collaboration in writing-up police notebooks.[57] By creating an exception for the police, the judges thereby handicapped the defence, opened the door to police perjury and created a loophole for mendacious police officers to exploit.[58]

The fifth design change focused on the defendant's plea. The common law rule was clear: the defendant must have *complete freedom* to decide whether to plead guilty or not guilty and improper pressure in this regard, such as the offer of a lesser sentence, nullified the plea.[59] That position was subverted in practice by the subterranean policy of the judges instituting state-induced guilty pleas (plea bargaining). Following this practice coming to the surface, in a series of rulings,[60] the Court of Appeal overturned the common law rule and authorized the threat of a substantially increased sentence should a defendant elect to plead not guilty and be convicted following trial, at the same time promoting the fiction that the choice over plea remained free.

[57] *R v Bass* (1953) 1 QB 680. A consequence flagged up by CGL Du Cann: 'Suddenly Mr Justice Byrne indicated during a trial that it was surely the natural, sensible and unobjectionable things for two police officers concerned in a case to put their heads—and notes—together in recollecting what had been said in their presence. *From that day, the police practice changed to its very opposite*': *Miscarriages of Justice* (Muller 1960).

[58] Indeed, in *Bass* (n 57), the court acknowledged changing the rule because the police were tendering false evidence of non-collaboration.

[59] *R v Harper* (1967) *The Times* 7 October (hereafter *Harper*).

[60] See *R v Turner* (1970) 54 Cr App R 352; *R v Goodyear* (2005) EWCA Crim 888. As *R v Jisl* [2004] EWCA Crim 696 made clear, citing *R v Chaaban* [2003] EWCA Crim 1012, the responsibility of judges was redefined in management terms: 'Active, hands on, case management, both pre-trial and throughout the trial itself, is *now regarded* as an essential part of the judge's duty. The profession must understand *that this has become and will remain part of the normal trial process*, and that cases must be prepared and conducted accordingly' (para 116 emphasis supplied) The significance of these cases, well-understood in professional circles, is underlined in the official Ministry of Justice (MOJ) explanatory notes accompanying the Criminal Procedure Rules, as the following extract makes clear: ' ... The Rules promote a culture change in the management of criminal cases, but that change is evolutionary ... Part 3 for the first time gives courts explicit powers to manage the progression of criminal cases. In the cases of *Chaaban* [2003] EWCA Crim 1012 and *Jisl* [2004] EWCA Crim 696 the Court of Appeal held that courts have a duty to manage criminal cases effectively. The new rules give them the framework of powers they need to fulfil that duty. Read with the overriding objective the Part 3 rules will help the courts to promote the culture change in criminal case management that the Committee wants': <www.Justice.gov.uk/courts/procedure-rules/criminal/notes> accessed 1 January 2020.

The sixth design change arose out of the institution of state-induced guilty pleas. This innovation could work only if established sentencing principles, repeatedly endorsed at common law, were torn up, which the judges indeed did. From then (1970) sentencing no longer depended on remorse or contrition but upon the fact of a guilty plea whether voluntarily proffered or induced; and the 'reward' of a lesser sentence or 'threat' of a more severe sentence had to be substantial enough to secure guilty pleas to satisfy the new sentencing rationale, namely 'efficiency' defined in terms of through-put of cases. Accordingly, into the jurisprudence of sentencing the judges introduced market-driven calibrations in which sentences could be sold and guilty pleas bought in a 'deal'. These transactions are detached from traditional sentencing principles and directed instead to achieving 'cost-efficiency' by maximizing guilty pleas and minimizing trials with insufficient regard to the ancillary effects such as the impact upon those (including victims) who conventionally judges were required to take into account.

The seventh design change, underpinned by the CrimPR, focused on the political economy of trials by further weakening the defence through co-opting the defence lawyer to be part of the prosecution. This was achieved by the unilateral decision on the part of the Court of Appeal[61] to change the courtroom 'culture' based around a reconfiguration of the role of the judge as a case manager and further changes such that the defence was required to engage in advance disclosure of its case, to work alongside the prosecution towards the 'progression' of cases in an 'efficiency-driven' environment and under a duty to point out weaknesses in the prosecution case so that these could, where possible, be repaired;[62] and where trial judges, as 'case managers', were enabled to pressurize defendants and their lawyers into pleading guilty. In such a setting, judges have endeavoured to keep the new system in place by emphasizing the dangers (to defence lawyers) of objecting to it.[63]

The eighth design change focused on the burden of proof. While the technical bar (the prosecution being required to establish its case beyond reasonable doubt) could not be lowered without major public controversy, as we have seen, the actions of judges have weakened adversarial defence protections, undermining the defence and assisting the prosecution. Additionally, as we have seen, in extrajudicial speeches, successive Chief Justices stimulated governments into attenuating the right to silence by making reliance on it hazardous and on penalty of adverse comment.

[61] See *Chaaban; Jisl* (n 60).

[62] Sometimes the errors are so basic that they cannot be repaired. See, eg, *R v Walker and Coatman* [2017] EWCA Crim 392.

[63] See Mike McConville and Luke Marsh, 'Adversarialism Goes West: Case Management in Criminal Courts' (2015) 19(3) International Journal of Evidence & Proof 172.

System-Change and Its Consequences

If we stand back, the impact of these system changes becomes clear. In combination, all suspects are at risk of custodial interrogation; all defendants, innocent and guilty, are under pressure to plead guilty through state-induced sentencing threats; defence lawyers are reassigned as the right hand of the trial judge; the role of the jury is attenuated; in practical terms the burden of proof is reduced; and reflective sentencing hearings are replaced by market-driven prefigured regimes. Trials, once seen to be instruments for the ascertainment of legal guilt, have become obstacles to rapid case-processing. Added to this, by diminishing the role of all lawyers,[64] the concept of the criminal process has been radically changed such that the trial has been rotated on its axis with a newly empowered 'Trial Judge' elevated to centre stage.

Unlike the rule of law and the adversarial system in which courts respond to a factual matrix presented by the parties, senior judges involved in policy-making may be entirely *proactive*, driving system-change under their own initiative. The Judges' Rules are the classic demonstration of political collaboration, although there are indications elsewhere of such liaison.[65] More recently, the decision by the LCJ to commission a report by Leveson LJ on 'efficiency' in criminal proceedings came after discussion with the Lord Chancellor and dovetailed with a stream of governmental papers amounting to a collaborative campaign for cost savings rather than, and arguably at the expense of, actuarial investigation of where the real (ie, both fiscal and systemic) inefficiencies lay.

The Uses of a Judge

The uses to which judges have been put by government in criminal justice are another indication of the political character of the system. For Robert Stevens, asking judges to head committees or undertake inquiries threatens judicial independence and blurs the separation of powers, amounting in the eyes of critics to a 'misuse' of the judicial office.[66] The examples he cites certainly show that governments resort to judges in a variety of situations from terrorism,[67] to industrial

64 Defence lawyers who stand up for their clients are at risk of being disparaged and even reported to their disciplinary authority, ibid. The firmness with which the court intends to enforce its precepts is made clear in *Marshall and Ors v R* [2015] EWCA Crim 1999.

65 Thus, eg, when the practice of 'jury vetting', authorized secretly by the executive, was exposed in 1978 at the ABC Trial (after probably going on since 1948), it appeared known to the trial judge, Willis J who said, when it was challenged, that the procedure was 'perfectly proper in a case like this': Thomas Grant, *Jeremy Hutchinson's Case Histories* (John Murray 2015) 312. See also John Platts-Mills, *Muck, Silk and Socialism* (Paper Publishing 2001) 465 where Platts-Mills says that the jury was vetted at the trial of the Krays in 1978.

66 See Stevens, *Independence of the Judiciary* (n 12) 170ff.

67 For example, Lord Parker, *Report of the Committee of Privy Counsellors Appointed to Consider Authorised Procedures for the Interrogation of Persons Suspected of Terrorism* (HMSO 1972), who

disputes,[68] from interrogation procedures[69] to street disorders;[70] and there have been many others since.[71] However, rather than viewing this as a threat to the independence of judges, we see it as a further indication of the political role of the judiciary. Indeed, in criminal justice, governments have continually relied upon the judiciary to further their policies,[72] help allay public concern, and restore 'confidence' in the system.[73] And, for their part, judges have acted to assist as a brief overview of some of the major inquiries in the area of criminal justice[74] over the past fifty years demonstrates.[75]

When John Reginald Christie confessed in the witness box to having killed Timothy Evans' wife, public concern forced the government into action and the Home Secretary informed the House of Commons on 6 July 1953 that he had instructed the Recorder of Portsmouth, Mr Scott Henderson QC, to examine the case in private, the report to be made public before 15 July 1953, the date set for Christie's execution. The Henderson Report, dashed off in nine days, exonerated the legal system by concluding that Christie's confession was false and that Evans had been rightly hanged.[76] Later, the Denning Report (1963) into the 'Profumo

shamefully disregarded evidence submitted to him by the British Society for Social Responsibility in Science (BSSRS) that the government technique of sensory deprivation torture (known as 'depth interrogation') was harmful and could cause long-term damage. Parker recommended that the torture technique continue to be used, dismissively remarking that 'in a small minority of cases some mental effects may persist for up to two months', quoted in Carol Ackroyd and others, *The Technology of Political Control* (Pelican 1977) 35.

[68] For example, Lord Scarman, *Report of a Court of Inquiry under the Rt. Hon. Justice Scarman* (Cmnd 6922, HMSO 1977).

[69] For example, Lord Diplock, *Report of a Committee to Consider, in the Context of Civil Liberties, and Human Rights, Measures to Deal with Terrorism in Northern Ireland* (1975).

[70] For example, Lord Scarman, *Report into The Red Lion Square Disorders of 15 June 1974, Report of an Inquiry* (HMSO 1975).

[71] For example, *The Grenfell Tower Inquiry* (established 2017) chaired by Sir Martin Moore-Bick, a former judge of the Court of Appeal. The *Independent Inquiry into Child Sexual Abuse* is another, as is the Mitting Inquiry into *Undercover Policing*.

[72] See, eg, the *Interdepartmental Committee on the Distribution of Criminal Business between the Crown Court and the Magistrates' Courts* (HMSO 1975) (hereafter *The James Committee* (1975)). The Committee was headed by Arthur James J and promoted a government agenda to remove some criminal cases from jury trial and place them into magistrates' courts. While those proposals relating to small thefts were ditched, others (including public order offences) were eventually adopted by Parliament (Criminal Law Act 1977).

[73] Apart from the reports discussed below, see also the *Committee of Inquiry into the Challenor Case* chaired by James J (1964) the first statutory inquiry held under the Police Act 1964; widely considered a whitewash, it is discussed by James Morton, *Bent Coppers: A Survey of Police Corruption* (Warner Books 1993) 117.

[74] In other areas judges have been used in highly political and volatile matters such as in Northern Ireland, one of which, by Lord Diplock, led to the restructuring of the system of trials with the introduction of 'Diplock Courts'. See, Lord Diplock, *Legal Procedures for Dealing with Terrorists* (1972). See also John Jackson and Sean Doran, *Judge Without Jury: Diplock Trials in the Adversary System* (OUP 1995).

[75] An honourable exception is the Report by Harry Woolf LJ (with the assistance of three Assessors: Gordon Lakes, Rod Morgan, and Mary Tuck) into the prison riots at Strangeways (1991) available at National Archives, HO 370.

[76] The badly flawed Report is forensically examined by Ludovic Kennedy in, *10 Rillington Place* (Panther Books 1971) 261ff.

Affair' set a path that others were able to follow. Setting aside forensic analysis of evidence and failing to even read the trial transcript, Denning found Stephen Ward guilty of being ready to arrange 'whipping and other sadistic performances' (for which no evidence had been offered at his trial) and also guilty of procuring girls, a charge of which he had been acquitted at his trial.[77] A subsequent report into the Timothy Evans case by Brabin J (1966)[78] sought to confirm the same outcome as achieved by Scott Henderson although by similar prestidigitation to that of Denning. Brabin concluded, using the *civil* standard of proof and contradicting the prosecution case at trial (that both murders had been committed by the same person), that Evans had killed his wife but had not murdered his daughter (with the inexplicable outcome that two murderers had lived side-by-side in the same house, using the same method for killing, each unaware of the activities of the other!)[79] Using the same warped template, Sir Henry Fisher's inquiry into the killing of Maxwell Confait (1977)[80] concluded that all three boys (subsequently wholly exonerated) had been involved on a balance of probabilities (the *civil* standard) and that one of them was guilty of involvement in the killing despite never having been charged with the offence.

Extraordinarily, a disdain for evidence and facts marks other judicial inquiries in this general area.[81] Thus, the report into the 'Bloody Sunday' massacre in Ireland by Lord Widgery (1972), now seen universally as a whitewash, contented itself with hearing witnesses principally from one side only.[82] The Roskill Report on Fraud (1986) adduced no evidence in support of its proposals regarding the removal of complex fraud cases from jury trial and the defence's duty to disclose.[83]

[77] Denning did not trouble himself with standards of proof, simply announcing that Ward took girls down to his cottage at weekends and 'procured them to be mistresses for his influential friends': *The Denning Report: The Profumo Affair* (1963) (Pimlico 1992) 7.

[78] Brabin J, *Inquiry into the case of Timothy John Evans 1965-66*, National Archives, CAB 143.

[79] A sensible Home Secretary (Roy Jenkins) disregarded the Report and immediately recommended a free pardon.

[80] Sir Henry Fisher, *Report of an Inquiry by the Hon. Sir Henry Fisher into the circumstances leading to the trial of three persons on charges arising out of the death of Maxwell Confait and the fire at Doggett Road, London SE6* (HMSO 1977).

[81] Other government-commissioned reports are also deficient in this respect. Thus, the report by Sir Bill Jeffrey into independent advocacy commissioned by the Justice Secretary rests upon no firm factual foundation as is made clear: Sir Bill Jeffrey, *Independent Criminal Advocacy in England and Wales* (Ministry of Justice 2014) 70 para 10.1.

[82] The Inquiry arose out of the shooting of civilians by members of the 1st Parachute Regiment. Although there was no proof that the dead or wounded had handled firearms, in an inquiry that was marked by the utmost haste, Widgery concluded that the soldiers had been fired on first. The Saville Inquiry (2010) undertook a wide-ranging investigation and its findings contradicted Widgery in every material respect. Established in 1998, the inquiry was expected to last up to two years and cost £11 million. By its conclusion it had lasted over twelve years and cost £200 million. For a highly critical account see Louis Blom-Cooper, *Public Inquiries: Wrong Route on Bloody Sunday* (Bloomsbury: Hart 2017). As of 2019, one British soldier, 'Soldier F', is facing murder prosecution arising out of the shootings: <https://www.bbc.co.uk/news/uk-northern-ireland-47540271>.

[83] Section 43 of the Criminal Justice Act 2003 allowed for non-jury trial in serious and complex fraud cases on application by the prosecution, a provision subsequently repealed: Protection of Freedoms Act 2012.

The Report of Auld LJ (2001) which formed the basis for substantial changes to the criminal justice system was undertaken without any systematic data in its support on any key issue and contrary to much of which existed. Similarly, the report by Leveson LJ (2015) into 'efficiency' in criminal proceedings was undertaken, in a matter of months, with 'no time and little opportunity for evidence gathering'[84] and no 'quantitative analysis of the effect of the changes' proposed'.[85] In these instances, the insistence upon evidence conventionally associated with court trials was not allowed to stand in the way of dispositive, sometimes, forceful conclusions.

Without a factual foundation, often disdainful of normal evidential protocols and lacking, indeed often not offering, plausible rationales for their conclusions, such reports are more likely to be *ideological*, derived from anterior presuppositions, appealing to narrow political segments, and serving the interests of the state however well-intentioned they might be. Some have met their end through the vindication of those they have traduced[86] but others have secured influence without honour,[87] or have been left on the shelf awaiting a sympathetic cherry-picking government. The themes they have canvassed, however, remain; and some remain because they have long attracted the instinctive prejudice of judges.

One underlying theme, a matter close to the hearts of government and the judiciary alike, is a suspicion, bordering on animus, of trial by jury. As we have seen, with the then impending democratization of the jury,[88] the government introduced a series of (what it saw as) 'damage-limitation' initiatives including abolishing (by statute[89]) the requirement of unanimity, restricting the grounds on which to challenge prospective jurors by removing jurors' occupations from the jury list,[90] removing certain cases from trial by jury,[91] and introducing at some unknown historical point, without parliamentary authority but with the knowledge of judges, the secret 'vetting' of potential jurors by the prosecution.

[84] Sir Brian Leveson, *Review of Efficiency in Criminal Proceedings* (Judiciary of England & Wales January 2015) (hereafter Leveson, *Review*) para 9.

[85] ibid para 10.

[86] As is the case with Henderson, Brabin, Widgery, and Fisher.

[87] As is the case with Auld.

[88] Following the recommendations of the *Report of the Departmental Committee on Jury Service* (1965) chaired by another judge, Lord Morris of Borth-y-Gest. The Committee was established following pressure from within Parliament and outside particularly focused on the exclusionary effect of the property qualification on women.

[89] Criminal Justice Act 1967.

[90] This was effected by an Order issued by the Lord Chancellor (Lord Hailsham) following the granting of overall control of jury panels by the Courts Act 1971 to the Lord Chancellor's Department although the Act itself appeared to assume no change in the right of a party to the proceedings to inspect the panel (s 32(2)). The Order came after failed prosecutions of building workers on charges of affray, intimidation, and damage to property following a defence challenge to a juror whose trade was listed as 'building contractor' and immediately prior to trials at Shrewsbury of striking building workers.

[91] *The James Committee* (1975) (n 72). The Criminal Law Act 1977, in addition to removing certain classes of case from jury trial, also restricted the defence right to challenge jurors.

In a similar fashion, inquiries of various sorts headed by judges have cast doubt upon jury trial in specified classes of cases[92] and just as Leveson LJ used his review of 'efficiency' to go 'out of scope' (ie, not within his terms of reference) and cast further doubt upon the right to jury trial by suggesting that in 'either-way cases' the decision on venue should be for the court not the defendant. Leveson came to this conclusion having 'heard the voices of many involved' in the system, no doubt some of whom may have had in mind the views expressed by another judge, Stephen J:[93]

> … I think that the great bulk of the working classes are altogether unfit to discharge judicial duties, nor do I believe that, rare exceptions excepted, a man who has to work hard all day long at a mechanical trade will ever have either the memory, or the mental power, or the habits of thought, necessary to retain, analyse, and arrange in his mind the evidence of, say, twenty witnesses to a number of minute facts given perhaps on two different days. Jurors almost never take notes, and most of them would only confuse themselves by any attempt to do so, and I strongly suspect that a large proportion of them would, if examined openly at the end of a trial as to the different matters which they had heard in the course of it, be found to be in a state of hopeless confusion and bewilderment … I think that the habit of flattering and encouraging the poor, and asserting that they are just as sensible and capable of performing judicial and political functions as those who from their infancy have had the advantages of leisure, education, and wealth, has led to views as to the persons qualified to be jurors which may be very mischievous.

Whatever one's view of the worth of individual proposals, it is clear that some senior judges have arguably not only taken up the mantle of Stephen J but in addition have not fully heeded the lesson given when John Horne Took was acquitted of a trumped-up charge of Treason in 1794 having warned the Attorney-General not to attempt to shed men's blood on 'lame suspicions and doubtful inferences'.[94]

Political Character of Judges

The political character of the judiciary is not accordingly dependent upon linking decisions in individual criminal cases to 'attitudes', although senior criminal judges (with some outstanding exceptions) have displayed a strong propensity towards

92 ibid; *Report of Fraud Trials Committee* (1986) (hereafter *The Roskill Committee*) and the Sir Robin Auld, *The Criminal Courts Review* (Royal Courts of Justice 2001) (hereafter Auld, *Review*).
93 James Fitzjames Stephen, *A History of the Criminal Law of England* (1883) 1 572.
94 See Minnie Clare Yarborough, *John Horne Tooke* (AMS Press 1966) 173.

state interests over individual rights both in key areas of criminal justice and in major modern 'State Trials'.[95] In secret collaboration with the executive, judges oversaw a fundamental change in police–citizen relations that would have caused enormous controversy if proposed in Parliament. There was a move from police officers' 'keep your eyes and ears open and your mouth shut' to investigation through compelled interrogation; from citizen to suspect; from no questioning after charge to detention for the purpose of interrogation; from individual constable responsibility to multiple-officer signatures and cover up. Once into the court system, defendants, stripped of the right to silence, became subject to a series of pressures designed to weaken their resolve and forego trial. For their part, defence lawyers have been further weakened not only by severe cuts to legal aid but by curtailment of their advocacy rights by senior judges.[96]

In all of this, it is clear that the senior judiciary has not been an inert part of the machinery of justice but, with the executive and Parliament, its joint architects. The process followed demonstrates both a political orientation and a link with another arm of the state, the executive, not apparent from the strictly formal arrangements celebrated in the separation of powers ideology. The idea of 'judicial independence' as taking decisions 'independently of interests' is unsustainable in the light of evidence both in Home Office files and in other areas discussed. Senior judges are not inanimate creatures, passive interpreters of the will of Parliament only warming up in the sun of judicial review. Rather, in the area of criminal justice some have been politicized individuals not merely initiating but promoting policies of a fundamental character and all have operated in a setting in which a future cherry-picking government might well implement their wishes in whole or in part.

The ideological roots of these views are the outcome of a combination of class backgrounds and interests, and the material conditions of the wider political economy. Ever since[97] the reorganization of the court system in the 1870s, those responsible for developing criminal justice policy have been drawn from a closed social and educational elite which provides the window through which they view the world. The lack of affinity with or empathy for and prejudices about those who form the daily diet of the courts becomes indelibly inscribed in the organizational rules to which they have contributed in no small measure. These underlying ideologies found resonance with an equally narrow cadre of civil servants at each stage of the development of the Judges' Rules. Then and thereafter, the political views of 'Judge

[95] The pro-prosecution leanings of some trial and appellate judges have regrettably been a feature of some notorious cases including, but not limited to, the Birmingham Six, Broadwater Four, and Cooper and McMahon.

[96] See Daniel Newman, *Legal Aid Lawyers and the Quest for Justice* (Hart 2013). In his empirical study, Newman documents the disjuncture between how legal aid lawyers describe themselves in pursuing justice and the realities of a debilitated system. See further Hannah Quirk, *The Rise and Fall of the Right of Silence: Principle, Politics and Policy* (Routledge 2016); Abenaa Owusu-Bempah, *Defendant Participation in the Criminal Process* (Routledge 2017).

[97] And, indeed, long before.

& Co', as Bentham put it,[98] found fertile soil in the efforts of successive governments to rein in the jury (an institution with a potential to, if not substantial track record in, upsetting governments) punish defendants for failings of the system,[99] and reduce state services (including legal aid) in the name of 'efficiency'.

The System and Its Members

The important point here is that it is the criminal justice *system* which has been made political. Lower ranking judges in criminal cases are 'political' only in the limited but important sense that they are working within a system that has been politically constructed and are accordingly captive to and must conform to its co-ordinates.[100] While the co-ordinates are constituted by political boundaries erected by the senior judiciary[101] those who operate the system do so within an increasingly confining bureaucracy in which their actions are controlled by detailed prescriptive rules. In criminal cases, modern judges are 'trained' to 'manage' the processing of cases so that throughput is maintained by applying the CrimPR and by extending essentially pro-forma[102] sentencing 'sweeteners' to defendants to anchor the (early) guilty plea system. In this bureaucratic system, there is little room (or need) for individual judges to be political in any other sense and, indeed, they may be censured if they act politically because they can do so only by non-compliance with its determinants. As low-level officials in a bureaucratically constructed system, judges who breach the CrimPR will themselves be liable to censure by the Court of Appeal; 'over-sweet' guilty plea inducements are at risk of being overturned as unduly lenient;[103] and egregious failings may result in action by the formal disciplinary agency, the Judicial Conduct Investigations Office (JCIO).

[98] Jeremy Bentham, 'Principles of Judicial Procedure' in *The Works of Jeremy Bentham*, vol ii (Bowring edn, 1843) 7.

[99] Thus, the coercive guilty plea regime is fashioned on the palpably false basis that defendants are responsible for 'cracked trials' when research evidence and official statistics demonstrate that the main causes lie elsewhere. This falsehood is attributable to a presupposition about the conduct of defendants 'playing the system' that was propagated by, among others, Auld.

[100] Judges may be criticized on appeal for their conduct in dealing with case management issues. So far as personal conduct is concerned, judges may find themselves subject to investigation and possible censure by the Judicial Conduct Investigations Office (JCIO). The JCIO operates in accordance with the Judicial Discipline (Prescribed Procedures) Regulations 2014 and the supporting rules.

[101] Initially through Court of Appeal guidelines in cases such as *Turner* and *Goodyear*, furthered in *Chaaban* and *Jisl* which have now morphed into Criminal Procedure Guidelines (see n 60).

[102] Thus, eg, sentencing must in general comply with the Sentencing Council 'Definitive Guidelines'. Guidelines are set out for specific offences and the maximum level of reduction for a guilty plea tendered at the first stage of the proceedings is one third (Guideline D1) after which the maximum is one quarter with a sliding scale thereafter (Guideline D2) each of which is subject to detailed exceptions (Guidelines F1–F5).

[103] On application by the Law Officers under the Criminal Justice Act 1988.

And there is one counter-factual outcome: in this new system, the class composition of lower-level judges, central to the thesis of Griffith, is rendered *irrelevant*. Precisely because discretion has been largely removed by the inauguration of standardization templates, the new system requires and will tolerate only faithful operatives, lieutenants who know the rules and can be trusted to implement them without, as it were, hesitation, repetition, or deviation. The traits of those who formulate prescriptions of policy at the top do not have to be replicated in those lower in the hierarchy, though the differences are not measured by great distance at present.

It follows that the increasingly bureaucratized system is another reason why the views and actions of individual judges are no guide on the question whether judges are political. Indeed, the criminal justice system today is so organized that it may be operated by individuals who, honestly and faithfully, do no more than implement its rules according to the protocols laid down and whose personal 'politics' are otherwise irrelevant: the mechanics of the system have had no hand in how it has been engineered and little discretion in how it operates.

Legitimation

Against a background of order maintenance, an essential role of the executive and the judiciary has been the protection of the criminal justice system's philosophical bedrock—its legitimacy—in more subtle ways than Stephen J chose to adopt. So far as the executive is concerned, a number of well-rehearsed strategies have been conventionally deployed. Wherever possible, governments are ready to stress the 'independence' of the judiciary. But it goes much further and involves attempts to protect the 'integrity' of the system in all its aspects.

Thus, where issues become of great public concern, governments seek to limit what can be looked into and hence what may be discovered. In relation to matters addressed in this book, as Paul O'Higgins documented,[104] the Report into the Challenor affair[105] was restricted to an essentially peripheral matter, namely whether any senior police officers were at fault in failing to detect the onset of paranoid schizophrenia in Challenor, a matter of great difficulty even for psychiatric specialists rather than the more general question as to how such irregularities could occur in a supposedly well-regulated police force; the Sheffield (rhino whip) Inquiry[106] was restricted to the question whether the police officers involved should have been asked to resign rather than dismissed from the service with the

[104] Paul O'Higgins, 'The Challenor Report—1' [1965] Criminal Law Review 633.

[105] Arthur Evan James QC, *Report by Mr A.E. James, Q.C. into the circumstances in which it was possible for Detective Sergeant Harold Gordon Challenor to continue on duty as a time when he appears to have been affected by the onset of mental illness* (HMSO 1965).

[106] Home Office, *Report of the Sheffield Police Appeal Inquiry* (Cmnd 2176, HMSO 1963).

result that interested parties not strictly being party to the proceedings were denied legal representation; and the Mars-Jones Inquiry (into the cases of Tisdall, Kingston, and Hill-Burton involving assault and planting of evidence)[107] was restricted to the narrow question whether there had been a breach of duty by any officer involved in certain inquiries instigated by the Home Secretary rather than with the general issue of the utility of the procedures then in force for inquiring into complaints against the police.

Similarly, it was no accident that when it became clear that the underpinnings of the case against the Birmingham Six had collapsed, the Crown did not contest the appeal with the result that detailed forensic examination of the failures of the police and prosecution in the investigation could not take place. And on the very day the Court of Appeal quashed the convictions in the Birmingham Six case, the Home Secretary[108] announced the establishment of a Royal Commission on Criminal Justice (RCCJ) but restricted its potential scope by ruling out an inquiry into the Birmingham Six case on the spurious basis that 'the essential facts of the case have now been fully established in the Court of Appeal'[109] and sowed the seeds for the subordination of principle to cost-efficiency (which both the Commission[110] and later the judges[111] readily grasped). Although the RCCJ (1993)[112] has been criticized for failing to look into miscarriages of justice, the files on many of the central cases, such as the Birmingham Six,[113] the Maguire Seven,[114] Judith Ward,[115] were already sealed and, indeed, many of the relevant papers may have been 'weeded' or destroyed.[116]

So far as senior judges are concerned, they have sought to overcome a core problem which their actions have presented: while part of the state's order maintenance regime they have to appear legitimate in a 'democratic' sense. They have sought to reconcile this core contradiction through two devices. First, the judiciary has been able to produce an endless stream of generalized, abstract rhetoric concerning 'independence' of judges as non-political actors and as custodians of individual freedoms. Second, particularized 'justifications' have been advanced for the policies pursued. The synthetic nature of the analytical grids utilized by the

[107] Report of Inquiry by Mr WL Mars-Jones, QC into the Inquiries made, for the Information of the Secretary of State for the Home Department, into the Case of Thomas Halloran and Patrick Joseph Cox and the Case of Patrick Albert Tisdall, Thomas Alfred Kingston and Sidney Hill-Burton (HMSO 1964).

[108] HC Debates 14 March 1991, vol 187, cols 1109–26.

[109] ibid at 1112.

[110] See Royal Commission on Criminal Justice, *Report* (Cm 2263, HMSO 1993).

[111] When adopting a 'change in culture' which eventually underpinned the CrimPR.

[112] RCCJ, *Report* (n 110). The Commission adverted to 'widely publicised miscarriages of justice'.

[113] The papers have been sealed for at least seventy-five years.

[114] See, eg, National Archives: BS 27 Core Bundles sealed for forty-three years.

[115] See, eg, National Archives: HO291/2132, sealed until 1 January 2050.

[116] On the general issue of state secrecy, see Tony Bunyan, *The History and Practice of the Political Police in Britain* (Julian Friedman 1977); Moran Christopher, *Classified: Secrecy and the State in Modern Britain* (CUP 2013).

judiciary, however, is demonstrated by their fungibility; propositions cast as enduring, even unqualified, principles may be suddenly replaced by contradictory propositions bearing an apparently permanent and unconditional status. Thus:

> 'Neither judge, magistrate nor juryman can interrogate an accused person unless he tenders himself as a witness, or require him to answer questions tending to incriminate himself'[117] was set aside because 'If this sort of investigation were not allowed very few crimes would ever be discovered'[118]; 'Every man's house is his castle'[119] fell away because 'honest citizens must help the police'[120]; where once only 'genuine remorse'[121] justified a lesser sentence, the passage of two years led to this being available for 'an element of remorse'[122] and later where there was no remorse at all.[123]

In the most recent era, by contrast, the arguments advanced in leading cases have rendered previous attempted rationalizations irrelevant.[124] The analytical grids utilized by judges today tend to be abstractions entwined with business and commercial ideologies favoured by government, although requiring citizens to pay unqualified allegiance to the police[125] has had to be set down in the face of established police malpractice.[126] Statistics, empirical data, and research evidence, much of which made for uncomfortable reading for judges, are now eschewed in favour of sales and market rhetoric in which abstractions and soft images displace reality. In judicial rhetoric, the underpinnings of social order are today found in a 'changing landscape'[127] in which there is 'personal freedom'[128] for defendants, represented by lawyers, also accorded 'complete freedom', with judges simply 'acceding to the wishes of defendants' acting alongside and in alignment with government policy, in pursuit of 'simplicity' and 'efficiency'.

117 Address of Lord Brampton (J) to the Police, 1882 (in *Sir Howard Vincent's Police Code* (National Archives 1889)).

118 *R v Booth and Jones* (1910) 5 Cr App R 177.

119 *Semayne's Case* (1604) 5 Coke Rep 91.

120 *Chic Fashions v Jones* [1968] 2 QB 299 (hereafter *Chic Fashions*).

121 *R v Harper* (1967) *The Times* 7 October, (1968) 52 Cr App R 21.

122 *Turner* (n 60).

123 See *Goodyear* (n 60).

124 This judicial tendency for 'unique' principles with no capacity for endurance, whereby the 'inconvenient' can be overturned has further manifested itself in the court's approach to the interpretation of the CrimPR. See Luke Marsh, 'The "Tommy Robinson" Case and Contempt of Court: Conflicting Interpretations of the Criminal Procedure Rules' (2020) 1 Criminal Law Review, 50.

125 '... honest citizens must help the police and not hinder them in their efforts to track down criminals': *Chic Fashions* (n 120) 313 *per* Denning J.

126 See, eg, *R v Maxwell* [2010] UKSC 48 in which the House of Lords was confronted with an 'appalling history of misconduct' by police officers.

127 The image utilized by Leveson, *Review* (n 84) para 1.3.

128 This was the effect of the recommendation of Auld, *Review* (n 92) and adopted in *Goodyear* (n 60) that the defendant could request (through his or her advocate) an advanced indication of sentence.

Because 'efficiency' cannot be understood internally to the courts but has arisen through state pressure to which the judges have responded, this is masked by appeal to a 'change in culture' which is divorced from the political economy within which the courts actually operate. However, mimicking the sloganized environment of commercial tag-lines, ('*Just do it*';[129] '*We try harder*'[130]), investigators and courtroom actors are now abstracted from their real and conflicted environments and simply enjoined to '*get it right*'.[131] In this procedural nirvana, the mediocre is the message.

While the judges have an alignment with government policy, their relationship in criminal justice is one which is at base *dependent* in the sense that they are vulnerable to direct political pressure. Just as Lord Parker was given a dressing down by Charles Cunningham, so the judiciary was forced to knuckle under in the face of parliamentary denunciation when formulating the Judges' Rules. And judges and their defenders felt exposed during the 'Enemies of the People' furore precisely because the Lord Chancellor, who has a statutory duty to uphold the independence of the judiciary, was not seen to have done so when she said that the independence of the judges was the fountain upon which the rule of law was built but failed to condemn press attacks on the High Court judges who had decided the legal challenge to Brexit under Article 50 of the Treaty on European Union.

Conclusion

The search for the politics of senior judges through an analysis of judgments in criminal cases is accordingly insufficient. Historically, key elements of the senior judiciary have proved political in every sense of the word but the evidence lies

[129] Trademark of Nike.

[130] Trademark of Avis.

[131] In the Leveson *Review* (n 84) the police and prosecutors are advised that 'the first overarching principle must be Getting it Right First Time' 2.1 para 25. For discussion on this principle see Luke Marsh, 'Leveson's Narrow Pursuit of Justice: Efficiency and Outcomes in the Criminal Process' (2016) 45(1) Common Law World Review 51. The recent notorious collapse of rape trials involving Liam Allan, Isaac Itiary, and Oliver Mears demonstrates the ineffectiveness of such judicial invocations in the face of deep-seated structural failings. See 'Metropolitan Police Review of Rape Case Evidence' (*BBC News* Online, 20 December 2017) <>; Stephen Walter and Jack Maidment, 'Oxford University Student Cleared of Rape Charge as yet another Case Collapses Days before Trial Begins' *The Telegraph* (18 January 2018). Such failings are, regrettably, replicated across the board not only in terms of the non-disclosure of relevant evidence (see 'Making it Fair' Joint Inspection Report of HMCPSI and HMIC (July 2017) which found 'revelation by the police to the prosecutor of material that may undermine the prosecution case or assist the defence case [to be] rare' 3) but also in terms of basic investigative quality and engagement (see, eg, 'Stolen Freedom: The Policing Response to Modern Slavery and Human Trafficking' HMICFRS Report (October 2017) which found, among other things: 'Victims are being let down at every stage. Identification, information flows, victim focus and investigative practice all need to be improved considerably, so that victims receive the full range of protections and safeguards to which they are entitled and more offenders are brought to justice') 13 HMIC (July 2017).

primarily in their role in the construction of the system itself. That involvement has intensified in line with government policy which has increasingly focused on a market economy based in 'efficiency'. Principles which once conditioned judicial actions are, we argue, now increasingly displaced by policies shrouded in the legitimating rhetoric of the market-place.

11
The Global Diaspora

Introduction

In spite of the technical shortcomings of the Judges' Rules, their foothold around the world has been remarkably successful. Their transplantation into mixed-racial, mixed-cultural, mixed-religious, multi-lingual, and economically diverse territories was not, however, fortuitous; it followed the spread of the British Empire and its economic imperatives.[1] While their proliferation across colonial territories[2] remains an under-researched part of Imperial legal history,[3] in greater or lesser degree the Rules helped shape the justice apparatus of these occupied states and the actions of officials administering them, who were throughout the colonial period, often British personnel[4] or their non-tenured appointees.

In dispatching the Rules to the far corners of the Empire,[5] the Colonial Office was to have powerful influence on the regulation of police questioning in these

[1] Often, the flag followed trade rather than the other way around. The introduction of colonial police forces and ancillary legal regimes were usually predicated upon the protection of primarily British personnel and their commercial interests. See, eg, for JH Pain, ' The Reception of English and Roman-Dutch Law in Africa with Reference to Botswana, Lesotho and Swaziland' (1978) 11 Comparative & International Law Journal of Southern Africa 137 (hereafter Pain, 'English and Roman-Dutch Law in Africa'); James Opolot, 'The Resilience of the British Colonial Police Legacies in East Africa, Southern Africa, and West Africa' (1992) 15 Police Studies: International Review of Police Development 90; TA Okonkwo, *On the Culture of Social Structure* (Chicago University Press 1966); Joseph Ogbonnaya Irukwu, *Nigeria at the Crossroads* (Witherby 1983); Etannibi Alemika, 'Policing and Perceptions of Police in Nigeria' (1998) 11(4) (Winter) Police Studies 161.

[2] For brevity, this term covers all dominions, protectorates, and other mandates of the British Empire including concession territories.

[3] For a critique of colonial criminal justice covering the period of the 1912 Judges' Rules, with focus on interracial homicide trials, see Martin Wiener, *An Empire on Trial* (CUP 2009) (hereafter Wiener, *Empire*). See more generally Barry Godfrey and Graeme Dunstall (eds), *Crime and Empire 1840-1940—Criminal Justice in Local and Global Context* (Routledge 2005). For a critical account of colonial law see also Hussain Nasser, *The Jurisprudence of Emergency: Colonialism and the Rule of Law* (Michigan University Press 2003).

[4] This was true of those in charge of the police and the judiciary as well as the governors and administrators. Administrators, in turn, lacking the necessary resources and personnel themselves, had to utilize local power structures wherever possible: Isaac Schapera, *Tswana Chiefs and Social Change 1795–1940*, London School of Economics Monographs on Social Anthropology no 43 (Athlone Press 1970); William Cohen, *Rulers of the Empire: The French Colonial Service in Africa* (Hoover Institution Press 1971).

[5] In many territories, the general law had already been drafted by the British (as in India) or was imposed (as, eg, the Gold Coast Colony Supreme Court Ordinance of 1876 which introduced the 'common law, the doctrines of equity, and the statutes of general application' in force in England into the coastal trading areas of Nigeria; and the 1889 Africa Order in Council and the East Africa Order in Council 1897 which did the same in East Africa). Other examples include: Criminal Law and Procedure Act 1873 (Antigua and Barbuda) and Criminal Procedure Act 1891 (Barbados). For fuller discussion,

The Myth of Judicial Independence. Mike McConville and Luke Marsh, Oxford University Press (2020). © Mike McConville and Luke Marsh. DOI: 10.1093/oso/9780198822103.001.0001

territories and with it bring about a global shrinkage of the rights and liberties of citizens.[6] In particular, whatever the contested claims regarding the 'rule of law',[7] the Rules—essentially expressed as normative rules of practice for the guidance of police conduct[8]—were to have a stultifying effect upon the progressive development of local law and suspects' rights.

For many places subject to occupation[9] or to some form of 'belonging' to the common law world,[10] archival evidence shows a dialogical process with the Home Office and its Colonial department at the helm during key evolutionary periods of the Rules. This reveals the extent to which Britain centralized control and how at least some occupied territories saw themselves unavoidably bound to the Rules as their personal 'law'.[11] It is this deeper question of how 'rules' became 'law' within the Imperial system and what implications this had that we outline in this chapter.

Rule Britannia: The Global Dimension

The structuring of police–citizen relations by the Rules was furthered by the standing of English judges and of the common law, itself integral to the

see Henry Morris and James Read, *Indirect Rule and the Search for Justice* (Clarendon Press 1972); Pain, 'English and Roman-Dutch Law in Africa' (n 1); and Robert Seidman, 'A Note on the Construction of the Gold Coast Reception Statute' (1969) 13 Journal of African Law 45.

6 Of course, policing, like the common law, was not applied in a uniform manner. Policing in white settlements tended to be mostly civilian (with the exception of Ireland) whereas it was paramilitary in 'colonies of rule'. See Bankole A Cole, 'Post-Colonial Systems' in Rob Mawby (ed), *Policing Across the World: Issues for the Twenty-first Century* (UCL Press 1999) (hereafter Cole, 'Post-colonial Systems'). See Emma Bell, 'Normalizing the Exceptional: British Colonial Policing Cultures Come Home' (2013) <https://mimmoc.revues.org/1286> accessed 1 January 2020.

7 For an overview, see Mark Brown, '"An Unqualified Human Good?" On Rule of Law, Globalization, and Imperialism' (2018) 43(4) Law & Social Inquiry 1391. See also Morton Horowitz, 'The Rule of Law: An Unqualified Human Good?' (1977) 86 Yale Law Journal 561; Ranajit Guha, *Dominance Without Hegemony: History and Power in Colonial India* (Harvard University Press 1998); Lauren Benton, *Law and Colonial Cultures: Legal Regimes in World History, 1400–1900* (CUP 2002) (hereafter Benton, *Law and Colonial Cultures*); Brian Tamanaha, *On the Rule of Law: History, Politics, Theory* (CUP 2004).

8 Indeed, various commentators trace problems with modern law enforcement to the brutal, corrupt, and brutalizing practices in some colonial policing regimes. See, eg, Tekenya Nitonye Tamuno, *The Evolution of the Nigerian State* (Western Printing Sevices 1972).

9 The underlying tenets of imperial rule remained based in co-opting local collaborators (usually those already having a power base), gaining access to local labour markets while concurrently keeping both subordinated through the exercise of power, and depriving indigenous people of opportunities for self-development.

10 Windeyer J (writing extra-judicially) articulated this 'belonging' thus: 'Implicit and not analysed, but basic—of common law as the ultimate foundation of British colonial institutions, a belief that not even Parliament could properly deprive British subjects anywhere of their birthright' Sir Victor Windeyer, 'A Birthright and Inheritance—Establishment of the Rule of Law in Australia' University of Tasmania Law Review [1962] 635, 653.

11 For example, the courts of Western Samoa (Samoa) which see English law as a 'type of law', Michael Ntumy (ed), *South Pacific Islands Legal Systems* (University of Hawaii Press 1993) xxi (cited by H Patrick Glenn, *On Common Laws* (OUP 2005) (hereafter Glenn, *On Common Laws*) 93.

colonial enterprise.[12] This alliance led to a diaspora through which jurisdictions across the globe (including Antigua[13] and Barbuda,[14] Australia,[15] Bahamas[16], Belize,[17] Botswana,[18] British Virgin Islands,[19] Cayman Islands,[20] Cook Islands,[21] Dominica,[22] East Africa,[23] Fiji,[24] Hong Kong,[25] Ireland,[26] Jamaica,[27] Kenya,[28] Kiribati,[29] Mauritius,[30] Montserrat,[31] Namibia,[32] New

[12] As scholars have noted, law was a central part of the imperial project. See, eg, Sally Merry, 'Law and Colonialism' (1991) 25 Law and Society Review 879, 889; and Martin Chanock, *Law, Custom, and Social Order: The Colonial Experience in Malawi and Zambia* (CUP 1985).

[13] See Law Library of Congress, *Miranda Warning Equivalents Abroad* (Global Legal Research Center 2016) <www.loc.gov/law/help/miranda-warning-equivalents-abroad/miranda-warning-equivalents-abroad.pdf> accessed 1 January 2020 (hereafter Congress, *Miranda Warnings Abroad*) 1.

[14] ibid.

[15] With slight variation of substance, the Judges' Rules were adopted across Australian states: see Mark Aronson, Norman Stephen Reaburn, and Mark Weinberg, *Litigation—Evidence and Procedure* (2nd edn, Sydney Butterworths 1979); James Gobbo, *Cross on Evidence* (2nd Australian edn, Sydney Butterworths, 1979) 532–33. For further literature on this jurisdiction, see 'Admissibility of Confessions—Judges' Rules' (1960–62) 1 Adelaide Law Review 85. For an early ruling on the introduction of the Judges' Rules in Victoria, see Australian Law Journal (1937) 11(4) at 113, noting that the Chief Commissioner of Police had made it obligatory for the police to follow the English Judges' Rules. In the states of Queensland and Tasmania, the English Judges' Rules were adopted with certain modifications (see for Queensland *R v Juenszko* [1967] Qd R 128 and for Tasmania *R v Deverell* [1969] Tas SR 106). Where Australian states do (or did) not have a direct equivalent of the Judges' Rules the test outlined in *R v Lee* (1950) 82 CLR 133 is relevant. See also Karl Alderson, 'Powers and Responsibilities: Reforming NSW Criminal Investigation Law' (PhD thesis, UNSW 2001) <www.unsworks.unsw.edu.au/primo_library/libweb/action/dlDisplay.do?vid=UNSWORKS&docId=unsworks_541> ch 3.

[16] For example, *Shavargo McPhee v The Queen (Bahamas)* [2016] UKPC 29.

[17] See, eg, *Phillip Tillet v The Queen* [2011] UKPC 21.

[18] Congress, *Miranda Warnings Abroad* (n 13) 56–57.

[19] Although their precise status is unclear: ibid 2.

[20] While the Judges' Rules applied here, note Cayman Islands Constitution Order 2009, ss 5(3) and (4): Congress, *Miranda Warnings Abroad* (n 13) 5.

[21] *Police v Young* [2015] CKHC 1 23 quoting Rule III.B of the Judges' Rules, cited by Congress, *Miranda Warnings Abroad* (n 13) 15.

[22] See, eg, *Balson v State* [2005] UKPC [2005] 4 LRC 147.

[23] Initially the 1912 Rules applied to the East African states. With time, some countries sought to replace the Rules (wholly or partly) with instruments such as Uganda's Evidence (Statements to Police Officers) Rules 1961. See *Hassan s/o Waliseme* [1959] EA 800, 802–03. See generally Philip Durand, 'Confessions in East Africa' (1968) 4 East African Law Journal 70.

[24] See discussion of principles in *Varani v The State* [2015] FJCA 145. See also *State v Matacagi* [2003] FJHC 166.

[25] See *Rules and Directions for the Questioning of Suspects and the Taking of Statements* issued by the Secretary for Security in 1992 (Hong Kong Gazette No 40/1992, Special Supplement No 5, E3, 2 October), Note in *Butterworths Hong Kong Police Force Handbook* (LexisNexis 2004) (hereafter *Rules and Directions* (1992)) 1 1. See also discussion, *infra*.

[26] Congress, *Miranda Warnings Abroad* (n 13) 41–42. See, eg, *McGarrick v Leavy* (1964) I.R. 226.

[27] See *infra*.

[28] See generally Momanyi Bwonwong'a, *Criminal Procedures in Kenya* (East African Educational Publishers 1994) 66–67.

[29] Prior to the Kiribati Police Powers and Duties Act 2008, 'Kiribati courts referred to the English Judges' Rules with respect to cautioning suspects': Congress, *Miranda Warnings Abroad* (n 13) 19. See *Republic v Kimaere* [2004] KIHC 14.

[30] The 1964 Rules continue to apply.

[31] Congress, *Miranda Warnings Abroad* (n 13) 9.

[32] The *State v Malumo and Ors* (CC 32/201) [2011] NAHC (31 January 2011) in which Hoff J said '... though Judges Rules are administrative directives to be observed by the police, they are not completely without effect and that a breach thereof may influence whether an incriminating statement (or

Zealand,[33] Papua New Guinea,[34] Saint Vincent and the Grenadines,[35] Singapore,[36] the Solomon Islands,[37] South Africa,[38] Trinidad and Tobago,[39] Tuvalu,[40] Western Samoa (Samoa),[41] and Zambia[42] to name some)[43] were forced to 'adopt' the Rules in one of their iterations[44] or otherwise expressed themselves in compliance,[45] with long-term consequences (some continuing today) for their own systems. As such, far from symbolizing archaic vestiges of another era, the issue of the Rules remains a live one in the post-colonial world.

To underline the point, the post-colonial influence is even carrying the English Criminal Procedure Rules (CrimPR) into the vestiges of the Empire such as the Eastern Caribbean. Thus, Saint Lucia, having gained independence in 1979, continues along with other states[46] to feed off English law, the Saint Lucia Criminal Code importing through its Criminal Code 2004 and Criminal Procedure Rules 2008 essentially the English provisions on criminal procedure. Thus, section 909 ('Voluntary Disclosure by accused') of its Criminal Code tracks the English

in this instance a pointing-out) had been made freely and voluntarily or not'. See also *The State v Mafuya and Ors* [1992] 2 SACR 370 (W).

[33] See extensive discussion of the rules in the New Zealand context in Sir Francis Adams (ed), *Criminal Law and Practice in New Zealand* (Sweet & Maxwell (NZ) 1964) 695–714. The New Zealand Court of Appeal held in *Convery* [1968] NZLR 426 that the 1964 version of the Rules did not apply in New Zealand.

[34] Congress, *Miranda Warnings Abroad* (n 13) 23.

[35] Although now note the new caution under PACE 'may apply to Saint Vincent': ibid 11.

[36] See Amarjit Singh, 'S.121(5) C.P.C—A Policemen's Charter?' [1989] Singapore Academy of Law Journal 106-112.

[37] Congress, *Miranda Warnings Abroad* (n 13) 25–26.

[38] In 1931, 'Judges' Rules' akin to those in England were adopted. See Victor Hiemstra, 'Abolition of the Right Not to Be Questioned' (1963) 80 South African Law Journal 187 (hereafter Hiemstra, 'Abolition of the Right Not to Be Questioned') 218.

[39] The 1964 Judges' Rules were adopted in Trinidad and Tobago in 1965. See *Attorney General of Trinidad and Tobago v Whiteman* [1991] 2 AC 240; *Kumar v The State (Trinidad and Tobago)* [2000] UKPC 23; *Hunte and Khan v The State (Trinidad and Tobago)* [2015] UKPC 33; and *Pitman v the State (Trinidad and Tobago)* [2017] UKPC 6.

[40] Prior to the Tuvalu Police Powers and Duties Act 2009. See Congress, *Miranda Warnings Abroad* (n 13) 28–29.

[41] See Leulua' iali 'I Tasi Malifa, 'The Reception of Judges' Rules and the Right to Counsel in the Constitution of Western Samoa' (1997) 21 The Journal of Pacific Studies 161 (hereafter Malifa, 'The Reception of Judges' Rules').

[42] The English Judges' Rules were even referenced in the Zambia Police Act (s 9(3)(a)) (since removed).

[43] Other territories included: Aden; British Guiana; British Solomon Islands Protectorate; Gambia; Gibraltar; Guernsey; Seychelles; Tanganyika; and Zanzibar.

[44] Thus, in a Colonial Office Letter of August 1964 Northern Rhodesia (now Zambia) reported that it was not desirable to introduce the new rules 'at this time' and that the existing rules (those of 1930) were 'familiar to all officers whose duty it is to apply them and in practice they work well'.

[45] In substance, if not always in language. Thus, in response to the promulgation of the 1964 Rules, Malta (which became independent in 1964) reported that: 'The English Judges' Rules have no legal *locus standi* in Malta although in practice they are largely observed' (original emphasis).

[46] See, eg, Bermuda which provided for the introduction of Criminal Procedure Rules by s 540 of the Criminal Code Act 1907 (as amended) now set out in Criminal Procedure Rules 2013 BR 13/2013 which is, in essence, a copy of the English CrimPR. This is also the case for Trinidad and Tobago, The Criminal Procedure Act Chap 12, 02 (Criminal Procedure Rules 2016); Belize, Criminal Procedure Rules 2016.

provisions providing that, on initial prosecution disclosure, the accused must supply a written defence statement (a) setting out in general terms the nature of the defence; (b) indicating the matters on which he or she takes issue with the prosecution; and (c) setting out in the case of each such matter, the reasons why he or she takes issue with the prosecution. If a special defence is advanced the written statement must disclose particulars including (a) the name and address of any witness the accused believes is able to give evidence in support of the special defence if the name and address are known to the accused when the statement is given; and (b) any information in the accused's possession which might be of material assistance in finding any such witness, if his or her name and address are not given. On failure to comply with these and other detailed provisions, by section 912, the court or, with the leave of the court, any other party, may make such comment as appears appropriate or the court or jury may draw such inferences as appear proper in deciding whether the accused committed the offence concerned. A constitutional challenge to these local 'adaptations' was recently dismissed by the Privy Council.[47]

Archival evidence underlines three points.[48] First, prior to the release of the 1918 Rules, the British government was in receipt of requests for 'guidance' from colonial provinces in regard to police interrogation. Various appeals from far-flung subjects such as the government of Manitoba littered the desks of those in the Colonial Office and in the Home Office itself (see **Illustration 11.1**).

Second, English Judges were put on notice that the end-product would impact upon populations well beyond the jurisdiction of their own courts, amplifying, one would have expected, a sense of duty to ensure the 'rights' framework was carefully drafted and in good faith. By way of example, a letter to Darling J on 17 July 1918 by the Civil Service read as follows:

> A memorandum was drawn up by His Majesty's Judges of the King's Bench Division in October 1912 on the subject of statements made to the Police by persons suspected of crime. It is now proposed to revise this memorandum so as to cover points which have been raised from time to time and on which it is very important that the Police should have clear instruction. The memorandum would also be sent in reply to the inquiries which *are often received from the authorities of the Colonies and others on the subject.* I should be glad to know whether the Judges approve the revised memorandum.[49]

[47] *Sexius v The Attorney General of Saint Lucia* [2017] UKPC 26. The common law applicable in St Lucia prior to the adoption of the Constitution of St Lucia in 1979 placed an onus on an accused only to provide advance notice of any special defence, including alibi.

[48] Any study of British colonial history cannot ignore that large volumes of archival evidence relating to British activities in the colonies were destroyed or hidden under the auspices of 'Operation Legacy', run by a British Colonial Office tasked with the disposal of sensitive documents: see, eg, Shohei Sato, '"Operation Legacy": Britain's Destruction and Concealment of Colonial Records Worldwide' (2017) 45(4) The Journal of Imperial and Commonwealth History 697.

[49] Emphasis supplied. Letter held at National Archives.

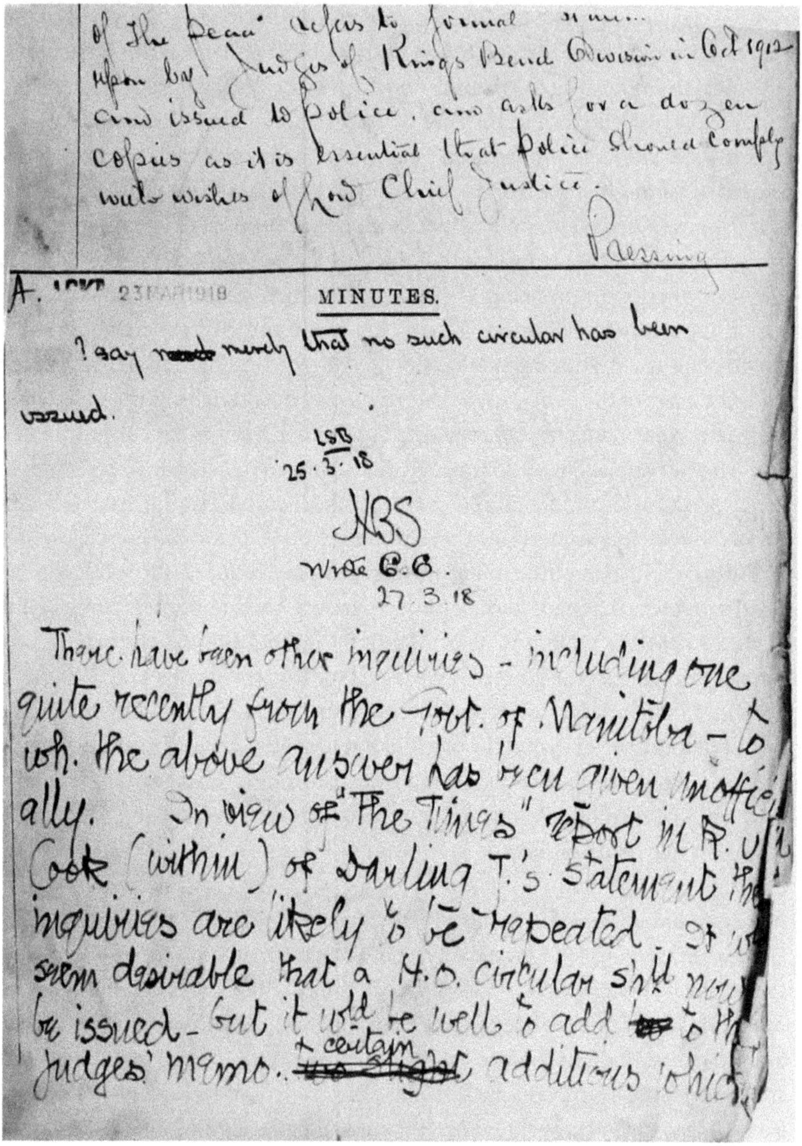
of The Bench' refers to formal ...
upon by Judges of Kings Bench Division in Oct 1912
and issued to Police, and asks for a dozen
copies as it is essential that Police should comply
with wishes of Lord Chief Justice.
Passing

MINUTES.

I say ~~...~~ merely that no such circular has been
issued.
LSB
25.3.18
HBS
Write C.C.
27.3.18

There have been other inquiries – including one
quite recently from the Govt. of Manitoba – to
wh. the above answer has been given unoffici-
ally. In view of "The Times" report in R. v.
Cook (within) of Darling J.'s statement the
inquiries are likely to be repeated. It w[d]
seem desirable that a H.O. circular sh[d] now
be issued – but it w[d] be well to add ~~...~~ to the
Judges' memo. certain ~~...~~ additions which

Illustration 11.1 Home Office Minute Recording Inquiries from the Colonies (March 1918) (National Archives)

Third, the archives also demonstrate the existence of an organized system of distribution and control, one which facilitated the long-distance reach of the Rules. Correspondence within the Colonial Office following the release of the 1964 Rules (see **Illustration 11.2**), for example, gives some sense as to the level of subordination with this operation.

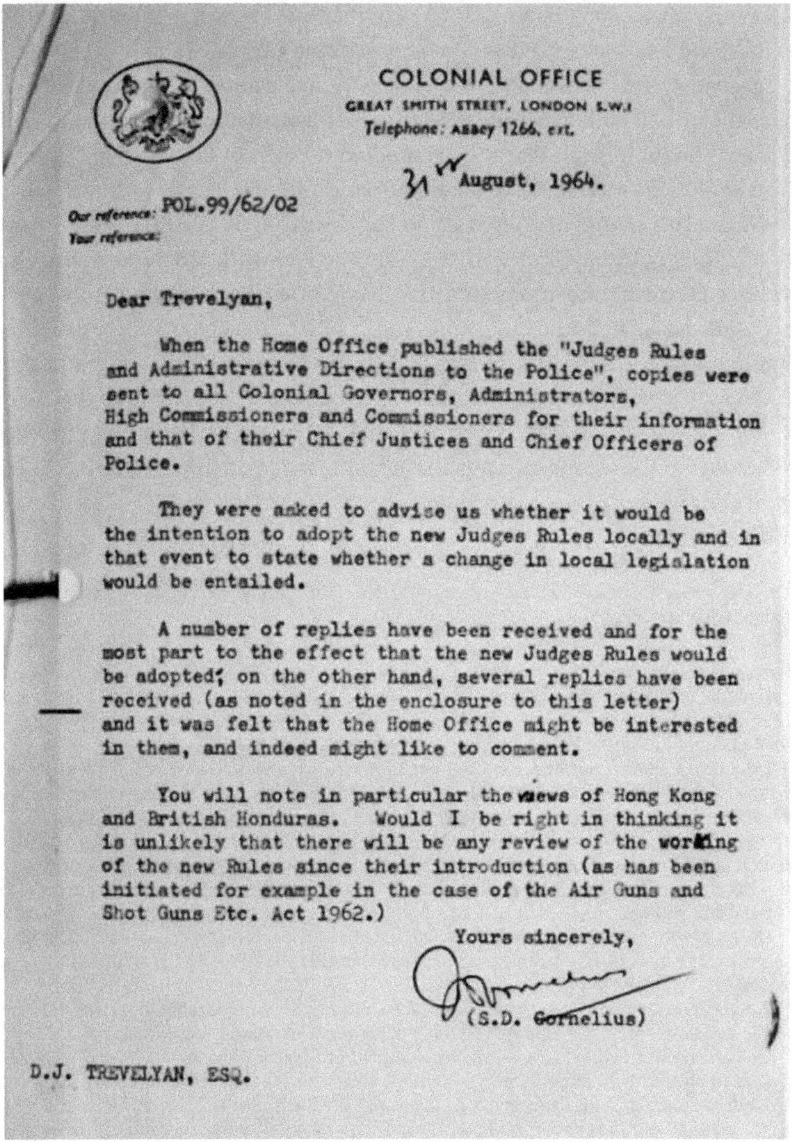

COLONIAL OFFICE
GREAT SMITH STREET, LONDON S.W.1
Telephone: ABBey 1266, ext.

31st August, 1964.

Our reference: POL.99/62/02
Your reference:

Dear Trevelyan,

When the Home Office published the "Judges Rules and Administrative Directions to the Police", copies were sent to all Colonial Governors, Administrators, High Commissioners and Commissioners for their information and that of their Chief Justices and Chief Officers of Police.

They were asked to advise us whether it would be the intention to adopt the new Judges Rules locally and in that event to state whether a change in local legislation would be entailed.

A number of replies have been received and for the most part to the effect that the new Judges Rules would be adopted; on the other hand, several replies have been received (as noted in the enclosure to this letter) and it was felt that the Home Office might be interested in them, and indeed might like to comment.

You will note in particular the views of Hong Kong and British Honduras. Would I be right in thinking it is unlikely that there will be any review of the working of the new Rules since their introduction (as has been initiated for example in the case of the Air Guns and Shot Guns Etc. Act 1962.)

Yours sincerely,

(S.D. Cornelius)

D.J. TREVELYAN, ESQ.

Illustration 11.2 Letter Recording Distribution of Judges' Rules to the Colonies (August 1964) (National Archives)

Not only did Colonial administrators embrace the pre-1964 Rules, but 'for the most part' put up little resistance to the transportation of the 1964 Rules across their borders.[50] Despite having no statutory authority in England, there was almost

[50] Given the reach of the Empire and the diverse territories occupied, transplantation of the common law and ancillary policing systems took root in some areas but not in others within the same territory

blanket acceptance (at least until 1964[51]) of the Rules' policing 'formula' abroad.[52] The Rules were not presented as conventional common law rules[53]—they did not emerge incrementally through cases—but as 'practice notes' for police officers and judges alike. Their authority was therefore dependent on the prestige of the English judiciary; the impression that they embodied the will of the judiciary (the 'protectors of liberty') was pivotal to their global reception.

Why did this impression resonate so convincingly? While judges are invested with an inherent legitimacy[54] deriving from their constitutional position, it is not unconnected to the self-promotion that has carried British judges through the ages.[55] Judges claimed to be the *moral conscience* of the colonial network,[56] contributing to a general sentiment that British justice is a widely admired tradition and the judiciary its most vaunted instrument;[57] one that persists to the current day.[58] Ironically, this acted to cover over not only an often unthinkingly repressive system but the second-rate qualities of those who administered it. For, as Lord Devlin said:[59]

particularly where areas occupied by settlers were policed differently from those occupied by mostly indigenous people: Cole, 'Post-Colonial Systems' (n 6).

[51] In some instances, well beyond 1964. Thus, it was not until 1992 that the New Zealand Court of Appeal, in the context of its own Bill of Rights, ruled that 'the Judges' Rules of 1912 and 1930 [are] in their literal form largely obsolescent in New Zealand. It is important not to confuse ... the New Zealand Bill of Rights and the Judges' Rules': *R v Butcher* [1992] 2 NZLR 257 266.

[52] The archives show that immediately upon the 1964 Revision reservations as to implementing the new rules were voiced by Northern Rhodesia (because the old rules were 'familiar to all officers' and 'work well'), Swaziland (new rules being 'too complicated for local conditions'), Aden ('the time is not ripe'), New Hebrides (the new rules were 'even less likely to be understood and properly applied'), Hong Kong (which wished to stall implementation until comments in legal publications were available), and British Honduras (also wishing to wait and 'assess their practicality in light of experience in the Courts of England and Wales').

[53] The Rules did not purport to be a complete statement of the law governing the admissibility of statements made by accused persons, nor did their issue alter the law as to the admissibility of such statements.

[54] David Pannick put it well, 'Laymen treat judges as a priestly caste to whom they are reluctant to apply the standards of criticism imposed on other public servants': *Judges* (OUP 1987) 105.

[55] See ch 1. Hewart LCJ felt able to announce at the Lord Mayor's Banquet in 1936: 'Her Majesty's judges are satisfied with the almost universal admiration in which they are held', quoted by David Heath MP in a debate on judicial independence in the House of Commons: HC Deb 20 October 2003, vol 411, cols 392–411, 407. It is understood that Hewart borrowed this sentiment from Justice Avory: see Beverley McLachlin, 'Role of Judges in Modern Commonwealth Society' (1995) 53 The Advocate 681, 688, footnote 1. In 1979, Lord Devlin wrote: 'The English judiciary is popularly treated as a national institution—and tends to be admired to excess' *The Judge* (OUP 1979) 25.

[56] As Peter Fitzpatrick observes, imperialists generally thought that they were, through moral superiority, donating gifts to the world. See Peter Fitzpatrick, '"The Desperate Vacuum": Imperialism and Law in the Experience of Enlightenment' in Anthony Carty (ed), *Post-Modern Law: Enlightenment, Revolution and the Death of Man* (Edinburgh University Press 1990) 90–106.

[57] This claim has manifested variously, including the description of the British judiciary as 'the weakest and least dangerous department of government' in an article of the same title, Lord Steyn [1997] Public Law 84.

[58] 'The judiciary of England and Wales has earned a well-deserved reputation for being the best in the world ... because it is impartial, independent and incorruptible': Burnett, *Speech* (2017).

[59] Devlin, 'Judges and Lawmakers' (1976) 39 Modern Law Review 1, 8.

> It is British justice rather than English or Scots law that has been the gift of British lawyers to the world. You cannot visit the countries of the Commonwealth without realizing that. Those who brought the gift to these countries were the second-best, for naturally the best stayed at home; they were, if you like, the judicial blimps. But it is the handiwork of the blimps that has survived.

Yet the British government took as its basic principle the superior *moral quality* of its judicial ranks as a way of easing global dispersal of the Rules. Under its aegis, the Colonial Office was able to maintain dominion over and give facial legitimacy to a system of police control of more than doubtful pedigree[60] for many decades to come. And facial it was because the colonial policing system was in many territories an order maintenance system[61] designed to protect trade, the Judges' Rules throwing a canopy of legitimacy over a system in which 'justice' did not in reality exist.[62]

The Challenge of Indigeonizing Rights

The notion that the Rules could take root in systems with conditions that bore little resemblance to those in England,[63] presented a fresh set of difficulties. Firstly, the (legal and local) cultures of Britain and the Colonies were starkly divergent.[64]

[60] British rule in many territories was not marked by the Metropolitan model but by that of the military style Royal Ulster Constabulary (formed in 1836 to control British-occupied Ireland), centralized and armed. See Philip Stead, *The Police of Britain* (Macmillan 1985); Charles Jeffries, *The Colonial Police* (Parrish 1952); John Tobias, 'The British Colonial Police—An Alternative Police Style' in Philip Stead (ed), *Pioneers in Policing* (Patterson Smith 1977); Mike Brogden, 'The Emergence of the Police—The Colonial Dimension' (1987) 27 British Journal of Criminology 4; David Anderson and David Killingray (eds), *Policing the Empire: Government Authority and Control, 1830–1940* (Manchester University Press 1991); Charles Gwynn, *Imperial Policing* (Macmillan 1934); Mark Brown, 'The Politics of Penal Excess and the Echo of Colonial Penality' (2002) 4 Punishment and Society 403. This was of course known to the Home and Colonial Office. Indeed, Sir John Anderson, eg, having overseen the re-issue of the Judges' Rules in 1930 was then posted in 1932 as Governor of Bengal. Additionally, colonial officers often returned to Britain to join or head police forces there. In almost all territories the structure and delivery of colonial policing transitioned over time and had different inflections. In colonial Kenya, eg, the regime of police regulation was imported from British India: Mathieu Deflem, 'Law Enforcement in British Colonial Africa: A Comparative Analysis of Imperial Policing in Nyasaland, the Gold Coast, and Kenya' (1994) 17(1) Police Studies 45. See also Georgina Sinclair, *At the End of the Line: Colonial Policing and the Imperial Endgame 1945–80* (Manchester University Press 2006).

[61] With a residual emphasis upon coercion in the post-independence state: Upendra Baxi, *The Crisis of the Indian Legal System* (Vikas Publishers 1980).

[62] See, eg, Dilip Das and Arvind Verma, 'The Armed Police in the British Colonial Tradition' (1998) 21(2) Policing: An International Journal of Police Strategies & Management 354; Anand Yang (ed), *Crime and Criminality in British India* (University of Arizona Press 1985).

[63] For examples, see Douglas Brown, 'Reform of the Administration of Criminal Justice' (1966) 2 East African Law Journal 248; Chilwell J in *R v Lee* [1978] 1 NZLR 481 was of the opinion that the Rules were 'ambiguous and unsuited in style to modern conditions' 482.

[64] As Wiener argues: 'Colonial courtrooms were arenas for struggle in which both sides often appealed to the British inheritance of "the rule of law," but interpreted this heritage in different ways' *Empire* (n 3) 230. See also Elizabeth Kolsky, 'Codification and the Rule of Colonial Difference: Criminal Procedure in British India' (2005) 23(3) Law and History Review 631. Kolsky demonstrates how the

Nurtured in different historical, political, social, and legal cultures these were multi-racial populations[65] with minority European populations[66] or indigenous peoples with their own culture and heritage.[67] Secondly, variations in practical implementation of the Rules would only exacerbate in the fast evolving circumstances of these new territories where much depended on the precise temporal and geographical context.[68] Thirdly, the need for an indigenous judiciary who could mitigate these difficulties was often not met.[69]

The problems posed by multi-jurisdictional differences were highlighted by Kirby J (as he was then):

> Some features of the investigation in crime in Australia are special. The Federal system, the vast geographical distances which must be policed, the presence of

nineteenth century Indian codification process 'was prompted by the growing and uncontrollable problem of European criminality and shaped by the colonial insistence on the peculiarities of Indian culture' 683.

[65] The race dimension had significant effects on those suspected of crimes. In the Indian context, Elizabeth Kolsky, highlights that '[t]he colonial promise of uniform legal equality was blatantly undermined by the institutionalization of race-based privileges and by the discriminatory practices of police, judges and juries that consistently tipped the scales of justice': *Colonial Justice in British India—White Violence and the Rule of Law* (CUP 2010) ch 5 186.

[66] See, eg, the account of the diverse population of the Canadian prairie provinces beginning in the nineteenth century: Gerald Friesen, *The Canadian Prairies: A History* (University of Toronto Press 1987). Thus, in the early part of the twentieth century, following huge immigration from Eastern Europe, in the prairie provinces (Manitoba, Saskatchewan, and Alberta), ethnic diversity was reflected in the fact that more than half the population did not speak English with the area marked by undersocialization, radical politics, and a strong labour movement. See Wesley Pue, 'British Masculinities, Canadian Lawyers: Canadian Legal Education, 1900–1930' (1999) 16(1) Law in Context 80. It was against this background that the request for help in regard to regulating police questioning came from Manitoba, set out in Illustration 11.1.

[67] See, eg, the Aboriginal People of Australia and the inappropriateness of the Judges' Rules to their culture which brought about the *Anunga Guidelines* (*R v Anunga and Ors* (1976) 11 ALR 412) which have their own implementation problems. See: Heather Douglas, 'The Cultural Specificity of Evidence: The Current Scope and Relevance of the *Anunga Guidelines*' (1998) 21(1) UNSW Law Journal 27; Dina Yehia, 'Admissibility of Admissions: Aboriginal and Torres Straits Islanders Suspects' (2012) <www.publicdefenders.nsw.gov.au/Documents/admissibilityofadmissionsatsisuspects.pdf> accessed 1 January 2020.

[68] H. Patrick Glenn explains: 'In the common law world there was a general technique which was that of determining the "suitability" of common law (including here English statute) for local circumstance. The case law on this question is vast, spread over many continents, and the "suitability requirement was imposed by the courts even where omitted by reception legislation. Results varied greatly, and *the application, or not, of the common law was always a matter of judicial interpretation*' *On Common Laws* (n 11) 68 (emphasis supplied). In this way, colonial judges helped pave the way for the monopolistic position of the Judges' Rules as a key source of common law.

[69] The ratio between indigenous judges who understood the local legal-political culture and the less culturally aware British 'imports', was far from evenly spread across the colonies. Some 'new' colonies, eg, Upper Canada, faced less difficulty in building an indigenous judiciary, whilst others with a more 'embryonic legal culture' (such as Australia) were reliant on 'strong guidance in the form of a judiciary long comprised of English and Irish barristers sent out from "home" who 'often got into trouble by relying on idealized conceptions of the "rule of law" or "British justice" that had undergone subtle transformations in a particular colonial context' See Philip Girard, 'Review of *Bewigged, Bothered, & Bewildered: British Colonial Judges on Trial, 1800–1900* (by John McClaren) (The Osgoode Society for Legal History 2011)' (2012) 39(4) Journal of Law & Society 631–34.

> large communities of people not fluent in English and used to a different criminal justice system and the special disadvantages of Aboriginals confronted with authority are just a few of the particular Australian problems which local laws should address. *It is scarcely surprising that the English judges of 1912 did not give special thought to our local problems.* What is surprising is that we have struggled on for more than half a century with a complex body of law made up of a little legislation, much case law, (in most jurisdictions) the Judges' Rules and administrative directions of varying authority issued by Police Chiefs.[70]

While Kirby lent an excusatory tone towards the British judiciary, it is misplaced. Putting aside that the practice of the English courts with regard to the admissibility of confessions might be inappropriate to local conditions, the fact remained that colonial governments acquiesced in Rules inherited from England on the basis of an elemental undisclosed misrepresentation as to their true provenance.

Had the executive-judicial subterfuge surrounding the Rules been exposed, colonial provinces might have questioned their authority, been more inclined to be 'untied from the apron strings of English law',[71] and develop rules more faithful to geographical, cultural, societal, and political realities that existed locally. As VG Himestra explained in the South African context:

> The English are a settled community and their system of criminal prosecution is designed for a fundamentally law-abiding country. We are a young country afflicted by social restlessness and conflict. What is for England sufficient can represent for us an uncorrected obsolescence which clogs a logical onward development towards greater efficiency.[72]

As it turned out, the opportunity for these disparate jurisdictions to develop their own rules[73] was largely eclipsed by the steady entrenchment of the English Judges' Rules.[74]

[70] The Hon Mr Justice Kirby, 'Criminal Investigation & The Rule of Law' 20th Australian Legal Convention Adelaide (7 July 1979) (hereafter Kirby, 'The Rule of Law') 12.

[71] Albert Fiadjoe, 'An Overview of the Public Revolution in the Commonwealth Carribean' (1992) Anglo-American Law Review 310, 340.

[72] Hiemstra, 'Abolition of the Right Not to Be Questioned' (n 38) 190.

[73] Lauren Benton explains that it was historically commonplace for colonizing forces to make 'conscious efforts to retain elements of existing institutions and limit legal change as a way of sustaining social order': Benton, *Law and Colonial Cultures* (n 7) 2.

[74] Challenge to the Judges' Rules was made unlikely by a colonial judiciary comprising of what John McClaren describes (in an echo of Lord Devlin), 'the "also rans" of the English, Irish and Scottish bars'. Sending out 'aspirants [who] were desperate enough to accept judicial preferment at almost any cost' was compounded by deep-set political patronage and reflected in the policy of the imperial order: ' … dependent upon balancing the grant of a representative legislature with the provision of a strong executive power through the Crown's representative in the colony … In this system there was to be no doubt about where the judges would stand in political terms: firmly behind the executive': John McClaren, 'Navigating the Scylla of Imperial Politico-Legal Aspirations and Charybdis of

The Spirit of the Rules

Although with the decline of the Empire the influence of the Rules has diminished, they live on in one form or another.[75] The replacement of the Rules by the Codes of Practice under the Police and Criminal Evidence Act 1984 (PACE) in England did not automatically lead to disintegration elsewhere although this has often added to the sense of confusion. Their continuing effect is still felt in a number of colonial and former colonial jurisdictions, as was made clear by the Lords of the Judicial Committee of the Privy Council in *Shabadine Peart v The Queen*,[76] an appeal from Jamaica. Lord Carswell outlined the position:

> The Judges' Rules constitute a striking example of judge-made law. Although classed formally as administrative directions for the guidance of police officers interviewing suspects, they were afforded over time a higher status, and a general requirement became established that police officers had to observe them if confessions received were to be admitted in evidence. They have been replaced in England and Wales by the provisions of Code C made under the Police and Criminal Evidence Act 1984, which have similar strong persuasive force, but in jurisdictions such as Jamaica which have not replaced them by legislative provisions the Judges' Rules retain considerable importance.

The appeal with which the Lords were concerned, focused on the status of the Judges' Rules (in Jamaica), the requirements of Rule III(*b*), and the way in which trial judges may exercise their discretion to admit evidence if there has been a breach of the Rules. That such matters—of centrality to the criminal process—are still being litigated, nearly one hundred years after their infelicitous beginnings and subsequent demise in England, only reinforces the unclarity and inconsistency in interpretation flowing from the Rules.

While the Lords in *Shabadine Peart* reiterated that there was a general claim that the rules 'are administrative directions, not rules of law', this familiar proposition sits uneasily with their Lordships' opening statement that the rules have since been afforded a 'higher status', going as far to openly declare them to be 'judge-made law'. Their route to bridging this divide was to adopt a line of reasoning that the Judges' Rules 'possess considerable importance as *embodying the standard of*

Colonial Micro-Politics in the British Empire: The Case of the Judges' in Shaunnagh Dorsett and John McClaren (eds), *Legal Histories of the British Empire—Law, Engagements and Legacies* (Routledge 2014) 16, 18.

[75] For example, Mauritius remains wedded to the 1964 Rules despite continual calls within its legal community for the introduction of a PACE-style Code of Practice.

[76] UKPC 5 [2006] 1 WLR 970.

fairness which ought to be observed'.[77] This judicial observation is a useful backcloth to understanding the real impact of the Judges' Rules across the colonies.

The spread of the Judges' Rules underlined the confusing and haphazard effects of the imperfect reception of English laws into colonial regimes. This is exemplified in a recent Privy Council case from Trinidad and Tobago:[78]

> The essential rule in relation to the admissibility of a confession is that it must be shown to be voluntary, in the sense that it has not been obtained by fear of prejudice or hope of advantage exercised or held out by a person in authority, or by oppression. That rule is reflected in principle (e) of the Judges' Rules of 1964, adopted by the judges in Trinidad and Tobago in 1965. A trial judge has additionally the power, sometimes called a discretion but better described as an exercise in judgment, to refuse to admit evidence tendered on behalf of the prosecution if its effect will be unfair to the defendant: *Noor Mohamed v The King* [1949] AC 182, 192. In some jurisdictions there are in addition rules of conduct or codes of practice binding the police in relation to dealings with suspects. The English Codes of Practice made under the Police and Criminal Evidence Act 1984 are an example. Where there is a breach of such a code, that is a relevant factor in the exercise of the judgment whether evidence obtained in consequence ought to be excluded as unfair. Even if there is such a specific provision, exclusion of evidence depends on a judgment that its effect will be unfair and does not follow automatically from a breach. England does have such a code which requires an appropriate adult to be present at the interview of a mentally disordered or mentally vulnerable suspect: see Code C under the 1984 Act, para 11.15. *But Trinidad does not have such a rule, and contrary to [counsel for the appellant's] submission so specific a provision cannot be imported on the grounds that it represents an essential feature of the common law. That would be to impose on Trinidad a rule which it has not chosen to make* (emphasis supplied).

Case law also demonstrates, however, that many colonial courts clung robustly to the malleable symbolism the Rules bestowed. For example, the Australian High Court in *Lee* (1950) 82 CLR 133, explained that the Rules 'are not rules of law and the mere fact that one or more of them has been broken does not of itself mean that the accused has been so treated that it would be unfair to admit his statement ... The rules may be regarded *in a general way as prescribing a standard of propriety* and it is in this sense that what may be called the *spirit of the rules* should be regarded'.[79] In New Zealand, the Court of Appeal in *R v Convery* [1968] NZLR 426,

[77] ibid judgment, para 24(i). This restatement of the Rules as having embodied 'a standard of fairness' was approved by the Privy Council in *Ricardo Williams v The Queen* [2006] UKPC 21.

[78] *Pitman v The State* (Trinidad and Tobago) [2017] UKPC 6.

[79] See also *R v Bailey* [1958] SALR 301 and 'Admissibility of Confessions—Judges' Rules' (1960) Adelaide Law Review 85.

stated it was the spirit and purpose of the rules that is important, not the letter.[80] In Canada, again, it was reported that the 'spirit' of the Judges' Rules 'if not the letter . . . prevails throughout Canada'.[81]

Even when the future of the Rules lay in question, the symbolism of the Rules has served as a judicial tool to fix cracks in the edifice of the police-suspect interrogation process. In Hong Kong, where judges differed as to the status of the 1964 Rules,[82] Sir Michael Hogan CJ of the Full Court in *Li Wai-leung* [1969] stated that *both* the original Rules *and* the 'spirit' of the 1964 revision should be observed by police officers and judges in the territory.[83]

In this regard, colonial practices show how the Judges' Rules were accessed, by colonizer and colonized alike. This disjointed legal patchwork of suspects' rights across the Commonwealth is illustrative of the damage done by the Rules under the veil of 'common law' juridical regulation. As seen in previous chapters, the English judges experienced difficulties in consistently applying the confessions rule partly because the Rules were never intended to replace the common law rules regulating the admission of confessions; rather they were intended to provide *guidance* as to the application of the common law confessions rule.[84] In essence, judges were required to consider the failure of a police officer to abide by the Rules in deciding upon the issue of voluntariness. It is for this reason that while the Rules officially never had the force of law usually accorded to judicial precedent or legislative

[80] See also *R v Horsfall* [1981] 1 NZLR 116 at 122; and *R v Hartley* [1978] 2 NZLR 199 at 218. For an example of a serious breach, see *R v Smith* (CA 76/87, 11 December 1987). cf *R v Mason* (CA 114/88), 7 September 1988) where in spite of a breach of the rules, a statement was still deemed voluntary and there was no unfairness in the way it was obtained.

[81] 'Discussion' (1960–61) 3 Criminal Law Quarterly 351, 357. Although note that the importance of the Rules in Canada is contested: 'Despite *dicta* underlining the usefulness of the Judges' Rules as guidelines in adjudication, they are not regularly applied in Canada. Mark Shrager, 'Recent Developments in the Law Relating to Confessions: England, Canada and Australia' (1981) 23(3) McGill Law Journal 435, 436. cf Dame Sian Elias, 'Righting Criminal Justice' in *Fairness in Criminal Justice: Golden Threads and Pragmatic Patches* (CUP 2018) 78. Regardless, the dangers of relying on the 'spirit' alone of a protective device for suspects rather than the 'letter' were forcefully made by the Royal Commission in 1929: '. . . generally speaking the spirit of the Judges' Rules is faithfully observed, but the "letter" is productive of frequent misunderstanding' quoted in Thomas Eric St Johnston, 'The Legal Limitation of the Interrogation of Suspects and Prisoners in England and Wales' (1948–49) 39(1) Journal of Criminal Law and Criminology 89, 98.

[82] The 1912 Rules applied: 'Suffice it to say that the rules, propounded in 1912 for the guidance of the police, continue to be relevant in this territory in the sense that the code of conduct which they recommend continues to be regarded in these courts as generally appropriate to the conduct of investigations in this territory': *R v Leung Cheuk-fan* [1984] HKC 374 *per* McMullin VP at 391D–E. Although the 1964 Rules were never formally adopted in Hong Kong they were drawn upon: *Li Wai-leung* [1969] HKLR 642. See also the cases cited in Bernard Downey, 'Confessions to Police Officers' (1971) 1 Hong Kong Law Journal 131 (hereafter Downey, 'Confessions').

[83] *Li Wai-leung* (n 82) 653–54 *per* Hogan CJ. In regard to the 'spirit' of the Rules, Hon Mr Justice Bokhary NPJ (ed-in-chief) and Graham Harris QC (gen ed), *Archbold Hong Kong* (Sweet and Maxwell 2017)—the Hong Kong version of Archbold (hereafter Archbold, *Hong Kong*)—remarks: 'It has *never* been clear to practitioners or judges what this phrase meant' 15–22 (emphasis supplied).

[84] *Thompson* [1893] 2 QB 12. See also Mark Berger, 'Legislating Confession Law in Great Britain: A Statutory Approach to Police Interrogations' (1990) 24(1) University of Michigan Journal of Law Reform 11–12.

provision, they *conditioned*[85] the common law to such an extent that they took on its appearance.[86]

While the common law is said to be customary, in that it is 'discovered' and interpreted by judges in cases that come before them, the Judges Rules' halted this in relation to the interrogation process. As Peter Wesley-Smith, writing in the context of Hong Kong, argued:

> As [a colonial] legal system steadily grows more sophisticated, and as it matures it should become less dependent on the English model. A source of rules to fall back on when necessary is convenient and useful. But the Judges' Rules seem to be retrogressive, for it not only provides for a source of rules which always apply unless specifically excluded, but it limits the power of the local courts to adapt and modify them to suit local conditions.[87]

Hong Kong is a compelling case of the legislative inertia that often results once foreign rules of practice crystallize.[88] The continuation of the Judges' Rules in Hong Kong was initially thrown into doubt by judicial prevarication as to whether the 1964 Rules should apply locally[89] but the question of their formal adoption soon became of limited importance with successive generations of Hong Kong judges consistently attaching significance to them.[90] And although attempts were made by the Hong Kong government to steer its legal system towards its own path of

[85] Rules of practice can be said to have entered the common law. John Eekelaar has argued: 'it is not uncommon for comparatively weak normative provisions to gain in strength so that "practices" are said to "harden into rules of law"', see ch 2 in Alfred William Brian Simpson (ed), *Oxford Essays in Jurisprudence* (Second Series) (Clarendon Press 1973) 33. The English House of Lords appeared to confirm this legal phenomenon when discussing jury warnings as to uncorroborated evidence: 'This rule, although a rule of practice, now has the force of a rule of law': *Davies v DPP* [1954] AC 378, 399. Also: 'The common law is shaped as much by the way in which it is practiced as by judicial dicta', *Jayasena v R* [1970] AC 618, 625 *per* Lord Devlin.

[86] Two factors have contributed to this: the very title 'Judges' Rules' is a misnomer which has created an impression that the sanction of the judges has somehow elevated the rules from mere administrative directions to a definitive text. The second is that the courts have tended to analyse the Rules in the same way as a legislative provision and case law abounds with discussions on the construction of individual words and phrases found in the Rules: Patrick Devlin, *The Criminal Prosecution in England* (OUP 1960) 39.

[87] 'English Practice and Procedure in Hong Kong' (1979) 9 Hong Kong Law Journal 255, 289.

[88] It is also an example of the way in which colonial law was utilized as an oppressive instrument. See Michael Ng, 'Rule of Law in Hong Kong History Demythologised: Student Umbrella Movement of 1919' (2016) Hong Kong Law Journal 46; Peter Wesley-Smith, 'Anti-Chinese Legislation in Hong Kong' in Ming Chan (ed), *Precarious Balance: Hong Kong between China and Britain, 1842–1992* (HKU Press 1994); and Richard Klein, 'The Empire Strikes Back: Britain's Use of the Law to Suppress Political Dissent in Hong Kong' (1997) 15(1) Boston University International Law Journal 1.

[89] The new Rules were formally sent to Hong Kong after their adoption in England and on 7 March 1964 the Governor informed the Secretary of State for the Colonies: 'It is not intended that the new Judges' Rules should be adopted in this Colony at the present time … The existing Judges' Rules will accordingly remain in force and continue to be applicable in the Courts of the Colony.'

[90] Downey, 'Confessions' (n 82).

reform,[91] the *Rules and Directions for the Questioning of Suspects and the Taking of Statements*[92] it eventually issued in 1992 to replace the Judges' Rules, were actually a knock-off copy (in all but title) of the original 1964 text![93] This charade typifies the obfuscation of the common law process in which 'judge-made' rules transform into 'judge-made law'.[94]

A further instructive example of the extraordinary process of 'reception' and 'implementation' is Western Samoa (Samoa),[95] itself merely emblematic of the process applied to the South Pacific Islands. The common law was received into Western Samoa under the Samoa Act 1921, an Act of the New Zealand General Assembly in Parliament because Western Samoa, as a Trustee Territory of the United Kingdom, was administered by New Zealand under the Covenant of the League of Nations for peace, order and good governance. The Samoa Act provided, among other things, that the legislative powers of the local administration must not be repugnant to any other Act of the Parliament of New Zealand or of the United Kingdom. In the result, the criminal law imposed on Western Samoa was a legislative adoption of the English common law in force in New Zealand,[96] including the Judges' Rules, without reference to the vastly different social, economic, and cultural conditions of Western Samoa itself. Court judgments were accordingly framed with reference to English cases such as *Voisin*[97] and *Ibrahim*[98] and, although the Rules were said to apply, the courts disregarded local cultural considerations and displayed a reluctance to exclude evidence of a confession notwithstanding an established breach of their provisions.[99] Moreover, despite the passage of the New Zealand Bill

[91] In July 1980 in the report of the Chief Justice's *Working Party on Voir Dire Proceedings and Judges' Rules* a majority of the Working Party was in favour of the adoption of a new set of Judges' Rules for Hong Kong which it drafted.

[92] See *Rules and Directions* (1992) (n 25).

[93] Despite slight expansion, the Hong Kong *Rules and Directions* (1992) (n 25) follow almost word for word the text of the English 1964 Rules. This trend of 'emulation' is not unique to Hong Kong. For example, the Judges' Rules 'were replaced by rules issued by the Chief Justice of the Solomon Islands as a practice direction in 1982' but remain '*essentially the same as the English rules*' (emphasis supplied), Congress, *Miranda Warnings* (n 13) 25.

[94] Adding to the charade, Archbold, *Hong Kong* (n 83) explains: 'The Judges' Rules may still have some relevance in interpreting the Rules and Directions. However, there is no suggestion in the Rules and Directions or elsewhere that Judges' Rules have been revoked. In principle the courts will apply the Rules and Directions in the same spirit as they did the Judges' Rules' 15–26.

[95] Our account here is drawn from Malifa, 'The Reception of Judges' Rules' (n 41).

[96] ibid 163. In turn, the 1840 Charter for New Zealand provided that the Legislative Council should not make ordinances 'repugnant to the law of England, but consistent therewith so far as the circumstances of [the] colony may admit'. The Legislative Council was to conform with all Royal Instructions (ie, instructions issued by the Queen-in-council): Damen Ward, 'Legislation, Repugnancy and the Disallowance of Colonial Laws' (2010) 41 Victoria University Wellington Law Review 381.

[97] (1918) 87 LJKB 574.

[98] [1914] AC 599.

[99] *Inspector of Police v Tagaloa & Fuataga* [1921–29] WSLR 18; and *Braisby v Tamasese* [1921–29] WSLR 48. See also *Police v Samasoni* [1950–59] WSLR 106 where the charges were dismissed on appeal after the Chief Justice concluded that there was a doubt as to whether the statement was free and voluntary.

of Rights Act 1990, which stimulated the New Zealand courts to adopt a global perspective on human rights in the process of application within the South Pacific itself, in Western Samoa 'little or no recognition is given to the same constitutional safeguard'.[100]

A similar lack of sensitivity to local conditions is evident in responses to the transmission by the Colonial Office of the 1964 Rules. Thus, the New Hebrides[101] (a territory colonized by both the British and the French) confirmed that the old Judges' Rules were applied in the territory. The Reporter, however, added:

> Even so the old Rules are not always thoroughly understood by the Police, nor are they appreciated by New Hebridean members of the public and the Police have the greatest difficulty in cautioning a defendant who is usually quite willing to make a voluntary statement.[102] Furthermore the Judges' Rules have no place at all in cases investigated by the French Police.
>
> The new Rules, as you will appreciate involve a considerably more complicated procedure and as such are even less likely to be understood and properly applied. I am advised that they were drawn up for a more literate community than is the case here and, consequently, I do not think that the adoption in the New Hebrides would be practicable.

Claims that the very foreign nature of colonial law gave it an advantage over customary and other rivals in offering predictability of procedure and outcome look barren when set against insensitivity to local culture and identity and the consequent impact upon the capacity for indigenous development[103] caused by the continuing ideology of the contrived superiority of English law.[104]

[100] Malifa, 'The Reception of Judges' Rules' (n 41) 180. Malifa does, however, draw attention to the approval given by Cooke P in *R v Goodwin* [1993] 2 NZLR 153 to the judgment of King CJ in *Micronesia v Edward* [1987] SPLR 44 which drew upon jurisprudence from the United States including *Miranda v Arizona* (1966) 384 US 436 on the right to counsel. More generally, new legislation is often laid down leaving difficult questions of interpretation as between the new laws and the Judges' Rules, account of which was not taken in the reform.

[101] Today, the Republic of Vanuatu.

[102] This important cultural observation was also said to be true in Western Samoa: Malifa, 'The Reception of Judges' Rules' (n 41).

[103] cf Benton, *Law and Colonial Cultures* (n 7). Other scholars have concluded that in certain (non-criminal) instances, colonial subjects might engage in 'forum shopping' with perceived self-interest determining the selection process: Mitra Sharafi, 'The Marital Patchwork of Colonial South Asia: Forum Shopping from Britain to Baroda' (2010) 28 Law and History Review 979.

[104] For a discussion of the challenges facing indigenous Canadian Aboriginal lawyers in the context of the contrived superiority of English law, see James (Sákéj) Youngblood Henderson, 'Postcolonial Indigenous Legal Consciousness' (2002) 1 Indigenous Law Journal 1; Moana Jackson, 'Justice and Political Power: Reasserting Maori Legal Processes' in Kayleen Hazelhurst (ed), *Legal Pluralism and the Colonial Legacy: Indigenous Experiences of Justice in Canada, Australia and New Zealand* (Avebury 1995).

The Ghost of Colonial Judges

Thus, colonial emancipation in the realm of criminal justice was not to follow with the fall of the Empire. Instead, the stultifying effect the Judges' Rules had on legal culture across former colonial lands outlived the formal end of imperial rule. This is despite two Royal Commissions on Police Powers and Procedure (1929) and Criminal Procedure (1981) which, between them, identified systemic deficiencies in the confessions framework as governed by the Rules (even with three distinct permutations and over seventy years to 'get it right'), subsequently deeming them 'unfit for purpose', leading to their eventual demise and triggering the creation of a new regime under PACE (1984). An important part of the story of the Rules is therefore how they have come to survive in multiple jurisdictions, notwithstanding their complete disposal in England and Wales. The answer lies in great measure in two bulwarks of the Empire: the Privy Council and itinerant judges.

The Last Bastion of the Empire: the Privy Council

Even with the decline of the Empire, the Judicial Committee of the Privy Council ('Privy Council') continued as a forum within which to ventilate concerns about the Judge's Rules abroad. The Privy Council[105] still acts as a court of *final appeal* for many countries,[106] comprising UK overseas territories and Crown dependencies, and for those Commonwealth countries that have retained the appeal to Her Majesty in Council or, in the case of republics, to the Privy Council.[107] The magnitude of its reach was breathtaking, spanning a quarter of the world's population in the 1930s.[108] Once known as the 'supreme tribunal of the Empire'[109] it was said that the 'real work' of the Privy Council was 'that of assisting in holding the Empire together'.[110] In modern times, as its jurisdiction contracted in line with the diminishing influence of the Empire,[111] its purpose is now contested by some.[112]

[105] The Privy Council was established as a statutory body under the Judicial Committee Act 1833. The institution's website explains: 'This council or court was the "Curia Regis" [Royal Council] from which springs the British judicial system.'

[106] Note it is further available to any state which wishes to avail itself of the Privy Council as a forum for appeals or dispute resolution.

[107] Privy Council Practice Direction 1.

[108] Frank Safford and George Wheeler, *The Practice of the Privy Council in Judicial Matters* (Sweet and Maxwell 1901).

[109] Richard Haldane, 'The Work for the Empire of the Judicial Committee of the Privy Council' (1922) 1 Cambridge Law Journal 143, 143–44 (hereafter Haldane, 'Work for the Empire').

[110] ibid 154.

[111] Daniel Clarry calculates this in the following way: '... the Privy Council now acts as the highest appellate court for just 0.1% of the world's population': 'Institutional Independence and the Privy Council' (2014) 3 Cambridge Journal of International & Comparative Law 46 (hereafter Clarry, 'Privy Council') 51. Such a figure, if correct, still represents over 7 million people worldwide, covering a range of disparate societies.

[112] Whereas Clarry speaks of assisting 'various countries on the path to realizing their own institutional judicial independence' others strongly disagree. Thus, Patrick Robinson argues that '[b]y

In spite of its dwindling hold over extra-territorial appellate systems, the Privy Council's prominence within the common law world remains. Clarry explains that:

> As the Committee's decisions often display the rigorous analysis of the judgments ordinarily delivered by the UK's top court, *having been penned by the same persons*, its judgments are regarded as being of *the highest persuasive value throughout the Commonwealth*, even though they are not binding on any jurisdiction beyond that in any particular appeal.[113]

Its prominence is further strengthened, Clarry argues, owing to the way in which the Privy Council addresses issues that have 'broad importance to the international community' and its parallel goal of developing a 'common stream of jurisprudence by taking a comparative and cross-jurisdictional approach to the development of principle that it then applies in appeals from various jurisdictions, *taking into account local conditions if need be*'.[114]

This legal methodology involving a supposed cross-fertilization of law between countries and cultures has two-fold importance to our account. Firstly, it demonstrates the extent to which senior judges can draw attention to issues of broad principle from outside the jurisdiction the appeal is centred on. Secondly, it alludes to legal principles of such 'universal' importance that local conditions do not trump all other considerations.

Speaking two years after the Judges' Rules first appeared in a judgment of a British court,[115] Haldane (a former member of the Privy Council)[116] explained:

> The Judges try to look for the common principle underlying systems of jurisprudence of differing kinds. They know that the form often veils over a very similar substance. We are constantly finding that, where *great broad principles of justice* are concerned you find—veiled, but still there, and only distinguished by technicalities—the same substance as belongs to other systems. The human mind is much the same all the world over.[117]

far the worst relic of . . . colonialism is that Jamaicans have been left with a muddled sense of their identity.' He continues: 'In Jamaica the symbols at the apex of the political and judicial systems are all wrong. The . . . Privy Council, comprised of foreigners, ignorant of Jamaican culture, living thousands of miles away, many of whom . . . have precious little in common with the Jamaican people, are an anachronism that Jamaicans should not be asked to endure any longer': 'The Monarchy, Republicanism and the Privy Council: The Enduring Cry for Freedom' (2012) 101(5) (October) The Round Table 447, 450, 451.

[113] Clarry, 'Privy Council' (n 111) 68, emphasis supplied. See authorities cited therein.
[114] ibid 70, emphasis supplied.
[115] *R v Voisin* [1918] 1 KB 531.
[116] Lord Alverstone and Lord Brampton were also former members.
[117] Haldane, 'Work for the Empire' (n 109).

This statement exemplifies a key *colonial* function underpinning the work of the Privy Council throughout its history. Mitchell puts it succinctly: developing 'universal principles in order to give transnational authority to English legal rules'.[118] Of course, articulating universal principles under the convenient juridical device of a 'common law' avoided the obvious difficulties that might arise were accusations from foreign jurisdictions of a 'British legal hegemony' to surface. Perhaps conscious of this, the Privy Council sought to distance itself from its former imperial ambitions by repeatedly claiming that it is *not* a 'British tribunal'.[119]

There are many reasons why a 'foreign' court would choose not to interfere, legally speaking, with the rights regime of another jurisdiction, even where specifically mandated to as with the Privy Council. A central argument historically raised against the capacity of the Privy Council to effect legitimate legal change has been the court's 'distance' from the jurisdiction it adjudicates upon during any one appeal:

> It is obvious, that the mere distance of those colonies, and the immense variety of matters arising in them, foreign to our habits, and beyond the scope of our knowledge, any judicial tribunal in this country must, of necessity, be an extremely inadequate court of review.[120]

Mitchell gives contemporary weight to this concern by outlining the difficulties faced by the Privy Council in establishing 'two traditionally compelling bases for recognizing a court's (moral) authority'.[121] These are, firstly, '*technical expertise*' that is the inability of the Privy Council to claim to possess 'superior knowledge' of systems from which it heard appeals, in light of the plethora of jurisdictions (and array of local laws) within its once vast purview. The second, which Mitchell describes as 'particularly powerful in a common law system', is '*social solidarity*' that is the notion that law is grounded in 'social acceptance' and its judicial members being 'in touch with the relevant society's needs and aspirations'[122]—a claim

[118] Paul Mitchell, 'The Privy Council and the Difficulty of Distance' (2016) 36(1) Oxford Journal of Legal Studies 26 (hereafter Mitchell, 'Difficulty of Distance') 53.

[119] *British Coal Corporation v The King* [1935] AC 500, 521–22 *per* Viscount Sankey LC. See also *Ibralebbe v R* [1964] AC 900, 922 *per* Viscount Radcliffe. This is buttressed by the extra-curial claims of judges, eg, the court 'sits not as a ghost of the colonial past': Lord Neuberger, 'The Judicial Committee of the Privy Council in the 21st Century' (2014) 3(1) Cambridge Journal of International & Comparative Law 30 (hereafter Neuberger, 'JCPC in the 21st Century') 37.

[120] HC Deb 7 February 1828, vol 18, cols 154–55 (Henry Brougham). See also David B Swinfen, who highlights that mistakes in specific cases were made by the Judicial Committee owing to their dilution of expertise when it came to legal matters of Commonwealth countries and local conditions remote from London: *Imperial Appeal—The Debate on the appeal to the Privy Council, 1833–1986* (Woleboro, N.H: Manchester University Press 1987).

[121] Mitchell, 'Difficulty of Distance' (n 118) 28.

[122] ibid.

stretched thin by the thousands of miles distance between the Privy Council and those societies its rulings affect.

In addressing the Privy Council's treatment of the Judges' Rules it is hard to see how 'incapacity' of the court caused by 'ignorance of the [local] law and unfitness to judge of the facts'[123] would have arisen. Not only did the Privy Council have a wealth of technical expertise in regard to the Judges' Rules, having handpicked its members from the jurisdiction where they originated, but it would have been more than able to draw upon a fund of information on the Rules and their corresponding deficiencies (not least from the reports of the Royal Commission). The common law is said to be based on 'experience not logic'.[124] If so, why was experience disregarded in the instance of the Judges' Rules?

There is a dualistic feature of 'British justice' whereby episodic engagement with modern thinking arose from the negative experience of the Judges' Rules *at home*, eventually resulting in, at least partially, beneficial developments. And yet, *abroad*, the most critical area in criminal procedure (the production of evidence; how facts are produced; what rights belong to criminal suspects) is left largely untouched. Historical evidence should have cast new light upon the Privy Council's interpretation of old Rules in foreign contexts, where problems demonstrably inherent to them would only be amplified (as the Colonial Office files attest). Instead the conflagration of suspects' rights was—inexplicably—allowed to prevail. Rules which had effectively become a constitutional overlay in a colonial context left the door open to oppressive and capricious police practices.

Equally, while it is accepted that '[s]ometimes, their Lordships did not have a full appreciation of the local conditions that made it difficult for them to reflect all of the factors necessary to a lawful and just resolution of the cases',[125] this scenario did not apply where the Judges' Rules featured. This was an *English* court applying Rules *it* had formulated and *it* had since abandoned. Arguments that local law is paramount are, accordingly, irrelevant. So are those which suggest its judges were not conversant with the procedural niceties of overseas jurisdictions (for they had imposed the *English* Rules in the first place and were most familiar with them).

What is more, the Privy Council has always been in a position to rectify legal wrongs of its own making—or even to pronounce that, in the past, it took a 'wrong turn'.[126] This is not a court which can shirk responsibility on the basis that

[123] HC Deb 7 February 1828, vol 18, col 155 (Henry Brougham).

[124] Oliver Wendell Holmes Jr, *The Common Law* (Little, Brown 1881) 1 cited by Neuberger, 'JCPC in the 21st Century' (n 119) 30.

[125] Michael Kirby, 'Address to the Justices of the Supreme Court of Nigeria' (12 June 2012) (hereafter Kirby, 'Supreme Court of Nigeria') 8 cited by Neuberger, 'JCPC in the 21st Century' (n 119) 38–39.

[126] As has been done in some other cases: see, eg, the overturning of the *Chan Wing-Siu* principle (regarding accessory liability) in *R v Jogee and Ruddock v The Queen* (Jamaica) [2016] UKSC 8. Although *Ruddock* was a Privy Council case, it was dealt with by way of conjoined appeal with *Jogee* in the Supreme Court which is housed in the same building as the Privy Council and staffed by the same judges: see <www.jcpc.uk/about/biographies-of-the-justices.html and www.supremecourt.uk/about/biographies-of-the-justices.html> accessed 1 January 2020.

a higher court will rescue it from error.[127] Nor is this unfamiliar terrain, for the Privy Council frequently engages with questions of policy.[128] Yet in spite of this, judges within the Privy Council have given insufficient weight to the evidence even though much has been notorious and in the public domain.

Bearing in mind the 'Privy Council sits as the guardian Justice to take care to see that justice is done'[129] and its court is stocked with members of 'integrity, intelligence and efficiency [who] set a very high standard for the performance of judicial duties by judges far from London',[130] it remains a source of puzzlement why these judicial figureheads remained mute, even when the issue was brought before them by litigants.

The Itinerant Bastions

This conundrum is not exclusive to the inner workings of the Privy Council. The silence of senior judges from England and Wales extends under their robes worn in other legal systems *even where appeals to the Privy Council have been abolished.* Through invitation, senior English (and other common law) judges find themselves sitting in overseas courts to help determine appeals. Hong Kong is an illuminating example of how foreign judges perpetuate the *survival* (as with the Privy Council) of the Judges' Rules abroad.[131]

Since 30 June 1997, the former British colony has allowed eminent outsiders to sit as non-permanent judges (NPJs) on its Court of Final Appeal (CFA),[132] through which 'the Privy Council's legacy continues to live on'.[133] Hong Kong's post-handover constitution ('the Basic Law') established a 'local judiciary of final adjudication and promised to maintain the *underlying principles* and institutions for the administration of criminal justice *which were inherited from the British*'.[134]

[127] See Peter Mirfield, 'A Novel Theory of Privy Council Precedent' (Case Comment) (2017) (January 1–6) Law Quarterly Review 133 on *Willers v Joyce* [2016] UKSC 44, which establishes that the JCPC may overturn a decision of the Supreme Court, the House of Lords, or the Court of Appeal 'for the purposes of the applicable English common law and in the jurisdiction for which it is ruling, but it does so also for the purposes of the common law of England and Wales itself' 1.

[128] Indeed, the JCPC 'had greater freedom to manoeuvre on policy matters than its English counterparts': Mitchell, 'Difficulty of Distance' (n 118) 54.

[129] Haldane, 'Work for the Empire' (n 109).

[130] Kirby, 'Supreme Court of Nigeria' (n 125) 8.

[131] Indeed, although Hong Kong has since jettisoned the Privy Council as its final appellate court, its judges continue to take direction from its decisions on the Judges' Rules. For example, various propositions relating to the rules articulated by Lord Carswell in *Peart v The Queen* [2006] 1 WLR 970 were followed in *HKSAR v Kong Pui Lam* [2012] 4 HKLRD 167, CA.

[132] The CFA sits as a court of five judges, of which one is foreign, and invariably from England and Wales.

[133] Simon Young, 'Human Rights in Hong Kong Criminal trials' in Paul Roberts and Jill Hunter (eds), *Criminal Evidence and Human Rights* (Hart 2012) 55 (hereafter Young, 'HK Criminal Trials').

[134] ibid 56. See in particular Article 87 ('the principles previously applied in Hong Kong and the rights previously enjoyed by parties to proceedings shall be maintained').

While the establishment of a self-sufficient judiciary is a natural stage in the evolution of an independent state,[135] the irony here is that English (or foreign) judges were invited onto the CFA[136] in order to bolster the 'independence' of the Hong Kong judiciary (their local counterparts portrayed as a possible threat to it).[137] In addition, is the other primary reason for judicial invitations being sent out, as underlined by the Hon Mr Justice Fok PJ (of the CFA):

> By dint of their backgrounds, the overseas NPJs bring enormous judicial experience and wisdom to the Court. They are all judges who have had *significant influence in shaping the jurisprudence of their own jurisdictions* and *they bring that wealth of experience to bear* when they participate in the deliberations and decisions of the Court.[138]

It is the fact that Hong Kong judges did not initially have any prior experience of appellate work at 'the apex of the court hierarchy'[139] when the CFA was created, coupled to the other fact that non-local common law judges are still flown in to provide 'a deep pool of specialist expertise on which the Chief Justice draws'[140] which allowed English judges to entrench their prominence outside the jurisdiction of the Privy Council. But the more important point is that these judges (while officially labelled as Hong Kong judges) are entrusted with the following unique function:

> … I think that it may be inferred that, in appropriate cases, a function of a judge from other common law jurisdictions is to give particular consideration to whether a proposed decision of this Court is *in accord with generally accepted principles of the common law*.[141]

Again, this echoes the task of the Privy Council ('to look for the common principle underlying systems of jurisprudence of differing kinds') and their influence beyond the Privy Council is reflected by the high proportion of leading judgments

135 Note Hong Kong is a Special Administrative Region (SAR) of China.

136 See Article 82 of the Basic Law ('… may as required invite judges from other common law jurisdictions to sit on the Court of Final Appeal'.)

137 Young, 'HK Criminal Trials' (n 133) 56.

138 The Hon Mr Justice Joseph Fok PJ, 'The Use of Non-local Judges in Overseas Jurisdictions—Judges from other Common Law Jurisdictions in the Hong Kong Court of Final Appeal' Commonwealth Law Conference 2017 (22 March 2017) (hereafter Fok, 'Non-local Judges') para 19 8. As is the case domestically, the 'experience and wisdom' of the Overseas Non-Permanent Judges is conditioned by their homogenous background. Of the nine British judges serving on the Court, all are Oxbridge educated and all are white (there is one female, Lady Hale): see <https://www.hkcfa.hk/en/about/who/judges/npjs/index.html> accessed 1 January 2020.

139 ibid para 21 9.

140 ibid para 22 9.

141 *Chen Li Hung and Ors v Ting Lei Miao and Ors* (2000) 3 HKCFAR 9 at 23B *per* Lord Cooke.

which the NPJs author (or contribute to), many of which 'establish important binding precedents on the courts of Hong Kong in all areas of the law'[142] and also the courtroom reality that '... common law norms under the stewardship of judges continue to steer the direction of criminal trials'.[143]

With such a heavy contingent of English judges[144] in Hong Kong's most authoritative court, their relationship towards the existence of the Judges' Rules there is not merely irrational; it has verged towards the schizophrenic. On the one hand, confronted with some twenty years' experience of the 1964 Rules in action, judges declared them moribund in England and Wales, consigned them to the inglorious annals of '*Judicial History: best forgotten*', and saw in a new era of suspects' rights under PACE (itself far from perfect). On the other, when confronted with the dead body of the Judges' Rules (in all but name), the judges (including former Chief Justices) sat on the Hong Kong CFA and appeared to be struck by a kind of judicial amnesia,[145] appearing to have very little influence in bringing the territory to up to date,[146] even on English practices.[147]

142 Fok, 'Non-local Judges' (n 138) 11–12 para 27.

143 Young, 'HK Criminal Trials' (n 133) 56.

144 The mechanism is actively engaged with NPJs present in more than 95 per cent of all CFA appeals: ibid 64.

145 This could not be for want of cases being brought to their attention. A well-spring of criminal jurisprudence on confessions came from Hong Kong, including the classic case of *Ibrahim v R* [1914] 14 AC 599 (see ibid 58–59 for discussion of other confession cases). See generally Archbold, *Hong Kong* (n 83) ch 15. The underlying point is this: since 1997 Hong Kong courts have been at liberty to develop the common law in a way that is different from the approach taken in England and Wales. Despite this, almost every criminal case that goes before the CFA will involve individuals who are questioned or interrogated under the Hong Kong version of the Judge's Rules. By their very membership of the CFA, the existing law (unless directly challenged) is endorsed by overseas judges since this court has final authority. Based on available judgments (and extra-curial writings), no judge has raised questions as to the continued efficacy of defunct English rules operating in Hong Kong, or called for legislative interference, remaining silent on deep-seated problems that were widely exposed at their point of origin. This concern is all the more worrying when set against the unique political landscape of Hong Kong, a feature of which is the 'the dominant power of the police in a government of unelected bureaucrats ... without its own army'. The reality of abuse of police powers in the territory was manifested following city-wide peaceful protests against the now-withdrawn extradition bill to amend the Fugitive Offenders Ordinance (Cap 503) in June 2019 (which subsequently morphed into a public demand for an independent inquiry into police conduct and revolt for democratic reform). Throughout what became the largest ever demonstrations in the history of Hong Kong, the politico-legal arrangements allowed respected commentators to claim 'policy on the ground has been in the hands of the police': Philip Bowring, 'Lessons from 1970s Hong Kong: The Danger of Unchecked Police Powers, and how a Judge-Led Inquiry and an Amnesty Can Work' *The South China Morning Post* (20 October 2019).

146 By way of example of the stultifying effect that British occupation had on Hong Kong's own legal system, Young has explained: 'Hong Kong's law of criminal evidence currently resembles English evidence law in the early 1980s. Hong Kong has not adopted ... any of the statutory interventions that have since transformed criminal procedure in England and Wales': Young, 'HK Criminal Trials' (n 133) 56.

147 Arguments against overseas judges (such as those with the Privy Council) interfering with colonial and former colonial legal structures because of a lack of requisite local knowledge are particularly weak in the Hong Kong context. Not only was the British colony awash with police corruption (many of whom were British born personnel) in the 1970s and 80s but police maltreatment towards suspects was rife: Carol Jones and Jon Vagg, *Criminal Justice in Hong Kong* (Routlege Cavendish 2007) 453, 466, 505; see also Downey, 'Confessions' (n 82).

It is astonishing that a procession of senior overseas judges continues to dignify the Rules through an historical blind spot, which has resulted in their ducking the issue as to what to do with them. As dead body parts of the Rules washed up on the shores of colonial outposts like Hong Kong, life was breathed into them by the legitimating presence of English (and other common law) judges at the apex of the system and whose silence on the issue of their rejection in England and Wales has left permanent scars on suspects' rights.

Rules which were buried in England therefore continue to rule Hong Kong (and elsewhere)[148] from their grave, having attained extended shelf life for more than thirty years now. Inevitably, had the existence of what were thought to be *Judges'* Rules been called into question by the very people they sprung from, within court walls of the highest standing, then key pillars of the common law architecture—including judicial 'expertise', 'legitimacy', and 'moral authority'—would have risked toppling down. While the exact reasons for their silence remain unknown, at the very least, their failure to draw *any* attention to the plight of the Rules back home raises questions both about the extent of the protection offered by the common law to criminal suspects, and the integrity of its judicial decision-making.

Policing the Common Law

The general effect (intended or otherwise) of the Judges' Rules in other jurisdictions has been to discourage suspects from challenging the admissibility of alleged confessions.[149] Moreover, they have evinced a greater willingness to tolerate questioning of suspects in the years since 1964. Far from handcuffing colonial law enforcement personnel with the 'standard of fairness'[150] enunciated in the Privy Council, the Rules encourage oblique practices which flow from 'largely ill-defined powers and duties, the content of which is obscure to the police and largely unknown to most citizens'.[151]

In light of known dangers: (i) that the Rules put police regulation in the hands of judges who did not have the constitutional authority to police them;[152] (ii) that once power was given to police, the respective legislatures seldom supervised it; and (iii) that this did not merely appear to be law-making by servants of the state without popular mandate at home or abroad, but was, in fact, policy-making, formulated

[148] For example, Mauritius: *The Queen v Boyjoo* (1991) MR 284; *Samserally v State* (1993) MR 94; *Wadud v State* (1999) SCJ 187; *State v Bundhun* (2006) SCJ 254.

[149] As demonstrated by the dearth of case law where a breach of the Rules was successfully argued.

[150] The argument that the 'standard of fairness' should not change according to whether a suspect is English, Kenyan, or Samoan is fallacious. Each foreign jurisdiction presents its own difficulties, be they of language, cultural attitudes towards the police, or even legal representation.

[151] Kirby, 'The Rule of Law' (n 70) 12.

[152] The evidence in this book demonstrates efforts of courts in this respect are not effective in any event.

without adequate publicity, nor arising out of adversarial determinations; it can only be concluded that the Judge's Rules were inflicted upon or adopted by a variety of jurisdictions on the basis of *unwarranted prestige*. And setting aside colonial imposition, while there is nothing in principle against a country 'borrowing' legal precepts from another, those which did so bought a pig in a poke unaware of the Rules' adulterated origins.

Conclusion

The available evidence leaves a disturbing reality: the Judge's Rules embodied executive-judicial reform of the common law, one which, resting on a contradiction between its tainted private origins and its public claim to moral purity, led to a doctrinaire and much-maligned approach to suspects' rights. Mass exportation elevated the Judges' Rules into a faux-constitutional prescription around the world, providing cover for military-style policing methods that were alien to England and Wales (though not to Ireland), devaluing the privilege of silence and presumption of innocence wherever it went, and inhibiting local jurisprudential development. Not only were the Rules ineffectual as an individual instrument but they tended to complicate a pivotal point in the timeline of a criminal case, one where legal certainty was needed but instead left fragmented,[153] turning the integrity of the system very much into another of the Empire's conquests.

[153] An important aspect of the rule of law is that citizens know in advance what the nature of official encroachment on their liberties is to be before that power is used against them: Trevor Allan, 'Legislative Supremacy and the Rule of Law: Democracy and Constitutionalism' (1985) 44 Cambridge Law Journal 111, 117.

12
Appraisal and Review

Introduction

In this chapter we reflect upon the principal findings of our research. We concentrate on the main constitutional issues to which this has given rise including the role-performance of Home Office civil servants first seen in handling the Beck Petition at the end of the nineteenth century and thereafter in their involvement in drafting the 1918 and 1964 Rules. Alongside the Civil Service, we examine the role of the judges in the creation of the Judges' Rules, the introduction into England and Wales of 'plea bargaining', and of the redesignation of judges as 'managers'. We explain why consideration of personnel is important in the light of how the constitution works and its alignment with the proclaimed Westminster Model which we examine in the context of executive relations with the legislature. We also reflect on the dispersal of the English rules (in various disguises) around the world.

Qualifications

We re-emphasize that, despite the universalistic tenor of claims of judicial independence outlined throughout this book, our findings are located within the criminal justice system. The story is necessarily incomplete because, as a result of official 'information interment' policies, key documents have been weeded, destroyed, or withheld from public view.[1] In addition, the minutes of meetings that took place are not recorded in the files and other meetings which doubtless took place (signified in indirect ways) go unmentioned. And the surviving files have to be read with care given that they have been created by officials aware that one day they might be read by others.

[1] By way of further example, repeated attempts to secure access to a Report by Detective Superintendent Hannam on behalf of the Commissioner of Police into wrongdoing by Metropolitan Police officers in 1955 have been unsuccessful. Similarly, repeated FOI requests succeeded in securing only a heavily redacted report by Assistant Commander Ronald Hay in 1985 into the activities of detectives in the (later publicly discredited) Serious Crime Squad of the West Midlands Police. Many files are sealed for years to come including those relating to the Birmingham Six, Judith Ward, the Guildford Four, Stephen Ward, and Operation Countryman. Recently declassified files reveal the depth of despair Gerry Conlon, one of the Guildford Four, who had contemplated suicide twelve years into his life term of imprisonment: 'Guildford Four Man Gerry Conlon's "Living Hell" Revealed' (*BBC Website*, 29 December 2017).

The Myth of Judicial Independence. Mike McConville and Luke Marsh, Oxford University Press (2020). © Mike McConville and Luke Marsh. DOI: 10.1093/oso/9780198822103.001.0001

The roles of the executive and the judiciary are accordingly encrypted by the filtration of records, and social and political history is necessarily a victim. The lack of transparency makes it difficult to discover where decisions are made and to attach accountability when things go wrong. This has wider implications because it may mean that no lessons are learned for the future and also that the collective experience is stultified. When decisions are taken by individuals or a select group, even if *they* learn from experience,[2] no one else can; and when they move on, the experience goes as well.

Regulatory Impropriety

A distinctive feature of the whole period under review is the lack of compliance with available procedures. The decision to inaugurate[3] a regime of regulating police interrogations by means of the Judges' Rules was contrary to established practice and in disregard of the Court of Criminal Appeal. This was no mere 'procedural' oversight (though that in and of itself would be of concern): the creation of an ad hoc measure resulted in the bypassing of a forensic trial process whose very purpose was to test the soundness of proposed principles, rules, and interpretation of laws. Without such testing, the risk of dubiety, ambiguity, and confusion in any 'rule' is magnified and, as it turned out, became apparent as soon as the Rules were in force.

From their establishment, the Rules were the source of confusion not only for lawyers but for judges themselves and all of this on one of the gravest of matters in a democratic polity: the point at which the liberty of the subject can be subject to interference by force of the law. No one knew then or subsequently the precise status of the Rules—judicial guidance, policy, law—yet they purported to control (and still control in some overseas jurisdictions) the conditions under which the police can lawfully question citizens and detain them as well as the rights of citizens in such circumstances.

Not only was this style of irregular decision-making repeated in 1918, 1930, and 1964 but the judges and the executive[4] thereafter took it upon themselves to further restructure the relationship of suspects and defendants to the criminal justice system. Without *any* public airing, the judges first introduced an 'under-the-counter' form of pressurizing defendants to plead guilty and then, beginning in 1970, formalized a 'plea bargaining' system while purporting to ban the practice.[5] More than twenty years later, they introduced a formal system of state-induced

[2] Which, as we have seen, is by no means a given.

[3] They were not 'promulgated' nor were they accompanied by an official Circular.

[4] The exact role of the executive cannot be determined because of the incompleteness of records.

[5] For an in-depth study of these developments, see Mike McConville and Luke Marsh, *Criminal Judges* (Edward Elgar 2014) (hereafter McConville and Marsh, *Criminal Judges*) ch 3.

guilty pleas in the context of enhanced defence disclosure requirements and the restructuring of defence lawyers as aides to the prosecution all mandated by a 'change in culture' supposedly visited upon them by some innominate force.[6]

The departure from the principles and procedures embodied in the rule of law also raises fundamental questions regarding the *moral* standing of the process. Among other things, adherence to the rule of law involves transparency of decision-making thereby giving credence to the claim that the judgment of the court can be relied upon as being the best statement that the court can make of its reasoning[7] and, more fundamentally, as an affirmation of the integrity by which it was reached. The story of the evolution of the Judges' Rules in and of itself destroys any notion of openness and accessibility of law-making and, together with the secretive introduction of state-induced guilty pleas and the sleight of hand accompanying the inauguration of 'case management', puts a stake through unmediated claims of integrity in decision-making.

The Personnel of the Law

Any assessment of the personnel involved in this restructuring process from the outset until today—civil servants, ministers, and judges—raises fundamental questions not only as to their role and institutional capacities but also about the constitution and its enforcement. The assessment of the personnel is not assisted by the secrecy which has attended critical moments but the concerns, as we have seen, go even deeper.

After the middle of the nineteenth century, the much-vaunted 'Northcote-Trevelyan' reforms were intended to lead to the replacement of time-serving bureaucrats by a modern, albeit elitist, professional Civil Service staffed by individuals

[6] The Ministry of Justice website authoritative account (<www.justice.gov.uk/courts/procedure-rules/criminal/notes>) which sets out the heritage in the Review of Auld LJ, states, inter alia: ' . . . The Rules promote a culture change in the management of criminal cases, but that change is evolutionary . . . And they make explicit and particular the powers and duties of judicial case management identified in decisions of the Court of Appeal . . . Part 3 for the first time gives courts explicit powers to manage the progression of criminal cases. In . . . Chaaban [2003] EWCA Crim 1012 and Jisl [2004] EWCA Crim 696 the Court of Appeal held that courts have a duty to manage criminal cases effectively. The new rules give them the framework of powers they need to fulfil that duty. Read with the overriding objective the Part 3 rules will help the courts to promote the culture change in criminal case management that the Committee wants.'

[7] This is more fully expressed by Ronald Dworkin, *Law's Empire* (Harvard University Press 1986). See also Lord Neuberger, 'Some Thoughts on Judicial Reasoning across Jurisdictions' Mitchell Lecture 2016 <www.supremecourt.uk/docs/speech-161111.pdf> accessed 1 January 2020. Neuberger discredits extra-curial comments by judges to emphasize the centrality of the judgment: 'The judgment contains the legal reasoning of the judge who makes the order, and it is the judgment, not the order, which is normally published and reported and it is the judgment, not the order, which is subsequently referred to in legal arguments, judgments and articles. In other words, judges communicate and lay down the law publicly through their judgments, in the same sort of way as Parliament lays down the law in statutes, albeit with far more reasoning.'

of outstanding ability, carrying out their duties on the basis of honesty, integrity, objectivity, and impartiality. The technical performance of the new recruits did not, however, produce results commensurate with their proclaimed intellectual excellence, nor did the new group unfalteringly exhibit the honesty and integrity that was promised. This first clearly emerged in the handling of the case of Adolf Beck.

As the Beck Inquiry was to determine, the Petitions submitted on his behalf were summarily rejected without *any* inquiries being made by Home Office officials despite resting upon facts which suggested a miscarriage so grave as to demand interference. The officials involved, one a qualified barrister, were criticized for drafting a Minute which was not 'such a minute as a trained lawyer ... could possibly have written for the guidance of his superior'. Officials made no effort to compare the handwriting of the documents in Beck's case with those in Smith's case, or to obtain a statement as to the 'distinctive marks' until prompted by Beck's solicitor. Once the separate identities of Beck and the real culprit, Smith, were established through prison records, this was not communicated by the Home Office to the trial judge in a clear manner and no effort was made by officials to clarify the status of the Distinctive Marks document (**Illustration 2.1**) after the judge had written to say that he was unsure of its provenance. At this stage, a further Home Office Minute (approved by the permanent Under-Secretary—a barrister and County Court judge) was found to disclose 'a want of appreciation of the facts and the legal aspect of the case'.

While there are serious moral as well as competence questions concerning the fact that no one in the Home Office did anything to secure Beck's release from prison after the separate identities had been established, worse was to follow. Despite a public uproar when Beck was re-arrested in 1904, *no one* in the Home Office responded to requests for help and *no one* informed the Public Prosecutor or the court of the lack of identity between Beck and Smith. Extraordinarily, Edward Troup, the acclaimed Poster Boy of the Northcote-Trevelyan reforms, told the Beck Inquiry that the Home Office knew nothing of Beck's second arrest until *after* his trial and conviction. This is scarcely believable; in fact, it is not believable at all.

The malaise was not only individual; it was *institutional*. Although the fault lines ran throughout the Home Office chain of command, the principal players were all allowed to remain as they were. The structure, training, work habits, and reliance on departmental precedent were continued on the absurd basis that outside barristers who would be attracted by the salaries paid to junior clerks would be of less general ability than the latter and would not be likely to possess legal knowledge or training of any value. Accordingly, the moving force in dealing with police powers of detention and the rules relating to the compulsory questioning of citizens remained with the very clerks responsible for the Beck fiasco.

These clerks were then transferred into the area of legal drafting without displaying a talent for this challenging task or given training in lieu. Suggestions for adding to the 1912 Rules displayed a failure to understand their basic shortcomings by clerks acting without close supervision or guidance. On top of this, Troup, without the benefit of legal practice, pronounced the existing 1912 Rules fit for purpose when they clearly were not and then proposed additional Rules which, far from clarifying existing problems, magnified them further. These problems were to continue for over thirty more years because the clear and unambiguous advice of Home Office lawyers was unaccountably set aside by Sir John Anderson, (a brilliant intellect but no lawyer), in favour of a bizarre note signed off by Lord Chief Justice (LCJ) Hewart but drawn up by the very judge (Mr Justice Avory), then seventy-seven years old, whose negligence as a barrister had been the major cause of Beck's initial wrongful conviction.

The Home Office legal advisers were also fully aware of the dubious way in which the Rules were being presented, beginning their internal advice with the words: 'The Judges' Rules are not rules laid down by the Judges, but rules approved by them.' This technical and moral ambiguity arose directly from the process by which the 1918 Rules came into existence. Although the reformulation was essentially the work of Troup (appropriating the work of Harry Simpson), he sought to pass them off as having been 'laid down' by the judges. The attempted 'correction' of this misrepresentation by Justice Darling—that the Rules had been 'approved' by the judges—in fact furthered the misunderstanding that the judges had authored the Rules.

While the 1930 iteration of the Rules continued the technical disarray and moral dubiety, much worse followed in the 1964 revision. Not only were the judges browbeaten into abandoning their preferred formulation, and then into accepting the executive version, the new Rules were distributed under false colours. Although the original Circular stated that the Rules had been *approved* by the judges and had superseded those previously *approved* by the judges, the permanent Under-Secretary altered this by hand to state that the new Rules had been *made* by Her Majesty's judges of the Queen's Bench Division and that the Rules superseded those previously *made* by the judges.

This calculated act of deception placed a capstone on a pattern of Home Office duplicity and dissimulation traceable at least to its mishandling of Beck's case and the early formulation of the so-called Judges' Rules. The shoddy history demonstrates technical failings that were to dog the regulation of policing for some eighty years. More than this, it shows moral failings by scores of individuals involved in the formulation and dissemination of the Rules at relevant historical moments. And more than this, it provides clear evidence of dishonourable conduct at an institutional level. The lack of moral compass shown in the Beck case was passed to successive administrations infecting everyone from bottom to top.[8] On these

[8] After many subsequent revamps there remain calls to reform the Civil Service and even for another Northcote-Trevelyan Review. See, eg, Chris Huhne, 'The UK's Civil Service Needs Reform for Government to Work Better' *The Guardian* (15 December 2013): 'A new Northcote-Trevelyan—the seminal 1854 report that established the modern civil service—is essential because the world that

grounds alone, the Home Office, as an institution, debased the concept of public administration.

Home Office officials were not alone in carrying blame for this catastrophic failure. So far as the Beck case is concerned, the prosecution barrister, Horace Avory and the trial judge, Forrest Fulton, had much to answer for but were in effect given a 'Get out of Jail Free' card by the Inquiry. While judgment on Avory's subsequent aberrant memorandum regarding the Judges' Rules may be softened by reason of his age, a harsher view must be taken of later judges. The behaviour of Lord Parker and his fellow judges in dealing with the perjury of Christine Keeler so that its impact on the trial of Stephen Ward was to strengthen rather than undermine the prosecution was nothing short of discreditable and amounted in our view to misconduct in public office.

What is more, in rewriting the Rules, senior judges, under pressure from the executive, weakened their grip on principles which had underpinned their view of the 'public interest' and bowed to what were openly described as 'police interests'. This was, however, merely a modern lineage of high-ranking judges, led by Lord Parker, acting in concert with an executive that would pick away at individual rights over the next fifty years.

This occurred, as the judges knew full well, in the context of violations of suspects' (slender) rights and notorious police corruption. The standing of the Rules as mere 'administrative directions' for the police combined with their ambiguous nature resulted in extended detention and questioning practices. Alongside this, the plain clothes division's close links to the criminal fraternity presented opportunities for wrongdoing that proved irresistible. For their part, rather than attempting to arrest this malpractice, senior judges, utilizing what they euphemistically labelled 'elasticity' of the Rules, in fact provided officers with *pro forma* explanations they could give as lawful accounts for unlawful actions which were

government is trying to influence is so much more complex.' See also UK Government, *The Civil Service Reform Plan* (June 2012) <www.gov.uk/government/uploads/system/uploads/attachment_data/file/305148/Civil-Service-Reform-Plan-final.pdf> accessed 1 January 2020 National Audit Office, *Capability in the Civil Service* (HC 919 Session 2016-17, 24 March 2017). Regrettably, in other areas of its responsibility the Home Office has displayed a failure to comply with the law and breaches of the duty of candour and cooperation to the courts as in the area of child refugees. See, eg, *R (on the application of citizens of the UK) v Secretary of State for the Home Department* (2018) EWCA Civ 1812. In addition, Home Office civil servants came out badly in the Review by Sir Alex Allan (the Prime Minister's adviser on Ministers' interests) of the 'Amber Rudd Affair' which resulted in the then Home Secretary being forced to resign having misled Parliament over immigration targets: Richard Johnstone, 'Civil Servants Let Down Amber Rudd over Immigration Targets, Ex-Perm Sec Finds' (2018) <https://www.civilserviceworld.com/articles/news/civil-servants-let-down-amber-rudd-over-immigration-targets-ex-perm-sec-finds>. A Report by the National Audit Office (2018) into the immigration scandal surrounding the 'Windrush' generation, concluded, among other things, that the Home Office 'in its implementation of the policy with few checks and balances and targets for enforcement action, we do not consider, once again, that the Department adequately prioritised the protection of those who suffered distress and damage through being wrongly penalised, and to whom they owed a duty of care. Instead it operated a target-driven environment for its enforcement teams. The clarity of briefing to the former Home Secretary on this issue has also been called into question.' National Audit Office, 'Handling of the Windrush Situation' (2018) <https://www.nao.org.uk/wp-content/uploads/2018/12/Handling-of-the-Windrush-situation-1.pdf>.

supplemented by an extended extra-judicial inclination towards the attenuation of the right to silence and access to legal advice.

Against a history of papering over miscarriages of justice or contributing to them judges introduced a covert system of state-induced guilty pleas brought out into a twilight zone in 1970 before later undertaking 'reviews' of the criminal justice system at the behest of the executive or on the initiative of the then Chief Justice. Further papering over miscarriages, exhibiting bias in summing up evidence in serious cases, and making extra-judicial comments of a discreditable kind, judges often sought to undercut jury trial while purporting to laud it as central to the British justice system.

The System Created

Although growth has been non-linear, the resulting system is one focused upon the defendant population. Under the current regime, the defendant is expected to capitulate at the earliest possible moment so as to relieve the state of the expense and trouble of proving guilt at an adversary trial necessarily regarded as an impediment to 'truth' and 'justice'. In this way, the intrusion of the state into society is now openly incorporated into criminal procedure and legitimates the opening of decision-making to extra-legal (social) criteria around race, gender, and class.

As a necessary consequence of this, the system is structured to deny individual autonomy, the defendant population (innocent and guilty alike) treated both as a class and as a class outside respectable society. This system will not tolerate lawyers who raise 'technical' defences, confining them to perfunctory 'conferences' (preferably disengaged from the defendant through video links), and requiring them to help correct prosecution mistakes.[9] *The collective effect is to refigure the defendant into a client of the court.*

In this new age of managerialism, the task of the judge, as a manager,[10] is to educate all defendants and their lawyers that challenge to the state's case is fruitless and attempts to do so will be heavily penalized. In a system whose rationale is detached from actual caseload, judges will nonetheless be rated according to their ability to rapidly dispose of cases without trial and at the earliest opportunity.

The successive official actions spread over the century have amounted to a bonfire of vanities of which Savonarola would have been proud. On the flames have

[9] *R v Gleeson* [2003] EWCA Crim 3357 in which Auld LJ adopted a key provision from his own *Review*. The general responsibility placed on the defence has now been incorporated into the CrimPR.

[10] See *R v Jisl* [2004] EWCA Crim 696: 'Active, hands on, case management, both pre-trial and throughout the trial itself, is now regarded as an essential part of the judge's duty. The profession must understand that *this has become and will remain part of the normal trial process*, and that cases must be prepared and conducted accordingly' 116 (emphasis supplied). See *R v Chaaban* [2003] EWCA Crim 1012.

been thrown objects thought by senior judges to be conducive to sin; these have included: the right to be free from custodial detention for questioning; the right to silence in the face of police questioning before charge; the right of defendants to be free from questioning following charge; the right of defendants to enter a free and voluntary plea; the right of defendants to put the prosecution to the proof without disclosing lines of defence and without penalty; the right of defence counsel to give advice freely; the right of defence counsel to stand aside from the prosecution's management of its case; the right to defence counsel being *physically* present; the right of defendants to trial free of penalty; the right of victims to a sentence that reflects the gravity of the offending behaviour; and the right of the public to an open and transparent system based in principle not short-term expediency. In this process, the residual trappings of 'freedoms' and 'rights' have been reduced to a formalistic canopy in which defendants are disempowered by the actions and expectations of those who define the process. Order is not, however, severed from law: indeed, 'law' and 'legitimacy' is served up in new forms.

The Vertical System

While this system seeks to impose control and discipline on sections of the community perceived as guilty and unworthy, it has widespread consequences which have little to do with and, indeed, contradict, the 'efficiency' judges proclaim. While depleted defence services[11] are an achievement of the system there are also unintended consequences. Routine case processing outside the trial court reinforces the actions and expectations of all the system actors so as to produce the very inefficiencies it purports to cure. As long as police and prosecutors can rely upon a system which does not meaningfully test the state's case, the system will continue to be saturated with cases, many of which are worthless or should (and commonly do) result in discontinuance before trial or acquittal,[12] because prosecutors are hospitable to rubber-stamping police decisions.[13] Moreover, police and prosecutors

[11] For an example see *R v K* [2017] Crim LR 716 in which the defendant pleaded guilty without being advised of an available statutory defence, the conviction being quashed following referral by the Criminal Case Review Commission. See also *R v Alfie Good* [2016] EWCA Crim 1054; and *Maxwell v R* [2017] EWCA Crim 1233. For research evidence, see McConville and others, *Standing Accused: The Organisation and Practices of Criminal Defence Lawyers in Britain* (OUP 1994); Daniel Newman, *Legal Aid Lawyers and the Quest for Justice* (Hart 2013); Hannah Quirk, *The Rise and Fall of the Right of Silence: Principle, Politics and Policy* (Routledge 2016). For a detailed account of the 'crisis' in criminal legal aid and the criminal defence profession, see: Tom Smith and Ed Cape, 'The Rise and Decline of Criminal Legal Aid in England and Wales' in Asher Flynn and Jacqueline Hodgson (eds), *Access to Justice & Legal Aid: Comparative Perspectives on Unmet legal Need* (Hart Publishing 2017) 63–86 .

[12] The Criminal Statistics for England and Wales show that for the year ending December 2018, of those cases that went to trial in the Crown Court (n=23, 111), some 56 per cent (n=12, 942) resulted in acquittal.

[13] Recent Crown Court statistics from the Crown Prosecution Service (CPS) (2018–19) show, eg, that 11.80 per cent of all prosecutions (n=8, 264) were dropped (discontinued, no evidence offered, or

are encouraged to act as if they can safely dispense with a professional model which focuses on the acquisition of legally persuasive evidence because witnesses rarely need to be produced, technical shortcomings will be (forcibly) supplemented by the defence, and the barriers to challenge are such as to minimize the risk of trial. As a consequence, at a time when criminal law, procedure, evidence, and sentencing[14] are all becoming intensely more complex,[15] institutional inefficiency and unprofessional conduct are magnified.

The results are everywhere to be seen.[16] Police malpractice is facilitated where the mechanisms for oversight are weak,[17] the chances of discovery are

withdrawn) before the case went to trial. This figure is slightly higher than the previous year (11.0 per cent) despite intense scrutiny from HM Crown Prosecution Service Inspectorate (HMCPSI) and public criticism. Added to this, there were 6.9 per cent (n=4, 776) additional 'unsuccessful' (judge directed acquittals or acquittals after trial) outcomes. The problem of non-disclosure is a discrete but significant indication of the lack of prosecution professionalism. As a result of a FOI request, the CPS revealed the number of prosecutions dropped because of non-disclosure over the period April 2018–October 2018 was 928 (3.1 per cent total prosecutions dropped; up from 1.6 per cent 2017–18): CPS FOI. After it was revealed that more than 900 cases a year were dropped because of disclosure issues, the Chief Constable of Surrey Police attributed part of the problem to a police mindset with the CPS admitting that there were still 'systemic disclosure issues': Matthew Weaver and Jamie Grierson: 'Police Chief Admits "Cultural Problem" with Evidence Disclosure' *The Guardian* (24 January 2018).

[14] See, eg, *R v Maxwell* [2017] EWCA Crim 1233 in which Treacy LJ emphasized the importance of vigilance on the part of advocates to ensure that the court passes a lawful sentence; a warning that merely repeated that given by the Court of Appeal in *R v Cain* [2006] EWCA Crim 3233. See also *R v C and D* [2018] Crim LR 564. The Court of Appeal recently expressed the hope that 'the Sentencing Code proposed by the Law Commission will be adopted by the government and so permit all the relevant legislation to be found in one place, avoiding the correction of costly mistakes and thereby aiding the proper administration of justice' *Thompson v R* [2018] EWCA Crim 639, in which the court also said: 'In the meantime, it is necessary to remind all advocates (and, in particular, the Crown Prosecution Service and those who prosecute on its behalf) that their obligation, in the public interest, is to ensure that the judge is correctly informed of the powers of the court and timeously reminded of any failure to comply with the many legislative requirements in place.'

[15] Jonathan Sumption underscores the point in his first Reith lecture, 'Law and the Decline of Politics' (25 May 2019): 'In a single year, ending in May 2010, more than 700 new criminal offences were created, three-quarters of them by government regulation ... the rate of increase continues to be high. On top of that, there is the relentless output of judgments of the Courts, many of them on subjects which were hardly touched by law a century ago (transcript available via the BBC website).

[16] For example, police ineptitude in the handling of fraud cases (see 'Placebo Policing' *The Times* (15 August 2019), has led to serious concerns being noted by HM Inspectorate of Constabulary and Fire and Rescue Services in its 2019 report, 'State of Policing—The Annual Assessment of Policing in England and Wales 2018': We have seen demand suppression manifest itself ... for example, in some forces' failure to record a significant proportion of the crimes which are reported; and with some crime types—fraud being a good example—the often wholesale failure to carry out investigations' 35. This has been masked in part by the manipulation of crime figures by the Home Office: Paul Morgan-Bentley, 'Home Office "Manipulates Crime Figures by Telling Action Fraud to Dismiss Identity Theft"' *The Times* (18 September 2019). Widescale police failure to properly report serious sexual offence allegation has also surfaced: Caelainn Barr, 'Thousands of Rape Reports Inaccurately Recorded by Police' *The Guardian* (19 September 2019). See also Fiona Hamilton, 'Police Making Basic Disclosure Errors, Says Attorney-General' *The Times* (29 January 2018). This must be viewed alongside a litany of slipshod prosecution work, too innumerable to list here, which has been an abiding feature of the justice system: see, eg, Jonathan Ames and Catherine Baksi, '"Inept" Prosecutors Blamed for Fall In Rape Convictions' *The Times* (19 September 2019).

[17] The historical failings of the Home Office in discharging its responsibilities in this regard which we have discussed have been more than matched by the official 'watchdogs', the latest incarnation of

small, and the system of resignation and early retirement (together with force indulgence[18]) provides escape hatches for uncooperative[19] or deviant officers even though the system costs (in terms of consequent investigations, reviews, commissions, inquiries,[20] and ancillary legal expenses) are incalculable.[21]

which is the Independent Office for Police Conduct set up in January 2018 to replace the Independent Police Complaints Commission (about which concerns were raised by the Public Accounts Committee, 9 March 2009). The Metropolitan Police has been able to act without fear of investigation or meaningful external governance with results that remain to be fully catalogued. Among the casualties of its covert policing operations have been at least ten women deceived into relationships by false identities and more than fifty campaigners whose convictions have now been overturned having been wrongly prosecuted or subject to false police evidence at trial (with up to eighty-three further cases to be resolved) as well as interference in the Stephen Lawrence case. See Dominic Casciani, 'Undercover Policing Inquiry: Why It Matters' *The Guardian* (28 July 2015) and Mark Ellison QC and Alison Morgan, 'Review of Possible Miscarriages of Justice: Impact of Undisclosed Undercover Police Activity on the Safety of Convictions' Report to the Attorney General, House of Commons (HC Paper No 291, 16 July 2015). In a recent review, the National Audit Office found that the Home Office had overseen substantial cuts to police office numbers (44,000 officers and staff since 2010) without forecasting the effect on policing, that it lacked 'a long-term plan for policing and significant gaps remain in its understanding of demand for police services and their costs. The way the Department chooses to distribute funding has been ineffective and detached from the changing nature of policing for too long, and it cannot be sure overall funding is being directed to the right places:' National Audit Office, *Financial Sustainability of Police Forces in England and Wales 2018*. Concerns have been repeatedly raised over the effectiveness of the Independent Office for Police Conduct (IOPC). In a recent case, eg, the IOPC found proof that demands from Chinese officials, including its security service, may have informed the decision to arrest Shao Jiang (a Tiananmen Square survivor) for 'conspiracy' as a result of a protest during the visit to the United Kingdom of President Xi Jinping. According to solicitors for Shao Jiang, the IOPC initially concluded that there was evidence of a breach of professional standards involving two officers but subsequently reversed its findings following objections from the Metropolitan Police. See Bindmans Press Release <https://www.bindmans.com/news/shao-jiang-releases-statement-on-the-iopcs-final-report> (1 July 2019). See also the heavily redacted IOPC Report: *Dr Shao Jiang, Investigation into the complaints made by DR Shao Jiang and Ms Johanna Jiang following Dr Shao's arrests during the Chinese State Visit October 2015.*

[18] See, eg, an investigation managed by the Independent Police Complaints Commission (IPCC) arising out of the murder of Kevin Nunes in 2002 the background to which is reported in *R v Joof and Ors* [2012] EWCA Crim 1475. The investigation, known as *Operation Kalmia*, found that three Chief Constables, an Assistant Chief Constable, and two Detective Constables had a case to answer for gross misconduct. The findings were rejected by the relevant authorities in respect of all the senior officers and the IPCC decided not to direct that hearings be held. The police force accepted the finding of misconduct in relation to one Detective Constable who was given 'management advice'; the other Detective Constable retired on health grounds. As a general rule, a Chief Constable is supposed to take into account public interest before permitting an officer to retire: *R (Coglan and Ors) v Greater Manchester Police* [2004] EWHC 2801 (Admin).

[19] See, eg, Daniel De Simone, 'Stephen Port: Officers Refuse to Answer Watchdog's Questions' (*BBC News Online*, 26 July 2018) reporting that all but one of seventeen Met officers under investigation for the initial response to the serial killer Stephen Port refused to answer questions during interviews with the Independent Office of Police Conduct in response to misconduct notices.

[20] An indication of the system costs is provided by the ongoing costs of the *Undercover Policing Inquiry* (Mitting Inquiry) into undercover police operations in England and Wales since 1968 which were already in excess of £21 million, as of September 2019, not including civil damages and legal costs of the various police forces involved; and the costs arising out of the Hillsborough Inquiry are expected to exceed £100 million (the Home Office spending £63.6 million on the legal costs of the families of the ninety-six victims of the disaster, with the South Yorkshire Police costs exceeding £25 million and further substantial costs to be incurred).

[21] See, eg, the devastating report by the former High Court judge, Sir Richard Henriques, into the 'Nick' (Carl Beech) affair which resulted in an abortive Scotland Yard investigation into a claimed

Setting aside the massive consequences of under-resourcing,[22] police failures to comply with standard investigative rules[23] and principles are widespread[24] with tragic consequences for victims, unnecessary dislocation to the lives of defendants, and significant system costs; and repeated invocations to improve fall on deaf ears.[25] Prosecutors charge people with crimes that do not

sinister paedophile ring costing in excess of £2.5 million and untold distress to the alleged perpetrators and their families. According to Sir Richard, officers used false information to obtain search warrants to raid the homes of retired Armed Forces chief, Lord Bramall, the widow of ex-Home Secretary Lord Leon Brittan, and ex-Conservative MP Harvey Proctor by falsely asserting that 'Nick' was a 'consistent' witness. Beech was subsequently convicted of twelve counts of perverting the course of justice and sentenced to eighteen years in prison. Sir Richard also stated that during his investigation of this affair the Metropolitan Police did not give him all relevant documentation and that the Met sought to protect itself from effective outside scrutiny when its conduct was investigated. Shortly after Beech was convicted, the Independent Office for Police Conduct announced that three officers accused of misconduct over search warrant applications had been cleared. See: Stephen Wright, *Mail Online* (30 July 2019) (in which Sir Richard published a comment piece on 6 October 2019); See also Martin Evans, *The Telegraph* (30 July 2019). It has been estimated that the total cost to the Met for this fiasco may eventually reach £4 million including compensation payments.

22 Many police chiefs have warned about the impact of reduced funding and reduced numbers of police, police numbers declining by some 22,000 since 2010. Under-resourcing leading, it is claimed, to 'poor service': including not investigating car thefts, criminal damage, and shoplifting: Sima Kotecha, 'West Midlands Police Chief Constable Says Force Offers "Poor Service"' (*BBC News Online*, 28 July 2018).

23 This is all the more necessary given the massive complexity that has been introduced into investigations and evidence production over the past thirty years with the proliferation of computers, tablets, the internet, and mobile phones. As the Director of Public Prosecutions has pointed out, the CPS typically receives each day 1 terabyte (1 million megabytes) of data from the police with the average mobile smartphone containing the equivalent of 5 million A4 pages of data: Max Hill, QC 'Disclosure—A Response from the CPS' (2019) Criminal Law Review 611.

24 See, eg, Rt Hon Dame Elish Angiolini DBE QC, *Report of the Independent Review into The Investigation and Prosecution of Rape in London* (2015). This Report followed on the back of other major reports including: HMCPSI and HMIC, *Investigation and Prosecution of Cases involving Allegations of Rape* (April 2002); Liz Kelly, Jo Lovett, and Linda Regan, *A Gap or Chasm? Attrition in Reported Rape Cases* (Home Office Research Study 293, HMSO 2005); HMCPSI and HMI, *Without Consent: A Report on the Joint Review of the Investigation and Prosecution of Rape Offences* (2007); The Stern Review, *A Report by Baroness Vivien Stern CBE of an Independent Review Into How Rape Complaints are Handled by Public Authorities in England and Wales* (Government Equalities Office and Home Office 2010). Extraordinarily, the Report found among other things that untrained and inadequately trained officers were assigned to deal with rape complaints; the guidance provided to them failed to meet the needs either of police or prosecutors; there was an absence of early consultation between the specialist rape prosecutor and the investigator; and non-specialist officers were seconded to deal with rape complaints. Despite these Reports, rape has seen the biggest fall in police charging suspects with, as of July 2019, the rate slashed by two-thirds in just a year with women victims of rape now having a 1.4 per cent chance of the offence resulting in a charge or summons, down from 3.3 per cent in the previous year: Lizzie Dearden, 'Only 1.7% of Reported Rapes Prosecuted in England and Wales, New Figures Show' *The Independent* (25 April 2019). A second Report by Rt Hon Dame Elish Angiolini DBE QC into deaths in police custody similarly points up deficiencies in police training for dealing with persons taken into custody, the inappropriateness of using ex-police officers to staff the IPCC, and the opportunity for improper police collusion which the current investigative system presents: *Report of the Independent Review of Deaths and Serious Incidents in Police Custody* (January 2017).

25 Thus, eg, the recent report of HMCPSI, *Making it Fair: The Disclosure of Unused Material in Volume Crown Court Cases* (2017), reporting on a joint inspection by HMCPSI and Her Majesty's Inspectorate of Constabulary, found widespread failures by both police and prosecutors in relation to disclosure of unused material which it considered a key component of the investigative and prosecution process. Police routinely failed to comply with guidance and legal requirements and prosecutors failed

exist;[26] under defective indictments[27]; under legislation that has been repealed; or is not yet in force; or without a basis in evidence.[28] And there is some evidence of a more general falling in standards of professional practice.[29]

to challenge substandard police accounting. The inspection additionally found poor decision-making by prosecutors on the requirements of the Criminal Procedure and Investigations Act and more than half the disclosure records deficient. In 2017, 916 individuals had charges dropped because of non-disclosure of prosecution evidence, a feature which continues thereafter. See Tom Harper, 'Drug Barons Walk Free as Police Hide Evidence' *The Sunday Times* (27 May, 2018) describing how two drug traffickers were freed after a judge ruled that police, the CPS, and a leading barrister behaved in a way that was an 'affront to the integrity of the trial' and would 'undermine public confidence'. See further Clive Coleman, 'Red Diesel Trial Collapse Shows "Systemic Disclosure Failings"' (*BBC News Online,* 29 April 2018) detailing the collapse of a £500,000 fraud trial because of non-disclosure by investigating officers of HMRC, the former LCJ Lord Thomas attributing blame for widespread disclosure failures to the cut in resources for criminal justice.

[26] See, eg, *R v Shields* [2011] EWCA Crim 2343; *R v Maciejczyk* [2018] EWCA 2665 where, as the Court of Appeal stated, the trial judge who had proposed the invalid addition to the indictment would have been better assisted by counsel had careful research been undertaken before the indictment was amended.

[27] See, eg, *R v McKenzie* [2011] EWCA Crim 1550; *R v Stocker* [2013] EWCA Crim 1993; *R v Boateng* [2016] EWCA Crim 57; *Darroux v The Crown* [2018] EWCA Crim 1009; and *R v J* [2018] EWCA Crim 2485 (a case involving nine defendants in a high value burglary in which the Court of Appeal variously described the prosecution case as too fragmentary and speculative to be left to the jury and as 'unacceptably tenuous'). See further *R v Naveeda Ikram* [2018] EWCA Crim 440 in which the failure of an appeal against a refusal of leave to amend the indictment and a ruling of no case to answer was due 'essentially because an insufficient consideration as to how the case was to be framed, and an insufficiently rigorous analysis of what the evidence available could prove' (at para 57). It should be added that counsel on both sides may be at fault in not assisting the court on matters of law, procedure, or evidence, as, eg, in *R v Leathem and Mallett* [2017] EWCA Crim 42.

[28] See McConville and Marsh, *Criminal Judges* (n 5). See also *Evans and Ors v SFO* [2015] EWHC 63; *R v Lewis and Marshall-Gunn* [2017] EWCA Crim 1734; *R v SA and Ors* [2019] EWCA Crim 144. For a graphic illustration of a prosecution that collapsed with information so slight that the judge was unable to carry out a pre-trial management hearing: Megi Rychlikova, 'Top Judge Calls for CPS to Explain Case Collapse' *York Press* (14 June 2019). The weaknesses in appraising prosecution evidence are also repeatedly shown in costly failures by the Serious Fraud Office as recently in the collapse of the prosecutions against Tesco executives launched originally in 2016 and collapsing in 2018 when Sir John Royce terminated the case after the jury had heard months of prosecution evidence, a decision upheld by the Court of Appeal: Zoe Wood and Sarah Butler, 'Two Tesco Directors Cleared of Fraud as Judge Labels Case "Weak"' *The Guardian* (6 December 2018).

[29] See, eg, *Leatham and Hallett v R* [2017] EWCA Crim 42 at para. 61 'The Court was disappointed that Counsel did not take us to any of the various authorities mentioned above, notwithstanding the fact that in advance of the hearing we had invited their specific attention to the passage in Blackstone's *Criminal Practice 2017*, which provides references to some of the cases and a customarily helpful introduction to the topic in issue.' *R v A* [2019] EWCA Crim 106 paras 41 and 42: 'Counsel on both sides recognised that they had not given the Honorary Recorder of Manchester the accurate assistance to which he was entitled, and that the need for an appeal to put that right had added to the distress of the victim's family and friends. In the result, both counsel made fulsome apologies at the outset of their submissions to us. However, we regret to record that, initially, both failed to give accurate assistance to this Court as well. Mr Johnson QC had not discovered *Anderson*, and neither he nor Ms Duckworth had obtained the judgment in *R v D & H* (which is referred to in *Anderson*). Ultimately, at our request, the judgment in *R v D & H* was provided by the Registrar and the appeal had to be adjourned for a time whilst the parties re-considered their submissions.' See also *R v Blerim Hajdarmataj* [2019] EWCA Crim 303—failure of prosecution counsel to adduce evidence of bad character of (alleged victim) at re-trial; *Pamela Darroux v R* [2018] EWCA Crim 1009 where the wrong charge (theft instead of fraud) had been brought (and the legal difficulty in doing so had not been identified before trial by either counsel (only later by the Criminal Appeal Office) with the result that the convictions were quashed on appeal; *R v Mohammed Hussain* [2019] EWCA Crim 362—failure of counsel (on both sides) to refer the trial

A System of Rules

Not only is it a vertical system, *it is also a system of rules*. This has important constitutional implications. Historically, one of the great values of law—one that people have fought and died for—is its potential to place limits upon authoritarian state power. Indeed, it can be said that the great struggles of the eighteenth and nineteenth centuries were supposed to have secured *legal control of government as a constitutional principle* such that even fierce critics, including EP Thompson, have affirmed its centrality:[30]

> [T]here is a difference between arbitrary power and the rule of law. We ought to expose the shams and inequities which may be concealed beneath this law. But the rule of law itself, the imposing of effective inhibitions upon power and the defence of the citizen from power's all-intrusive claims, seems to me to be an unqualified human good.

However, in the realm of criminal justice in which the order maintenance role of the state is most apparent, senior judges have not only acquiesced in *governmental control of the judges* but also instituted a system of *governance by rules*.

'Rule by rules' markedly differs from the rule of law both in terms of process and substance. At common law, the rule of law requires judges to be independent of, not captive to, government. It requires that laws be made openly 'not in holes and corners'. It requires that judges should preside over the court rather than strong arm the parties under the guise of 'management'. The well-spring of the common law has been the crucible of the trial, a participatory process in which the matrix of facts and the arguments of counsel frame the judgments of the court. It is in this way that the principles of the common law are forged but remain provisional, forever to be tested.

By contrast, the system of dispositive rules which has been inaugurated—principally the Judges' Rules, the state-induced guilty plea rules, and the Criminal Procedure Rules (CrimPR)[31]—has been the lode-carrier for the views and policies of a small group of judges historically hatched in secret, untested by forensic argument, and with the active support of the executive and now fashioned in the non-public setting of the Rule Committee, all in contradiction to notions of

judge at the sentencing stage to decisions of the Court of Appeal concerned with the issue of exceptional circumstances in the context of a disguised gun; and *R v RR* [2019] EWCA Crim 866 (in which the Court of Appeal remarked that, at the trial, it was 'unfortunate that the judge was not given more assistance by counsel in formulating the legal directions in relation to count 3').

[30] Edward Palmer Thompson, *Whigs and Hunters* (Pantheon Books 1975) 266.

[31] Albeit that so-called 'sentence indications' and the CrimPR received retrospective legislative sanction of a form that spoke eloquently to their dubious heritage and standing.

participatory democracy and now enforced through a disciplinary matrix. The common law was never thought to be the preserve of the few: it was understood and is ironically flaunted by judges themselves to be a constitutional asset that belongs to everyone.

Such rule by rules is the mark of a command economy in which the principal decisions are taken centrally and in which the judges and government, in private collaboration, own the territory and control the means of production. Whereas the market economy of law which preceded it functioned democratically, in great measure according to what was brought to it by the parties, the significant ingredients of the new order are the things brought to it by judges. While under the old system, judicial power was shrouded in ambiguity and 'elasticity' with such effect that they forgot whether they were engaged in 'judge-made law', 'administrative directions', or a mysterious something that is of a 'higher status', under the new peremptory regimen such gobbledygook is of less relevance in a climate which admits of little or no flexibility as the push for a trial-less system accelerates although it remains part of the fixture and fittings of those jurisdictions still burdened by the colonial inheritance where the imaginative work of rhetorical legitimation must continue.

The Legitimation Project

The continuation of judicial unintelligibility is, in fact, a necessary part of their claims to legitimacy. Today, the skeletons of the rule of law and the common law are clothed with the rags of judicial rhetoric but it is rhetoric that has been adjusted to paper over unsustainable claims previously advanced, to allow for changes of direction, and to make new formulations consonant with executive demands. When the judicial defence—'Plea bargaining has no place in the English criminal law'[32]—was exposed to mean: 'We do it all the time clandestinely'; and when the public were told that they should not think 'that the results of cases are agreed out of court'[33] meant: 'They shouldn't but they are', the language of legitimation had to change. It had to change for reasons fully in accord with classic Newspeak: first to project the world view of criminal judges as neutral, independent, and apolitical *and* to make other modes of thinking impossible. Other classic techniques were also employed: removing undesirable words and creating new ones.

Thus, 'plea bargaining' had to be replaced with 'advanced sentence indications'. Similarly, 'heavy increases in sentence' on conviction after trial became 'sentence discounts' for a guilty plea; punitive sentence additions became 'loss of credit'; loss of 'credit', in turn, became a fictional construct as expediency displaced remorse

[32] *R v Atkinson* [1978] 2 All ER 460.
[33] *Warring-Davies* (1978) Unreported 5854/c/77.

from the sentencing equation; the door to judicial bullying was opened by 'active case management'; 'freedom of plea' became 'involuntary plea styled as free'. Old legitimating forms based in (fictitious) factual claims (interests of victim; genuine remorse of the defendant; voluntariness of plea) had to be replaced by generic claims about 'efficiency' and 'interests of justice' within a market model. As bureaucratic mechanisms increasingly framed participants in the process (witnesses, lawyers, or defendants) as 'court-users', 'customers', and 'stakeholders',[34] the commodification of justice required that traditional understandings of 'efficiency' in the criminal justice context (ie, procedures and rules aimed at preventing wrongful convictions)[35] be supplanted by argot tolerable to the marketplace: 'efficiency' entails 'cost reduction' rather than 'system effectiveness';[36] and notions of 'economy' involve ever-diminishing obligations of the state towards defendants and ever-increasing obligations of defendants towards the state.

The legitimation project did not, however, rest only upon the manipulation of verbal formulations. It also required a change to a *methodology* which had left discretion in the hands of trial court judges. Plea bargaining was an uncertain delivery system. Research showed that while some judges extracted guilty pleas through threats of very severe sentences, others were not muscular enough and yet others mistakenly gave greatest rewards to those who were convicted after trial![37] This led to the so-called 'standard discount' aimed at taking much of the sentencing discretion out of the trial judge's hands. This too remained vulnerable because it was simply a standard which trial judges could not be relied upon to enforce. Hence the creation of a new delivery system: the judge as 'case manager' operating under a more rigid set of rules which required a more assertive approach to securing guilty pleas in the certain knowledge that they would be supported by the Court of Appeal. This too had to be reinforced by redefining defence lawyers as part of the prosecution project under threat of being reported to their disciplinary authority.

[34] The LEAN initiative that has been developed within HM Courts and Tribunals Service since 2008 describes itself as an attempt both to save money and improve 'service' to 'customers'. See Andrew Langdon QC, 'A Right, not a Commodity' *Counsel* (September 2017), who argues that this language-creep of officious directives is 'predicated on the basis that the courts deliver a product—justice, presumably—as a "service", which comes at a measurable cost, and that if the business case for the service does not add up then, one way or another, the users will have to pay, if they have the means, through court fees, if not through the removal of, or cuts to, legal aid.' An attempt to introduce criminal court charges on a scale according to the stage at which guilty pleas were entered was given a legislative footing but soon crumbled under the weight of complaint it attracted. cf *R (on the application of UNISON) (Appellant) v Lord Chancellor (Respondent)* [2017] UKSC 51 66.

[35] '… [W]hen the innocent become victims of the law, the law is not *merely inefficient*,—it does not merely fail of accomplishing its intended object—it injures the persons it was meant to protect; it creates the very evil it was to cure, and destroys the security it was made to preserve': Samuel Romily, *Observations on the Criminal Law of England* (1810) Note D, emphasis supplied.

[36] The recommendations are not cost-effective in the long term in light of all the dis-benefits: Luke Marsh, 'Leveson's Narrow Pursuit of Justice: Efficiency and Outcomes in the Criminal Process' (2016) 45(1) Common Law World Review 51.

[37] See, eg, David Moxon, *Sentencing Practice in the Crown Court* (Home Office Research Unit Study No 103, 1988); and Ralph Henham, *Sentence Discounts and the Criminal Process* (Ashgate 2001).

Even that delivery mode is not yet enough to move the system to the state's desired end: further diminution of jury trial and maximum reliance on guilty pleas. This remains work in progress, the Leveson Review breaking its own terms of reference and thereby offering cherries for future government picking.

The Leveson Review is, indeed, a reminder that law is not simply a set of internal rules and procedures advanced by legal institutions and legal actors but has a direct relationship to the political, social, economic, and cultural conditions of society. In the case of the criminal justice system, the architecture of 'justice', once disguised by claims of universality and equal treatment, is now directly related to the political economy of a state committed to an austerity philosophy, portended for more than fifty years in efforts to limit jury trial, marked by squeezing public services and attacking welfare provision. The new ideology is accordingly institutionalized not by data (to which it is in contradiction) but by incorporation into procedural rules redolent of central command and discipline and an overlay of government-inspired austerity neologisms.

In the result, senior judges, in close accord with the government, have rotated the criminal system on its axis. In place of an adversarial system run in co-operation with counsel, trial judges have been elevated to a position of managerial command, with the position of the Bar and defendants correspondingly lowered. Attempts to paper over this transformation by resort to claims of judicial independence and freedom from interests are no longer plausible.

Measurable outcomes of this political arrangement include the movement of cases out of the Crown Court into the Magistrates' Courts, where research evidence shows bias towards the prosecution and particularly police evidence. Alongside this, in a climate of ever-diminishing rights of defendants and defence lawyers, senior judges, using the language of 'system efficiency' (ie, reductions in legal aid and the right to jury trial) and 'advanced plea indications' (ie, state-induced guilty pleas), are normalizing miscarriages of justice by transferring them out of the public arena of jury trials and into the routinized processing of cases in the lower courts and through the guilty plea regime.[38]

The Politics of the Judiciary

A critical insight into the politics of the system is the way in which senior judges were subordinated into accepting reformulations demanded by the executive.

[38] See an early assessment of this in Lee Bridges and Mike McConville, 'Keeping Faith With Their Own Convictions: The Royal Commission on Criminal Justice' (1994) 57(1) Modern Law Review 75. Many miscarriages of justice do not involve distortion by the enmity seen in recent notorious cases such as the Birmingham Six and Maguire Seven cases. It is the distortion by 'efficiency' that is now most likely to cause casualties of the innocent and ones which will not call forth campaigning champions (outside the families involved) such as Ludovic Kennedy, Chris Mullin, Robert Kee, and Paul Foot.

During a period in which breaches of investigative rules placed political pressure on judges to regulate the police in ways that the 1918 formulation had manifestly failed to do, the attempt to bring in a PACE-type form of regulation was summarily thrown out by the executive acting as a mouthpiece of the police. Indeed, such was the influence of the police lobby on Home Office thinking that, to coin a phrase, it meant that 'there were four in this constitutional marriage; so it was a bit crowded'.

When, soon afterwards, departures from the Rules and deep-seated corruption within the police emerged in dramatic form, attempts by the judges at more closely regulating the police in 'the interests of the public' were shot down by naked threats that the judges would be subject to severe criticism by the Home Secretary in Parliament acting on an agenda that was constructed 'in the interests of the police'.

Accordingly, to classify this system as a *legal* system is to misunderstand its mission and character. To define this system as a *social* system is to make a category error which underplays its manufacture, structure, and purpose. To ask if an analysis of individual cases can answer the question whether the system is political is to ask the wrong question and is a failure of method. As we have seen, it is a *political* system, in the politicization of which the senior judiciary have taken more than an active role. It is one thing to fashion a system, as was openly done for many years, in which it was hard to distinguish the judges from the police; it is quite another to have covertly created a system which has hardened the task of distinguishing the judges either from the police or the executive.

Compounding this, the political character of the system has been perpetuated in colonial settings. It is in this context, home and afar, that senior judges as moral entrepreneurs, have bestowed on occupied territories 'superior' wisdom, guidance, and leadership. In the afterglow of the Empire, senior judges, whether sitting in the Privy Council in London or reposing in the highest courts of former colonial outposts, continue as legal missionaries proselytizing the common law and overseeing the implementation of rules, discredited and long-discarded in England and Wales.

The Westminster Model

On one constitutional formulation, in Britain the core functions of the state are described as an allocation of powers between the legislature, executive, and the judiciary; whereas, on another, sovereignty is bipolar, residing in the power of Parliament to decide what the law is to be and the power of the courts to decide, case by case, what the law is.[39] Whatever formulation is preferred, however, the

[39] Stephen Sedley, *Lions Under the Throne: Essays on the History of English Public Law* (CUP 2015) 173. As stated in *R (on the Application of Miller) (Appellant) v The Prime Minister (Respondent)* [2019] UKSC 41, para 55: 'The Government exists because it has the confidence of the House of Commons. It has no democratic legitimacy other than that.'

fundamental understanding is that it is contrary to the constitution for the executive to seek to invade the province of the other arms particularly by using unseen and undeclared means.[40] Yet this is precisely what happened in the criminal justice system when the executive subordinated the judiciary to its political will. But that regrettably is not the end of the story because, in the process, the executive also interfered with the role and function of Parliament.

Indeed, the construction of the modern criminal justice system was undertaken by the executive and the judiciary *out of sight of and with the purpose of actively misleading Parliament*. Thus, when the reformulation of the Judges' Rules was being undertaken over the period 1961–64, efforts by Members of Parliament to play a role in the process were actively deflected by misinformation. MPs were repeatedly misled into believing that the judges *and the judges alone* were reviewing the Rules whereas in fact the process, at all stages, was directed by the Home Office who came to mastermind it.[41] Thus, from the outset, to prevent debate and to deflect questioning, the account given to MPs by the Home Secretary (Rab Butler) was crafted (no doubt with the assistance of briefs written by Charles Cunningham and Philip Allen) to appear that the matter was for the judges alone but that the Home Secretary would use his good offices to relay questions or information to the LCJ: 'The judges have given me an assurance that they will look into the question of interrogation ... before a man is charged'; as to whether submissions could be presented to the judges: 'I shall be glad to get in touch with the Lord Chief Justice on the point ... so that we can be sure that if they wish to be made there is a quarter where this can be received'; as to whether the result would be made public: 'I shall have to consult the Lord Chief Justice. This is a matter for the judges.'[42]

Whatever excuse for conveying the impression of dissociation from the process at the outset, there could be none after June 1962 when the LCJ submitted the First Draft and following which the Home Office assumed full management of the process. Yet, in reporting to Parliament, the deception continued and was indeed intensified. The Home Office repeatedly used the passive voice to convey the impression that it was merely the recipient of information *from* the judges. Thus, the Under-Secretary of State informed the House of Commons:

> '[The Rules] are being re-examined by the Lord Chief Justice and his colleagues, and *I am informed that they have made substantial progress*. I have no doubt that

[40] And *R (on the Application of Miller) (Appellant) v The Prime Minister (Respondent)* [2019] UKSC 41 emphatically demonstrates that there are limits (supervised by the courts) to the way in which the prerogative power is used by the executive holding, in the particular case, that the executive could not use the prerogative to prorogue Parliament if prorogation has the effect of 'frustrating or preventing, without reasonable justification, the ability of Parliament to carry out its constitutional functions as a legislature and as the body responsible for the supervision of the executive' (para 50).

[41] With the assistance of the Lord Chancellor's Department.

[42] HC Deb 30 March 1961, vol 637, cols 1512–14 at col 1514 (Home Secretary, Rab Butler).

all the points raised by the hon. Member will come within their purview, but he will appreciate *that it is not for me to interrogate the Lord Chief Justice on exactly what he is doing* (emphasis supplied).[43]

The same pretence was continued by the next Home Secretary, Henry Brooke:

I am informed that progress is being made with the review and that any revised Rules will in due course be published and brought to the attention of the police and others concerned (emphasis supplied).[44]

I understand that it is hoped that *the review now being carried out by the judges* will be completed by the end of the year (emphasis supplied).[45]

The new Rules are the responsibility of the judges and not of the Home Secretary; but I know that the views of chief officers of police were available to the judges before the Rules were made (emphasis supplied).[46]

In the result, MPs were belittled, being treated like 'loyal and dutiful subjects'.[47] Requests by MPs for the review to be in the form of a public inquiry or one to which oral evidence could be submitted were summarily dismissed, as in the following exchange:[48]

Mr Fletcher MP: asked … whether those desirous of making representations on the subject will have an opportunity of doing so; and what procedure is contemplated for this purpose.

David Renton (JOINT UNDER-SECRETARY OF STATE): … The Lord Chief Justice has authorised [the Home Secretary] to say that while the judges—who have themselves the widest experience of the operation of the existing Rules—do not propose to invite evidence, they will take account of any representations which may be made to them in writing, through the Secretary to the Lord Chief Justice at the Royal Courts of Justice.

Mr Fletcher: While appreciating that reply, may I ask the Joint Undersecretary to consider the desirability of people who so desire making verbal representations to the judges … ?

Mr Renton: No, this would not have been appropriate. This is not a public inquiry. It is the desire of [the Home Secretary] to obtain the opinion of the judges about this matter in the light of their own very great experience, but if anybody has

43 HC Deb 9 May 1963, vol 677, cols 680–799, 677–78.
44 HC Deb 23 May 1963, vol 678, cols 629–30629.
45 HC Deb 1 August 1963, vol 682, col 128W.
46 HC Deb 28 January 1964, vol 688, cols 209–12209.
47 HC Deb 26 November 1963, vol 685, cols 81–210 113 (Mr Leslie Hale MP).
48 HC Deb 1 May 1961, vol 639, cols 905–6905.

any information which he thinks may be of help to the judges and delivers it to them in writing, the judges will be glad to consider it.

The clear message throughout all the debates was that MPs were not to interfere, a message summarized by Leslie Hale MP as being virtually told to 'keep off the grass'.[49] Whatever the legal technicality, with some MPs (like commentators afterwards) regarding the Rules as legislation,[50] it is of the highest constitutional significance that the House of Commons was shut out of the review by a storyline carefully constructed by civil servants and their Ministers comprising a concoction of half-truths, casuistry, and downright lies.

With one arm of the state—Parliament—placed at the margins and deceived, a second—the executive—was able to run the show, breaking the resistance of the third arm—the judges—through strong-arm tactics familiar to regimes that are something other than democratic. Not only was a key element, the Civil Service, unelected and unrepresentative[51] it was also unaccountable, as were the judges. Once, however, the warm shower of rhetoric visited upon the judges (often self-applied it has to be said) was replaced with the acid bath of threats and public humiliation, these two arms linked in such a way that defendants were marginalized, the role of their lawyers and the jury diminished over all of which actions the third arm, the legislature, was induced to throw a retrospective veneer of respectability.

In all of this, the competence and integrity of the personnel of the executive—civil servants and Ministers—are of fundamental importance precisely because the constitution is not self-implementing. Much of it is, as Geoffrey Wilson[52] has pointed out, regulated by *convention*. Accordingly, while Ministers may withhold information from the elected representatives on various grounds, including but not limited to national security, they are supposedly under a solemn duty not to actively mislead or lie to Parliament,[53] a duty which is not to be found in any

[49] HC Deb 26 November 1963, vol 685, cols 81–210 113 (Mr Hale MP).

[50] See, eg, Reginald Paget MP: '... [I]s [the Home Secretary] aware that I, at any rate, have always been brought up to believe that it was for us to make laws and for the judges to interpret them? This appears to be an act of legislation by the judges.' The Home Secretary (Henry Brooke) replied: 'This is not an act of legislation ...' HC Deb 28 January 1964, vol 688, cols 209–12209 211.

[51] Like the LCJs, permanent Under-Secretaries at the Home Office have been drawn, almost exclusively, from either Oxford or Cambridge (Sir John Anderson, 1922–32, being a graduate of Edinburgh).

[52] Geoffrey Wilson, 'Postscript: The Courts, Law and Convention' in Rt Hon Lord Nolan and Sir Stephen Sedley, *The Making & Remaking of the British Constitution* (Blackstone Press Ltd 1997). Whether the courts can enforce conventions is a highly contentious matter. On the so-called 'education convention' and 'tripartite convention' see *R (Evans) v Attorney-General [2015] UKSC 21* discussed in Mark Elliott, 'A Tangled Constitutional Web: The Black-Spider Memos and the British Constitution's Relational Architecture' (2015) Public Law 539; TRS Allan, 'Law, Democracy and Constitutionalism: Reflections on Evans v Attorney-General' (2016) 75(1) Cambridge Law Journal 38; Richard Ekins and Christopher Forsyth, 'Judging the Public Interest: the Rule of Law vs. the Rule of Courts' (Policy Exchange 2015) (responses to which are available on the Policy Exchange website).

[53] It was breach of this convention (not any law) that led to the resignation of John Profumo, the Secretary of State for War, following lying to the House of Commons about his affair with Christine Keeler (discussed in ch 6). By contrast, telling a blatant lie in a television programme

statute but in a convention which lies at the heart of the constitution.[54] However, this convention was disregarded because members of the executive lacked the integrity that self-enforcement relies upon. Contrary to what MPs were told, the master-builders were not the judges but the executive acting covertly. The confidential internal papers, filleted and filtered as they are, provide a shocking glimpse into the activities of this Secret State[55] operating through partially recorded confidential meetings and wholly unrecorded private encounters, all protected by the withholding or destruction of historical records and misinformation given to Parliament.

Echoing the sentiments of the nineteenth century political reformist William Cobbett who spoke of the need to avow sentiments in a public, constitutional manner 'not in holes and corners', Gross LJ recently said[56] that the rule of law was a priceless asset and that open justice was both a hallmark and a safeguard, 'a fundamental principle of the common law and a means of ensuring public confidence in our legal system . . .' In place of such constitutional fictions, the Home Office papers lay bare an executive lacking in integrity, without respect for the 'independence' of the judiciary, and with an agenda that may be far removed from that of Parliament, which it too is willing to subvert. They also reveal a senior judiciary, hidden behind the shibboleths of the 'rule of law' and 'judicial independence', which became at a critical point in the history of criminal justice, a cat's paw for the executive. When properly unpacked, the mask of rhetoric reveals more than the face of justice.

about a parliamentary matter, though considered dishonourable, will not necessarily lead to resignation: see, eg, Alistair Carmichael who leaked an inaccurate memorandum from the Scottish Office and denied all knowledge of it when interviewed on *Channel Four News*, 'Alistair Carmichael Admits Trying to Mislead Leaked Memo Investigation' *BBC News* (10 November 2015). Under today's Ministerial Code: 'It is of paramount importance that Ministers give accurate and truthful information to Parliament, correcting any inadvertent error at the earliest opportunity. Ministers who knowingly mislead Parliament will be expected to offer their resignation to the Prime Minister; Ministers should be as open as possible with Parliament and the public, refusing to provide information only when disclosure would not be in the public interest, which should be decided in accordance with the relevant statutes and the *Freedom of Information Act* 2000' (*Ministerial Code*, August 2019, 1.3c and 1.3d).

[54] Where information is withheld, it may be possible for the House of Commons to hold the government 'in contempt of parliament'. This occurred for the first time under Theresa May's government on 4 December 2018 after persistent refusal by Ministers to release the legal advice given by the Attorney-General Geoffrey Cox to the Prime Minister and her cabinet on her Brexit deal. See Sam Coates, 'MPs Find Ministers in Contempt over Brexit Legal Row' *The Times* (4 December 2018).

[55] See also Edward Palmer Thompson, 'The Secret State' in Edward Palmer Thompson, *Writing by Candlelight* (Merlin Press 1980).

[56] *Guardian News and Media Ltd v AB CD* [2014] EWCA Crim (B1) 2: 'The Rule of Law is a priceless asset of our country and a foundation of our Constitution. One aspect of the Rule of Law—both a hallmark and a safeguard—is open justice, which includes criminal trials being held in public and the publication of the names of defendants. Open justice is both a fundamental principle of the common law and a means of ensuring public confidence in our legal system; exceptions are rare and must be justified on the facts. Any such exceptions must be necessary and proportionate. No more than the minimum departure from open justice will be countenanced.'

In the result, the purity of the 'Westminster Model'[57] assiduously exported around the globe,[58] is now clearly tainted. The internal files give glimpses of a clandestine world in which private undertakings were able to be given on prosecution policy by the Director of Public Prosecutions,[59] private advice offered on the interpretation of the law by the LCJ,[60] and where meetings between the senior judiciary and the police[61] and between the executive and the senior judiciary,[62] most unrecorded and many not even noted, were allowed to settle matters of policy bearing upon the 'public interest'. The Westminster Model—based around accountability through Parliamentary supremacy located within a representative democracy in which the conventions of the constitution are respected—as broadly descriptive of the British political arrangements, at least in the area of criminal justice, is falsified by the evidence in the Home Office files and no longer tenable.

[57] See, eg, Andrew Gamble, 'Theories of British Politics' (1990) 38 Political Studies 404; and Patrick Dunleavy, 'The Westminster Model and the Distinctiveness of British Politics' in Patrick Dunleavy and others (eds), *Developments in British Politics* 8th Series (Palgrave Macmillan 2006). The Model has come in for criticism over such things as government overload, the activities of pressure groups, special advisers, and the influence of the executive. See, eg, Anthony King, 'Overload: Problems of Governing in the 1970s' (1975) 23(2 & 3) Political Studies 162; Anthony Birch, 'The Theory and Practice of Modern British Democracy' in Jeffrey Jowell and Dawn Oliver (eds), *The Changing Constitution* (Clarendon Press 1989). For an overview and critical appraisal, see Mark Bevir, *Democratic Governance* (Princeton University Press 2010).

[58] See, eg, the discussion in *DPP v Mollison (Jamaica)* [2003] UKPC 6 where Lord Bingham said: 'Whatever overlap there may be under constitutions on the Westminster model between the exercise of executive and legislative powers, the separation between the exercise of judicial powers on the one hand and legislative and executive powers on the other is total or effectively so.' The alleged separation, based on the rule of law, was recently described by Lord Steyn as 'a characteristic feature of democracies': *R (Anderson) v Secretary of State for the Home Department* [2002] 3 WLR 1800, 1821–22, para 50. Similar observations were made in *The State v Khoyratty* [2006] UKPC 13 in respect of the Constitution of Mauritius and *Fuller v The Attorney General of Belize* [2011] UKPC 23 in respect of Belize. See also William Dale, 'The Making and Remaking of Commonwealth Constitutions' (1993) 42 (1) International & Comparative Law Quarterly 67; Andrew Harding, 'The "Westminster Model" Constitution Overseas: Transplantation, Adaptation and Development in Commonwealth States' (2004) (Winter) Oxford University Commonwealth Law Journal 143; Harshan Kumarasingham, *A Political Legacy of the British Empire—Power and the Parliamentary System in Post-Colonial India and Sri Lanka* (I.B. Tauris 2013); Kevin Tan, *The Constitution of Singapore: A Contextual Analysis* (Bloomsbury 2015) and *Tan Seet Eng v Attorney General* [2015] SGCA 59 1.

[59] See above, eg, ch 5, 1.

[60] Above, ch 7.

[61] Above, ch 5; ch 6.

[62] Above, ch 5 and 6 *passim*.

Bibliography

Abrahams Gerald, *Police Questioning and the Judges' Rules* (Oyez Publications 1964).

Ackroyd Carol, Margolis Karen, Rosenhead Jonathan, and Tim Shallice, *The Technology of Political Control* (Pelican 1977).

Adams Francis Sir (ed), *Criminal Law and Practice in New Zealand* (Sweet & Maxwell (NZ) 1964).

Advisory Council on National Records and Archives, *14th Annual Report 2016–17*.

'Admissibility of Confessions–Judges' Rules' (1960–62) 1 Adelaide Law Review 85.

Alderson Karl, 'Powers and Responsibilities: Reforming NSW Criminal Investigation Law' (PhD thesis, Faculty of Law, UNSW 2001).

Alemika Etannibi, 'Policing and Perceptions of Police in Nigeria' (1998) 11(4) (Winter) Police Studies 161.

Allan Trevor, 'Legislative Supremacy and the Rule of Law: Democracy and Constitutionalism' (1985) 44 Cambridge Law Journal 111.

Allan Trevor, 'Parliamentary Sovereignty: Law, Politics and Revolution' (1997) 113 Law Quarterly Review 443.

Allan Trevor, 'Interpretation, Injustice, and Integrity' (2016) 36(1) Oxford Journal of Legal Studies 58.

Allan Trevor, 'Law, Democracy and Constitutionalism: Reflections on Evans v Attorney-General' (2016) 75(1) Cambridge Law Journal 38.

Allen Lord, 'State Service: Reflections of a Bureaucrat' in *The Home Office: Perspectives on Policy and Administration* (Royal Institute of Public Administration 1983) .

Allison John, *The English Historical Constitution* (CUP 2007).

Alverstone Viscount, *Recollections of Bar and Bench* (Edward Arnold 1914).

Ames Jonathan, 'Fraud Trial Delayed by Ten Months as Court "Crisis" Deepens' *The Times* (London, 24 September 2019).

Ames Jonathan and Baksi Catherine '"Inept" Prosecutors Blamed for Fall in Rape Convictions' *The Times* (London, 19 September 2019).

Anderson David and Killingray David (eds), *Policing the Empire: Government Authority and Control, 1830–1940* (Manchester University Press 1991).

Angiolini Rt Hon Dame Elish DBE QC, *Report of the Independent Review into The Investigation and Prosecution of Rape in London* (2015).

Angiolini Rt Hon Dame Elish DBE QC, *Report of the Independent Review of Deaths and Serious Incidents in Police Custody* (January 2017).

Annison Harry, 'Interpreting the Politics of the Judiciary: The British Senior Judicial Tradition and the Pre-emptive Turn in Criminal Justice' (2014) 41(3) Journal of Law & Society 339.

Annison Harry, 'Weeding the Garden: The Third Way, the Westminster Tradition and Imprisonment for Public Protection' (2014) 18(1) Theoretical Criminology 38.

Annison Harry, *Dangerous Politics: Risk, Political Vulnerability and Penal Policy* (OUP 2015).

Archbold John Frederick, *A Digest of the Law, Practice and Procedure Relating to Indictable Offences* ('Archbold) (2nd edn, Sweet & Maxwell 1918).

Aronson Mark, Reaburn Norman Stephen, and Weinberg Mark, *Litigation—Evidence and Procedure* (2nd edn, Butterworths 1979).

Arvind TT and Stirton Lindsay, 'Legal Ideology, Legal Doctrine and the UK's Top Judges' [2016] Public Law 418.

Ascoli David, *The Queen's Peace* (Hamish Hamilton 1979).

Ashley Frederick William, *My Sixty Years in the Law* (John Lane, The Bodley Head 1936).

Aspden Kester, *The Hounding of David Oluwale* (Vintage 2008).

Auld Robin Sir, *The Criminal Courts Review* (Royal Courts of Justice 2001).

Australian Law Journal (1937) 11(4) 113.

Bailey Stephen '"Nuff said": Ridge v Baldwin' in Juss Satvinder and Sunkin Maurice (eds), *Landmark Cases in Public Law* (Hart 2017).

Baldwin John, 'Legal Advice in the Police Station' (1992) 142 New Law Journal 1762.

Baldwin John, 'Review of Judicial Discretion in the House of Lords (David Robertson)' (1999) 19 Legal Studies 580.

Baldwin John and McConville Mike, *Negotiated Justice* (Martin Robertson 1977).

Baldwin John and McConville Mike, *Jury Trials* (Clarendon Press 1979).

Bar Council, *Well-being at the Bar* (The Positive Group April 2015).

Barendt Eric, 'The Separation of Powers and Constitutional Government' [1995] Public Law 599.

Barnes John Arundel, *Who Should Know What? Social Science, Privacy and Ethics* (CUP 1979).

Barr Caelainn, 'Thousands of Rape Reports Inaccurately Recorded by Police' *The Guardian* (19 September 2019).

Baxi Upendra, *The Crisis of the Indian Legal System* (Vikas Publishers 1980).

BBC News, 'Alistair Carmichael Admits Trying to Mislead Leaked Memo Investigation' (*BBC website*, 10 November 2015).

BBC News, 'Guildford Four Man Gerry Conlon's "Living Hell" Revealed' (*BBC website*, 29 December 2017).

BBC News, 'Julian Cole: Three Bedfordshire Police Officers Sacked' (*BBC website*, 22 October 2018).

BBC News, 'Bloody Sunday: Soldier F Faces Murder Charges' (*BBC website*, 14 March 2019).

BBC News, 'Essex Police Child Abuse Officers Jailed for Misconduct' (*BBC website*, 10 May 2019).

BBC News, 'Kwasi Kwarteng Criticised for "Biased Judges" Comment' (*BBC website*, 12 September 2019).

Beatson Rt Hon Lord Justice, 2017 Atkin Lecture: 'Judicial Independence: Internal and External Challenges and Opportunities' (The Reform Club, London 14 November 2017).

Bell Emma 'Normalizing the Exceptional: British Colonial Policing Cultures Come Home' (online 2013).

Bentham Jeremy, 'Principles of Judicial Procedure' in *The Works of Jeremy Bentham*, vol ii (Bowring edition, 1843).

Bentham Martin, 'Rush for Gender Equality with Top Judges "Could Have Appalling Consequences for Justice"' *Evening Standard* (London, 21 September 2015).

Benton Lauren, *Law and Colonial Cultures: Legal Regimes in World History, 1400–1900* (CUP 2002).

Berger Mark, 'Legislating Confession Law in Great Britain: A Statutory Approach to Police Interrogations' (1990) 24 University of Michigan Journal of Law Reform 1.

Berlins Marcel, 'Call to Ease Police Questioning Methods' *The Times* (London, 17 July 1971).

Better Government Initiative, *Good Government: Reforming Parliament and the Executive* (Institute for Government 2010).

Bevir Mark, *Democratic Governance* (Princeton University Press 2010).

Bevir Mark and Rhodes Roderick, *Governance Stories* (Routledge 2006).

Bickel Alexander, *The Least Dangerous Branch: The Supreme Court at the Bar of Politics* (2nd edn, Yale University Press 1986).

Bindman Geoffrey, 'Keep an Eye on the Judges' (2010) 160 New Law Journal 880.

Bingham Lord, 'The Judges: Active or Passive?' in Marshall Peter James (ed), *Proceedings of the British Academy, 2005 Lectures* (OUP 2007) 139.

Bingham Tom, *The Rule of Law* (Penguin Books 2010).

Birch Anthony, 'The Theory and Practice of Modern British Democracy' in Jowell Jeffrey and Oliver Dawn (eds), *The Changing Constitution* (Clarendon Press 1989).

Birch Diane, 'Suffering in Silence: A Cost-Benefit Analysis of Section 34 of the Criminal Justice and Public Order Act 1994' [1997] Criminal Law Review 769.

Blackwell Michael, 'Old Boys' Networks, Family Connections and the English Legal Profession' [2012] Public Law 425.

Bleakley Paul, 'Cleaning up the Dirty Squad: Using the Obscene Publications Act as a Weapon of Social Control' (2019) 8(1) State Crime Journal 19.

Blom-Cooper Louis, *Public Inquiries: Wrong Route on Bloody Sunday* (Hart 2017).

Bogdanor Vernon, *Politics and the Constitution: Essays on British Government* (Dartmouth 1996).

Bokhary Hon Mr Justice NPJ (ed-in-chief) and Harris Graham QC (gen ed), *Archbold Hong Kong* (Sweet & Maxwell 2017).

Bork Robert, *The Tempting of America: The Political Seduction of the Law* (Sinclair-Stevenson 1990).

Bottomley A Keith, Coleman Clive, Dixon David, Gill Martin, and Wall David, *The Impact of PACE: Policing in a Northern Force* (Hull Centre for Criminology and Criminal Justice 1991).

Bottoms Anthony and Stevenson Simon, '"What Went Wrong?": Criminal Justice Policy in England and Wales, 1945–70' in Downes David (ed), *Unravelling Criminal Justice* (Macmillan 1992).

Bourne JM, *Patronage and Society in Nineteenth-Century England* (Edward Arnold 1986).

Bovens Mark, 'Analyzing and Assessing Accountability: A Conceptual Framework' (2007) 13 European Law Journal 447.

Bowcott Owen, 'More than Half of Judges under 40 in England and Wales are Women' *The Guardian* (30 July 2015).

Bowcott Owen, 'Criminal Cases Delayed across England and Wales as Courts Lie Idle' *The Guardian* (19 August 2019).

Bowker Archibald Edgar, *A Lifetime with the Law* (W. H. Allen 1961).

Bowring Philip, 'Lessons from 1970s Hong Kong: The Danger of Unchecked Police Powers, and how a Judge-Led Inquiry and an Amnesty Can Work' *The South China Morning Post* (20 October 2019).

Boyle Andrew, *Trenchard—Man of Vision* (Collins 1962).

Brace Matthew, 'PC Gets 10 Years for Drug Smuggling' *The Independent* (25 February 1997).

Brabin Mr Justice, *Inquiry into the Case of Timothy John Evans 1965–66* (National Archives CAB 143).

Braddick Michael, *The Common Freedom of the People: John Lilburne and The English Revolution* (OUP 2018).

Bridges Lee and McConville Mike, 'Keeping Faith with their Own Convictions: The Royal Commission on Criminal Justice' (1994) 57(1) Modern Law Review 75.

Brogden Mike, *The Police: Autonomy and Consent* (Academic Press 1982).

Brogden Mike, 'The Emergence of the Police—The Colonial Dimension' (1987) 27 British Journal of Criminology 4.

Brown David, *Detention at the Police Station under the Police and Criminal Evidence Act 1984* (HMSO 1989).

Brown David, *Investigating Burglary: The Effects of PACE*, Home Office Research Study No 123 (Home Office 1989).

Brown Douglas, 'Reform of the Administration of Criminal Justice' (1966) 2 East African Law Journal 248.

Brown John, *Policing by Multi-Racial Consent* (Bedford Square Press 1982).

Brown Lord, 'The Unaccountability of Judges: Surely their Strength not their Weakness' in Forsyth Christopher, Elliot Mark, Jhaveri Swati, Ramsden Michael, and Scully Hill Anne (eds), *Effective Judicial Review: A Cornerstone of Good Governance* (OUP 2010).

Brown Mark, 'The Politics of Penal Excess and the Echo of Colonial Penalty' (2002) 4 Punishment and Society 403.

Brown Mark, '"An Unqualified Human Good?" On Rule of Law, Globalization, and Imperialism' [2018] 43(4) Law & Social Inquiry 1391.

Browne Douglas, *The Rise of Scotland Yard* (George Harrap & Co 1956).

Bryan Ian, *Interrogation and Confession* (Dartmouth Publishing Co 1997).

Bunyan Tony, *The History and Practice of the Political Police in Britain* (Julian Friedman 1977).

Burden Peter, 'More and More Muggers: But the Police Fight Back' *Daily Mail* (21 January 1982).

Burnett Ian Sir, 'Sir Ian Burnett Sworn in as Lord Chief Justice of England and Wales' (*Courts and Tribunals Judiciary website*, 2 October 2017).

Burnett Lord CJ, 'A Changing Judiciary for a Modern Age' (Judiciary of England & Wales 2019).

Burnton Rt Hon Stanley Sir, *Delivering Justice in an Age of Austerity* JUSTICE (London 2015).

Butterworths, *Hong Kong Police Force Handbook* (LexisNexis 2004).

Bwonwong'a Momanyi, *Criminal Procedures in Kenya* (East African Educational Publishers 1994).

Cabinet Office, *The Cabinet Manual* (October 2011).

Campbell Duncan, 'Man Convicted of Theft in 1976 Cleared after Googling his Arresting Officer' *The Guardian* (17 January 2018).

Campbell Duncan and Evans Rob, 'Files Shed Light on Alleged Efforts to Hide 1970s Police Corruption' *The Guardian* (19 August 2018).

Casciani Dominic, 'Undercover Policing Inquiry: Why It Matters' *The Guardian* (28 July 2015).

Cawley Laurence, 'Magistrate Court Cases Take a Week Longer to Complete' (*BBC News online*, 17 November 2016).

Challenor Harold and Draper Alfred, *Tanky Challenor* (Leo Cooper 1990).

Chanock Martin, *Law, Custom, and Social Order: The Colonial Experience in Malawi and Zambia* (CUP 1985).

Chapman Leslie, *Your Disobedient Servant* (Chatto & Windus 1978).

Cheltenham Chronicle (21 May 1904).

Chibnall Steve, *Law and Order News* (Tavistock 1977).

Clarry Daniel, 'Institutional Independence and the Privy Council' (2014) 3 Cambridge Journal of International & Comparative Law 46.

Coates Sam, 'MPs Find Ministers in Contempt over Brexit Legal Row' *The Times* (London, 4 December 2018).
Coates Tim (ed), *The Strange Story of Adolf Beck* (TSO 1904, 1999 reprint).
Cobain Ian, Bowcott Owen, and Norton-Taylor Richard, 'Britain Destroyed Records of Colonial Regimes' *The Guardian* (18 April 2012).
Cohen Phil, 'Policing the Working Class City' in Fine Bob, Kinsey Richard, Lea John, Picciotto Sol, and Young Jock (eds), *Capitalism and the Rule of Law* (Hutchinson 1979).
Cohen Stanley, *Images of Deviance* (Penguin 1970).
Cohen Stanley, *Folk Devils and Moral Panics* (Paladin 1972).
Cohen William, *Rulers of the Empire: The French Colonial Service in Africa* (Hoover Institution Press 1971).
Cole Bankole, 'Post-Colonial Systems' in Mawby Rob (ed), *Policing Across the World: Issues for the Twenty-first Century* (UCL Press 1999).
Coleman Clive, 'Red Diesel Trial Collapse Shows "Systemic Disclosure Failings"' (*BBC website*, 29 April 2018).
Committee on Minister's Powers, *Donoghmore Committee Report* (Cmd 4060, 1932).
Cowell David, Jones Trevor, and Young Jock, *Policing the Riots* (Junction Books 1982).
Cox Barry, Shirley John, and Short Martin, *The Fall of Scotland Yard* (Penguin Books 1977).
Craig Paul, 'Formal and Substantive Conceptions of the Rule of Law: An Analytical Framework' [1997] Public Law 467.
Craig Paul, 'Limits of Law: Reflections from Private and Public Law' in Barber Nicholas, Ekins Richard, and Yowell Paul (eds), *Lord Sumption and the Limits of the Law* (Hart 2016).
Crawford Ian, *The Profumo Affair* (White Lodge 1963).
Criminal Law Review, 'Comment' [1963].
Criminal Law Revision Committee, *Eleventh Report: Evidence (General)* (Cmd 4991, HMSO 1972).
Critchley Thomas Alan, *A History of Police in England and Wales* (2nd edn, Patterson Smith 1972).
Daily Herald (3 March 1961).
Daily Mail (2, 20 May 1904;21, 22 September 1906; 18 November 1955; 5 July 1963; 4 November 2015).
Daily Mail, 'Hannam of the Yard Guards Secret File'—'Confidential to the Home Office' (19 November 1955).
Daily Telegraph (2 May 1904; 8 August 1904; 3 March 1961).
Daily Telegraph, 'Muggings of Women Double' (4 February 1982).
Dale William, 'The Making and Remaking of Commonwealth Constitutions' (1993) 42 International & Comparative Law Quarterly 67.
Das Dilip and Verma Arvind, 'The Armed Police in the British Colonial Tradition' (1998) 21(2) Policing: An International Journal of Police Strategies & Management 354.
Davies Anthony, 'Sentences for Sale: A New Look at Plea Bargaining in England and America' [1970] Criminal Law Review 150.
Davis John, *Youth and the Condition of Britain* (Athlone Press 1990).
De Simone Daniel, 'Stephen Port: Officers Refuse to Answer Watchdog's Questions' (*BBC News website*, 26 July 2018).
Dearden Lizzie, 'Only 1.7% of Reported Rapes Prosecuted in England and Wales, New Figures Show' *The Independent* (25 April 2019).
Deflem Mathieu, 'Law Enforcement in British Colonial Africa: A Comparative Analysis of Imperial Policing in Nyasaland, the Gold Coast, and Kenya' (1994) 17(1) Police Studies 45.

Denning Lord, *The Denning Report: The Profumo Affair* (Pimlico Edition 1992).
Dennis Ian, 'Prosecution Disclosure: Are the Problems Insoluble?' (2018) 10 Criminal Law Review 829.
Denyer Roderick, 'The Changing Role of the Judge in the Criminal Process' (2010) 14 International Journal of Evidence & Proof 96.
Denyer Roderick, *Case Management in the Crown Court* (Hart 2008).
Departmental Committee on Jury Service, *Report* (Morris Committee) (Cmd 2627, HMSO 1965).
Derby Daily Telegraph (2 May 1904).
Devlin Lord, 'Judges and Lawmakers' (1976) 39 Modern Law Review 1.
Devlin Lord, 'Judges, Government and Politics' (1978) 41(5) Modern Law Review 501.
Devlin Lord, *The Judge* (OUP 1979).
Devlin Patrick, *Trial by Jury* (Stevens 1956).
Devlin Patrick, *The Criminal Prosecution in England* (OUP 1960).
Devlin Patrick, *Easing the Passing* (The Bodley Head 1985).
Dicey Albert Venn, *An Introduction to the Study of the Law of the Constitution* (Macmillan and Co 1885).
Dilnot George, *The Trial of the Detectives* (Charles Scribner's Sons 1928).
Diplock Lord, *Legal Procedures for Dealing with Terrorists* (Cmd 5185, 1972).
Diplock Lord, *Report of a Committee to Consider, in the Context of Civil Liberties, and Human Rights, Measures to Deal with Terrorism in Northern Ireland* (Cmd 5847, 1975).
'Discussion' (1960–61) 3 The Criminal Law Quarterly 351.
Dixon David, 'Common Sense, Legal Advice and the Right to Silence' [1991] 7 Public Law 233.
Doig Alan, *Corruption and Misconduct in Contemporary British Politics* (Penguin Books 1984).
Doran Sean, 'Trial by Jury' in McConville Mike and Wilson Geoffrey (eds), *The Handbook of The Criminal Justice Process* (OUP 2002).
Douglas Heather, 'The Cultural Specificity of Evidence: The Current Scope and Relevance of the *Anunga Guidelines*' (1998) 21(1) UNSW Law Journal 27.
Doward Jamie and Felstrom Carl, 'Brutal Ganglord Who Fell Victim to his Own Drugs' *The Guardian* (5 August 2007).
Downes David, 'The Gang Myth' *The Listener* (14 April 1966).
Downey Bernard, 'Confessions to Police Officers' (1971) 1 Hong Kong Law Journal 131.
Drewry Gavin and Butcher Tony, *The Civil Service Today* (Wiley-Blackwell 1988).
Dunleavy Patrick, 'The Westminster Model and the Distinctiveness of British Politics' in Dunleavy Patrick, Gamble Andrew, Heffernan Richard and Peele Gillian (eds), *Developments in British Politics* 8th Series (Palgrave Macmillan 2006).
Durand Philip, 'Confessions in East Africa' (1968) 4 East African Law Journal 70.
Dworkin Ronald, *Taking Rights Seriously* (Harvard University Press 1972).
Dworkin Ronald, *Law's Empire* (Harvard University Press 1986).
Du Cann Charles Garfield Lott, *Miscarriages of Justice* (F. Muller 1960).
Dyer Clare, 'Lane "Ruled himself out of Appeal"' *The Guardian* (28 April 1990).
Easton David, 'An Approach to the Analysis of Political Systems' (1956–57) 9 World Politics 383.
Editorial, 'The Judges' Rules' [1964] Criminal Law Review March 161.
Editorial, 'I did it' *The Observer* (12 February 1961).
Editorial, 'Matters of Life and Death' *The Guardian* (17 February 1961).
Edwards J L J, *The Law Officers of the Crown* (Sweet & Maxwell 1964).

Eekelaar John, 'Chapter 2' in Simpson Alfred William Brian (ed), *Oxford Essays in Jurisprudence* (Second Series) (Clarendon Press 1973).
Ekins Richard and Forsyth Christopher, *Judging the Public Interest: the Rule of Law vs. the Rule of Courts* (Policy Exchange 2015).
Elias Dame Sian, *Criminal Justice: Golden Threads and Pragmatic Patches* (CUP 2018).
Elks Laurie, *Righting Miscarriages of Justice? Ten Years of the Criminal Cases Review Commission* JUSTICE (London 2010).
Elliott Mark, 'A Tangled Constitutional Web: The Black-Spider Memos and the British Constitution's Relational Architecture' [2015] Public Law 539.
Elliott Mark, 'The Rule of Law and Access to Justice: Some Home Truths' (case comment) (2018) 77(1) Cambridge Law Journal 5.
Ellison QC Mark and Morgan Alison, 'Review of Possible Miscarriages of Justice: Impact of Undisclosed Undercover Police Activity on the Safety of Convictions' Report to the Attorney General, House of Commons (16 July 2015) HC Paper No 291.
Emsley Clive, *The English Police: A Political and Social History* (2nd edn, Longman 1996).
Emsley Clive, *The Great British Bobby: A History of British Policing from the 18th Century to the Present* (Quercus 2010).
Endicott Timothy, 'The Impossibility of the Rule of Law' (1999) 19 Oxford Journal of Legal Studies 1.
Etherton Terence, 'Liberty, the Archetype and Diversity: A Philosophy of Judging' [2010] Public Law 727.
Evans Martin and Mendick Robert, 'Police Chief Resigns after Two Female Officers Make Accusations of Inappropriate Behaviour against him' *The Telegraph* (21 January 2019).
Evans Martin, 'Home Secretary is urged to launch independent inquiry into Scotland Yard following Operation Midland scandal' *The Telegraph* (30 July 2019).
Evening Post, 'The Great Judicial Scandal' (New Zealand, 14 October 1904).
Evening Telegraph (21 May 1904).
Evening Telegraph (Dundee, 3 May 1904; 14 May 1904).
Farrar Salim Ali, 'The Role of the Accused in English and Islamic Criminal Justice' (PhD Thesis, University of Warwick 1999).
Fiadjoe Albert, 'An Overview of the Public Revolution in the Commonwealth Carribean' (1992) 310 Anglo-American Law Review 340.
Findlay Mark and Duff Peter (eds), *The Jury Under Attack* (Butterworths 1988).
Finnis John, 'Judicial Law-Making and the "Living" Instrumentalisation of the ECHR' in Barber Nicholas, Ekins Richard, and Yowell Paul (eds), *Lord Sumption and the Limits of the Law* (Hart 2016).
Fisher Henry Sir, *Report of an Inquiry by the Hon. Sir Henry Fisher into the Circumstances Leading to the Trial of Three Persons on Charges Arising out of the Death of Maxwell Confait and the Fire at Doggett Road, London SE6* (HMSO 1977).
Fitzpatrick Peter, '"The Desperate Vacuum": Imperialism and Law in the Experience of Enlightenment' in Carty Anthony (ed), *Post-Modern Law: Enlightenment, Revolution and the Death of Man* (Edinburgh University Press 1990) 90–106.
Fok Hon Mr Justice Joseph PJ, 'The Use of Non-local Judges in Overseas Jurisdictions—Judges from other Common Law Jurisdictions in the Hong Kong Court of Final Appeal' Commonwealth Law Conference 2017 (22 March 2017).
Foley Conor, 'Police Violence and Death: An Old Story' *The Guardian* (26 April 2009).
Foster Christopher Sir, 'Letter' *The Times* (London, 10 November 2003).
Foot Paul, *Murder at the Farm* (Sidgwick & Jackson 1986).

Fouzder Monidipa, 'Virtual Court Pilot is 'Not Fit for Purpose' *Law Society Gazette* (26 September 2016).
Fox John Sir, *The History of Contempt of Court* (Clarendon Press 1927).
Fraud Trials Committee, *Report* (The Roskill Committee) (HMSO 1986).
Freeman Michael, 'Law and Order in 1984' (1984) Current Legal Problems 175.
Friesen Gerald, *The Canadian Prairies: A History* (University of Toronto Press 1987).
Fulton Report, *The Civil Service, Report of the Committee 1966–68* Vol 1 (Cmd 3638, HMSO 1968)
Gamble Andrew, 'Theories of British Politics' (1990) 38 Political Studies 404.
Geary Adam, Morrison Wayne, and Jago Robert, *The Politics of the Common Law* (Routledge-Cavendish, 2009).
Gee Graham, Hazell Robert, Malleson Kate, and O'Brien Patrick, *The Politics of Judicial Independence in the UK's Changing Constitution* (CUP 2015).
Gibb Frances, 'Profumo Scapegoat's Conviction "Would Not Stand Today"' *The Times* (London, 9 September 2017).
Gibb Frances, 'Toughen Sentencing Powers of Magistrates, Says Law Chief' *The Times* (London, 19 September 2017).
Gibb Frances and Ames Jonathan, 'Judges Guilty of Bullying in Legal World that 'Stinks of Testosterone' *The Times* (1 January 2019).
Gibbs Penelope, 'Defendants on Video—Conveyor Belt Justice or a Revolution in Access?' *Transform Justice* (October 2017).
Girard Philip, 'Review of *Bewigged, Bothered, & Bewildered: British Colonial Judges on trial, 1800–1900* (by John McClaren) (The Osgoode Society for Legal History 2011)' (2012) 39(4) Journal of Law & Society 631.
Gittings Danny, 'Separation of Powers in Hong Kong: Inching Towards a More Flexible Judicial Interpretation' (2019) 49 Hong Kong Law Journal 187.
Glasgow Herald, 'Criminals Too Well Protected? Lord Shawcross Deplores Sentiment and Emotion' (6 November 1963).
Glenn H. Patrick, *On Common Laws* (OUP 2005).
Gobbo James, *Cross on Evidence* (Butterworths, 1979).
Godfrey Barry and Dunstall Graeme (eds), *Crime and Empire 1840–1940—Criminal Justice in Local and Global Context* (Routledge 2005).
Goodhart Arthur, 'Determining the Ratio Decidendi of a Case' (1930) 40 Yale Law Journal 161.
Gove Rt Hon Michael MP, 'What Does a One Nation Justice Policy Look Like?' Speech delivered at the Legatum Institute (23 June 2015).
Grant Thomas, *Jeremy Hutchinson's Case Histories* (John Murray 2015).
Green Chris, 'Ali Dizaei Most Senior Scotland Yard Officer to be Convicted of Serious Crime since 1977' *The Independent* (8 February 2010).
Greenaway John, 'Celebrating Northcote/Trevelyan: Dispelling the Myths' (2004) 19(1) Public Policy and Administration 1.
Greenwood George and Gibb Frances, 'Thousands Cleared by Evidence Failures' *The Times* (London, 17 December 2018).
Greer Steven, 'The Right to Silence: A Review of the Current Debate' (1990) 53(6) Modern Law Review 22.
Griffith JAG, 'Lord Denning Rolls the Dice against London' *New Society* (19 November 1981) 311.
Griffith JAG, 'The Law Lords and the GLC' *Marxism Today* (February 1982).
Griffith JAG, *Judicial Politics since 1920: A Chronicle* (Blackwell 1993).

Griffith JAG, *The Politics of the Judiciary* (5th edn, Fontana Press 1997).
Griffith JAG, 'The Brave New World of Sir John Laws' (2000) 63(2) The Modern Law Review 159.
Griffiths Emma, 'Nick Gargan Profile: Troubled End for High-Flying Police Chief' (*BBC website*, 16 October 2015).
Grigg Mary, *The Challenor Case* (Penguin 1965).
Guha Ranajit, *Dominance Without Hegemony: History and Power in Colonial India* (Harvard University Press 1998).
Gwynn Charles, *Imperial Policing* (Macmillan 1934).
Gyorfi Tamas, Review of *Final Judgment: The Last Law Lords and the Supreme Court* (Alan Paterson)' (2015) 19(2) Edinburgh Law Review 289.
Haddon Catherine, 'Developments in the Civil Service' in Heffernan Richard, Hay Colin, Russell Meg and Cowley Philip (eds), *Developments in British Politics* (Palgrave 2016).
Haldane Report, *Report of the Machinery of Government Committee* (Cmd 9230, HMSO 1918).
Haldane Richard, 'The Work for the Empire of the Judicial Committee of the Privy Council' (1922) 1 Cambridge Law Journal 143.
Hale Brenda, 'Equality and the Judiciary: Why Should We Want More Women Judges?' [2001] Public Law 489.
Hale Lady, 'Georgetown Commencement Speech' (23 May 2010).
Hall Andrew, 'Where Do the Advocates Stand when the Goalposts Have Been Moved' (2010) 14 International Journal of Evidence & Proof 107.
Hall Sarah, 'From the Yard to Shadow World' *The Guardian* (13 September 1999).
Hall Stuart and Jefferson Tony, *Resistance through Rituals* (Hutchinson 1998).
Hall Stuart, Critcher Charles, Jefferson Tony, Clarke John and Roberts Brian, *Policing the Crisis: Mugging, the State, and Law and Order* (Macmillan 1978).
Halliburton Rachel, 'When the Law Attacks the Lawyers' *New Statesman* (23 August 1999).
Hansard (1828; 1833; 1899; 1905; 1906; 1953; 1955; 1956; 1957; 1959; 1961; 1963; 1964; 1973; 1974; 1989; 1991; 1994; 2003; 2014).
Harding Andrew, 'The "Westminster Model" Constitution Overseas: Transplantation, Adaptation and Development in Commonwealth States' (2004) (Winter) Oxford University Commonwealth Law Journal 143.
Harper Tom, 'Drug Barons Walk Free as Police Hide Evidence' *The Sunday Times* (London, 27 May 2018).
Harper Tom, 'Elite London Met Police Shielded from Corruption' *The Times* (London, 22 July 2018).
Hart James S Jnr, *The Rule of Law 1603–1660* (Routledge 2003).
Heffernan Richard, Hay Colin, Russell Meg, and Cowley Philip (eds), *Developments in British Politics* (Palgrave 2016).
Helm Rebecca, 'Conviction by Consent? Vulnerability, Autonomy and Conviction by Guilty Plea' (2019) 83(2) Journal of Criminal Law 161.
Henderson James (Sákéj) Youngblood, 'Postcolonial Indigenous Legal Consciousness' (2002) 1 Indigenous Law Journal 1.
Henham Ralph, *Sentence Discounts and the Criminal Process* (Ashgate 2001).
Hennessey Peter, *Whitehall* (Secker & Warburg 1989).
Hewart Lord, *The New Despotism* (Ernest Benn Ltd 1929).
Hiemstra Victor, 'Abolition of the Right Not to Be Questioned' (1963) 80 South African Law Journal 187.
HMCPSI, *Better Case Management—A Snapshot* (November 2016).

HMCPSI, *Transforming Summary Justice: An Early Perspective of the CPS Contribution* (February 2016).
HMCPSI, *Making it Fair: The Disclosure of Unused Material in Volume Crown Court Cases* (2017).
HMCPSI, *Annual Report* (2017–18).
HMCPSI and HMI, *Without Consent: A Report on the Joint Review of the Investigation and Prosecution of Rape Offences* (2007).
HMCPSI and HMIC, *Investigation and Prosecution of Cases Involving Allegations of Rape* (April 2002).
HMICFRS, 'State of Policing—The Annual Assessment of Policing in England and Wales 2018' (2019).
Hobbs Dick, *Doing the Business* (OUP 1988).
Hodder-Williams Richard, 'Six Notions of "Political" and the United States Supreme Court' 1992 22(1) British Journal of Political Science 1-20.
Hoffmann Leonard, 'The Judges' Rules' (1964) 7 The Lawyer 23.
Hoffmann Lord, 'Separation of Powers' (2002) 7 Judicial Review 137.
Holden, Richard, 'Months of Hell, 15 Minutes for my Name to Be Cleared' *The Sunday Times* (London, 8 July 2018).
Hollander Barnett, *The English Bar: A Priesthood* (Bowes 1956).
Holmes Oliver Wendell Jr, *The Common Law* (Little, Brown and co 1881).
Home Office, *Criminal Justice: The Way Ahead* (Cmd 5074, HMSO 2001).
Home Office, *Delivering Simple, Speedy, Summary Justice* (Department for Constitutional Affairs 2006).
Home Office, *Justice for All* (Cmd 5563, HMSO 2002).
Home Office, *Penal Practice in a Changing Society* (Cmd 645, HMSO 1959).
Home Office, *Policing Statistics* (May 2018) <https://www.ethnicity-facts-figures.service.gov.uk/crime-justice-and-the-law/policing/stop-and-search/latest>
Home Office, *Report of the Sheffield Police Appeal Inquiry* (Cmd 2176, HMSO 1963).
Home Office, *Report of the Working Group on the Right to Silence* (HMSO 1989).
Home Office, *Review of Delay in the Criminal Justice System: A Report* (The Narey Report) (HMSO 1997).
Horne Juliet, 'A Plea of Convenience' (PhD thesis, University of Warwick 2016).
Horowitz Morton, 'The Rule of Law: An Unqualified Human Good?' (1977) 86 Yale Law Journal 561.
Horwell Richard, *Mouncher Investigation Report* (HC 292, July 2017).
House of Commons, 'The Role of the Magistracy' Justice Committee Report (17 October 2017).
House of Lords Constitution Committee, 1st Report (2001–2002): *Reviewing the Constitution: Terms of Reference and Method of Working* (HL Paper 11).
House of Lords Constitution Committee, *The Process of Constitutional Change—Constitution Committee* (2011).
Huhne Chris, 'The UK's Civil Service Needs Reform for Government to Work Better' *The Guardian* (15 December 2013).
Hungerford-Welch Peter, 'Unrepresented Defendants: R. v Conaghan (Terence)' (Case Comment)' (2017) 12 Criminal Law Review 1009.
Hunt Adrian, 'Review of *Politics of the Judiciary* (by JAG Griffiths)' (1988) Civil Justice Quarterly 346.
Hyde Harford Montgomery, *Norman Birkett* (Hamish Hamilton 1964).

Independent Police Complaints Commission (IPCC), *Operation Kalmia Staffordshire Police* (Final Report) (online, 2017).
Interdepartmental Committee, *The Distribution of Criminal Business between the Crown Court and the Magistrates' Courts* (Cmd 6323, The James Committee, (HMSO 1975).
Irukwu Joseph Ogbonnaya, *Nigeria at the Crossroads* (Witherby 1983).
Jackson John, 'Recent Developments in Criminal Evidence' (1989) 40 Northern Ireland Legal Quarterly 26.
Jackson John, 'Curtailing the Right to Silence: Lessons from Northern Ireland' [1991] Criminal Law Review 404.
Jackson John, 'Inferences from Silence: From Common Law to Common Sense' (1993) 44 Northern Ireland Legal Quarterly 103.
Jackson John, 'Silence Legislation in Northern Ireland: The Impact after Ten Years' (2010) 6(2) Journal of Civil Liberties 134.
Jackson John and Doran Sean, *Judge Without Jury: Diplock Trials in the Adversary System* (OUP 1995).
Jackson Moana, 'Justice and Political Power: Reasserting Maori Legal Processes' in Hazelhurst Kayleen (ed), *Legal Pluralism and the Colonial Legacy: Indigenous Experiences of Justice in Canada, Australia and New Zealand* (Avebury 1995).
Jackson Robert, The *Chief—The Biography of Gordon Hewart, Lord Chief Justice of England (1922–40)* (Harrap & Co Ltd 1959).
Jackson Stanley, *Mr. Justice Avory* (Victor Gollancz Ltd 1935).
Jacobs Francis Sir, *The Sovereignty of Law: The European Way*, The Hamlyn Lectures (CUP 2007).
James Arthur Evan QC, *Report by Mr A.E. James, Q.C. into the Circumstances in which it Was Possible for Detective Sergeant Harold Gordon Challenor to Continue on Duty at a Time when he Appears to Have Been Affected by the Onset of Mental Illness* (Cmd 2745, HMSO 1965).
Jeffrey Bill Sir, *Independent Criminal Advocacy in England and Wales* (Ministry of Justice 2014).
Jeffries Charles, *The Colonial Police* (Parrish 1952).
Johnston Ed, 'The Adversarial Defence Lawyer: Myths, Disclosure and Efficiency—A Contemporary Analysis of the Role in the Era of the Criminal Procedure Rules' (2020) 24(1) The International Journal of Evidence & Proof 35.
Johnston Ed and Smith Tom, 'The Early Guilty Plea Scheme and the Rising Wave of Managerialism' (2017) 181(13) Criminal Law and Justice Weekly 210.
Johnston Thomas Eric St, 'The Legal Limitation of the Interrogation of Suspects and Prisoners in England and Wales' (1948–49) 39(1) Journal of Criminal Law and Criminology 89.
Johnston Thomas Eric St, 'Judges' Rules and Police Interrogation in England Today' (1966) 57(1) Journal of Criminal Law and Criminology 85.
Jones Brian Christopher, 'The Rule of Law in UK Public Law Textbooks: From Critique to Acceptance?' [2018] Public Law 594.
Jones Carol and Vagg Jon, *Criminal Justice in Hong Kong* (Routlege Cavendish 2007).
Jowell Jeffrey, *Letter The Times* (London, 13 November 2003).
Judge Igor Sir, 'The Criminal Justice System in England and Wales—Greater Efficiency in the Criminal Justice System, Time for Change?' Speech delivered at University of Sydney (August 2007).
Judge LCJ, Speech delivered at Lord Mayor's Banquet (3 July 2013).
Judicial Diversity Statistics 2018 (Courts and Tribunals Judiciary website 12 July 2018).

Judicial Executive Board, *Guidance to the Judiciary on Engagement with the Executive* (July 2017).
Judiciary of England and Wales, *Disclosure: A Protocol for the Control and Management of Unused Material in the Crown Court* (Courts and Tribunals Judiciary website, undated).
Judiciary of England and Wales, 'The Judiciary, the Government and the Constitution' (Court and Tribunals Judiciary website, undated).
Justice of the Peace, 'Questioning or Cross-examination of Persons under Arrest by the Police—Important Warning by the Lord Chief Justice' (29 June 1912) vol LXXVI.
Kaye Tim, *Unsafe and Unsatisfactory? Report of the Independent Inquiry into the Working Practices of the West Midlands Police Serious Crime Squad* (Civil Liberties Trust 1991).
Keel Paul, 'Senior Police to Call for End of Right to Silence' *The Guardian* (22 September 1987).
Kellner Peter and Crowther-Hunt Lord, *The Civil Servants: An Inquiry into Britain's Ruling Class* (Macdonald 1980).
Kelly Liz, Lovett Jo, and Regan Linda, *A Gap or Chasm? Attrition in Reported Rape Cases*, Home Office Research Study 293 (HMSO 2005).
Kelsall Roger Keith, *Higher Civil Servants in Britain* (Routledge 1955).
Kennedy Ludovic, *10 Rillington Place* (Victor Gallancz 1961 and Panther Books 1971).
Kennedy Ludovic, *On My Way to the Club* (Fontana 1989).
Kettle Martin and Hodges Lucy, *Uprising!* (Pan Books 1982).
King Anthony, 'Overload: Problems of Governing in the 1970s' (1975) 23(2&3) Political Studies 162.
King Anthony, *Who Governs Britain?* (Pelican 2015).
Kingsley John, *Representative Bureaucracy: An Interpretation of the British Civil Service* (Yellow Springs 1994).
Kirby Hon Mr Justice, 'Criminal Investigation & The Rule of Law' 20th Australian Legal Convention Adelaide (7 July 1979).
Kirby Michael, *Address to the Justices of the Supreme Court of Nigeria* (12 June 2012).
Kirby Terry, 'Two Cleared over "Tainted Police Evidence": Convictions Quashed after Court of Appeal Told Officers Could not Be Relied upon' *The Independent* (15 December 1993).
Klein Richard, 'The Empire Strikes Back: Britain's Use of the Law to Suppress Political Dissent in Hong Kong' (1997) 15(1) Boston University International Law Journal 1.
Knightley Phillip and Kennedy Caroline, *An Affair of State: The Profumo Case and the Framing of Stephen Ward* (Jonathan Cape 1987).
Kolsky Elizabeth, 'Codification and the Rule of Colonial Difference: Criminal Procedure in British India' (2005) 23(3) Law and History Review 631.
Kolsky Elizabeth, *Colonial Justice in British India—White Violence and the Rule of Law* (CUP 2010).
Kumarasingham Harshan, *A Political Legacy of the British Empire—Power and the Parliamentary System in Post-Colonial India and Sri Lanka* (I.B. Tauris 2013).
Kyle David, 'Correcting Miscarriages of Justice: The Role of the Criminal Cases Review Commission' (2004) 52 Drake Law Review 657.
Kyritsis Dimitrios, 'Constitutional Review in Representative Democracy' (2012) 22 Oxford Journal of Legal Studies 297.
Lammy David, *The Lammy Review* (September 2017).
Langbein John, 'The Criminal Trial Before Lawyers' (1978) 45 University of Chicago Law Review 263.
Langbein John, *The Origins of Adversary Criminal Trial* (OUP 2003).
Langdon Andrew QC, 'A Right, not a Commodity' *Counsel Magazine* (September 2017).

Law Library of Congress, *Miranda Warning Equivalents Abroad* (Global Legal Research Center 2016).
Law Reform Commission of Hong Kong, *Report on Confession Statements and their Admissibility in Criminal Proceedings* (1985).
Laws John Sir, 'Law and Democracy' [1995] Public Law 72.
Lee William Melville, *A History of the Police in England* (Methuen 1901).
Leigh David, *The Frontiers of Secrecy* (Junction Books 1980).
Leng Roger, *The Right to Silence in Police Interrogation: A Study of Some of the Issues Underlying the Debate*, The Royal Commission on Criminal Justice Research Study No 10 (1993).
Le Sueur Andrew, 'Developing Mechanisms for Judicial Accountability in the UK' (2004) Legal Studies 73.
Leveson Brian Sir, *Review of Efficiency in Criminal Proceedings* (Judiciary of England & Wales January 2015).
Leveson Brian Sir, 'Modernising Justice through Technology' Keynote lecture (24 June 2015).
Leveson Brian Sir, 'Valedictory Speech' Judiciary of England & Wales (21 June 2019).
Lewis Paul, 'Blair Peach Killed by Police at 1979 Protest, Met Report Finds' *The* Guardian (27 April 2010).
Lloyd Gary and Mounter Julian, 'London Policemen in Bribe Allegations: Tapes Reveal Planted Evidence' *The Times* (London, 29 November 1969).
Loughlin Martin, 'Sumption's Assumptions' in Barber Nicholas, Ekins Richard, and Yowell Paul (eds), *Lord Sumption and the Limits of the Law* (Hart 2016).
MacDermont Lord, *Protection from Power under English Law* (Stevens 1957).
Magistrate, 'Stop Delaying Justice! A New Training Programme' 2011, 67(9) 6.
Maguire Mike and Norris Clive, 'Police Investigations: Practice and Malpractice' (1994) 21 Journal of Law & Society 72.
Majoribanks Edward, *For the Defence: The Life of Sir Edward Marshall Hall* (Macmillan co 1930).
Majoribanks Edward, 'Introduction' to *Famous Trials of Marshall Hall* (Advanpress Ltd 1989).
Malifa Leulua' iali 'I Tasi, 'The Reception of Judges' Rules and the Right to Counsel in the Constitution of Western Samoa' (1997) 21 The Journal of Pacific Studies 161.
Malleson Kate, 'The Evolving Role of the Supreme Court' [2011] Public Law 754.
Malleson Kate, 'Little Progress towards a Diverse Judiciary on either Gender or Race' *The Guardian (Letters)* (3 August 2015).
Malvern Jack, 'National Archives: Dossier on Profumo Affair Proved Too Good to Miss' *The Times* (London, 28 December 2018).
Mangold Tom, 'The Fall Guy for Profumo' *The Telegraph* (19 May 1963).
Mangold Tom, *Profumo Confidential* (*BBC Radio 4: Archive 4*, 25 May 2013).
Mark Robert, *Minority Verdict*, Dimbleby Lecture (BBC Publications 1973).
Mark Robert, *Policing a Perplexed Society* (Allen & Unwin 1977).
Mark Robert Sir, *In the Office of Constable* (William Collins & Sons 1978).
Mars-Jones William QC, *Report of Inquiry made for the Information of the Secretary of State for the Home Department, into the Case of Thomas Halloran and Patrick Joseph Cox and the Case of Patrick Albert Tisdall, Thomas Alfred Kingston and Sidney Hill-Burton* (Cmd 2526, HMSO 1964).
Marsh Luke, 'All the King's Men, Police Powers and the Reining in of Liberty' (2014) 78 Journal of Criminal Law 4.

Marsh Luke, 'Leveson's Narrow Pursuit of Justice: Efficiency and Outcomes in the Criminal Process' (2016) 45(1) Common Law World Review 51.
Marsh Luke, 'The "Tommy Robinson Case" and Contempt of Court: Conflicting Interpretations of the Criminal Procedure Rules' (2020) 1 Criminal Law Review 50.
Marshall Geoffrey, 'Comment' (1964) (Summer) Public Law 97.
Marshall Geoffrey, *Constitutional Theory* (OUP 1971).
Mason Anthony Sir, 'The Judiciary in the Modern World' Speech delivered to the Judicial Studies Board at High Court, Hong Kong (13 November 1998).
Masterman Roger and Wheatle Se-shauna, 'Unpacking Separation of Powers: Judicial Independence, Sovereignty and Conceptual Flexibility in the UK Constitution' (2017) (July) Public Law 469
Matthew Henry Colin Gray, *Gladstone 1809–1874* (OUP 1986).
McBarnet Doreen, 'The Fisher Report on the Confait Case; Four Issues' (1978) 41(4) Modern Law Review 455.
McClaren John, 'Navigating the Scylla of Imperial Politico-Legal Aspirations and Charybdis of Colonial Micro-Politics in the British Empire: The Case of the Judges' in Dorsett Shaunnagh and McClaren John (eds), *Legal Histories of the British Empire—Law, Engagements and Legacies* (Routledge 2014).
McClintock Frederick Hemming and Avison Neville Howard, *Crime in England and Wales* (Heinemann Educational Books 1968).
McConville Mike 'Videotaping Interrogations: Police Behaviour on and off Camera' [1992] Criminal Law Review 552.
McConville Mike and Bridges Lee, *Criminal Justice in Crisis* (Edward Elgar 1994).
McConville Mike and Hodgson Jacqueline, *Custodial Legal Advice and the Right to Silence* (HMSO 1993).
McConville Mike and Marsh Luke, *Criminal Judges* (Edward Elgar 2014).
McConville Mike and Marsh Luke, 'Adversarialism Goes West: Case Management in Criminal Courts' (2015) 19(3) International Journal of Evidence & Proof 172.
McConville Mike and Marsh Luke, 'Factory Farming and State-Induced Pleas' in Hunter Jill, Roberts Paul, Young Simon, and Dixon David (eds), *The Integrity of Criminal Process* (Hart 2016) 99–116.
McConville Mike, Hodgson Jacqueline, Bridges Lee, and Pavlovic Anita, *Standing Accused: The Organisation and Practices of Criminal Defence Lawyers in Britain* (OUP 1994).
McConville Mike, Sanders Andrew, and Leng Roger, *The Case for the Prosecution* (Routledge 1991; Routledge Revival Edition, 2019).
McEwan Jenny, 'From Adversarialism to Managerialism: Criminal Justice in Transition' (2011) 31(3) Legal Studies 519.
McEwan Jenny, 'Truth, Efficiency and Co-operation in Modern Criminal Justice' (2013) 66(1) Current Legal Problems 203.
McLachlin Beverley, 'Role of Judges in Modern Commonwealth Society' (1995) 53 The Advocate 681.
McLagan Graeme, *Bent Coppers: The Inside Story of Scotland Yard's Battle Against Police Corruption* (Orion 2004).
McLaughlin Eugene, 'Forcing the Issue: New Labour, New Localism and the Democratic Renewal of Police Accountability' (2005) 44(5) Howard Journal 473.
McNee David Sir, *McNee's Law* (Collins 1983).
Mendick Robert, 'Police Chief Resigns after Two Female Officers Make Accusations of Inappropriate Behaviour Against Him' *The Telegraph* (21 January 2019).
Merry Sally, 'Law and Colonialism' (1991) 25 Law and Society Review 879.

Miller Phil and Wright Oliver, 'Whitehall Addiction to Secrecy Getting Worse, Warns Watchdog' *The Times* (London, 3 August 2017).
Ministry of Justice, *Criminal Court Statistics Quarterly* (January–March 2016).
Ministry of Justice, *Criminal Court Statistics* (2017).
Ministry of Justice, *Criminal Court Statistics: January to March 2019* (27 June 2019).
Ministry of Justice, *Modernising the Criminal Justice System, The CJS Efficiency Programme* (21 December 2011).
Ministry of Justice, *Swift and Sure Justice: The Government's Plans for the Reform of the Criminal Justice System* (Cmd 8388, HMSO 2012).
Ministry of Justice, *Transforming Legal Aid: Delivering a More Credible and Efficient System* (2013).
Ministry of Justice, *Transforming Our Justice System* (2016).
Ministry of Justice, 'Virtual Courts Brings Swifter Justice' 28 November 2011 (online).
Mirfield Peter, 'A Novel Theory of Privy Council Precedent' (Case Comment) (2017) January 1–6) Law Quarterly Review 133.
Mirfield Peter, *Confessions* (Sweet & Maxwell 1985).
Mitchell Paul, 'The Privy Council and the Difficulty of Distance' (2016) 36(1) Oxford Journal of Legal Studies 26.
Moran Christopher, *Classified: Secrecy and the State in Modern Britain* (CUP 2013).
Morgan Rod, 'The Process is the Rule and the Punishment is the Process' (1996) 59 Modern Law Review 306.
Morgan-Bentley Paul, 'Home Office "Manipulates Crime Figures by Telling Action Fraud to Dismiss Identity Theft"' *The Times* (London, 18 September 2019).
Morris Henry and Read James, *Indirect Rule and the Search for Justice* (Clarendon Press 1972).
Morton James, *Bent Coppers: A Survey of Police Corruption* (Warner Books 1993).
Morton James, *Gangland* (Piatkus 2008).
Moxon David, *Sentencing Practice in the Crown Court* (Home Office Research Unit Study No 103 1988).
Mullin Chris, *Error of Judgement: Truth About the Birmingham Bombings* (Chatto & Windus 1986).
Muncie John, *The Trouble with Kids Today* (Hutchinson 1984).
Napley David Sir, *Not Without Prejudice* (Harrap 1982).
Nasser Hussain, *The Jurisprudence of Emergency: Colonialism and the Rule of Law* (Michigan University Press 2003).
National Archives, *Records Management Retention Scheduling* (2012).
National Audit Office, *Efficiency in the Criminal Justice System* (Ministry of Justice 2016).
National Audit Office, *Capability in the Civil Service*, HC 919 Session 2016–17 (24 March 2017).
National Audit Office, *Financial Sustainability of Police Forces in England and Wales* HC 1501 Session 2017–19 (11 September 2018).
Neuberger Lord, 'The Judicial Committee of the Privy Council in the 21st Century' (2014) 3(1) Cambridge Journal of International & Comparative Law 30.
Neuberger Lord 'Some Thoughts on Judicial Reasoning across Jurisdictions' 2016 Mitchell Lecture, Edinburgh (11 November 2016).
Neuberger Lord, 'Reflections on Significant Moments in the Role of the Judiciary' Personal Support Unit Fundraising Breakfast (16 March 2017).
Neuberger Lord, 'Judges, Access to Justice, the Rule of Law and the Court of Final Appeal under "One Country Two Systems"' Lecture delivered at the University of Hong Kong (13 September 2017).

Newman Daniel, *Legal Aid Lawyers and the Quest for Justice* (Hart 2013).
Ng Michael, 'Rule of Law in Hong Kong History Demythologised: Student Umbrella Movement of 1919' (2016) Hong Kong Law Journal 46.
Northcote Stafford Sir and Trevelyan Charles Sir, *Northcote-Trevelyan Report* (February 1854).
Ntumy Michael (ed), *South Pacific Islands Legal Systems* (University of Hawaii Press 1993).
Obituary, 'Lord Allen of Abbeydale' *The Guardian* (11 December 2007).
O'Connor Denis, *Closing the Gap* (HMIC 2005).
O'Donnell Bernard, *The Trials of Mr. Justice Avory* (Rich & Cowan 1935).
O'Higgins Paul, 'The Challenor Report—1' [1965] Criminal Law Review 633.
O'Toole Barry, *The Ideal of Public Service: Reflections on the Higher Civil Service in Britain* (Routledge 2006).
Okonkwo T A, *On the Culture of Social Structure* (Chicago University Press 1966).
Oliver Dawn, 'Book Review of *The Politics of the Judiciary* (3rd edn, Fontana Books 1985) (by J.A.G. Griffith)' (1986) (July) Legal Studies 6.
Opolot James, 'The Resilience of the British Colonial Police Legacies in East Africa, Southern Africa, and West Africa' (1992) 15 Police Studies: International Review of Police Development 90.
Owusu-Bempah Abenaa, *Defendant Participation in the Criminal Process* (Routledge 2017).
Padfield Nicola and Hawker Tom, 'Sentencing via Video Link' [2017] Criminal Law Review 585.
Pain J H , 'The Reception of English and Roman-Dutch Law in Africa with Reference to Botswana, Lesotho and Swaziland' (1978) 11 Comparative & International Law Journal of Southern Africa 137.
Palmer H, 'The Brighton Conspiracy Case' [1958] Criminal Law Review 422.
Pannick David, *Judges* (OUP 1987).
Parker Graham, 'Copping a Plea,' (1971) 135 Justice of the Peace and Local Government Review 408.
Parker Howard, *View from the Boys* (David & Charles 1974).
Parker Lord, *Report of the Committee of Privy Counsellors Appointed to Consider Authorised Procedures for the Interrogation of Persons Suspected of Terrorism* (Cmd 4901, HMSO 1972).
Parker Nick General Sir, *Independent Review of ACPO* (2013).
Parker Robert, *Rough Justice* (Fontana 1981).
Parris John, *Under My Wig* (Arthur Barker 1961).
Paterson Alan, *The Law Lords* (Macmillan 1982).
Paterson Alan, 'The Judges, the House of Lords and Politics' (2009) 16(1) International Journal of the Legal Profession 43.
Paterson Alan, *Final Judgment* (Hart 2013).
Paterson Alan, '*Final Judgment* revisited' (2015) 21(1) European Journal of Current Legal Issues 1.
Pearson Geoff, *Hooligan: A History of Respectable Fears* (Macmillan 1983).
Peirce Gareth, 'The Birmingham Six: Have We Learned from Our Disgraceful Past?' *The Guardian* (12 March 2011).
Pellew Jill, *The Home Office 1848–1914* (Fairleigh Dickinson University Press 1982).
Phillips Lord, 'Judicial Independence' Lecture given at Constitution Unit, UCL (7 February 2011).

Phillips Owen Hood, 'A Constitutional Myth: Separation of Powers' (1977) 93 Law Quarterly Review 11.
Pilkington Colin, *The Civil Service in Britain Today* (MUP 1999).
Platts-Mills John, *Muck, Silk and Socialism* (Paper Publishing 2001) 465
Plucknett Theodore, *A Concise History of the Common Law* (Liberty Fund 1929, The LawBook Exchange 1956 edition).
Police Chronicle (24 February 1913).
Police Officer, 'The Judges' Rules and the Police' [1964] Criminal Law Review 173.
Police Review, (18 June 1915; 7 March 1958).
Police Review, 'The Constable and the Law' (24 March 1961).
Police Review, 'The Constable and the Law: A Weekly Commentary' (31 January 1964).
Policy Studies Institute, *Police and People in London* (1983).
Ponting Clive, *The Right to Know* (Sphere Books 1985).
Poole Thomas and Shah Sangeeta, 'The Law Lords and Human Rights' (2011) Modern Law Review 79.
Preston Peter, 'A Source of Great Regret' (2005) 16(3) British Journalism Review 47.
Private Eye (21 March 1963).
Proctor Michael, 'Criminals Are Not Getting Swift Justice' (*CambridgeshireLive* (online), 23 August 2019).
Pue Wesley, 'British Masculinities, Canadian Lawyers: Canadian Legal Education, 1900-1930' (1999) 16(1) Law in Context 80.
Punch Maurice, *Conduct Unbecoming: The Social Construction of Police Deviance* (Tavistock 1985).
Punch Maurice, *Police Corruption* (Routledge 2009).
Quirk Hannah, *The Rise and Fall of the Right of Silence: Principle, Politics and Policy* (Routledge 2016).
Radcliffe Lord, *Not in Feather Beds* (Hamish Hamilton 1968).
Redmayne Mike, 'Disclosure and its Discontents' (2004) Criminal Law Review 441.
Reid, Lord, 'The Judge as Lawmaker' (1972) The Journal of Public Teachers of Law 22.
Reiner Robert, *The Politics of the Police* (3rd edn, OUP 1985).
Rennell Tony, 'King of the Corrupt Cops' (*Daily Mail online*, 24 May 2019).
Rhodes Rod, *Everyday Life in British Government* (OUP 2011).
Rhodes Rod, Wanna John, and Weller Patrick, *Comparing Westminster* (OUP 2009).
Robbins Jon, *The First Miscarriage of Justice* (Waterside Press 2014).
Roberts Alasdair, *Blacked Out: Government Secrecy in the Information Age* (CUP 2006).
Roberts Robert, *The Classic Slum: Salford Life in the First Quarter of the* Century (Penguin 1973).
Robertson David, *Judicial Discretion in the House of Lords* (Clarendon Press 1998)
Robertson Geoffrey, *Stephen Ward Was Innocent, OK* (Biteback Publishing Ltd 2013).
Robinson Patrick, 'The Monarchy, Republicanism and the Privy Council: The Enduring Cry for Freedom' (2012) 101(5) (October) The Round Table 447.
Robson William Alexander, *Justice and Administrative Law* (3rd edn, Stevens 1951).
Romily Samuel, *Observations on the Criminal Law of England* (1810).
Root Neil, *Crossing the Line of Duty* (The History Press 2019).
Royal Commission on Criminal Justice, *Report* (Cmd 2263, HMSO 1993).
Royal Commission on Criminal Procedure, *Report* (Cmd 8092, HMSO 1981).
Royal Commission on Police Powers and Procedure, *Report* (Cmd 3297, HMSO 1929).
Royal Commission Upon the Duties of the Metropolitan Police, *Report* (Cmd 4156 vol i, 1908).

Rychlikova Megi, 'Top Judge Calls for CPS to Explain Case Collapse' *The York Press* (14 June 2019).
Ryder Ernest Sir, 'Implementation and Application of the Law: The Governance of Justice' (Courts and Tribunals Judiciary website, 4 September 2019).
Safford Frank and Wheeler George, *The Practice of the Privy Council in Judicial Matters* (Sweet & Maxwell 1901).
Salewicz Chris, 'Lucky Gordon' *The Guardian* (24 March 2017).
Sanders Andrew, Bridges Lee, and Mulvaney Adele, *Advice and Assistance at Police Stations under the 24-Hour Duty Solicitor Scheme* (Lord Chancellor's Department 1989).
Sato Shohei, '"Operation Legacy": Britain's Destruction and Concealment of Colonial Records Worldwide' (2017) 45(4) The Journal of Imperial and Commonwealth History 697.
Saville Lord, *Report of The Bloody Sunday Inquiry* (HMSO 2010).
Scales Philip Sir, 'The Common Law: Context and Method' (2019) 135 Law Quarterly Review 47.
Scarman Lord, *Report of an Inquiry into The Red Lion Square Disorders of 15 June 1974* (Cmd 5919, HMSO 1975).
Scarman Lord, *Report of a Court of Inquiry under the Rt. Hon. Justice Scarman* (Cmd 6922, HMSO 1977).
Scarman Lord, *The Brixton Disorders 1-12 April 1981* (Cmd 8427, HMSO 1981).
Schapera Isaac, *Tswana Chiefs and Social Change, 1795–1940*, London School of Economics Monographs on Social Anthropology no 43 (Athlone Press 1970).
Scott Harold Sir, *Your Obedient Servant* (Andre Deutsch 1959).
Scott Henderson Committee, *Report and Recommendations on the Security Arrangements* (National Archives 1952).
Scraton Phil, *The State of the Police* (Pluto Press 1985).
Scraton Phil (ed), *Law, Order and the Authoritarian State* (Open University Press 1987).
Scrivener Anthony, 'Tough Justice on the Cheap' *The Independent* (7 October 1993).
Sedley Stephen, 'Law and State Power: A Time for Reconstruction' (1990) 17 Journal of Law & Society 234.
Sedley Stephen, 'Review of *Judicial Discretion in the House of Lords* (David Robertson)' (1999) 58(3) Cambridge Law Journal 627.
Sedley Stephen, *Ashes and Sparks* (CUP 2011).
Sedley Stephen, 'Judicial Politics' *London Review of Books* (23 February 2012).
Sedley Stephen, *Lions Under the Throne: Essays on the History of English Public Law* (CUP 2015).
Sedley Stephen, 'Judicial Independence is a Fragile Thing' *Financial Times* (London, 22 January 2017).
Sedley Stephen, 'A Boundary Where There Is None' *London Review of Books* (12 September 2019).
Seidman Robert, 'A Note on the Construction of the Gold Coast Reception Statute' (1969) 13 Journal of African Law 45.
Sekar Satish, *The Cardiff Five* (Waterside Press 2012).
Sentencing Guidelines Council, *Reduction in Sentence for a Guilty Plea Definitive Guideline* (June 2017).
Sharafi Mitra, 'The Marital Patchwork of Colonial South Asia: Forum Shopping from Britain to Baroda' (2010) 28 Law and History Review 979.
Shawcross Hartley Sir, 'Address Delivered at the Law Society's Hall' (18 February 1953).

Shetreet Shimon and Turenne Sophie, *Judges on Trial: A Study in the Appointment and Accountability of the English Judiciary* (CUP 2013).
Shrager Mark, 'Recent Developments in the Law Relating to Confessions: England, Canada and Australia' (1981) 23(3) McGill Law Journal 435.
Shrewsbury Chronicle and Advertiser (4 February 1961).
Sim Joe, 'Scarman: The Police Counter-Attack' (1982) Socialist Register 57.
Simon Viscount, *Retrospect: The Memoirs of The Rt. Hon. Viscount Simon* (Hutchinson 1952).
Sims George, *The Martyrdom of Adolf Beck Daily Mail* (London, 1904).
Sinclair Georgina, *At the End of the Line: Colonial Policing and the Imperial Endgame 1945-80* (Manchester University Press 2006).
Singh Amarjit, 'S.121(5) C.P.C—A Policemen's Charter?' [1989] Singapore Academy of Law Journal 106-112.
Skinns Layla, *Police Custody: Governance, Legitimacy and Reform in the Criminal Justice Process* (Willan 2011).
Slack James, 'Enemies of the People' *Daily Mail* (London, 4 November 2015).
Smith John Cyril, 'The New Judges' Rules—A Lawyer's View' [1964] Criminal Law Review 176.
Smith Phillip, *Policing Victorian London* (Greenwood Press 1985).
Smith Tom, 'The "Near Miss" of Liam Allan: Critical Problems in Police Disclosure, Investigation Culture and the Resourcing of Criminal Justice' (2018) 9 Criminal Law Review 711.
Smith Tom and Cape Ed, 'The Rise and Decline of Criminal Legal Aid in England and Wales' in Asher Flynn and Jacqueline Hodgson (eds), *Access to Justice & Legal Aid: Comparative Perspectives on Unmet legal Need* (Hart Publishing 2017) 63–86.
Smoker Barbara, 'The Challenor Case' (1966) 6(1) The British Journal of Criminology 68.
Softley Paul, *Police Interrogation: An Observational Study in Four Police Stations* (HMSO 1990).
Soubise Laurène, 'Prosecuting in the Magistrates' Courts in a Time of Austerity' (2017) 11 Criminal Law Review 847.
Spector Malcolm and Kitsuse John, *Constructing Social Problems* (Transaction Publishers 2001).
Stead Philip, *The Police of Britain* (Macmillan 1985).
Stephen James Fitzjames, *A History of the Criminal Law of England* vol i, vol iii (1883).
Stern Review, *A Report by Baroness Vivien Stern CBE of an Independent Review Into How Rape Complaints are Handled by Public Authorities in England and Wales* (Government Equalities Office and Home Office 2010).
Stevens Philip and Willis Carole, *Race Crime and Arrests* Home Office Research Study No 48 (HMSO 1979)
Stevens Robert, 'A Loss of Innocence? Judicial Independence and the Separation of Powers' (1999) 19(3) Oxford Journal of Legal Studies 365.
Stevens Robert, 'Judicial Independence: The Case of England' (1999) 72 Southern California Law Review 101.
Stevens Robert, 'The Act of Settlement and the Questionable History of Judicial Independence' (2001) 1 Oxford University Commonwealth Law Journal 253.
Stevens Robert, *The English Judges: Their Role in a Changing Constitution* (Hart 2002).
Stevens Robert, *The Independence of the Judiciary* (OUP 1993).
Stevenson John, *Popular Disturbances in England* (Longman 1979).
Stevenson John and Cook Chris, *The Slump: Britain in the Great Depression* (Cape 1977).
Stewart Richard, *The Great Detective Case of 1877* (The Battered Silicon Dispatch Box 2000).

Steyn Lord, 'The Weakest and Least Dangerous Department of Government' [1997] Public Law 84.

Storch Robert, 'The Plague of Blue Locusts' (1975) International Review of Social History 20.

Stryker Lloyd Paul, *For the Defence* (Staples Press 1949).

Sullivan Serjeant Alexander Martin QC, *The Last Serjeant* (Macdonald 1952).

Sumption Jonathan, 'Judicial and Political Decision-Making: The Uncertain Boundary' FA Mann Lecture, 2011 (2011) 16 Judicial Review 301.

Sumption Jonathan, *Trials of the State: Law and the Decline of Politics* (Profile 2019).

Sumption Jonathan, '2019 Reith Lectures: Law and the Decline of Politics' (*BBC* Online).

Sumption Lord, 'The Limits of the Law' the 27th Sultan Azlan Shah Lecture, Kuala Lumpur (20 November 2013).

Sumption Lord, 'The Limits of the Law' in Barber Nicholas, Ekins Richard, and Yowell Paul (eds), *Lord Sumption and the Limits of the Law* (Hart 2016).

Sunday Telegraph, 'Anything you Say' (11 August 1963).

Sutton Trust and Prime, 'Top Judges and QCs Ten Times More Likely to be Privately Educated' (November 2015).

Sutton Trust and Social Mobility Commission, *Elitist Britain* (25 June 2019).

Symonds John Alexander, *Romeo Spy* (online, 2010).

Tamanaha Brian, *On the Rule of Law: History, Politics, Theory* (CUP 2004).

Tamuno Tekenya Nitonye, *The Evolution of the Nigerian State* (Western Printing Sevices 1972).

Tan Kevin, *The Constitution of Singapore: A Contextual Analysis* (Bloomsbury 2015).

Tapper Colin, 'Evidence (General) Eleventh Report of the Criminal Law Revision Committee' (1972) 35(6) Modern Law Review 4.

Taylor Lord, 'Continuity and Change in the Criminal Law' Lecture at King's College London (6 March 1996)

The Guardian (Manchester, 3 March 1961).

The People, 'New Bribery Case Sensation: Gaoled Bookie Confesses' (8 June 1958).

The Proceedings of the Old Bailey: London's Central Criminal Court 1674–1913 (online).

The Sun, 'The Menace of the Muggers' (18 February 1982).

The Times, (London, 3 February 1899; 20 June 1912; 25 March 1953; 19 February 1954; 18 May 1957; 3 March 1961; 25 January 1964).

The Times, 'Bullying Judges "Driving Women to Quit Bar"' (London, 12 February 2019).

The Times, 'Challenor's Ideas of Grandeur' (London, 29 October 1964).

The Times, 'Juries Ill-Equipped for Fraud Trials, Supreme Court Judge Says' (London, 26 October 2018).

The Times, 'Fewer Women Advocates Make QC Grade' (London, 11 January 2019).

The Times, 'Forensic Budget Cuts Risk Wrongful Convictions, Says Lord Chief' (London, 21 November 2018).

The Times, 'Four Questions for the Chanellor Inquiry' (London, 6 July 1964).

The Times, 'Justice Denied' (London, 28 June 2019).

The Times, 'Male Barristers Get the Big Cases Says Top Judge' (London, 8 March 2019).

The Times, 'Malicious Officer Caught out by Bad Spelling' (London, 29 July 2017).

The Times, 'Secret State' (London, 6 October 2018).

The Times, 'Study of the Rights of the Individual' (London, 28 June 1961).

The Times, 'Why Shouldn't We Kill?—The Mentality of the Criminal Classes as Seen by the Retiring Lord Chief Justice' (London, 8 April 1971).

The Times, 'Youths Questioned in Stabbed P. C. Case' (London, 18 December 1958).

Thomas David Arthur, 'The Revised Judges' Rules' (1963--64) British Journal of Criminology 383.
Thomas Donald, *Villain's Paradise* (John Murray 2005).
Thomas LCJ 'Judicial Independence in a Changing Landscape' (17 September 2015).
Thomas LCJ, 'Reshaping Justice' Speech delivered to JUSTICE (3 March 2014).
Thomas LCJ, 'Developing Commercial Law through the Courts: Rebalancing the Relationship between the Courts and Arbitration' *Bailii Lecture* (9 March 2016).
Thomas LCJ, 'The Judiciary within the State—The Relationship between the Branches of the State' Michael Ryle Memorial Lecture (15 June 2017).
Thomas Lord, 'The Centrality of Justice: Its Contribution to Society, and its Delivery' The Lord Williams of Mostyn Memorial Lecture (10 November 2015).
Thomas Philip, 'An Exploration of Plea Bargaining' [1969] Criminal Law Review 68.
Thomas Philip, 'Plea Bargaining in England' (1978) 69(2) The Journal of Criminal Law & Criminology 169.
Thompson Edward Palmer, *Whigs and Hunters* (Pantheon Books 1975).
Thompson Edward Palmer, 'The Secret State' in Thompson Edward Palmer, *Writing by Candlelight* (Merlin Press 1980).
Thorseby Robert, 'Is Due Process Fleeing Its English Home?' (1973) 59 American Bar Association Journal 1046.
Tobias John, 'The British Colonial Police—An Alternative Style' in Stead Philip (ed), *Pioneers in Policing* (Patterson Smith 1977).
Tominey Camilla, 'Revealed: The 189 Police Officers Convicted of crimes Including Murder, Child Pornography and Drug Dealing since 2013' *The Telegraph* (20 January 2019).
Tonry Michael, *Punishment and Politics—Evidence and Emulation in the Making of English Penal Policy* (Willan 2004).
Travis Alan, 'After 44 Years Secret Papers Reveal Truth about Five Nights of Violence in Notting Hill' *The Guardian* (24 August 2002).
Trew Winston, *Black for a Cause. Not Just Because: The Case of the 'Oval 4' and the Story It Tells of Black Power in 1970s Britain* (Black for a Cause 2015).
Troup Edward (Charles) Sir, *The Home Office* (Putnam's Sons 1925).
UK Government, *The Civil Service Reform Plan* (June 2012).
UK Government, *The Civil Service Code* (London 2015).
UK Government and Bridge Group, *Socio-Economic Diversity in the Fast-Stream* (February 2016)
UK Parliament, *Report of the Justice Select Committee on Disclosure of Evidence in Criminal Cases* (House of Commons Select Committee 2018) (online).
United Nations, *Universal Declaration of Human Rights* (UDHR), General Assembly Resolution 217A (III) UN Doc A/810 at 71 (1948).
Vincent David, *The Culture of Secrecy: Britain 1832–1998* (OUP 1997).
Vincent Howard Sir, *Vincent's Police Code* (National Archives 1889).
Wade William and Forsyth Christopher, *Administrative Law* (11th edn, OUP 2014).
Walter Stephen and Maidment Jack, 'Oxford University Student Cleared of Rape Charge as yet another Case Collapses Days before Trial Begins' *The Telegraph* (18 January 2018).
Walker-Smith Derek, *The Life of Lord Darling* (Cassell and Company 1938).
Ward Damen, 'Legislation, Repugnancy and the Disallowance of Colonial Laws' (2010) 41 Victoria University Wellington Law Review 381.
Ward Jennifer, *Transforming Summary Justice—Modernisation in the Lower Criminal Courts* (Routledge 2017).

Watson Eric (ed), Notable British Trials, *The Trial of Adolf Beck* (William Hodge & Company 1924).

Weaver Matthew and Grierson Jamie: 'Police Chief Admits "Cultural Problem" with Evidence Disclosure' *The Guardian* (24 January 2018).

Weiner Martin, *An Empire on Trial* (CUP 2009).

Wesley Smith Peter, 'English Practice and Procedure in Hong Kong' (1979) 9 Hong Kong Law Journal 255.

Wesley Smith Peter, 'Anti-Chinese Legislation in Hong Kong' in Ming Chan (ed), *Precarious Balance: Hong Kong between China and Britain, 1842–1992* (HKU Press 1994).

Wheeler-Bennett John, *John Anderson: Viscount Waverley* (Macmillan 1962).

Whitaker Ben, 'The Challenor Case Re-Examined' *The Spectator* (29 January 1965).

Wigmore John Henry, *Evidence in Trials at Common Law* (first published 1904, revised by Chadbourn 1970).

Williams David, 'Bias; the Judges and the Separation of Powers' [2000] Public Law 45.

Williams Glanville, 'Police Interrogation, Privileges and Limitations: England' (1961) 52 Journal of Criminal Law, Criminology and Police Science 50.

Williams Glanville, *The Proof of Guilt* (Stevens & Sons 1963).

Willis Carole, *The Use, Effectiveness and Impact of Police Stop and Search Powers*, Home Office Research and Planning Unit Paper No 15 (1983).

Willis Carole, *The Tape-Recording of Police Interviews with Suspects: An Interim Report*, Home Office Research Study No 82 (HMSO 1984).

Wilson Geoffrey, 'Postscript: The Courts, Law and Convention' in Nolan Rt Hon Lord and Sedley Stephen Sir, *The Making & Remaking of the British Constitution* (Blackstone Press Ltd 1997).

Windeyer Victor Sir, 'A Birthright and Inheritance—Establishment of the Rule of Law in Australia' [1962] University of Tasmania Law Review 635.

Wood Zoe and Butler Sarah, 'Two Tesco Directors Cleared of Fraud As Judge Labels Case "Weak"' *The Guardian* (6 December 2018).

Woodhouse Diana, 'Politicians and the Judiciary: A Changing Relationship' (1995) 48 3(1) Parliamentary Affairs 401.

Woodhouse Diana, 'Politicians and the Judges: A Conflict of Interest' (1996) July 3(1) Parliamentary Affairs 49.

Woodhouse Diana, 'The Judiciary in the 1990s: Guardian of the Welfare State?' (1998) 26(4) Policy & Politics 457.

Woodhouse Diana, *The Lord Chancellor* (Hart 2001).

Woodland David, *Crime and Corruption at Scotland Yard* (Pen & Sword Books 2016)

Woolf, Harry LJ, *Report into the Prison Riots at Strangeways* Cmd 1456 (1991).

Wyles Lilian, *A Woman at Scotland Yard* (Faber 1952).

Yang Anand (ed), *Crime and Criminality in British India* (University of Arizona Press 1985).

Yarborough Minnie Clare, *John Horne Tooke* (Columbia University Press 1926; reprint by AMS Press, Inc 1966).

Yehia Dina, *Admissibility of Admissions: Aboriginal and Torres Straits Islanders Suspects* (2012) (online).

Yorke Richard, 'Questioning by the Police' *Daily Telegraph* (11 February 1961).

Yorkshire Post, 'More Reorganisation of Leeds CID' (23 November 1954).

Young Hugo, 'In Tune with the Times' *The Guardian Weekly* (2 August 1992).

Young Simon, 'Human Rights in Hong Kong Criminal Trials' in Paul Roberts and Jill Hunter (eds), *Criminal Evidence and Human Rights* (Hart 2012) 55.

Zander Michael, 'The Criminal Law Revision Committee Report: A Survey of Reactions' (1974) (2 October) Law Society's Gazette 953.

Zander Michael, 'Abandoning an Ancient Right to Please the Police' *The Independent* (6 October 1993).

Zander Michael, *Lord Justice Auld's Review of the Criminal Courts: A Response* (LSE 2001).

Zander Michael and Henderson Paul, *Crown Court Study*, RCCJ Research Study No 19 (HMSO 1993).

Name Index

Note: *For the benefit of digital users, indexed terms that span two pages (e.g., 52–53) may, on occasion, appear on only one of those pages.*

Subject Index

Note: *For the benefit of digital users, indexed terms that span two pages (e.g., 52–53) may, on occasion, appear on only one of those pages.*
Tables and figures are indicated by *t* and *f* following the page number